THE
LIGHT
of ITALY

JANE STEVENSON has taught at the universities of
Cambridge, Sheffield, Warwick and Aberdeen, and
is now a Senior Research Fellow at Campion Hall,
Oxford. She is the author of *Baroque Between the Wars*,
a study of alternative currents in the interwar arts,
and *Edward Burra: Twentieth-Century Eye*.

By the same author

Edward Burra: Twentieth Century Eye

Baroque Between the Wars: Alternative Style in the Arts,
1918–1939

Siena: The Life and Afterlife of a Medieval City

THE
LIGHT
of ITALY

The Life and Times of
FEDERICO DA MONTEFELTRO,
DUKE OF URBINO

JANE STEVENSON

HEAD
of
ZEUS

An Apollo Book

Head of Zeus Ltd
5–8 Hardwick Street
London EC1R 4RG

WWW.HEADOFZEUS.COM

for Duncan Rice:

vir magnificus

Contents

Preface   9

The Origins of the City of Urbino   15

PART I

Federico da Montefeltro, Lord of Urbino

1   Gubbio, Urbino & Mercatello, 1422–1431   25

2   Growing up: Venice & Mantua, 1432–1437   33

3   Dutiful Son, 1437–1444   41

4   Taking Control, 1444–1450   55

5   Consolidation, 1451–1460   71

6   Battista, 1460–1472   81

7   Magnificence, 1472–1482   113

PART II

Federico's Legacy

8   The Palace at Urbino   143

9   Gubbio & Beyond: Other Architectural Projects   165

10   Federico as Patron of the Arts   177

11   Urbino: the Ducal Library   215

PART III
The Duchy after Federico

12	Guidobaldo	235
13	Francesco Maria della Rovere	261
14	The Later della Rovere dukes	287
15	The Eighteenth Century: Clement XI & The Stuarts	305
16	The Last Duke of Urbino	311

Bibliography	323
Picture credits	341
Notes	343
Acknowledgments	363
Index	365

Preface

There are few paintings more famous than Piero della Francesca's double portrait of Battista and Federico da Montefeltro. Facing one another in profile, their presentation suggests a pair of coin portraits: the reference to the antique that is so characteristic of the Renaissance. Battista is portrayed as a woman in her twenties, with the waxen pallor admired in her time; she is festooned with jewels, her golden hair is elaborately dressed, and her expression is neutral. Federico's image shows a man in his fifties, lips thoughtfully pursed, with sagging jowls. On his jaw is the scar of an abscess, which nearly killed him when he was eleven. In contrast to the idealized image of his wife, his portrait has something of the unflinching realism of ancient Roman funerary sculpture. Also, in contrast to his wife's brocade and jewels, he is plainly dressed in scarlet. But though his garb is plain, it is made of very costly cloth: kermes, the dye from which scarlet was made, was fabulously expensive.

The painting is not exactly lying, but it is certainly being economical with the truth. When it was painted, Battista was dead, aged only twenty-six, her tiny body worn out by as many as ten pregnancies in twelve years of marriage. In life, she was diminutive, and her complexion was sanguine. That means there was colour in her face, and she lost her temper easily, though she cooled just as quickly. She also wasn't blonde; her hair was chestnut brown. She was clever, she was an eager student of the classics, Greek as well as Latin, and she spoke up for herself. Piero della Francesca's image is not a portrait of a living woman, it is a picture of how her husband wanted her remembered. And Federico, as he appears here? He looks every inch *Pater patriae*, the father of his country, and, as an admiring observer of the Urbino court, Baldassare Castiglione, called him, the light of Italy: *la luce dell'Italia*. His is one of the most curated images in the history of the world. One immediate truth the painter conceals is that the duke is in profile not merely to evoke antique coinage, but because his right eye was missing, lost in a tournament when he was twenty-eight. Due to this disfigurement, he was almost never depicted full-face,[1] and consequently there are no sculptural representations of him made in his own time. But there are dozens of images of this mild, fatherly profile: he often appears in the manuscripts he commissioned for his famous library, and he is also represented in a number of full-sized paintings and relief sculptures.

Urbino was indelibly fixed in the minds of a generation as the quintessential Renaissance city by episode four of Sir Kenneth Clark's BBC TV documentary series *Civilisation*, first aired in 1969. 'Urbino is such a sweet place – so compact, so humane… as for the palace of Urbino, it is the most ravishing interior in the world,' he wrote from Italy to his close friend Janet Stone while he was working on his Renaissance episode, 'Man, the measure of all things'.[2] In the programme itself, he observes that 'life in the court of Urbino was one of the high benchmarks of Western civilisation'. Florence, he thought, was the intellectual centre of the Renaissance, but Urbino, the ultimate expression of its ideals. He devotes a great deal of the programme to the spacious, dignified rooms of Federico da Montefeltro's palace, but also includes enchanting long vistas of the timeless order of the surrounding country, with its dusty white farmhouses and dark cypresses on disciplined, terraced hillsides, and the blue Apennines rising up in the distance, the landscapes of Bellini and Giorgione.

Fifty years later, Urbino is still an idyllic hill town of steep streets lined with houses and palazzi of weathered brick. The life of the city is dominated by a large modern university, which has been inserted behind the façades of some of these structures with rare architectural tact: students make up a substantial sector of the population. Because it has been brought into the modern world with such sensitivity and loving care, it has the air of a Renaissance time capsule. It remains little visited by tourists and art lovers, partly because it is only accessible by car or bus. Only determined art lovers and the discerning take the trouble, so for many of its visitors it feels like a private discovery.

The image of Duke Federico is central to any exploration of Urbino: the humanist warrior; the man who kept his promises in a faithless age; the Christian prince. Throughout the city, and his palace in particular, we are confronted by his personality. We see his values, his concerns, set forth in the art he commissioned. In the exquisite intarsia panels of his *studiolo*, copies of Cicero and Seneca lie piled up in fictive cupboards accompanied by musical instruments, and his Garter hangs casually from a hook. In another portrait hung in the *studiolo*, probably by Joos van Wassenhove, he sits rather stiffly upright, reading Gregory the Great's *Moralia in Job*, wearing full armour under his ducal robes, with his Garter buckled round his calf, and the insignia of the Order of the Ermine on his shoulders. He is accompanied by his little son, Guidobaldo.

The image is both familiar and compelling, so much so that it draws the eye away from other, also relevant, facts. It might be useful to remember that one of Federico's personal emblems, or *imprese*, was a whisk-broom, a handheld device for tidying away dirt and dust, stains and inconveniences, which he adopted from the Sforzas after marrying Battista. In our own day, there are reasons for thinking that he might have chosen an airbrush. Perhaps the most important of the facts that we might now think worth retrieving from the dustbin of history, to which they have been whisked, is that all this image-making dates to the later 1470s. Federico became lord of Urbino in 1444, when his legitimate half-brother Oddantonio was assassinated by the citizenry, and Federico happened rather conveniently to be in the immediate vicinity. The people of Urbino presented him with a list of demands before letting him through the gate, and he accepted all of them, suggesting that he did not feel himself to be in a position to dictate terms. He was made duke – that is, confirmed in the exercise of legitimate power *de jure* rather than merely ruling *de facto*, only in 1474, which is thirty years later. In that same year, he was invested with the Order of the Ermine by the King of Naples, and the Order of the Garter by Edward IV of England. These styles and titles are prominently on display in all the books and artefacts he commissioned in his wealthy late-middle years; it is as if the first thirty years of his rule have been whisked into oblivion by that useful little broom: we see the final glory, not the graft.

Joos, if he is the painter of the portrait of Federico and Guidobaldo, gives us an image of a dynast: a man in his mid-fifties, with a son and heir who is about four. What this father–son dyad encourages us not to see is that his attempts to beget this heir must have been increasingly desperate. His first marriage, to Gentile Brancaleoni, lasted twenty years, and was childless. There were two illegitimate sons who functioned as a dynastic insurance policy from that period of his life, the older of whom, a boy who had been groomed as a potential heir, had died of the plague in 1458. The younger son he seems never to have taken very seriously. His second marriage, to Battista Sforza, had been fertile, but year on year she gave him another daughter. Five or six of these girls seem to have survived to adulthood, but their lives are so obscure it is hard to know for sure: only those who married are historically visible. Guidobaldo, the last child she bore, was an only son, and the hope of legitimate succession rested upon his fragile shoulders alone. He was afflicted by early-onset gout in his twenties; it would not be surprising if, even aged four, his father might be wondering how robust he was turning out. Federico cannot but have been conscious of all this, because his marital history replicated his father's: his father, Guidantonio, had had a barren first wife, and Federico had been born during her lifetime. His father's second marriage had produced three daughters and a single son: when this boy, Oddantonio, was born, Federico himself was set aside and exiled. The impression of stability that this picture exudes is quite misleading: the history of the dukedom was, and would continue to be, marked by a series of succession crises, because dynastic will was expressed through frail human vessels.

Duke Federico was not a writer. Letters of his, mostly military dispatches, survive, but he turned to professionals to shape his image for posterity. The only work attributed to him is a treatise on cryptography. Like his artists, his writers were appropriately rewarded, so the picture they present shows us how he wished to be seen. Their efforts were highly persuasive: Federico was celebrated as the archetypal Renaissance prince by the influential nineteenth-century historian Jacob Burckhardt, whose seminal work *The Civilization of the Renaissance in Italy* (1886) opens with a chapter on 'The State as a Work of Art', principally based on Federico's Urbino.

But the image of Federico as the ideal virtuous ruler was very carefully crafted. All Renaissance princes and their ruling consorts were extremely self-conscious about how they presented themselves and how they chose to be depicted by others, but for Federico in particular, his sole claim to legitimate rule was in being a good Christian prince, in strong contradistinction to both his legitimate half-brother, Oddantonio, whom he had succeeded, and his arch-enemy, Sigismondo Malatesta. The picture given of him by his biographers, his humble, unassuming manner, his temperance and liking for the simplest food, suggests that he modelled himself on Suetonius's pen portrait of Augustus, first Emperor of Rome, and one of the most successfully self-made monarchs of all time.

Thus we know less about Federico than we think we do. The fact is, whether a prince of the Italian Renaissance went down in history as the Good Duke or the Tyrant of Rimini depended not so much on what he did, as on whether he was able to keep tight control of the narrative of his life. Sigismondo Malatesta's posthumous reputation is based on a campaign of character assassination led by Pope Pius II and Federico himself. But Federico as well as Sigismondo kept mistresses, and though he was famous for keeping his word as a condottiere once it was given, he would lie if he considered it expedient, and not all his professional activities were strictly honourable. He was capable of writing (heavily encrypted) to Pope Sixtus IV pledging his support in the enterprise to control the Medici known to history as the Pazzi conspiracy (1478), while simultaneously writing in clear to Lorenzo de' Medici, declaring his continued respect and trust, since both letters survive.

Some things we are told about Federico by his chroniclers are undoubtedly true: he was a man of tremendous physical courage and determination. He had a long history of physical injuries: for example, among other serious mishaps, he wrenched his back so badly in 1460 he probably did himself lasting damage, and he nearly lost a leg in 1477. He must have lived with chronic pain through most of his life, while doggedly pursuing the condotta commissions that gave him his wealth, since forensic examination of his skeleton revealed that he was gouty and arthritic.[3] Modern doctors have also noted collapsing vertebrae in his upper back, probably caused by the amount of time he spent riding in armour, starting before he was fully grown. He was also capable of great ruthlessness: the sack of Volterra might well have gone down in history as an atrocity, though his image-makers contrived to turn it into a triumph.

Thus, there is more to the great duke than meets the eye. His achievements were extraordinary, but the man behind the mask was more complicated and more challenged than his portraits aim to suggest.

The Origins
of the City of Urbino

Urbino is a city built on two hills; a natural fortress, since it also has a reliable water supply. It has been strategically valuable since the days of the Romans, who constructed a fort there called Urvinum Mataurense, referencing its shape, the curve of a Roman ploughshare (*urvus*), and its river, the Metauro. It's not just the river that keeps a Roman identity: Roman origins are still implicit in the street plan, which retains a hint of the cruciform layout of all Roman fortified sites. The old *decumanus*, part of which is now the Piazza Duca Federico, can still be discerned, dividing the city in half lengthways, crossed by the *cardo*, now Via Giuseppe Mazzini and Via Cesare Battisti. This layout created four quarters, as so often in old Italian cities, Pusterla and Vescovata in the north-east and north-west, Santa Croce and Portanova to the south-east and south-west, which retained a distinct identity as late as the fifteenth century.[1] The principal approach to Urbino from the days of the Roman empire onwards was to turn off the ancient Via Flaminia at Acqualagna, take the increasingly mountainous road leading up to Fermignano, and then to tackle the steep and dangerous final hill crowned by the city walls.

Urbino continued to be a valued defensive site through the early Middle Ages. During the Byzantine emperor Justinian's attempted reconquest of Italy in the sixth century, it was one of the cities garrisoned by the defending Ostrogothic king, Vitigis, and was held by an Ostrogothic captain called Moras with 2,000 troops. It was one of the largest garrisons that Vitigis appointed, which suggests that he set considerable store by the place. His strategy appears to have backfired, however, because the spring ran dry, and thirst forced the Goths to surrender.

In Francia (the western part of which would later become France), in the year 751, Pepin the Short deposed the last of the Merovingian dynasty on grounds of incompetence and made himself king of the Franks, a move Federico da Montefeltro would doubtless have approved. Pepin was both deeply pious and aggressively expansionist: though his power base was in France, he intervened in the struggle between Pope Stephen II and the Lombards, a Germanic people (as were the Franks) who had established themselves in northern and central Italy; their name survives in Lombardy, the region centred on Milan. Also in 751, Aistulf, king of the Lombards, conquered Ravenna, the last toehold the Byzantine empire had in Italy. The following year, he demanded the submission of the pope, and a poll tax of one gold *solidus* per citizen. Thus put under pressure, Stephen II appealed to Pepin for help. In 754, he travelled to Paris to formally anoint and crown Pepin as 'Patrician of the Romans' in the basilica of St Denis, adding his spiritual authority to what had been straightforward usurpation on Pepin's part. The term 'Patrician' was a vague honorific, invented in the fourth century by Constantine, the first Christian Roman Emperor, to honour a ruler without defining his status. As applied to a Frankish king, its meaning could evolve along with the changing political situation.

The coronation of 754 was the first occasion on which a pope had validated a king's right to rule. There were Old Testament precedents – the prophet Samuel anointed first King Saul, and when he proved unsatisfactory, King David. But the underlying question was, did a pope have the right to do so? For eight hundred years, the authority to invest an individual with power had lain in the hands of the emperors; but Constantine V, who was emperor in Constantinople at the time, was hardly likely to legitimate Pepin. The new kings of the Franks were determined that the pope's gesture should be meaningful, and in the course of the next twenty years, a forger, active either at the papal chancery or the Frankish court, evolved an elaborate explanatory fiction in which Constantine I had been cured of leprosy by Pope Sylvester I and, in gratitude, had ceded rule over the Western Empire to the papacy.[2] There was a certain plausibility to the story, since the papacy was the only institution in the West whose roots extended back to the Roman empire. As the political philosopher Thomas Hobbes observed in the seventeenth century, 'if a man consider the original of this great ecclesiastical dominion, he will easily perceive that the papacy is no other than the ghost of the deceased Roman Empire, sitting crowned upon the grave thereof: for so did the papacy start up on a sudden out of the ruins of that heathen power'.[3]

However, the narrative of Constantine's gift to Pope Sylvester is untrue from start to finish. Constantine never suffered from leprosy, and what had actually happened was that the Eastern emperors lost control of the West in the course of the fifth century. But the Donation of Constantine, as this invention came to be called, made the papacy the rightful fountainhead of political authority in the West. This suited the popes, since it increased their power; and it suited the Frankish kings, since it increased their legitimacy. The whole concept of a Holy Roman Emperor originates from this chicanery, which was accepted as true for seven hundred years, until Federico's contemporary, the humanist scholar Lorenzo Valla, applied sophisticated linguistic analysis to the text and demonstrated that its Latin was not that of Constantine's era, but considerably later.[4]

By the fifteenth century, however, the popes' temporal power was so established in law and in fact that merely pointing out that it rested on a fiction made no practical difference.

Meanwhile, back in the eighth century, in 756, thus two years after his coronation, Pepin crossed the Alps and forced the Lombards to cede the imperial territories they had seized. He then gave the pope a substantial swathe of largely mountainous country in central Italy. In practice, the problem of exercising effective authority over this difficult terrain meant that the Papal States, as they became known, continued to consist of smallish independent territories, each ruled from a suitable *rocca*, or fortress. What had changed was that, in theory, these rulers were exercising authority vicariously on behalf of the pope. This fiction gathered force and solidity over the centuries until, by the time Federico da Montefeltro came to power, the idea of a papal vicariate was a political reality. As a result, for practical purposes, Renaissance popes were secular rulers before they were anything else, which is one reason why almost all of them were Italians. Their principal focus was on defending and, if possible, extending their territories in Italy. They were not theologians or pastors, they were lords, and sometimes warlords, and the counts of Urbino came to be among their trusted subordinates.

Visitors to Urbino are often struck by the number of representations of the imperial eagle in the palace. The reason for this goes back to the coronation of Frederick Barbarossa as king of Italy in Rome in 1154. Count Antonio di Carpegna, signor of Montecopiolo and San Leo (in what is now the Marche region of central Italy), was granted the area of Montefeltro *in feudo* as a reward for suppressing a riot against the emperor. He adopted the imperial eagle as an emblem, and with it the name of Montefeltro, taken from the original name of San Leo, which had been known as the mountain of Jupiter Feretrius before it became the home of a saintly hermit.[5] The newly minted Montefeltri thus owed their loyalty to the Holy Roman Emperors. This implied membership of the pro-imperial faction. The understorey of medieval Italian politics was a struggle for power between the popes and the emperors, expressed via the two great factions of medieval Italy, the Guelphs, supporting the pope, and the Ghibellines, supporting the Holy Roman Emperor.

The struggle between Guelphs and Ghibellines underscores the best-known poem from medieval Italy, Dante's *Divine Comedy*. Dante was a Guelph, as was his native city of Florence, while the Montefeltri, who owed their title to an emperor, were staunchly Ghibelline. Two Montefeltro counts feature in his great poem, a father and son. The father, Guido da Montefeltro, is one of the damned souls in *Inferno* 27. Guido was a wily and successful soldier, a fox rather than a lion, according to Dante.[6] He conducted several important military campaigns against Florence in the 1270s and 1280s. In the campaign of 1288–92, he captained the Ghibellines of Pisa against Florence, and was excommunicated. Boniface VIII rescinded his excommunication, and he became a Franciscan monk in 1296, inaugurating the Montefeltri's connection with the monastic order founded by Francis of Assisi in the 1220s. He died two years later. Again according to Dante, Pope Boniface VIII asked him for advice on how to destroy the Colonna family's stronghold at Palestrina, absolving him in advance of the sin of doing so when he had put the soldier's life behind him. St Francis duly came to rescue him after he died and demons came to drag him off to hell, but they hung on to him, pointing out that he hadn't repented his action, since a man can't be penitent and, at the same time, go on intending to commit the crime in question. Boniface VIII, a pope Dante loathed, had given Guido fraudulent advice, either intentionally or because he was a bad theologian. However, it is also true that if Guido's conversion to the Franciscan way of life had been a true one, he would not have fallen in with the pope's suggestion.[7]

Dante could not of course actually know what went on in Guido's mind. While it is impossible to tell whether he is to some extent politically motivated in making Guido condemn himself out of his own mouth, the *Divine Comedy* is not about settling scores. The second Montefeltro to appear in the *Comedy* is Guido's son Buonconte, who was killed at the battle of Campaldino on 11 June 1289, where he was leading the Ghibelline cavalry. His body was never recovered, so nobody could actually have known how he died, let alone in what frame of mind. Dante himself fought on the other side in this battle, which the Guelphs won, but he decides to use Buonconte to demonstrate his understanding of the infinite mercy of God. He assigns him to a section of Purgatory given over to people who sinned all their lives and died by violence, but sincerely repented: so, although Buonconte in the poem is currently in a state of suffering, Dante is declaring that he will ultimately enter Heaven. The soul of Buonconte explains to the poet that when he was defeated, he fled from the battlefield on foot, with a mortal wound in his throat. But as he toppled, dying, to the ground, the name of Mary was on his lips, and a tear of penitence was in his eye. For this blink-of-an-eye compunction alone, an angel grabbed him at the moment of his death, and took him to Purgatory to expiate his many sins. While Dante suggests that his father's two years in a Franciscan habit had been a sort of cynical insurance policy, he presents Buonconte's penitence as momentary, but entirely sincere.

In thirteenth-century Italy, many of the territorial jurisdictions were independent city republics: some, such as Florence, very large; others tiny. Italy was precociously urbanized, compared to other European countries, and Milan, Florence and Venice were among the biggest cities in Europe. However, in the course of the fourteenth century, most of the small republics devolved into signorie, or lordships. Because Italian states existed in a state of intense rivalry with one another, many little republics came to feel that seigneurial rule offered them both more security and more stability.[8] The Montefeltri acquired Urbino in 1378, when the city rose up against the papal legate who governed it and welcomed Antonio da Montefeltro (1348–1404), Federico's grandfather, acclaiming him as their lord and protector. Nine years later, the nearby town of Gubbio, having seen how Urbino was faring, also sought his protection. Thus, in the Montefeltro signoria that Federico inherited, effective rule was based on a combination of dynastic succession, popular acclamation and papal approval. These new signori of the fourteenth century were frequently men like Antonio da Montefeltro, soldier-princes who became a characteristic feature of the Italian political landscape. Such men were members of a dynasty, ruling their city by inheritance, but at the same time selling their services as mercenaries to win wealth, experience and influence. By 1400, the Papal States in particular were a patchwork of semi-independent cities, whose rulers were theoretically papal vicars but, in practice, independent. The fact that from 1378 to 1417 there were at least two men claiming to be 'the pope' at any one time meant that the Papal States were pretty much left to get on with things for forty years. Only after the election of Martin V in 1417, five years before Federico's birth, were the popes able to pay attention to their landholdings in Italy.

The first symptoms of the Renaissance at Urbino appeared in the mid-fourteenth century, under the rule of Federico's grandfather Antonio da Montefeltro. He owned three copies of Dante's *Divine Comedy*, the earliest of which was written for him in 1352, and two essays by Petrarch, 'On His Own Ignorance and that of Many', and 'On a Solitary Life'.[9] He also invited a Florentine poet, Fazio degli Uberti, to Urbino. Guidantonio, Federico's father, was a patron of learning. Letters to the signoria of Siena survive in which he recommends learned men: two on behalf of lawyers, Benedetto de Bresis and Zucha de Cagli, and a third recommending a doctor, Piero de Pergalotti.[10] One of these letters is in Latin, and Guidantonio also wrote poetry in Italian. A poem on the theme of Good Friday survives, collected in a manuscript of miscellaneous verse and prose, Italian and Latin, written in Urbino by Antonio Petrucci of Siena in 1464 to pass the time while he was a prisoner of war in Federico's reign. Other poems of the count's were appended to a Dante manuscript in the Royal Library in Naples, and were printed in 1817 by Luigi Bertozzi.[11] Petrucci's manuscript is of some interest, because it provides a snapshot of the literary culture of Urbino before Federico's major spending on his library in the 1470s. It contains poems by Dante and Petrarch, and verse by minor humanist contemporaries such as Alberto Orlando, Chancellor of Florence, Tommaso Moroni, a servant of the Sforza, and Giusto de'Conti, a lawyer who served Sigismondo Malatesta. There is also Latin verse by authors renowned throughout Italy, such as Francesco Filelfo and Antonio Panormita, both of whom visited Urbino. Another poet represented in this volume who was a native of Urbino was Angelo Galli, secretary in turn to Guidantonio, Oddantonio and Federico.[12] All in all, Petrucci's book, and other verse collected at the court, suggests a lively literary culture was developing even before Federico became count.

Another early Urbino humanist was Fra Bartolomeo dei Carusi, also called Bartolomeo de Urbino (d. 1350), a friend of Petrarch's, and a student of Classical Latin. He wrote a theological treatise for men of war, 'On Military Matters, Spiritually', which he dedicated to the condottiere captain Count Galasso da Montefeltro, lord of Cesena, who was the son of Federico's great-grandfather Nolfo, Count of Urbino. This is one of the first indications of the Montefeltri directly dispensing literary patronage.[13] Typically, after he became duke, Federico updated the fourteenth-century manuscript presented to his great-uncle by adding illuminated pages at the front with his own *imprese*, the ermine and the flames of love, and his coat of arms.

PART I

Federico da Montefeltro, Lord of Urbino

1

Gubbio, Urbino & Mercatello
1422–1431

Federico da Montefeltro was born on 7 June 1422, in Gubbio, but not to his father's wife. His father, Guidantonio da Montefeltro, had been married to Rengarda Malatesta for twenty-five years (they wed in 1397), but there were no children of the marriage. He did, however, in the course of his first marriage, beget an illegitimate daughter called Aura (mother unknown), around 1405. All we can know about Aura is that she seems to have been an educated woman, since, when her husband died, she went to Milan, where her teenaged son Ottaviano then was, to help him sort out the estate.[1] In fifteenth-century Italy, it was only prudent for a ruler with a barren wife to take a mistress in the hopes of producing an insurance-policy heir. While most European countries barred the succession of illegitimate children, even when legitimized, in Renaissance Italy bastardy was not an insurmountable obstacle, and it was not uncommon for a dynasty to number one or more bastard heirs in the succession.[2] In 1420, Aura married Bernardino Ubaldini della Carda, a condottiere captain in Guidantonio's employment. Federico passed for the son of Guidantonio, but there was a persistent rumour that he was actually Guidantonio's grandson. Which is to say, when Aura's first child turned out to be a promising boy, her own father, who was forty-five and desperate for an heir, carried him off and put him in the charge of a wet-nurse. Alternatively, a single document, the will of Matteo degli Accomanducci of Gubbio, names Federico's mother as Matteo's daughter Elisabetta.[3]

Federico's contemporary and biographer, Pierantonio Paltroni, offers two possibilities: either that Federico was the illegitimate son of Count Guidantonio and an unknown mother, or Federico was the son of Aura and Bernardino.[4] The contemporary *Cronache Malatestiane* simply describes him as 'son of Bernardino della Carda',[5] and Pope Pius II, who knew Federico well, gives two different versions in his *Commentaries*, first published in Rome in 1584 and then again in 1589. The draft manuscript gives a radically different version of Federico's origins, and names Bernardino as his true father (the words deleted in the published version are in italics):

> at this time Federigo of Urbino waited on the Pope. He was an able and eloquent man, but blind in one eye, which he had lost in a tournament. *They say* he was the son of *Bernardo della Carda once a famous captain, but that when he was a tiny baby the mistress of* Guido, Prince of Urbino, *substituted him for his own child whom she had lost.*[6]

It looks as if the rumour that Federico was not Guidantonio's son whistled persistently round the courts of Italy for years. Even in distant England, the story was repeated in William Thomas's *Historie of Italie*, published in 1549: 'Guido Conte di Vrbino, havyng no heire male by his firste wife, feigned that he had gotten a Concubine with childe, and so secretly toke the sonne of his nere kinnesman Bernardino della Corda, whiche even than was newly borne, and namyng it Federike, caused it to be nourished as his owne.'[7] Much later, Federico called one of his daughters Aura, which may be a clue.

Two years later, in 1424, an acknowledged child, Ottaviano Ubaldini della Carda, was born to Aura and Bernardino, and raised as their first son. The truth can never be known, but the closeness of the lifelong bond between Federico and Ottaviano suggests that this version of Federico's parentage may well be the correct one. The nineteenth-century historians Alessandro Luzio and Rodolfo Renier noticed, for instance, that Vespasiano dei Bisticci tells us that Ottaviano was the only man other than their father allowed to visit Federico's daughters, when even their half-brother Antonio was banned from going near them, and deduced on this ground alone that the two men must be brothers.[8] Two more recent historians, Leonello Bei and Stefano Cristini, suggest that it was the della Rovere dukes of the early seventeenth century who tried to suppress what had been a fairly open secret.[9]

In the 1420s, Guidantonio was closely allied with Pope Martin V, born Oddone Colonna, who had been Bishop of Urbino before his elevation. Guidantonio had been rewarded with the title of Duke of Spoleto in 1419, though in the event he was not able to hold the territory. After the years of schism in which there were at least two contenders for the see of St Peter at any one time, Martin V had finally got the situation under control: in 1417 he was universally acknowledged as pope, and used this regained authority to restore order in the Papal States and to begin building up a papal army. While these developments would shape Federico's entire life and career, Martin V also intervened personally in his future. He and Guidantonio between them came up with an ingenious solution for securing Federico's future without weakening Urbino. Though the baby was potentially Guidantonio's heir, if there was a legitimate son by a second marriage (as, it turned out, there would be), it would be better if some provision was made for him in a way that would not compromise Montefeltro lands. Guidantonio's territorial neighbours included the Brancaleoni, a Guelph family with whom the Montefeltri, as good Ghibellines, had long feuded on and off, while peace was sometimes patched up by means of intermarriage.[10] The Brancaleoni controlled Sant'Angelo in Vado, Castel Durante and Mercatello, marching alongside Montefeltro territory.

In 1424, Bartolomeo da Brancaleoni died, leaving no son, having named his daughters, Piera and Gentile, as his heirs. Piera died in the following year, making Gentile her father's sole heir. Earlier in the same year, Guidantonio had seized Castel Durante, and on the death of Bartolomeo, he arranged the betrothal of Federico with Gentile, then possibly as old as seven, though she may have been younger. Guido Arbizzoni has argued that Federico and Gentile were in fact closer in age than used to be thought, and that they were both about eight when plans for their marriage were consolidated in 1430.[11]

This marriage required a dispensation from Martin V, since they were related, though not closely: Gentile's paternal grandmother was Agnese, daughter of Nolfo da Montefeltro, and therefore Guidantonio's aunt, so the children were distant cousins. The dispensation was granted on 11 October 1425, and Federico thus became effective heir to Bartolomeo's estates, though legally it was actually his fiancée who inherited them. The fief had lapsed to the papacy on the death of Bartolomeo, and Martin V was understandably reluctant to appoint a young girl as papal vicar. The agreement reached between the parties concerned was that Bartolomeo's widow, Giovanna degli Alidosi, should rule the Brancaleoni lands as regent, with the promise of a new investiture to Federico once he was of age and married to Gentile. Thus, Guidantonio successfully provided his bastard with a territory of his own, without compromising the Montefeltro inheritance.

In September 1423, the Countess of Urbino, Rengarda Malatesta, died. In the circumstances, there was no room for sentimentalizing about the end of a long marriage, and in January 1424 Guidantonio married Caterina Colonna, Martin V's niece, cementing his position as a close ally of the pope and his family: by the fifteenth century, Guelph and Ghibelline no longer mattered as they once had. When there was no sign of a pregnancy after eight months of marriage, Federico, who had been looked after by a wet-nurse, perhaps in Gubbio, where he was born, was brought to court and officially legitimized. But the bull of legitimization granted by Martin V on 22 December 1424 protected the rights of his niece and her children, by specifically excluding Federico from succeeding to the papal vicariate in the event of his father having a legitimate son. If the new young countess bore a son in wedlock, this child would have the right of inheritance over his older brother.[12]

In 1427, Guidantonio and Caterina welcomed a son and heir, Oddantonio, whose given name linked him with both his father, Guidantonio, and with his great-uncle, the pope (baptismal name Oddone). Federico's presence at court thus became an embarrassment, so he was sent away from Urbino to live with his future mother-in-law, Giovanna degli Alidosi. Oddantonio remained an only son, though Caterina went on to give birth to three daughters, Violante (born 1430), Agnesina (1431) and Sveva (1434).

Federico, meanwhile, was growing up among the Brancaleoni. Giovanna degli Alidosi, Federico's foster mother, was clearly a woman educated for rule, which is to say, Latin-literate and well read, because if she had not been educated in this way, she would not have been mandated as regent by the pope. Women like Giovanna were a new development in Italian culture, and emerged out of the circumstances of condottiere lords such as Bartolomeo da Brancaleoni, who had come to realize that having an educated wife who could step up to ruling their territories if they were absent fighting, or died leaving an under-age heir, was a powerful safeguard for the dynasty. Giovanna was clearly one such, and Guidantonio's sister Battista, her contemporary, was another. Battista's learning was famous. She was the recipient of Leonardo Bruni's widely circulated treatise on education, *De studiis et litteris* (On the Study of Literature), written *c.* 1424–9, which offers a curriculum for the education of a future ruler. This essay ends: 'I have not written to you as master to pupil (I should not presume so much) but simply as one of the crowd of your admirers.'[13] In the event, she was far more competent as a ruler of Pesaro than her husband (a story that belongs later in this narrative).

After her husband's death, Giovanna erected a commemorative epitaph at his elaborate tomb in the church of San Francesco in Mercatello sul Metauro (now the town museum), with this inscription: 'During her lifetime, Giovanna Alidosi erected this monument of fidelity to herself and Bartolomeo Brancaleoni, most faithful spouse, and prince of this town.'[14] It is she who is the grammatical subject of the sentence, and in it, she firmly associates herself with her husband as a ruling pair. Men in Renaissance Italy were not often praised for conjugal fidelity, and she is almost certainly the author of the inscription.

We know very little of Mercatello in the 1420s, except that, like Urbino, it was a town up in the Apennines, but much smaller, perched high above its river. There are two churches there now, San Francesco and the Pieve Collegiata, which would have been familiar to Federico, but the Brancaleoni palace itself was rebuilt by Francesco di Giorgio Martini after Federico gave Mercatello to Ottaviano Ubaldini della Carda in 1474. This had the incidental effect of obliterating the house in which he was brought up. The home of Giovanna degli Alidosi and her daughter was almost certainly smaller than the later palace, and though it was doubtless defensible, life there was probably rather rustic and not very luxurious, given that the local economy was based on agriculture and sheep.

Giovanna was evidently a most conscientious foster mother, and there is every reason to think that the relationship between her and Federico was a close one. The first of Federico's many brushes with death occurred when he was eleven. He developed an inflamed spot on his jaw, which turned into an acutely painful and life-threatening suppurating mass. Both Guidantonio and Giovanna were frantic with anxiety; Guidantonio sent the best doctors he could find post-haste to Mercatello, while Giovanna nursed the sick boy devotedly. Eventually, scientific medicine having failed, Giovanna asked a peasant wise woman to see what she could do. She washed the sore with a mystery lotion, and it began to heal, though he carried the scar for the rest of his life.[15]

The episode suggests that Giovanna was strongly committed to Federico's welfare, and this was remembered: a poem by a court poet of Federico's, Giambattista Cantalicio, evokes her anxious care of him, and compares her with the famously maternal Roman matron Cornelia, mother of the Gracchi.[16]

One area where her long-term influence on her fosterling is clear is as an educating mother. Federico's biographers always say that he was educated by Vittorino da Feltre, and the presence of Vittorino's image in the *studiolo* suggests Federico's sense of affectionate debt to this preceptor. But two facts, not in dispute, are worth observing. Federico went to live with Giovanna degli Alidosi when he was four, and stayed with her until he was sent to Venice as a hostage in 1433 (see Chapter 2), when he was eleven. In Venice, where he remained for fifteen months, he gave a speech to the doge (Francesco Foscari) and the Venetian Senate, which greatly impressed them with its eloquence and rhetorical sophistication. But at this point in his life, Federico had never even set foot in Mantua, where Vittorino had his school.[17] And it is worth remembering that when he was with Giovanna, she knew that she was educating the future signior of the domain, Mercatello, which claimed her own loyalty, so she would have had every reason to make sure he was up to the challenge.

Federico's upbringing must have left him with a wholesome respect for women's intellectual and political capabilities, since he was raised and educated by a thoroughly intelligent woman ruler, and, once at Vittorino da Feltre's school, he learned alongside the brilliant Cecilia Gonzaga. However, Federico's ruthless curation of his personal history in the last decade of his life has successfully airbrushed out both his foster mother and his first wife, even though Giovanna had been devoted to him and Gentile was loved and honoured by his children. At Mercatello itself, Brancaleoni's mausoleum in the church of San Francesco now faces profile portraits of Federico da Montefeltro and his brother-adviser, Ottaviano Ubaldini della Carda.[18]

2

Growing Up: Venice & Mantua
1432–1437

By our way of thinking, Federico was still a little boy in 1433, when he left Giovanna degli Alidosi's care, but many young nobles in the fifteenth century had to grow up very quickly: Federico's second wife, Battista Sforza, gave her first public address in Latin when she was four. Federico's sojourn in Venice came about through papal régime change. Martin V died in 1431 after a fourteen-year papacy. He was succeeded by Eugenius IV, who was a Venetian, and took a dim view of his predecessor's tendency to advance members of his own family, the Colonnas. This made the position of Guidantonio, married to a Colonna, somewhat difficult. Additionally, in the last year of Martin V's reign, he had led an army against Lucca on behalf of the Florentines, and been roundly defeated by the well-known condottiere Niccolò Piccinino. His competence as a commander had thus been put in question, and for this reason also, he was out of favour with the new pope. Eugenius IV signed a peace treaty at Ferrara with Filippo Maria Visconti of Milan. Such a deal was frequently secured by hostages, but Visconti had no children other than an illegitimate daughter. However, Guidantonio's father, Antonio, had formed a league with the Visconti in 1376, and Guidantonio himself had maintained this alliance into the next generation. Because of this established link with Visconti, the Venetians asked Guidantonio to send Federico to Venice in 1433 as a security measure. He had already experienced being a hostage: for a few months, probably in 1432, he was sent to Rimini as surety for his father's truce with the Malatesti – his first encounter with his inveterate enemy Sigismondo, who was five years older, and may even have already been the ruler of Rimini, since he succeeded his brother in 1432.[1] Given the long-standing tensions between the families, and his own character, Sigismondo is likely to have tried to dominate the young hostage, who would thus gain insight into Sigismondo's psychology, making this a useful, though doubtless very unpleasant, experience.

Federico arrived in Venice on 28 February 1433, according to the chronicler Ser Guerriero de' Berni da Gubbio, who knew him in the 1430s.[2] After a childhood spent in a small town in the Apennines, Venice must have been a revelation. It was beautiful, opulent and wealthy beyond anything Federico had ever seen, or could have imagined, though much of the Venice we know did not yet exist – the Rialto of 1433 was a wooden structure that looked a bit like the Ponte Vecchio in Florence, with two rows of shops along its length. But many-domed, Byzantine St Mark's was already much as we know it today, with the horses of Lysippos standing proudly on the façade. St Mark's must have been the biggest building Federico had ever seen by a long way, and astonishing to a country boy, its cavernous interior encrusted with gold-ground mosaics, and its spectacular altar retable, the Pala d'Oro, a great sheet of Byzantine gold, enamel and gems. The distinctive Venetian-Byzantine style had developed in the course of the thirteenth century, and when he arrived in the city, Federico found a building boom in full swing. The Doge's Palace had recently been extended by Francesco Foscari with a ground-floor arcade on the outside and open first-floor loggias running along the façade; but it is probably more significant that the noble families of Venice were throwing up fantastic palaces along the canals: the exquisite Ca' d'Oro, built for the Contarini, was brand new, since it was finished only in 1430. Though its elaborately interlacing ogee arches are now white, the façade was originally covered in gilt and polychrome decoration. So, in addition to expanding his understanding of the complicated politics of his time, eleven-year-old Federico will have observed the impressive effect of elaborate and beautiful buildings as statements of family pride and power.

In Venice, he not only distinguished himself as precociously literate, but he was invited to join the Compagnia della Calza, or 'company of the stockings', an elite group of young nobles governed by chivalric ideals, who organized entertainments and events such as tournaments – they wore distinctive hosiery, hence the name. They called themselves the *Accessi* ('the inflamed ones') and adopted as their badge, or *impresa*, a row of wiggling Gothic flames, representing the flames of love. Federico would use this as one of his *imprese* for the rest of his life.[3] His induction into the Compagnia della Calza was obviously of considerable significance to him. All his life, he was a man who valued professional and social recognition, because, for all his ambition and determination, almost nothing had come to him as of right. He was invited to become an *Accesso* as a consequence of his own merits and a self-discipline astonishing for a boy barely into his teens. No wonder he set store by the honour.

Federico stayed in Venice for fifteen months, according to Bernardino Baldi, his sixteenth-century biographer, who was writing around 1600.[4] The city was liable to outbreaks of plague, and Guidantonio, concerned for Federico's health, arranged for him to be received in the Gonzaga court at Mantua as a safer alternative, perhaps in June 1434. The wife of Count Antonio, officially his grandmother, perhaps in reality his great-grandmother, had been Giovanna, daughter of Ugolino Gonzaga; but perhaps more relevantly, Guidantonio's sister Battista, who had married a

Malatesta, and the Marquise of Mantua, Paola Malatesta Gonzaga, were sisters-in-law and friends, so there was a loose family connection with the Mantuan court.

When Federico went to live in Mantua, it was not in the sprawling Palazzo Ducale, with its rooms decorated with Gonzaga family devices. Instead, he came under the influence of one of the most remarkable educators of Renaissance Italy. Vittorino da Feltre was born in a small town in the foothills of the Dolomites. In his mid-teens, he went to Padua, where he received an education in Latin literature from Giovanni Conversino. He opened a Latin school of his own, and was awarded the degree of master in 1410. But he then gave up his school and offered himself as a servant to a mathematician to pay for instruction in mathematics. After that, he went to Venice, where he studied Greek under the famous educator Guarino Guarini of Verona and the Greek humanist George of Trebizond, whom he taught Latin in reciprocal exchange. In 1419 he returned to Padua, and in 1421 he was awarded the chair of rhetoric. But all he wanted to do was teach, and the other aspects of a professor's life bored him. In 1423, he was happy to accept the invitation of Paola Malatesta, wife of Gianfrancesco Gonzaga, Marquis of Mantua, to come to his city and open a school for the ducal offspring and other privileged or talented youngsters. Paola was deeply concerned with education: her intellectual abilities were widely acknowledged, and she was a patron of the arts.[5]

Vittorino set himself up in the Casa Gioiosa, a detached villa built in 1388 by Francesco Gonzaga IV as a trysting place (it is no longer extant), decorated with colourful painted images of birds and flowers. Vittorino changed its name from Gioiosa, joyous, with its overtone of sensual indulgence, to Giocosa, meaning playful. Mural painting was not expensive, so he had it redecorated with frescoes of playing children, but he removed any over-luxurious furnishings.[6] The house had its own grounds, an enclosed meadow with trees that bordered on the river Mincio, allowing plenty of space for children to play.[7]

His pupils included the Gonzaga children, Cecilia and Margherita as well as their brothers, and Barbara of Brandenburg, who had come to Mantua aged twelve as the future wife of Ludovico Gonzaga. Other known pupils, besides Federico and Ludovico and Carlo Gonzaga, included the future lords of Imola and Correggio, and several future bishops. Humanists of the next generation such as Niccolò Perotti and Lorenzo Valla also studied with Vittorino, and several major humanists sent their sons to the school, including Francesco Filelfo, whose son would later be a client of Federico's, and Guarino Guarini. There were also forty poor students boarded at Vittorino's own expense. A surviving contents inventory from 1406 includes seventy beds, so he was not just teaching a handful of young aristocrats.[8]

We know what Vittorino looked like, because Federico later included his portrait in his *studiolo*. He was thin and kind-faced, dressed simply in brownish black. As a teacher, he was both lovable and sensible, an educator who believed in leading students by affection and respect. He wanted his students to work hard but not obsessively. When he found two little boys sitting apart and earnestly discussing their lessons, he observed, 'that's not a good sign in a child', and sent them out to play. He was a great believer in exercise.[9]

He also refused absolutely to force education on the unwilling; if even his best efforts couldn't make study of the classics attractive to a child, he would ask the parents to take him away, recognizing that not everybody had a taste for academic studies. For those who did, his results were amazing. Ambrogio Traversari, one of the best Greek scholars of his generation, visited the Casa Giocosa, and was stunned to find Cecilia Gonzaga, aged ten, writing better Greek than his own pupils in Florence, who were almost adult. Vittorino was also deeply devout; he took his pupils to hear Mass daily, and himself recited the Office of Our Lady, so his pupils probably did too. He did not instruct pupils in theology, but the practice of piety was an integral part of life at the Casa.[10] The aim was to produce *Christian* humanists, fitted for high office either in secular or religious life, with habits of self-discipline and well-stocked minds.

Federico seems to have joined this exemplary academy in the summer of 1434. According to Vittorino's biographer Prendilacqua, the teacher recognized his remarkable quality. He encountered the boy moping because he had read (probably in Livy's history, a great favourite of his in later life) that Scipio Africanus had gained practical military experience when still only a child, something that was also true of Sigismondo Malatesta, who won his first battle aged thirteen.[11] With swift tact, the teacher said, 'I don't want you to be another Scipio, but an Alexander, because like you, he was the son of a prince.' It might be added that Alexander was also famous for having been tutored by Aristotle, so Prendilacqua is thus forging a flattering link between Vittorino and the classical Greek polymath. He claims that thereafter, Vittorino would sometimes ruffle the boy's hair and say, adapting a line of Virgil, 'tu quoque Caesar eris': 'you will be another Julius Caesar', a man remembered both as a conqueror and an author.[12] For what it is worth, this story suggests that Federico was no academic by temperament. He was ambitious to achieve rather than to learn. And also, his attention was divided, and there are only so many hours in a day. As Bernardino Baldi tells us,

> In wielding weapons and in chivalric activities, which he began
> to pursue as soon as he could, he had Gianfrancesco himself as
> a supreme master, and after him [he was taught by], the great
> numbers of knights who crowded that flourishing court as a
> most honourable school devoted to the exercise of arms.[13]

So for a significant part of the time, he, and probably Ludovico Gonzaga, who was similarly destined for the life of a condottiere, left their friends reading Livy in the Casa Giocosa, and went off for professional instruction to the marquis, who was a condottiere prince. Federico was knighted by the emperor Sigismund, who came to Mantua on 22 September 1433, on his way home from his coronation by the pope as Holy Roman Emperor, something of a puzzle. The emperor's movements are easy to verify, and his visit to Mantua occurred only six months after Federico went to Venice, so either the boy was sent on a first trip to Mantua specifically in order to meet him, or the Venice stay was shorter than Baldi believed.

Instruction from a competent general was invaluable to the boy's future. There was a lot to learn; not just fighting and how to manage a horse, but how to manage an army, how to keep the men fed, watered and in good heart, basic gunnery, logistics, and how to keep thousands of horses in good condition, to name only the most obvious. Proud as he was in later life of his sojourn in the Casa Giocosa, he was in Mantua for only two and a half years, and much of that time was spent with Gianfrancesco Gonzaga. He certainly learned some Greek and some mathematics before he was called home in 1437, since mathematics remained an interest for the rest of his life, but he was probably never quite the humanist prince he presented himself as, though he retained an enquiring mind. His book-purveyor, Vespasiano da Bisticci, tells us in his memoir that, in adult life, Federico studied Aristotle's *Ethics* with the assistance of a learned Dominican called Lazarus Racanelli, who later became Bishop of Urbino.[14]

However, the Mantua episode is important. One thing Federico did take away was an excellent humanist hand. His writing is neat, regular and well formed, though with touches of showiness: rather long ascenders and descenders, and dramatically swashed 'v's. And time spent learning from as inspirational a teacher as Vittorino da Feltre will have shown him what humanism actually was, even if there wasn't time for him to fully master the curriculum. He did at least have enough training to recognize a real humanist when he saw one, and to offer a fair semblance of informed interest. Vittorino will also have stimulated the uncomplicated piety that seems to have been a strong feature of his character. And from

Gianfrancesco Gonzaga and the life of the court more generally, he learned that success as a ruler in fifteenth-century Italy depended on four things: maintaining a good reputation, a thorough education, piety, and military effectiveness.

3

Dutiful Son
1437–1444

Federico's entry into his professional life was expedited by the death of the man who was quite possibly his father, Bernardino della Carda, Count Guidantonio's principal lieutenant, in 1437. In his will, he divided his company of 800 men-at-arms and their horses between Federico and his acknowledged son, Ottaviano Ubaldini della Carda. Ottaviano was thirteen at the time, living as a hostage in Milan, and he had no ambitions towards a military life. He passed his share over to Federico, aged fifteen, who thus returned to Urbino to find himself equipped with a small private army.[1] Eight hundred men-at-arms actually translated into at least 2,400 people. The armoured mercenary of the fifteenth century needed, at a minimum, a squire to help him don his armour and support him in battle, and a servant to look after baggage, prepare quarters, and care for at least four horses (a riding horse each for the men, one for the baggage cart, and perhaps a trained warhorse as well). This unit was known as a 'lance'.[2] Precise details of the number of people involved in a lance, and who did what, varied from country to country and over time, but the basic system of organizing men was the same throughout late medieval Europe, because so much about warfare was governed by dependence on horses, which have quite exacting physiological requirements.[3] These 800 lances were a resource for their young captain, but they needed to be paid, so they were also a responsibility. Federico accordingly took himself and his men to Milan, to take service under Filippo Maria Visconti, or rather, under his captain, the celebrated condottiere Niccolò Piccinino. From Piccinino, he learned the arts of making war in a prudent and calculated manner. He also reconnected with Ottaviano.

It was probably at this point that Federico invested in his first suit of armour. Personal armour was a professional necessity, but it was also very expensive, and only the very princeliest of rulers had armour made for a boy who was still growing. Milanese armour was considered the best in Europe: as a petition to the city governor observes, 'the *contrada* and the trade of the armourers here in the city of Milan is admired by all the world'. There were seventy-two master-armourers active in 1474, which suggests the scale of the trade.[4] Certainly, the armour Federico wears in Piero della Francesca's *Brera Madonna* portrait is Milanese work from *c.* 1455–60, since it is almost identical with a surviving suit that was discovered in 1930.[5] It is likely, therefore, that it was the second suit he purchased, since he can hardly have managed without one for his first twenty years of soldiering. In the *Brera Madonna*, two armourer's marks appear on the lower breastplate near the point of the elbow-guard, which may be those of a member of the famous Missaglia family of craftsmen.[6] He updated this necessary harness in response to new developments, since the armour that appears in the intarsia panels of the *studiolo* and in the painting by Justus of Ghent is of a later design. It is an indication of Federico's sober personality that whenever he had himself painted in armour, he chose to wear the harness he would actually go to war in, completely unadorned, rather than the decorative armour made for tournaments, which he also owned (a parade helmet with a Montefeltro eagle crest is depicted in the Gubbio intarsias), or even the vastly expensive silver-gilt parade casque made for him by Pollaiuolo in 1472.

Casing his body in steel will have enforced a new physical discipline on the young Federico. A made-to-measure harness allowed a surprising amount of freedom of movement, because the individual pieces were laced or buckled to a padded canvas under-jacket and slid smoothly over one another. The help of a squire was essential; no man could arm himself, and it could not be done swiftly. In some places, gauntlets were very subtly engineered with separate fingers, but fifteenth-century Milanese gauntlets were mittens rather than gloves; and it is gauntlets of this form that are represented both by Piero della Francesca and in the intarsia panels of the *studiolo*.

One major problem for the armoured man was lack of peripheral awareness. He could look forward, and some helmets had small holes around chin level to allow him some sense of what was happening on the ground (though contemporary Milanese helmets lack this feature), but a man in armour could not glance to the side unless he swivelled his whole body. These restrictions on movement will soon have become second nature.

Harness was heavy, and it was also hot to wear because it was unventilated. A helm effectively shut a man's breath in with him and must have got very steamy in hot weather. The distinguished Renaissance historian John Hale points out that the records show men in armour were sometimes killed because they couldn't stand the discomfort and removed the gorget or beaver to cool their heads.[7] An armoured man was soon pouring with sweat, so the risks of wearing armour included heatstroke and physical exhaustion. A full suit of armour weighs 50–60 lb: modern re-enactors have commented that if one is standing around doing nothing for hours, armour becomes very tiring, though in actual combat the weight isn't noticeable. Part of the discipline of making war effectively must therefore have been deciding when to go into armour so that one wasn't tiring oneself out just sitting around in it. Additionally, while squires could clean, oil and polish the harness itself – and to guard against rust, they would have to –

under camp conditions, daily laundry would hardly be possible, even for a captain. So the under-jacket and hose must often have been stinking and filthy; they would be sodden with sweat by the end of one day, and put on still clammy the next. Perhaps, given the difficulty of relieving oneself while in full armour, the hose might also have been not just sweat-soaked but, from time to time, damp with urine, since a man-at-arms had to pay attention to staying hydrated. Most of his liquid intake would boil off as sweat, but bodily processes aren't always obliging. Federico was a fastidious man to whom cleanliness was so important that he built the most elaborate bath-house seen in Italy since the end of the Roman empire. The unavoidable sordidness of his professional life must have been hard for him to tolerate.

Federico thus consolidated the military education he had received at the court of Mantua by actual service. A year later, in 1438, his father's second wife, Caterina Colonna, died. Guidantonio was sixty, and he seems to have been devastated by this loss. He evidently felt that Federico, then sixteen, was wholly competent, because he handed over his military responsibilities to him – his legitimate son, Oddantonio, was still only twelve. From then on, Guidantonio increasingly turned his mind to religion. He had established a friary of Observant Franciscans in Urbino in 1437, and spent more and more time with them. He was buried in a Franciscan habit, and represented thus on his tombstone. Another indication of his turn towards godliness is that he founded the Urbino church and convent of San Donato in 1439.

As Guidantonio became more and more preoccupied by attempting to make his peace with God, the situation of both half-brothers was awkward, for different reasons. Oddantonio was still growing up; he had lost his mother, and his father was increasingly disengaged from ordinary life. He will certainly have had a group of advisers, but he was effectively orphaned. On the other hand, he had a place in the world, he was being groomed to fill it, and he was so young that he may have been naïve enough to take Federico for granted.

Guidantonio had disposed his sons like pieces on a chessboard, which was rash of him, since they had their own points of view. As Guidantonio saw it, Oddantonio was his heir, he was to stay in Urbino and rule it, while Federico was to take mercenary service, make money and, presumably, funnel this wealth into increasing the glory of Urbino. Federico had his little fiefdom of Mercatello (he had married Gentile in 1437, aged fifteen), so from Guidantonio's point of view, he was properly provided for. Federico been trained in a hard school, and his Venetian experience suggests that he had acquired habits of self-command at a very early age. Guidantonio, blinded by his own partialities, does not seem to have worried about what Federico might be thinking about this comfortable forward planning. He perhaps did not reflect that he had not, after all, given his older son much reason to be personally loyal to him.

There is not much suggestion in the surviving evidence that Oddantonio was being raised as a warrior. He had a tutor, Agostino Dati, then a young Sienese humanist (born 1420). Though Dati was to become famous for his eloquence as a Latinist, this was his first job, and Oddantonio's civilian education was probably less rigorous and extensive than his half-brother's: Dati's later career suggests that he would have taught Latin but not Greek or mathematics.[8] Nor could Oddantonio's mother have been any help: the Colonna were papal nobility, not condottiere, and had no reason to train their daughters as future rulers. Caterina Colonna has not gone down in history as having made any of the formal public gestures of competence that the educated women of the period were beginning to make, such as a formal speech welcoming Emperor Sigismund when he visited the city. It was her sister-in-law, Battista de Montefeltro, then living in exile in Urbino, who did the honours.[9] Caterina is therefore unlikely to have been an educating mother like Giovanna degli Alidosi, and the precious only son of an elderly father may well have been rather indulged. His mother certainly had him painted, aged seven, by Ottaviano Nelli, since a letter from the painter survives, acknowledging the commission (though the fresco in question does not).[10] But according to Dati, Oddantonio was an eager student of the classics, and the night before his assassination, the two of them had spent the evening reading part of Cicero's *De Officiis* together.[11] Costanza Varano, the granddaughter of his aunt Battista, addressed a Latin poem to him, which indicates that she thought he was familiar with central schoolroom texts, Virgil's *Aeneid*, and the works of Julius Caesar.[12]

However, Federico, who was effectively operating as pre-cociously adult and making his own decisions when he went to Venice aged eleven, who had studied Latin, Greek, mathematics and astronomy under the brilliant Vittorino da Feltre, and was doing a man's service aged sixteen, may well have been profoundly unimpressed by his little blond half-brother.[13] There are also personal factors to take into account. Oddantonio had supplanted him; Federico, aged four, had been torn from the home he knew and sent away. No matter that his foster mother turned out to be warm and welcoming, it was a traumatic experience for a young child. Federico was profoundly ambitious, and he had no reason to love Oddantonio, something their father had evidently failed to take into account.

We have very little sense of what Federico was like, or looked like, as a young man. His image, as fixed by Piero della Francesca and Joos van Wassenhove, is of a man in his fifties, sobered, worn, and even deformed, by the rigours of his life. Two doctors who have recently looked at the famous portrait of Federico by Piero della Francesca from a medical point of view have pointed out a slight but definite hump in his back: they suggest that this arose from collapse of the sixth and seventh thoracic vertebrae caused by the long hours he had spent in harness. The *Brera Madonna*, in which he is kneeling in profile in full armour, confirms this since it shows his harness rounded out at the upper back.[14] However, contemporaries suggest that he had been handsome, well-knit, and dashing in his youth. Perhaps the nearest thing to a portrait of the young Federico is a portrait in the frescoes on the walls of San Giovanni di Urbino, painted by the brothers Lorenzo and Jacopo Salimbeni in 1416. This is of a rather splendid golden-haired young man in armour, wearing a red cloak and a captain's red felt beretta; his left profile is shown, and the resemblance to later portraits of Federico is clear: it is probably an image of his father, Guidantonio.[15] Federico's own hair was black and curly.

Pierantonio Paltroni's pen portrait of Federico in his prime gives a quite different impression of him from Piero's weary elder statesman. He is an excellent witness, since he had been Guidantonio's secretary, and started travelling with Federico around 1439. He remained an intimate associate and around 1470/76 wrote his life of Federico under its subject's direct supervision. He remembers the young Federico was sexy, and an excellent physical specimen. Additionally, he indicates that he was capable of acting a part.[16]

> He was of medium height, well shaped and well made, very agile
> and strong; able to withstand cold and heat, hunger and thirst,
> sleep and fatigue, as much as he wanted… he was cheerful, friendly
> and most generous… without any arrogance, any anger, so that
> nobody ever saw him troubled except if he wanted to appear as
> such, and not because he was overcome by emotion… extremely
> measured in his speech as in every other thing, he was overcome
> and vanquished only by his lust and love for women. Women
> generally loved him, and he generally loved and desired them.

Poems by Federico's secretary Angelo Galli, which record his pursuit of various women, suggest that even in 1442, when his father was still alive, Federico's womanizing was well known, and he was quite unabashed about it, though he had been married to Gentile since 1437.[17] The manuscript of Galli's verses made for the Urbino library includes ninety-three poems written for Federico to give a mistress, or about his affairs. Most of them refer only to 'his lover' (*la sua amorosa*), which perhaps allowed them to be presented to more than one girlfriend, but one mentions a woman called Casandra, and Francesca degli Atti, who later married Galli himself, was another of Federico's mistresses.[18] His oldest illegitimate child, Buonconte, was born in 1442, and given a Montefeltro family name, once borne by the thirteenth-century Montefeltro who led the Ghibellines at the battle of Campaldino. Nothing is known of his mother; he was given to Gentile to bring up.

Federico lost a woman who meant a great deal to him during this phase of his life; Giovanna degli Alidosi, who died in 1440. She had been the nearest thing to a mother he had ever had. His capacity to assess a woman's intelligence and capabilities and not just her sexual potential, which was abundantly demonstrated during his second marriage, must rest in part on the relationships established in Giovanna's little female monarchy at Mercatello.

From 1438 to 1442, Federico defended Urbino on his father's behalf. The principal problem Urbino faced was the predatory conduct of a neighbour, Sigismondo Malatesta of Rimini (1417–68). Like so many feuds in Renaissance Italy, the struggle between Sigismondo and Guidantonio started from landholding; in 1430, Pope Martin V, strongly predisposed towards Guidantonio, had detached some castles and towns from Malatesta jurisdiction and handed them over to the Montefeltri, creating a lasting grudge that Sigismondo inherited. In September 1441, aged nineteen, Federico was successfully deceived by Sigismondo, and fell into a Malatesta ambush at Montelocco, where he was injured, but contrived to cut his way out.[19]

In October that year, he went on the attack. The fortress of San Leo had particular significance for the Montefeltri, because their family originated there; it had once been the site of a Roman temple dedicated to Jupiter Feretrius, so it was the Mons Feretrius that had given the Montefeltri their name. However, it had passed to the Malatesti. The fortress was reached by a steep zigzag mountain path, with a sheer drop on the other sides, and it had a good water supply, so it was all but impregnable. On 22 October 1441, Federico took it with a small group of picked men, using scaling-ladders to climb one of the cliffs, a victory involving notable skill and daring, which did much to enhance his reputation as a soldier.[20] Francesco Sforza, the *de facto* ruler of Milan, intervened after that to broker a reconciliation between the Malatesti and the Montefeltri, and yet another temporary truce was declared.

In 1443, Guidantonio died, and was buried in a Franciscan habit. Oddantonio, aged fifteen, succeeded him. Federico promptly left the Marche and took service under Francesco Sforza of Milan, which turned out to be an excellent move, since he met Alfonso of Naples for the first time during this campaign, and the king was very favourably impressed by him. Alfonso, then forty-seven, was affable but dignified, self-controlled, and even-tempered. He dressed plainly, drank only diluted wine, was deeply religious, and had a passion for books. Looking at the young condottiere, he must have recognized him as a man of the same stamp.[21] This would turn out to be one of the most useful relationships of Federico's life.[22]

Meanwhile, soon after his father's death, Oddantonio went to ask for confirmation of his status from Pope Eugenius IV. He also asked for the dukedom of Spoleto. Although his father had been appointed Duke of Spoleto by Martin V, the formidable condottiere Braccio di Montone had, unfortunately, forced him out. Eugenius IV was reluctant to invest Oddantonio with Spoleto, which he thought would only create trouble, given Oddantonio's youth and lack of military experience, but softened the blow by investing him with the title of first Duke of Urbino on 26 April 1443, as a reward for siding with the papacy against Francesco Sforza. Oddantonio went to Rome and attended High Mass at St Peter's, and once the pope had taken his seat, knelt at his feet. He was made a Knight of St Peter, and swore to act in defence of the Holy Church. He was invested with a ducal cap and sceptre, and kissed the pope's foot.[23] The title was no empty honour. While Urbino was a papal vicariate, papal approval had to be obtained for each succession to power, even though the Montefeltri had been ruling Urbino since the thirteenth century. The ducal title changed Oddantonio's status in a fundamental way, securing rulership over Urbino for himself and his descendants. He married Isotta d'Este, sister of Lionello, the sophisticated and well-educated Marquis of Ferrara, two months later.

But the following year, Oddantonio was brutally assassinated in his palace, along with two of his advisers, on the night of 22 July 1444, after a reign of only fifteen months, which contemporaries represent as deeply unpopular. 'Evil counsellors' is a standard Renaissance explanation for malfunctioning rulers. Oddantonio's advisers, Manfredi Pio da Carpi and Tomaso Agnello da Rimini, were believed to be agents of Sigismondo Malatesta (one of them was Riminese, which lent some colour to the accusation), though as Federico's recent biographer Walter Tommasoli observes, given that the elimination of Oddantonio was more likely to benefit Federico than anybody else, Sigismondo probably had more sense than to involve himself.[24] Agostino Dati paints a picture of Oddantonio as a mild and studious youngster, but according to some contemporary chroniclers, Pio and Agnello encouraged the young duke in general debauchery, and he took to preying on the wives of respectable citizens. The *Chronicle* of Ser Guerriero de' Berni da Gubbio, for example, states that he died 'on account of violating feminine modesty'.[25] However, accusations of sexual misconduct are easy to make, and hard to prove; and the defence of outraged wives and daughters is a highly sympathetic reason for an assassination. It may be more to the point that the talented and ruthless Sigismondo Malatesta was nibbling away at Montefeltro territory and Oddantonio seemed helpless to prevent it.[26]

Additionally, Pius II accuses Oddantonio of revolting cruelty – though Pius had good reason to paint the legitimate duke in the blackest shades, since he was hand in glove with Federico.

For what it is worth, he asserts that a forgetful page neglected to provide candles at the proper hour, so Oddantonio had him wrapped in cloth coated with wax or pitch, and set fire to his head, leaving him to die in agony.[27] But the true nature of the 'evil counsel' may have been encouraging Oddantonio to live beyond his means, because one of the few things we can be certain about in this murky affair is that the young duke imposed new taxes, which were not acceptable to the people of Urbino. Marrying an Este was a highly prestigious testimony to Oddantonio's new status, but will also have been very expensive, since his bride, and the wedding party that arrived with her, had to be welcomed with suitable extravagance. He may well have imposed extraordinary taxes to pay for the wedding. In the months that followed Oddantonio's murder, Federico, Sigismondo Malatesta and their respective partisans engaged in a paper war accusing one another of complicity in the murder, questioning one another's parentage, generally exchanging abuse, and, like rival cuttlefish, emitting enormous quantities of ink.[28]

To what extent Federico was actually complicit in his half-brother's death is unknowable, but circumstantial evidence suggests that he was pretty sure it was going to happen.[29] In the immediate aftermath of the murderous attack on Oddantonio, Federico was in the vicinity, twenty-two miles away in Pesaro, in the service of Galeazzo Malatesta, who feared his cousin Sigismondo's territorial ambitions. He was thus conveniently poised to negotiate his succession. Sigismondo perhaps played into his hands by threatening Galeazzo, which gave Federico a colourable reason for being close by. Thus Federico arrived at the city gates of Urbino only hours after the night-time attack, where he was presented with a list of un-negotiable demands by the citizenry. It was only when he agreed to rescind the new taxes that he was allowed to enter. This exchange has an orchestrated feel to it.

The Urbinates' first demand was that there should be no reprisals. Most of the rest of the document restored citizen rights and duties to what they had been under Guidantonio, and they also extracted a promise not to raise extraordinary taxes, and to restore the price of salt to what it had been (the export of salt was important to the Urbino economy).[30] Federico agreed to everything.

The new taxes had undoubtedly been imposed; the rapes may have happened also; and it is possible that power had gone to Oddantonio's head, and his classical studies had led him to take the emperor Caligula as a role model. However, in order to assess the stories about him, it is important to remember that Federico had every reason to demonstrate that Oddantonio was both incompetent and wicked. Pierantonio Paltroni was happy to back him up, perhaps because he was one of the men who hacked Oddantonio down and threw his adolescent body out of the window of his palace. He is certainly named as one of the group of assassins by an anonymous chronicler in Verona.[31] Oddantonio's corpse was retrieved from the piazza and buried in Urbino's new Franciscan church, while his teenaged widow scuttled back to Ferrara (she later made a rather more successful second marriage to István II Frangepán, the Ban of Croatia).

Federico's contemporary image as a humanist ruler, good Christian prince, and one of Italy's foremost condottieri was crafted in contrast to this image of his half-brother, which presented him as none of these things. The complex relationship of Urbino with nostalgia therefore begins here, as Federico and his partisans worked to present the idea that things had gone back to the good old days of Count Guidantonio after an unfortunate interregnum. From the moment he seized power, Federico continued to wage what amounted to a full-time public relations campaign, which, in addition to highlighting his Christian devotion and his many and varied achievements, attempted to neutralize the handicap of illegitimate birth.

Within humanist political philosophy, the idea of the virtuous ruler was frequently invoked, and it was particularly useful for someone who came to power by questionable means. Within the terms of what the Renaissance scholar James Hankins has called 'virtue politics', legitimate government depended solely on the virtue of the individual ruler(s), and not on inheritance or legal or constitutional correctness; ultimately, this principle derives from Plato's theoretical treatise on governance, *The Republic*. According to the humanists, virtue is derived from classical education and refined by the practical exercise of virtuous rule.[32] Federico's strengths were therefore his character, his education under the renowned Vittorino da Feltre, and his skill set; his weakness was his illegitimacy and lack of a mandate. He had a vested interest in demonstrating that the legitimate Oddantonio had delegitimized himself by being a bad ruler.

One figure who was very useful in building this argument is the Cicero who, in a series of blistering speeches, defended the ancient Roman republic against Catiline. As another scholar of Renaissance Italy, Virginia Cox, observes, 'for a prince of weak ascriptive status, an elected magistrate like Cicero could serve as a more flattering alter ego than any ancient king or emperor, because he embodied a model of legitimacy that rested on virtue, not blood'.[33]

If the stories about Oddantonio were true, then one might argue that he had forfeited legitimacy through tyranny (like the pre-republican kings of Rome, the last of whom, Tarquin, fell as a result of the indiscriminate sexual appetites of his son). By contrast, if he continued to behave himself, Federico would legitimize himself through virtue and popular acclamation. In effect, he had been elected by the people of Urbino. According to Paltroni, who was still wiping Oddantonio's blood off his dagger at the time, 'the will of the citizens was universally good towards the count Federico', and they opened the gates to him accordingly.[34] However, the will of the citizens was not universally good, or anything like it. In the September of his first year as count, a rebellion was raised against Federico's rule by one Giovanni Gabrieli, possibly at the instigation of Sigismondo Malatesta, which he was able to repress quickly and effectively.[35] Some combination of charm, bluff, diplomacy and the brutal suppression of dissent kept him in power from day to day, if only because of the absence of any viable focus of opposition. The only real alternative to his rule was that of Sigismondo Malatesta, and, faced with a choice between a usurper who had given pledges of good behaviour and the volatile, impulsive and imprudent head of a family of ancient enemies, the majority of the citizenry settled down under the rule of the usurper. But for his first three years in power, Federico, as Eugenius IV says in a papal bull of 1447, 'tyrannically held and occupied [the Montefeltro] against the will of Our Lord… with no concession or title'.[36] Rather like the Papal States themselves, Federico's thirty-eight ever more glorious years of rule were a reality based on an initial fiction.

4

Taking Control
1444–1450

The Urbino ruled by Federico was a considerable improvement on the territory held by his father and half-brother. Not all of Oddantonio's holdings had been contiguous, but Federico, because of his marriage to the Brancaleoni heiress Gentile, controlled the whole of the Massa Trabaria from the river Foglia to the Cantiana, something like doubling the area previously ruled by his predecessors.[1] However, he needed to watch his step. He had undertaken not to raise taxes, and the one vice of which Oddantonio seems to have almost certainly been guilty was overspending, so Federico had inherited an empty treasury. His basic income derived from money granted by the various comunes of the Montefeltro every six months, plus rents and produce from his personal landholding.[2] But he also had an enemy. Even before he seized power, Federico had faced the hostility of Sigismondo Pandolfo Malatesta, the aggressive lord of the neighbouring state of Rimini, and this was exacerbated by the murder of Oddantonio and the accusations and counter-accusations that followed it.

The feud that unfolded between Sigismondo Malatesta and Federico from the 1440s onwards was exceptionally deep and bitter, and lasted for twenty years.[3] Sigismondo's family was Guelph, Federico's, Ghibelline. The two families had been making sly land grabs from each other's territories for a couple of hundred years, punctuated by truces and intermarriage. None of this need have added up to lifelong rancour were it not that the two men were so different. Sigismondo was brave, talented and precipitate, with the kind of headstrong ego that tempts an individual to follow immediate advantage and profit – indifferent to pre-existing agreements broken or animosity aroused. A brilliant and difficult man, Federico was also brave, but he was cool-headed and calculating, and he thought in the long term. In the end, he would destroy Sigismondo utterly, though in the 1440s it was Sigismondo who seemed marked for victory. Having been appointed commander of the troops of Milan, Naples and the Church, he had taken over the whole of the March of Ancona by December 1445, overrun the Montefeltro by the following autumn, and achieved his greatest military victory when he liberated Piombino from Alfonso of Naples in 1448.

One thing the fate of Oddantonio must have taught Federico is that it would be all but impossible to rule Urbino successfully unless he had money coming in from some external source. He had signed an undertaking not to raise more tax than his father, and he knew that if he was ever going to realize his ambitions, he would have to earn his money by fighting. He therefore deputized the management of the duchy, probably to his wife Gentile, and returned to his career of making war for money. The condotta system in fifteenth-century Italy is one of the few points in the annals of military history where, for the tough and skilled, warfare could be genuinely profitable.

Federico's professional life was governed by military contracts called condotte. A condotta was a document regulating the service a captain, or condottiere, promised to provide. A condottiere undertook to provide a certain number of troops for a set period in return for a negotiated payment, primarily in cash. In Italy, it was normally expected that a condottiere would lead his troops in person, though there were exceptions; there is a case of a condotta held by a widow for her infant son, which had presumably been negotiated by the deceased husband. The contract period was divided in two: the *ferma*, a set, contracted period of service, and *di rispetta/ad beneplacitum* (condotte might be written in Italian or Latin), a further period for which the employer could retain the troops if he wished, though if his objectives had been achieved he was required to give them several weeks' notice before they disbanded. Condotte were rarely issued for less than six months, so the condottieri had to bargain for leaving their own territories unattended for considerable periods of time: this explains the prevalence of education and character among the women they chose as their wives.[4]

Federico received his first independent condotta from Francesco Sforza at the age of twenty-two in 1444, so he must have left Urbino very shortly after taking control there. Francesco Sforza, son of a successful condottiere called Muzio, was at that time captain of the forces of the last Visconti Duke of Milan, Filippo Maria. But in 1441, Filippo Maria had permitted Francesco to marry his daughter, Bianca Maria Visconti, who was illegitimate but his only child. Filippo Maria Visconti subsequently died, still heirless, in 1447, and after a brief, determined, but abortive attempt by the Milanese to restore their city to the status of a republic, Francesco Sforza established himself as duke in 1450. His marriage provided some degree of dynastic continuity, despite specific provisions in the original 1395 imperial ducal investiture of the Visconti in Milan against succession through the female line. However, unlike the Visconti dukes, who derived their power legitimately from the Holy Roman Emperor, Francesco was 'elected' duke by general assembly. This meant that his title and claims lacked legal weight outside of his power base in Milan.

Francesco and Federico thus had problems in common, being both *de facto* rulers without any actual mandate. They were also rather similar in character, and over time moved from being patron and client to being allies, and perhaps friends. Both were, to an extent, self-made men, cautious and prudent; both strengthened their grasp on power by employing the tropes of 'the virtuous Christian prince' and avoiding arrogance. In 1460, someone, perhaps Bonifacio Bembo, painted two facing, profile portraits of Sforza and Bianca Maria, in which Francesco wears his noticeably worn and shabby old red captain's beretta, while his Visconti wife has an elaborate, pearl-strung hairdo and wears splendid brocades and much jewellery. Federico must have taken note of this picture, since he has Piero della Francesca repeat so many of its formal features in the double portrait he commissioned of himself and Battista Sforza in the 1470s, similarly representing himself as a plain man of war rather than an aristocrat.

When Federico set out on his military career, he was not considered the most ferocious warrior in Italy, or the most brilliant strategist, an honour that probably went to Sigismondo Malatesta.[5] His great strength was not his flair, but his trustworthiness. Once he signed an agreement, he was never known to break it. He revoked taxes as he had promised, when he took power, and for the duration of any one condotta, he served the interests of his patron scrupulously. His reputation for honesty served him well.

Federico, like most condottieri, waged war cautiously. The men-at-arms they employed, and the horses the men rode, were not cannon fodder but highly trained, valuable assets, not to be lightly expended. Familiar, like many captains, with Roman military manuals, such as Vegetius's *Epitoma rei militaris*, he tended to view warfare more from a scientific viewpoint than as an opportunity for glory and the display of conspicuous personal courage, a departure from the traditional values of the knight, but typical of his era. He considered it a better idea to outmanoeuvre his opponent and fight his ability to wage war, or to bluff his way to victory, rather than to risk his fortune in actual field battles. When Dante encountered Federico's ancestor Guido da Montefeltro in Hell, the damned soul described himself, famously, as more of a fox than a lion.[6] According to the mores of his and Dante's age, the thirteenth century, that indicated that he was not conducting himself as a true knight. Federico, living in changed times, would probably have taken this as a compliment.

Two years after the death of Oddantonio, Federico had trouble with his half-sisters. All three, the sixteen-year-old Violante, Agnesina, and even Sveva, who was only twelve in 1446, seem to have been implicated in a plot to assassinate Federico, which was brought to light that March by his former mistress Francesca degli Atti, who had since married the courtier-poet Angelo Galli; Baldi describes her as 'a noblewoman of great spirit'.[7] It was led by the lord of Casteldolce, Niccolò Perfetti, who was a client of Sigismondo Malatesta's, and the conspirators included one of Federico's own relatives, Antonio di Niccolò da Montefeltro, who had evidently been a confidant of Oddantonio, since it was he who had been sent to Ferrara to ask for the hand of Isotta d'Este on the latter's behalf. The others were Francesco di Vico, also related to the Montefeltri, albeit distantly, and Giovanni da San Marino, who had been chancellor under Oddantonio. This suggests that not everyone in Urbino had been as delighted by the régime change as Federico's propagandists suggest.[8]

According to the Gubbio chronicler Ser Guerriero de' Berni, Federico had the male conspirators decapitated in the piazza of Urbino, but spared his half-sisters' lives.[9] Since their involvement could very well be presented as an Antigone-like loyalty to Oddantonio, who was after all their full brother, punishing them would give his enemies a handle against him. He adopted the ermine device – it was believed that an ermine would die rather than dirty its beautiful white fur – around this time, apparently in allusion to his own clemency.[10] He wrote firmly to Cosimo de' Medici on the last day of March to say that he had dealt with five malefactors, and was in control of the situation.[11]

One aspect of taking control was that Federico threw his

half-sisters out of Urbino. The Marche historian Gino Franceschini suggests that they initially took refuge with their mother's sister Vittoria Colonna, widow of Carlo Malatesta (d. 1438), who was then in Fano. After a time, Agnesina then went to Rimini, where Sigismondo Malatesta hosted her marriage to Alessandro Gonzaga, which had been arranged by her father.[12] Federico and Sigismondo Malatesta were on particularly bad terms at this time, because Federico had been deeply implicated in the secret discussions that ended up with the valuable port town of Pesaro, held by Sigismondo's cousin Galeazzo, permanently alienated from the Malatesti towards the end of 1444. Between them, Federico and Elisabetta Varano, who was Galeazzo Malatesta's daughter and Federico's cousin, played on the incompetent, and cash-strapped, Galeazzo's fear of his cousin Sigismondo, and convinced him that Sigismondo was plotting to seize his territory. They persuaded him to cede Pesaro to his granddaughter Costanza Varano (who was engaged to Alessandro Sforza). The quid pro quo was a payment of 20,000 ducats from Francesco Sforza, Alessandro's older brother, for Pesaro; a deal that left Alessandro Sforza as the lord of Pesaro, after a hasty wedding, and Galeazzo's cousin Sigismondo incandescent with rage.[13] Two years later, in 1446, Galeazzo was also persuaded to sell Fossombrone to Federico himself for 13,000 ducats, on the rather shaky grounds that Federico was his wife's nephew. It was a useful addition to his territory, because it was on both the ancient Via Flaminia and the river Metauro, which flows into the Adriatic, essential for the trade and transportation of goods and food.

Eugenius IV did not love the Colonnas, and cannot have had much personal or political affection for Oddantonio, who was a Colonna on his mother's side, but having invested the young man with the title of duke only fifteen months before his sudden demise, he may have resented the challenge to papal authority implicit in his murder. He also regarded the Sforzas, and hence their ally Federico, as his enemies. He excommunicated Federico on 14 April 1446 for buying Fossombrone without asking papal permission.

Excommunication was regularly used as a political weapon in Renaissance Italy, but this was a major problem for Federico, since it cast a dark shadow over his status as 'good Christian prince', the main plank of his claim to legitimate succession, and drew attention to his lack of title. Whether he would manage to hold on to power in the face of this setback was very much in question: in 1446, his régime, and probably his life, was hanging by a thread. The Montefeltri held their territory as papal vicars, their vicariates being granted in fief by the pope. Hence the question of *de jure* authority remained crucial for Federico, since the dukedom had died with Oddantonio, and Eugenius had not invested him as papal vicar.[14]

Meanwhile, after leaving Fano, Violante and Sveva went to their cardinal uncle, Prospero Colonna, and spent a year in Rome with him.[15] Cardinal Colonna, evidently, was not pleased with the way his sister's children had been treated. With the full agreement of the pope, Cardinal Colonna, together with Cardinal Ludovico Scarampo, invested Violante, the oldest of the girls, with the comity of Montefeltro, Montegelli, Savignano di Rigo and Rotagnano on 2 September 1446, in return for a token annual fee of an ounce of gold to be paid to the Apostolic Chamber on the feast of Saints Peter and Paul.[16] Eugenius IV issued a bull confirming her status on 3 February 1447, which heavily underscored Federico's lack of legitimacy. It was one of the last documents he signed.[17]

But Federico was facing worse than a hostile pope at this time, because Sigismondo Malatesta was allied with the Colonnas. Violante had been betrothed to Sigismondo's younger brother, Domenico Malatesta, called Malatesta Novello, since 1442, though in 1446 she was yet to live as his wife (she left her uncle the cardinal's household for Novello's city of Cesena only in 1447, when she was seventeen). Sigismondo therefore vigorously supported Violante's legitimacy as countess, since, thus, Urbino would fall to the Malatesta via marriage, just as Costanza Varano's marriage to Alessandro Sforza legitimized Alessandro's purchase of Pesaro. The Malatesti were not, of course, fighting for the rights of women, but attempting a power grab using Violante as an excuse. At twenty-four, Federico was faced not only with a hostile pope and vengeful Colonnas, but with the most successful warrior in Italy, then at the height of his powers.

Fortunately for him, Eugenius IV was already in the grip of his final illness towards the end of 1446, which is probably why he did not respond to Violante's frantic plea for a solemn investiture as duchess. He died on 23 February 1447. Federico was therefore extremely lucky. Not only did the papal election not go in favour of his enemy Prospero Colonna, which would have finished him, it went to the humanist scholar Tommaso Parentucelli, as Nicholas V, who was not opposed to the Sforzas. Pope Nicholas ignored poor Violante's documents, ordered Malatesta Novello to suspend hostilities with Federico, and allowed the latter to make his peace with the Church. In September 1447, Nicholas lifted Federico's excommunication and granted him absolution and provisional investiture with the vicariates of Urbino, Gubbio, Cagli and the rest of the Montefeltro for the hefty sum of 12,000 ducats, stipulating, however, that Violante's dowry lands and dowry of 7,000 ducats must first be made over to her. But in defiance of law, natural justice and public opinion, Federico did not do so. A dowry was important to a woman: it was returned to her if her husband predeceased her, and gave her financial independence as a widow.[18] Federico's other half-sisters married people he considered allies (a Gonzaga and a Sforza), and he paid their dowries, but he refused to hand over the sinews of war to the Malatesti.[19] Nicholas's approval of Federico was conditional, however. He did not confirm that when Federico had a legitimate son, this boy would have the right to succeed him, a privilege Federico did not obtain until 1461, when it was granted by his friend Pius II.[20]

One of Federico's most important lifelong relations blossomed in 1447. It was with the man who was either his full brother or his nephew, Ottaviano Ubaldini della Carda, two years his junior. They knew each other as young boys, but in 1432, Ottaviano (then aged eight) was sent to the Visconti court in Milan as a hostage for his father's good behaviour as condottiere. Being both intelligent and sensible, he used his time in Milan to acquire an excellent academic education and networked with the humanists who visited that sophisticated court.[21] He gave particular attention to astrology and alchemy and, as an adult, became adviser to Filippo Maria Visconti.[22] His first important intervention in Federico's life was when he waived his right to his inheritance from his father in 1437, thus leaving Federico in sole charge of a small private army. It was not until 1447, when they were both in their mid-twenties, that Ottaviano returned to Urbino. The relationship that developed was based on complete collaboration and lasted for the whole of Federico's life. It was founded on mutual trust and a natural division of duties: Federico made the decisions, Ottaviano implemented them. Piero della Francesca's diptych of Federico and Battista is instantly recognizable; but Federico also had himself depicted more than once in shallow relief, similarly counterposed with Ottaviano.

The painter and courtier Giovanni Santi (father of Raphael) summed up Ottaviano in his immensely long and detailed rhymed chronicle on the life of Federico:

> Well versed was he in classic literature,
> And mastered readily theology,
> Whilst music's gentle art his pastimes shared
> The secrets of astrology to him
> Seemed nature's lesson. Never man than he
> A heart more trusty or more leal [loyal] could boast
> A shrine of truth his bosom. Friend of peace
> And justice, merit's steady patron still
> Painters and sculptors solace found in him
> Their almost father.[23]

This portrait of Ottaviano is endorsed by many other writers. He had an extensive humanist education, and must have given much more time to purely academic learning than Federico. Though Federico had studied Greek under Vittorino da Feltre, it is not very likely that he found time to read much Greek after he embarked on his military career. The Greek books in his library mostly turn out, on closer inspection, to be translations into Latin, commentaries in Latin, or parallel texts.

Giannantonio Campano wrote of the brothers in 1475/6, 'the rule of the state is well established between the two of them'.[24] It was Ottaviano, not Federico, who undertook diplomatizing with humanists. He maintained contact with the intellectual elite of his day, and invited poets and scholars to Urbino.[25] These included Francesco Filelfo, whom he had known in Milan, and his son Giovanni Maria Filelfo (who, like Federico, had attended Vittorino da Feltre's school in Mantua). Both father and son were frequent visitors. The Neapolitan poet Giovanni Antonio dei Pandoni, called Porcellio, and the Lombard Pier Candido Decembrio also came to the city, the latter in 1449.

Giovanni Maria Filelfo also emphasizes, in *Martiados*, the epic he wrote to flatter Federico in 1464, the importance of Ottaviano to the overall régime, his purely civilian role, and his relationship with humanists:

> In the same way, the other youth will protect the rites of peace and detest its destruction. He will, due to his noble character, surpass everybody through his generosity as patron of those studies for which Augustus once strove with admirable zeal.[26]

Ottaviano's personal name was the Italian version of Octavian, the personal name of the emperor Augustus, hence the reference to him. Augustus was the patron of Virgil and Livy, among others, and Ottaviano is repeatedly represented by grateful humanists as a prince of peace and patron of the arts.

One aspect of Federico's achievement that certainly owes a

great deal to Ottaviano is the restructuring of the palace, discussed in a later chapter. While Federico had very definite views about architecture, he was away too much to supervise building operations effectively. Knowing he could leave the humanist heavy lifting to his brother, he continued to support these developments by earning substantial sums as a mercenary and, through the 1450s, also continued to pursue his feud with Sigismondo Malatesta.

Since Nicholas V was evidently anxious to put a stop to the fighting, in 1448 Cardinal Colonna organized Sveva da Montefeltro's marriage to Alessandro Sforza, who had lost his first wife, perhaps with the hope of building a truce. This was less than effective, since Alessandro already had a legitimate heir, Costanzo, from his brief first marriage to Costanza Varano, and a mistress, Mattea Samperoli, gave him two more sons as dynastic back-up. He did not need Sveva. After twelve years of unhappy marriage, she was accused of having an affair, trying to poison her husband and plotting to surrender Pesaro to Sigismondo Malatesta.[27] Whether these accusations were true (her sister Violante, for one, was passionately convinced that they weren't) is of no importance: she was forced into a convent of Poor Clares, where she acquired a reputation for sanctity under the name of Suor Serafina.[28]

Federico's personality as a warrior was completely the opposite of that of his enemy. The manoeuvrings that took place in January 1450 illustrate their respective characters, and also show that Federico was by no means above dirty tricks when occasion called for them. In 1448, Sigismondo, as leader of the Venetian armies, had scored his greatest military victory at the siege of Piombino. He was still fighting for Venice in the following year, and in January 1450 his condotta was extended for another year. Since Milan and Venice were frequently at odds, Francesco Sforza, who had a wholesome respect for Sigismondo's talents in the field, began to feel that this cosy relationship was not in his interests. Knowing that Sigismondo had been obsessed with recovering Pesaro ever since his incompetent cousin Galeazzo had let it go, he got Federico, with a show of secrecy, to contact Sigismondo. Since there had been a truce between the pair of them since December 1447, Sigismondo was unsuspicious. Federico, apparently on his own initiative, offered a bargain: he would help Sigismondo regain Pesaro, provided he got back some disputed Montefeltro castles that Sigismondo had captured. This had precisely the effect Sforza had anticipated. Sigismondo promptly abandoned his condotta, enraging his Venetian employers, and consolidating his growing reputation for unreliability. But while he was racing homewards, Francesco Sforza sent a defensive force to back up his brother Alessandro's troops in Pesaro, entertained, en route, by Federico. Sigismondo arrived at Pesaro to find it bristling with Sforza soldiery, and had to abandon his attack, with nothing to show for his pains but having wrecked his relationship with the Venetian signoria. He must have forgotten that he had tried the same stunt on Federico in 1448, when he attacked Fossombrone while Federico was campaigning for the Sforzas, but Federico had had more sense than to fall for it.[29]

In the first decade of his marriage, Federico was frequently absent from Urbino. Many of these absences related to his military career, but they also had to do with his relationship with his wife. The fact that Federico and Gentile were children together, and that she may have been his senior, may have affected their interactions as adults. They must have known each other unusually well, encouraging trust and affection on one hand, but perhaps reducing physical passion. He left her to go on campaign five months after their marriage,[30] and often thereafter, since she had been reared as a future ruler and could be left in charge. Federico had the capacity to delegate. He travelled widely, pausing for visits at the Aragonese court in Naples as well as at the Visconti court in Milan where Ottaviano Ubaldini was a member of the court.[31] This obviously means that he could trust Gentile to deputize for him, since for the first three years of his rule, Ottaviano was not yet by his side.[32]

The year 1450 was a turning point in Federico's life. Given the close alliance between Federico and the Sforzas, it is not very surprising that, when the Milanese finally caved in after three years of dogged resistance and accepted Francesco Sforza as duke in succession to his father-in-law, Filippo Maria Visconti, Federico felt that this elevation demanded some formal recognition, and proclaimed a tournament. Even in the fourteenth century, jousting had lost any connection with training for actual warfare, but it continued to flourish as a sport and an arena for the display of knightly prowess. For the condottieri of the fifteenth century, chivalric valour remained a thoroughly useful concept. While in their professional lives they embraced the latest in projectile weaponry and military architecture, they were keen to represent themselves as civilized beings, and the trappings of chivalry gave them a model of the virtuous Christian soldier. Tournament culture was therefore slow to die: tournaments were held annually in Florence, resplendent civic occasions that allowed the Medici to assert their princely stature and gloss over the modesty of their origins.[33]

Federico had not intended to take part in his tournament personally. However, an Urbinate gentleman called Guidangelo de'Ranieri turned up, who had made himself conspicuous as a jouster, and had recently been victorious in one of these Florentine tournaments. Federico challenged him, a gesture that seems out of character. However, one aspect of Federico's personality that is acknowledged by his contemporaries is his pursuit of women, and this seems to have been his downfall. Pierantonio Paltroni, who was secretary of state for the dukedom during Federico's lifetime, commented darkly, with respect to the tournament accident that cost him his right eye, that the only aspect of Federico's life in which he failed to observe a high standard of virtue was chastity: 'and this drawback and missing virtue caused a great disaster in that tournament'.[34]

Precisely what this rather obscure statement meant was spelt out by Giovanni Santi in his rhymed chronicle. There is a single manuscript of this (Vatican Library, Ottobonensis 1305), and the art historian Roberto Papini discovered only in the 1940s that Santi had decided that his first account of the fateful tournament was unsuitable for the eyes of Federico's little son Guidobaldo, for whom the chronicle was composed, and had pasted plain paper over the relevant section of manuscript, and rewritten his stanzas. But Federico was still a womanizer in 1450, since the last but one of his known illegitimate children, Antonio, was born around 1450/52. In the original version of the rhymed chronicle, Santi explained what must have been common court gossip: that one day the duke had met an attractive young lady reposing pensively 'sotto una cerqua seccha' (under a dry, i.e., dead, oak) when he was out riding in the country. He had immediately seduced her, but forgot to ask her name, and after they parted he didn't know how to find her again. However, on the day of the tournament, he saw her in the crowd, and decided on the spur of the moment to joust in order to impress her.

Federico seldom acted on impulse, but women were his weak spot. In order to make clear to the girl that he was fighting in her (unknown) name, he sent a servant to find a bunch of dry oak, and fixed the twigs to his helmet and his horse's head. But to get them attached to the steel and sufficiently conspicuous, he had to leave his visor open.[35] This explains why the Venetian historian Girolamo Muzio describes his accident as 'shameful' rather than merely unfortunate.[36]

Jousting was never entirely without risk. The horses that were used were powerful and chosen for their strength and athleticism, not lumbering creatures like modern draught horses. At the point of impact, both beasts would be cantering at around twenty miles an hour, a combined velocity of forty mph, which must have felt like a car crash. The historian Ian Mortimer observes with respect to the English king Henry IV, who was a great jouster, that 'the man, armour and horse combined weighed more than half a ton, and all the pressure of the charge was focused on the point of the lance'.[37] In a tournament, steel-tipped lances were only used in unusual circumstances. The usual Italian practice at the time was to use lances with small three-pronged crowns on the end,[38] but the shock of impact meant that a wooden lance could, and often did, burst; indeed, 'breaking a lance' was a synonym for riding a course in a tournament. This is how, for example, Henri II of France came to be fatally injured while jousting in 1559. The combatants had to be able to see where they were going, so the eye slit was always a danger zone. Henri's accident shows precisely why this was a problem: the lance of his opponent, the young Scottish Count of Montgomery, hit his helmet squarely, and shattered, and there was an explosion of sharp wooden splinters, one of which went through the king's eye slit, pierced his eye, and entered his brain. Federico's accident was somewhat similar. Henri's fate suggests that even if Federico hadn't committed the major imprudence of leaving his visor up, he could still have sustained damage. What seems to have happened is that his opponent scored a direct hit somewhere on Federico's armoured body or head, the lance exploded, and one of the splinters destroyed his right eye. He was lucky that the angle of the blow was different from the one that killed Henri II: rather than the splinter going through the back of his eye into the brain, it punched out his eye and the bridge of his nose. For ever after, he chose to be depicted in left profile, and the curiously humped nose he was left with gave him one of the most recognizable profiles of any Renaissance man.

There is a persistent rumour that Federico actually had the bridge of his nose surgically removed after losing his eye, so as to improve his field of vision if he glanced to the right. He certainly had the necessary courage and fortitude, and, after decades of incessant warfare in the peninsula, there was considerable expertise in battlefield surgery to be found: a century later, Italy led the world in surgical reconstruction. However, two doctors who have looked at the evidence, such as it is (Federico's skull has never been produced, and examining it is the only actual way of settling the issue), are inclined to doubt the story.[39] Aged twenty-eight,

Federico had sustained his first major injury, and permanently handicapped himself. There must have been an element of chagrin in recognizing that he had done so in pursuit of something as frivolous as an agreeable little affair.

5

Consolidation
1451–1460

Federico made a good recovery from his injury. After six years of rule, his position was fairly secure. He was accepted by his people and on good terms with the pope, still Nicholas V, who was more concerned with international diplomacy, the architectural reconstruction of Rome and building up the Vatican library than he was with the affairs of the Papal States.[1] Ottaviano was at his side, or deputizing for him when he was away, and Gentile was perhaps also concerned with the administration of home affairs, as well as bringing up his three illegitimate children.

His lack of a legitimate heir will have been worrying him. Gentile's continued childlessness may have led to physical coolness between them, especially since at some point in her life she developed an illness that caused her body to swell, perhaps lymphatic dysfunction, congestive heart disease or diabetes. After her death, Bernardino Baldi paid tribute to the intelligence she shared with her mother, but acknowledged that she had a physical problem, saying that she was 'a woman of fecund mind, but with a body made sterile by excessive fatness'.[2] However, Federico named his daughter Gentile after her. The girl's mother was apparently a Jewish woman called Lucrezia, but the choice of his wife's name for the child might suggest that he, and perhaps even she, thought of Lucrezia as a surrogate.[3] Gentile da Montefeltro (1448–1529), born only two years later than Battista Sforza, was raised at court alongside her brothers (or, probably, half-brothers) Antonio and Buonconte. She was nine when the first Gentile died. Gentile the younger remained at court, and made a good marriage with a Genoese nobleman. Three of their children, Costanza, Federico and Ottaviano Fregoso, feature as interlocutors in Castiglione's *Book of the Courtier*.

It was fortunate for Federico that his situation at Urbino was relatively stable, since the overall political situation was changing in the 1450s in ways that brought new problems and new opportunities. Francesco Sforza's elevation as Duke of Milan, which had been so unfortunately celebrated at Urbino, inevitably focused the new duke's attention on northern Italy, and reduced his interest in the Marches. While his younger brother Alessandro was ensconced in the port town of Pesaro, and keeping the Malatesta out of it, which was to the good from Federico's point of view, Alessandro was a minor figure in Italian politics compared to his brother; an ally, but not a patron. But while Alessandro Sforza and Federico were much on a level in terms of their power and resources, the income of the King of Naples has been estimated as 830,000 ducats annually.[4] It was at this point that Federico and the King of Naples, Alfonso of Aragon, came to realize that they could be very useful to one another. The king had previously employed Sigismondo Malatesta as his principal condottiere, but in October 1447 the latter failed to appear with the troops required by the terms of his condotta, for which he had already been paid.[5] Alfonso was understandably furious, and in April 1448 offered a condotta to Federico, which he declined because he was still fighting for the Sforza. But after 1450, it was time for a rethink. On 2 October 1451, when his contract with the Sforzas and the republic of Florence expired, Federico signed an accord and condotta with the King of Naples, and from then until his death in September 1482 he was consistently under Neapolitan protection. Even when he took temporary service with another ruler, as, for example, when he took Volterra for Lorenzo de' Medici in 1472, he never accepted any role that would prejudice Alfonso's interests.

Alfonso was a magnificent figure, and a great patron of humanists.[6] Another bond between the king and his condottiere is that they both had an illegitimate son as their heir: Alfonso had Ferrante, whom he had made Duke of Calabria. He had been recently legitimized by a papal bull granted by Nicholas V, dated 27 April 1449, which specifically granted the duke and his heirs inheritance of the kingdom of Naples; Federico had yet to secure such a bull for Buonconte. Among Federico's duties was to bring Ferrante on as a leader of men by associating with him. In June 1452, Alfonso declared war on Florence, with Ferrante as the official leader of his army, but with Federico by his side as captain-general. This enterprise, Federico's first major battle fighting for the kingdom of Naples, was unsuccessful. The army poured into Tuscany via Cortona, took Foiano, and overran much of the Florentines' territory, coming within six miles of Florence, but to little effect. Alfonso had banked on being able to borrow artillery from the Sienese, traditional enemies of the Florentines, but who, in the event, refused to help him (Siena was a noted centre for gun manufacture). Nonetheless, during this campaign, Federico won the esteem and affection of both Alfonso and his son.

The use of gunpowder and gunnery was relatively new technology in Federico's time. Captains of his generation could see that the potential was great, but so, given the state of the art, were the practical problems. In Federico's time, giant guns called bombards were in use, devices for smashing large holes in city walls, or, when sited inside a city's defences, for smashing siege engines. One such enormous gun still survives at Edinburgh Castle, the well-known 'Mons Meg', built in 1449 for Philip the Good of Burgundy, and another, also cast at Mons, called 'Dulle Griet', is in the Friday Market in Ghent. Leonardo da Vinci's *Notebooks* contain detailed advice on casting big guns and how to work out the correct proportions: the problems of casting very large items in metal were common to sculptors in bronze, bell-founders and gun-manufacturers.[7] When da Vinci sought employment with Ludovico Sforza in Milan in 1482, it was first and foremost as a military engineer rather than an artist.

Federico's professional life was complicated rather than simplified by the palaeolithic era of gunnery. As early as 1449, he commissioned both bombards and handguns from the Florentine sculptor and bronze-caster Maso di Bartolomeo.[8] Bombards were extremely problematic. They had a slow rate of fire and were very inaccurate, and they fired stone balls weighing in the region of 300 lb. If they were used offensively rather than defensively, the first logistical problem they represented was getting them to where they were wanted in a country that had done very little about its roads since the days of the Roman empire. This was especially difficult if the place where they were wanted was either on a hill or marshy. It took at least forty pairs of buffalo or oxen to move a single bombard, and they halved the distance troops could travel in a day from twelve miles to six, even less in rainy conditions, which softened the ground; their effect on an army's speed is presumably why Federico did not bring bombards all the way from Naples, since they would have delayed him by a good month.[9] They also needed a swarm of support workers: drivers for the draught animals, smiths and carpenters to repair the gun carriage whenever it threatened to come apart, masons to chip cannonballs, and a mass of labourers to manhandle the bombards into position and throw up earthworks and so on, as well as actual master gunners to point and fire the things.

These monstrous guns were also liable to burst, often lethally: King James II of Scotland was killed at the siege of Roxburgh Castle in 1460 by a gun that exploded, and Federico lost one of his five bombards in the course of his 1478 campaign. Enormous balls of natural stone could easily be flawed in ways not apparent to the naked eye, and might respond to a charge of gunpowder by exploding in the barrel. As time went on, bombards also became less and less useful. They could do real damage to medieval-style high city walls, but military architecture hastily adapted to face these new challenges, and fortifications were rapidly redesigned to have massive earthworks with sloping walls, making it harder for a bombard to score a really damaging hit. As the military historian John Hale comments, 'they were as much symbols as weapons... the day of these impractical monsters was short'.[10] Nonetheless, some condottieri thought it worth the incredible effort of moving them about if a siege was in prospect, and Federico was one of them.

Handguns of a rudimentary kind were also coming into use during Federico's service. A letter from the Hungarian king Matthias Corvinus to Gabriele Rangoni, Bishop of Eger, written in 1488, reflects the way that war was changing during Federico's career.[11] The first part of the letter emphasizes the man-at-arm's need for support – the 'lance' remained a basic form of organization in the late 1480s:

> The third force of the army is the infantry, which divides into various orders, the common infantry, the armoured infantry, and the shield-bearers. The armoured infantry and the shield-bearers cannot carry their armour and shields without pages and servants, and since it is necessary to provide them with pages, each of them requires one page per shield and armour.

But he also indicates that handguns, or rather, a very primitive form of handheld firearm, had come into use. This could be supported with two hands, in which case the man-at-arm's page might be on hand to ignite it, using smouldering wood, coal, a red-hot iron rod, or slow-burning match cord. Alternatively, the hand cannon could be supported on a rest and steadied with one hand, so the gunner had the other hand free to touch his slow match or coal to the touch hole. These guns could fire just about anything, iron balls if they were to be had, pebbles if they weren't, and aiming was hardly a relevant concept. Matthias says,

Then there are hand-gunners… they are very practical, set behind
the shield-bearers at the start of the battle, before the enemies
engage, and in defence. Nearly all of the infantry and the hand-
gunners are surrounded by armoured soldiers and shield bearers,
as if they were standing behind a bastion. The large shields set
together in a circle present the appearance of a fort.

Federico was an early adopter of this new technology, and
included primitive handguns called *cerbottane* and a newly invented
kind of light cannon called *spingardi* among his forces.[12] He took
a contingent of hand-gunners to the siege of Fano in 1463, as well
as a bombard.[13]

Despite the limitations of bombards and *cerbottane* as weapons
of attack, Federico clearly perceived the usefulness of gunpowder,
since he chose a lit grenade as one of his personal *imprese*. These
were not yet the modern grenades triggered by pulling out a pin,
but they were still much more practical weapons than the great
bombards. Grenades were developed in the Arab world, where they
were in common use by the twelfth century. Early grenades were
made of unglazed ceramic, embossed with grooves and shaped like
a three-dimensional ace of spades, tapering to a point. They were
filled with incendiary material – petroleum or naphtha, crude oils
found at surface levels in various parts of the Middle East, or the
famous, and mysterious, 'Greek fire', a chemical compound that
was a Byzantine state secret, and ignited of its own accord in air.
There was a small hole in the top to pour the liquid in, and it was
stoppered with a wick once the grenade was loaded. It could then
be lit and hurled, using muscle power or some kind of catapult,
into a city under siege, creating fires that were hard to put out.
The grenades depicted in Federico's manuscripts are pear-shaped,
spouting fire from one end and presumably just on the point
of exploding; they appear to be metal rather than ceramic.[14]
They were presumably loaded with gunpowder and fitted with
slow-burning match cord, which can stand quite rough handling
without going out.

As an emblem, a grenade was probably intended to illustrate the concept of 'armed peace' developed by Aristotle,[15] that is, defence as a necessary protection for order and peace, because the point about a grenade is that it explodes only if triggered and at the appointed time.[16] It is sometimes accompanied by the motto *ardet ut feriat* (it burns so that it may strike). Grenades are depicted in different rooms of the Ducal Palace, including the *alcova* and the *studiolo*, and frequently appear in Federico's manuscripts.[17]

In 1454, the Peace of Lodi – a treaty between Milan and Venice that was quickly ratified by other states – established the hegemony of Venice, Milan, Florence, the kingdom of Naples and the Papal States over the peninsula, a balance of power that endured until 1495. These five powers maintained and expanded their holdings with the help of independent military contractors, of whom Federico was one of the most successful. This is the political context that shaped his mature career.

His oldest son, Buonconte, meanwhile, was doing well. Gentile the first seems to have been well named. She was gentle and loving as well as intelligent. She raised Buonconte, along with her husband's other children, Gentile and Antonio. Martino Filetico, in his funeral oration on Gentile, emphasizes her sweet nature and devotion to her stepchildren, whom, he claims, she considered 'dearer than her eyes'.[18] Buonconte was deeply attached to Gentile, whom he referred to as 'my mother and lady' (*me matre et madonna*) in a 1457 letter on her death to Bianca Maria Visconti in Milan, in which he also says, 'she loved me no less tenderly than if she had given birth to me'.[19] The two women were friends, because at a difficult moment for the Sforzas in 1446, Bianca Maria and her children had found a temporary refuge in Urbino, where Gentile had received them graciously.[20] Federico took a good deal of trouble with Buonconte. He asked Guarino Guarini of Ferrara to recommend a tutor, and the famous educator suggested his erstwhile pupil, Martino Filetico (1430–90), who accordingly came to Urbino *c.*1453–5 to teach both Buonconte and his cousin Bernardino Ubaldini della Carda, son of Ottaviano.

In 1456, Federico left Buonconte at the Sforza court, then in Pavia, as a token of goodwill towards Francesco Sforza. In Pavia, Buonconte will have met Battista Sforza, aged ten, who was Francesco's niece, the daughter of Alessandro Sforza and Costanza Varano. She and her younger brother Costanzo, whose mother had died at his birth, were receiving a full humanist education alongside her cousins, the clever and talented Ippolita Maria and Galeazzo Maria Sforza, at the hands of the court humanist, Baldo Martorello da Serra de'Conti, in accordance with the expectations of her aunt by marriage, Bianca Maria Visconti. She had been in Milan since she was four, partly as a hostage for her father's good conduct, and partly because Bianca Maria wanted to give the motherless children a home.[21] In 1456, Buonconte was fourteen. The two children must have got to know one another: Buonconte was being groomed as Federico's heir, and was receiving a thorough education in Latin and Greek at the hands of Martino Filetico,[22] so while he was in Pavia, it seems highly likely that he joined Battista, Costanzo, and Bianca Maria's own children in the schoolroom.

According to Bernardino Baldi, Buonconte was an attractive boy, witty, graceful, a good horseman and a good fencer. Sadly, he subsequently went to Naples in 1458 with Bernardino Ubaldini, on their first independent diplomatic mission, to offer condolences to Ferrante, the new king, on the death of his father, Alfonso, only to find that plague had broken out. They fled for home, but both boys died on the way, Buonconte at Aversa, and Bernardino at Castel Durante.[23] Federico was heartbroken. He wrote to Francesco Sforza, 'I know that because of my sins, the Lord has removed one of my eyes, and this son, who was my life and joy and that of my subjects, who never failed to do anything I might have wanted from him, and I cannot think of anything in which he would have displeased me.'[24]

Around the same time, Ottaviano lost his mother, Aura,[25] and a couple of months before the death of Buonconte, Federico lost his wife. Whatever was wrong with Gentile physically was not brought about by injudicious indulgence in pasta. She was a sick woman. Orfeo della Rovere wrote after her death that 'she died of an obesity which her doctors said would continue to make her larger and fatter and it was a monstrous thing to see'.[26] It sounds like some kind of oedema, which started to get dramatically worse. She died on 27 July 1457 in the convent of Santa Chiara, to which she had retired during her final illness. She was memorialized with a funeral oration by Martino Filetico, which emphasized her role in educating Buonconte, her husband's acknowledged heir.[27] Alessandro Sforza wrote a 152-line self-consciously Petrarchan consolatory poem dedicated to Federico on her death, focusing principally on her renunciation of the world. He describes her as 'temperate, prudent, humble and sagacious', and also as 'benign, honest and kind'.[28] Filetico wrote an epigram on a second illegitimate daughter of Federico's, born after the death of Gentile and, like the first, named after her, suggesting the sincerity of Federico's affection for his first wife. This baby was presumably conceived between 1457 and 1459, since the poem uses the past tense for Gentile the first, and she must have died in infancy, since no more is heard of her. Filetico says, 'the wife of your lord and father was Gentile, you, Gentile, will be a darling daughter to your father', as if the name was a sure password to his affection.[29]

6

Battista
1460–1472

Federico doubtless became aware of Battista Sforza while Buonconte was in Pavia. She was shaping up to be a thoroughly desirable prize. Apart from her personal qualities, she was herself legitimate, and descended from a legitimate Montefeltro, the learned Battista, sister of Count Guidantonio, who was her great-grandmother, so she would strengthen his claim to Urbino. A marriage would also forge links between the Montefeltro family, Alessandro Sforza in Pesaro, and the greater Sforza court at Milan. Meanwhile, the issue of a legitimate heir was an urgent one, so it seems that Gentile was barely cold before Federico began negotiations. Alessandro Sforza's poem of consolation was somewhat supererogatory. He agreed to betroth his daughter Battista, aged eleven, to Federico, though the marriage did not take place until she was nearly fourteen.[1]

While Federico was a lover of women, and Battista was an attractive girl, that would not have been his central motive. Sigismondo Malatesta, a man at the mercy of his impulses, fell in love with Isotta degli Atti when she was ten and married her on the death of his second wife, though she could bring him no political advantage and she had not been educated as the future

wife of a condottiere. The end result of this rashness was that
after Sigismondo died, she attempted to rule Rimini on behalf of
Sigismondo's designated heir, Sallustio, who was murdered within
the year by his illegitimate half-brother Roberto, who also set Isotta
aside and perhaps had her killed.[2] Federico would never have done
anything so quixotic. Mistresses were one thing, wives another. But
he had already sized Battista up as a powerful personality in the
making, and to all appearances she was healthy, and she possessed
fortitude, intelligence, character and piety as well as useful family
connections. With any luck, she might also possess the ultimate
wifely virtue of fertility.

From a twenty-first-century point of view, this marriage looks
like child abuse, but thirteen was a perfectly normal age for
aristocratic women to marry in fifteenth-century Italy. And it is
clear that, once married, Federico acquired Battista's total loyalty.
He was twenty-four years older than she, but he liked women,
which may be a euphemism for exploiting them sexually, but, in
the context of this particular marriage, may have allowed him to
make friends with this clever girl. On Federico's side, there were no
more illegitimate children, and he may even have been a faithful
husband. Unpromising though it might seem at the outset, this was
a marriage that worked. Battista was a girl-child with something
of Federico's own steely ruthlessness. She rapidly accepted her new
identity as the Countess of Urbino and unhesitatingly identified
her interests with those of her husband. It is as if she had been
waiting for a chance to prove herself as mistress of her own domain.
Her ambition met and matched with Federico's, and for the rest of
her life their project was a joint one, to make Urbino glorious, and
to found a dynasty.

But Battista was much more than the potential mother of his
heir – important though this was. Being legitimately descended
from Count Guidantonio's sister Battista, she thus not only had
Montefeltro blood but was the product of an extraordinary lineage
of competent women. On 31 May 1433, while the first Battista

and her husband, Galeazzo Malatesta, were exiled from Pesaro due to his ineptitude, she had welcomed Emperor Sigismund to Urbino with a Latin speech that moved rapidly from welcome to a series of specific requests concerning her own political life, in which she asked for support in restoring her husband to Pesaro, and in securing the release of her son-in-law, Piergentile da Varano, who was in prison.[3] Her poetic exchanges with her father-in-law, Malatesta 'dei Sonetti' Malatesta, were also circulated.[4] In addition to her public political profile, which she maintained even after her husband's virtual abdication from power, Battista directed the studies of her daughter, Elisabetta Malatesta, who was educated in the same way, and a patron of humanist studies.[5] Battista da Montefeltro also taught her granddaughter Costanza Varano, and when her great-grandchildren returned to Pesaro after spending their early years under the care of Bianca Maria and Francesco Sforza, she oversaw their education at the hands of Matteo Collenuccio da Sassoferrato and the humanist Martino Filetico. This lineage of learned, capable and politically astute women, each generation educating the next, was unusual, but far from unique. The Sforzas were doing the same, as were the Este and Gonzaga. In fact, it is around this time that a variety of writers, both male and female, began developing a narrative of female princeliness, while this growing band of illustrious women actively curated their own reputations for learning and rulership, and quite frequently made gestures of support towards one another.[6]

Additionally, the powerful Bianca Maria continued to regard her niece by marriage as something like an adopted daughter, and was keenly interested in her welfare, so Battista Sforza was no neglected child. Letters exchanged between Pesaro and Milan document Battista's return to Pesaro in 1458 and illustrate her relationship with Bianca Maria, Bianca's concern for Battista's physical and mental health and, above all, her desire that Battista should continue her education.[7] Alessandro Sforza therefore hired Martino Filetico, who was out of a job since the early death of

Buonconte da Montefeltro, to oversee the education of his two children. For the rest of her life, in writing to Bianca Maria, Battista Sforza signed herself as 'figlia', daughter, rather than 'Countess of Urbino'.[8] And Bianca Maria, the legitimating link who had allowed Francesco Sforza finally to impose his rule on Milan, provided the young Battista with a model for her own position.

Among the letters that document the relationship between Battista and Bianca Maria are two from the physician and diplomat Benedetto Reguardati di Norcia, written to Bianca Maria after Battista had been taken back to Pesaro, which sent good news about the way her character was developing, aged twelve or so. According to Benedetto, she showed every sign of becoming a great woman. She knew how to dress and conduct herself, but above all she knew how to speak appropriately, pleasing both in terms of her choice of words and her accent and way of speaking. He caps his description with a quotation from Plautus, '"nor is milk more like milk" than Battista is like the fond memory of her mother'.

Her mother, Costanza Varano, had been renowned for public speaking: orations to Bianca Maria, Francesco Sforza, Alfonso of Aragon, and to the people of Camerino were written down at the time, and survive. She also exchanged letters with other humanist women and addressed a poem to the famous Venetian woman humanist, Isotta Nogarola. We are here being told that, with her assured and educated speech, Battista was shaping up to be a woman of the same kind.[9] It is notable that Reguardati's description of her focuses primarily on her sophisticated use of words. He also tells us that she already had her own personal household, run by a matron aged fifty or so, Maddalena Almerici of Pesaro, but that she also had male staff, Ser Rolandino and Ser Antonio dell'Abbate, formerly of her mother's chancery. She had her own chaplain, and attended daily Mass in the family palace, which she rarely left, and then only for some important religious festival.[10] Aged twelve, she was no longer being treated as a child, something she had in common with her future husband.

Because of Piero della Francesca's famous profile portrait, we envisage Battista as pale, passive, blonde, and in fact dead (she had been dead for two or three years when it was painted, and Piero probably modelled her features from her death mask). But there is what may be a lifetime representation of her, which was commissioned by her father around the time of her marriage, in Rogier van der Weyden's Sforza Triptych, where she and Costanzo kneel facing their father at the foot of the cross.[11] Only Alessandro Sforza's careworn, middle-aged head is certainly a portrait: he spent eight months in Flanders and Burgundy in 1457–8, and commissioned a portrait of himself from Rogier van der Weyden, who thus had a drawing of him to hand.[12] By contrast, the two adolescents are shown in profile as fairly generic young aristocrats (apart from the fact that Costanzo, in Sforza livery, has apparently acquired the ability to hover in mid-air with his red beretta hitched on his knee). Van der Weyden could have been working from descriptions, drawings sent by his client, or his imagination. For what it is worth, his version of Battista's pale profile is similar to that of Piero della Francesca, but he records that her hair was actually chestnut brown. So why would Piero turn her blonde? The answer is fashion: every upper-class girl in fifteenth-century Italy was a pale, Nordic blonde, if we believe their portraits, because this was fashionable, if difficult to attain, and what was unattainable in reality could nevertheless be represented as truth by a painter. Netherlandic portraiture was already more realistic. It is therefore more probable that Piero has imposed this desirable feature on Battista retrospectively than that van der Weyden has darkened her colouring.[13] In his painting, she has neither cast down her eyes nor raised them in divine contemplation: she and her father are looking at one another, and she is almost smiling, whereas Costanzo's gaze seems to be fixed on St John, standing to the right of the crucified Christ.

Giovanni Sabadino degli Arienti wrote a collection of biographies of notable and politically active women for Battista's own half-sister, her father's illegitimate daughter Ginevra Sforza Bentivoglio, in 1483, when Battista's appearance would still have been remembered, and he gives us some sense of what she actually looked like in life. 'She was of moderate height, fair of skin and as fresh as a living rose. She had beautiful and most modest eyes, which rarely showed her incognizant of that which was within her chaste view. She had beautiful hands and white teeth. By nature and complexion, she was more sanguine than others: sometimes, for some offense, she would become enraged quickly, but just as quickly, the anger would leave her.'[14] This is an intriguingly unorthodox description of a fifteenth-century Italian lady. Chastity, of course, was regarded as the central female virtue, so naturally she is described as superbly chaste, but he also says that she was notably observant. This is at a time when the Archbishop of Florence, Antoninus Pierozzi, advised Lucrezia Tornabuoni, wife of Piero di Cosimo de'Medici, in his *Opera a ben vivere*, 'take good care of your sight, holding it well and mortified so as not to mar your spirit with scandal. Walk with the eyes so low that you do not see beyond the ground upon which you must place your feet.'[15] But Medici women played no part in public business: Battista, on the other hand, lived far more in the public sphere than a Florentine banker's wife, and she needed to keep her eyes open and her wits about her.[16]

Sabadino also tells us that she was pink-cheeked, and, surprisingly, that she was hot-tempered. The latter was normally considered a masculine quality in fifteenth-century Italy, where women were supposed to be able to control themselves. Battista's temper, to be mentioned at all, must have been quite a noticeable feature of her personality. He also notes that she enjoyed hunting, not the most ladylike of pastimes. Taking the two passages together, we see that, though physically on the small side, Battista was anything but passive, and a force to be reckoned with.

Battista was not quite fourteen years old when the marriage took place, and still a student. The marriage is recorded by Ser Guerriero de' Berni da Gubbio: it took place on 8 February 1460, amid grand celebrations.[17] These included dances: dancing by then was *de rigueur* at Italian courts, particularly in celebration of betrothals and nuptials, and the young Battista had not spent all her time at her desk. Her father supported perhaps the most famous dancing master in Italy, Guglielmo Ebreo da Pesaro, who was, as his name suggests, a Jew; there were a good few Jews living in the Marche in the fifteenth century. Around 1463, he wrote a defence of dancing as a noble art, *De pratica seu arte tripudii* (On the Practice or Art of Dancing), in which he describes qualities necessary for dancers, including posture, musicality, style and memory, and provides first-hand accounts of massive court celebrations in which he played a role. These included Battista and Federico's wedding.[18]

It was part of Battista's job to play a leading part on such occasions, beautifully dressed, and exhibiting an appropriate level of grace and skill, displaying an aristocrat's easy style, not the strenuous acrobatics of a professional.[19] The humanist Tideo Acciarini, who wrote a suite of poems on Alessandro, Costanzo and Battista Sforza dedicated to Alessandro, confirms that she was a good dancer, writing 'Terpsichore herself guides your feet'.[20] As the Renaissance historian Graham Pont has observed, 'dance was not only an essential part of aristocratic behaviour; it also provided a code of social emblems and a language of cosmic metaphors which were part of the Renaissance world-view. To the Renaissance mind, nurtured on Plato, a well-conducted life was essentially a noble dance.'[21] But once the festivities were over, Battista returned to her study. She brought Martino Filetico back to Urbino with her, and continued her formal education until 1467.

Her capacities as a leader were tested within months of her marriage. She was fourteen, pregnant with her first child, and Federico had left her in charge. Taking advantage of Federico's absence and assuming that Battista did not have the capacity to respond effectively, Sigismondo Malatesta attacked a small military outpost, Uffogliano, which had been recently conquered by Federico.[22] Battista sent a series of letters to Francesco Sforza in Milan, using her talent with words to keep him abreast of the situation and plead for his support.[23] Francesco did send troops, and she was able to re-secure the town. The victory consolidated her reputation, since it made it quite clear to the people of Urbino that her humanist training was thoroughly practical. Giovanni Sabadino degli Arienti stresses that when Federico was absent, she ruled on his behalf, 'with a manly soul, with no fear whatsoever, for which reason she was accused of being incautious'. The latter view was not his own. He was strongly supportive of these new-style educated women, and he says of Battista, 'she was so wary and shrewd, that she could have governed the kingdom of France'.[24] Federico had such trust in her that she was fully mandated as his proxy when he was on campaign from the age of fifteen, and her signature appears on many official documents, as 'Comitissa Montisferetri ac Urbini'.[25]

For Federico, the first three years of the marriage were dominated by his feud with Sigismondo Malatesta, which was pursued with grim pertinacity on both sides. His health was not always good; he wrote from one of his armed camps to his doctor in Urbino in 1461 that he was suffering so severely from gout he was considering suicide.[26] While this was certainly not an entirely serious statement, what we can take from it is that from 1461, if not earlier, he might find himself distracted from whatever he was doing by a sudden onset of intense pain. Gout is recurrent and chronic, caused by the build-up of uric acid in the joints, and is notoriously debilitating. Sufferers often find even the weight of a sheet intolerable, so forcing armour on over swollen, tender joints must have been agony. But despite the gout, Federico eventually triumphed over his enemy, and defeated Sigismondo in 1463, after which he and Battista spent two fairly quiet years together at Urbino, which he used to initiate another phase of expansion at the palace, discussed in a later chapter. Sigismondo lived on, defiant, bankrupt and desperate, until 1468.

Though fertility was not the only quality Federico esteemed in his young wife, his need for a male heir was extremely urgent. A woman could inherit: nothing prevented Federico from naming his oldest legitimate daughter, once he had one, as his heir. But the trouble was, if he did, Urbino was immediately vulnerable to takeover. His first wife, Gentile Brancaleoni, had been the heiress to a small independent fiefdom, but on her marriage to Federico it was absorbed into the territory of Urbino. Similarly, it was marrying Costanza Varano that gave Alessandro Sforza his title to Pesaro. Ruling solo, as Elizabeth I would do a century later in England, was unthinkable in fifteenth-century Italy, and in any case merely postponed the problem to the next generation. But the other problem was that a woman couldn't preserve his legacy. The wealth and power of Urbino did not come from rents and taxes, it came from condotte. There were some tough women in fifteenth-century Italy: Gentile Malatesta, the aunt of Federico's great enemy Sigismondo, became regent of Faenza on the death of her husband in 1417, and acquired such a reputation as a fighter that she was nicknamed Penthesilea, after the Queen of the Amazons.[27] But no woman, however ferocious in temperament, could become a professional soldier, because nobody would hire her, so the money would stop coming in. It was also relatively unlikely that the pope would ratify a woman as either papal vicar or duchess in her own right, and thus she would be vulnerable to challenge. Even if he did, a woman might have trouble making her claim stick: Eugenius IV had made Violante papal vicar over Montefeltro, and only death prevented him from solemnly investing her as Duchess of Urbino, but it had still been possible for Federico to brush off her claim. His one remaining insurance policy was his second son, Antonio, who in 1460 was only about eight. Ottaviano's only son Bernardino had died in 1458, along with Buonconte, so the whole future of the dynasty rested on Battista.

It's revealing that the décor of the first phase of Federico's great rebuilding, the rooms that Battista actually lived in, pullulates with fat-cheeked, naked boy babies. Putti frisk over doors, struggle with giant wreaths, or hold up shields over the fireplace of the Sala della Iole and Sala degli Affreschi. Even the return faces of the window cornice in the Sala della Iole have baby boys' heads in roundels on either side, carved by Michele di Giovanni, known as Il Greco.[28] A maternal head in the round, with a little boy's on either side, is carved in the pediment over the door to the Sala degli Affreschi. Wherever she went, Battista's eyes would have passed over images of pudgy little baby boys.

Battista became pregnant very soon after her marriage, since she married on 8 February and gave birth to a daughter on 26 December in the same year. This baby died two months later, which must have been sad for them both. Battista will also have grieved for her paternal grandmother, Lucia Sforza, who died in the same month,[29] but Federico could console himself with the thought that the baby's little life at least demonstrated that the marriage was fertile. However, they cannot but have been aware that Battista was risking her life with every pregnancy. Her mother, Costanza, had died aged nineteen, giving birth to her second child, Battista's brother, Costanzo. She had birthed Battista, her first child, only thirteen months previously. Battista's life would have been less endangered if Federico had held off consummating the marriage till his wife was more mature, which some fifteenth-century couples did, but he could not afford to wait. The doctor, Benedetto Reguardati da Norcia, who saw Battista aged twelve, noted that she promised to be tall.[30] Her smallness in adulthood is a witness to the toll pregnancy takes on an immature body.

An incident in July 1460 will have reminded Federico of the fragility of life. He was still allied with the Sforzas, though that condotta was coming to an end, when, in the course of indecisive manoeuvres at San Fabiano, a knight from the Aragonese army challenged one of Federico's men to a joust. Counter-challenges were issued, and the opposing forces agreed to take a break from official hostilities and hold a tournament. Federico, who doubtless remembered the tournament of 1450 only too well, did not offer to fight, but acted as marshal. But, spotting someone straggling off in the wrong direction, he spurred his own horse so as to catch him up, and it moved unexpectedly in such a way that he damaged his back. He was suddenly in agony, and incapable of movement, so he had probably slipped a disc. He had to be lifted off the animal and put to bed.[31] A couple of days later, when battle had been rejoined, he needed to make a show of leading his troops, but was incapable of putting his armour on, so he had himself swaddled in bandages and lifted onto a horse to encourage his men. His iron constitution triumphed and he recovered from this injury, but it probably weakened him, and will certainly have reminded him that he was far from immortal, and still had no legitimate heir. Both husband and wife, in different ways, were pushing their bodies to the limit in pursuit of dynastic glory. Battista joined Federico in his winter quarters at Magliano in Sabina early in 1461, and stayed with him till she was sure she was pregnant.

One thing that suggests a new sort of confidence in the Federico of 1461, who knew that finally he possessed a fertile wife, is that he commissioned an epic poem on his own life and times from the Neapolitan poet Porcellio Pandoni, who was then in Pesaro tutoring the young Costanzo Varano, though *Feltria*, as it was called, was not completed until 1475. In October 1461, Martino Filetico accompanied Battista to Rome, together with Ottaviano Ubaldini and his wife, Angela Orsini. Battista was well into her second pregnancy, and Federico had intended to rendezvous with her there, but was delayed, as we know from Porcellio Pandoni, since he wrote a consolatory poem for her, 'Exhortation to the divine Battista, because she did not find her lord and husband Federico in Rome'. In this, he compares the countess to the patient Penelope, and offers to amuse her with a guided tour of Rome.[32] Ulysses' wife, Penelope, was often invoked by humanists trying to put these new-style educated condottieri's wives in some kind of context, since Penelope was famous for cleverly preserving her chastity while simultaneously fending off challenges to her absent husband's kingdom. The highlight of Battista's Roman visit was an audience with the humanist Pope Pius II, in which she was again accompanied by Filetico, who presented Pius with his own Latin translation of Isocrates' Greek *De laudibus Helenae*, which extols the beauty of Helen of Troy. Doubtless in introducing his work, it was possible to work in a compliment to the youthful Countess of Urbino.

According to the papal court humanist Giannantonio Campano, who subsequently wrote a widely circulated funeral oration for Battista, Pius II was interested to meet Battista because he believed that women at this time were wrongly denied educational opportunities.[33] Pius honoured her by knighting twelve men in her retinue, and gave her a licence enabling her to seek entrance to any convent at any time and to receive lodgings during Holy Week.[34] This allowed her to travel throughout Italy as she chose, in a context where her conjugal chastity could not be aspersed. She was able thus to establish an alternative female-based network that gave her a certain kind of power and influence distinct from that which resulted from her marriage. Although Battista was motherless, her maternal grandmother, Elisabetta Varano, was alive. She had retired into the Clarissan convent of Santa Maria di Monteluce in Perugia after her husband was murdered, but when Federico founded a convent for Poor Clares in Urbino in 1445, shortly after he seized power, he requested the pope to allow her to transfer to Urbino and to become the convent's first abbess.[35] She was his cousin, as well as Battista's grandmother, and since it was she who had helped him to acquire Fossombrone, they were clearly allies, and perhaps friends.[36] He called on her once a week, according to Vespasiano da Bisticci, conversing through the convent grille; but, with free right of entry, Battista could go and have a private conversation with her politically astute grandmother at any time.

Battista was conspicuously pious, with particular connections with the Franciscan order, whom Federico also supported. But in fifteenth-century Italy, conspicuous piety in the ruling household was one of the essential underpinnings of a successful régime. A ruler needed to be seen to be a good Christian prince by his subjects and by his peers, though naturally it was only the wives who were expected to maintain scrupulous chastity, and to refrain from sins such as murder, grievous bodily harm, deception and theft, all of which were inevitable aspects of a mercenary's life. In the famous double portrait by Piero della Francesca, Federico is associated with the virtues of active life, Battista with the virtues of the interior life of a Christian.

After her visit to Rome, Battista accompanied the pope to Pienza, his natal village, which he was in the process of making glorious. The document giving her the right to hospitality in convents was signed there.[37] When he was growing up, his birth-place was a village called Corsignano, but he renamed it after himself, and reconstructed it as an ideal city with the aid of the Florentine architect Bernardo Rossellino. The visit may have been an added incentive to the Montefeltri's own building work, since some of the architectural details of the Urbino palace seem to be modelled on the Palazzo Piccolomini at Pienza. Having admired the construction site, Battista decided that she wished to have her baby in her own domains, left the pope there in December 1461 and returned to Gubbio, making an arduous winter journey through the Apennines. She gave birth there to her second daughter, Elisabetta, named for her grandmother, at the end of the same month.[38]

One important witness to Battista in the early years of her marriage is a dialogue by Filetico, *Iocundissimae disputationes*. It was written between 1462 and 1463, and survives in a single manuscript copy in the Urbino library. It is the first such work to feature a real woman (as distinct from a personification, such as Philosophy) as a principal speaker. Probably set in 1462, Filetico's dialogue purports to reproduce three days of conversation between Filetico, Battista and her brother, Costanzo, who is a guest at his sister's marital court in Urbino (a visit that did not occur), with occasional appearances from Battista's young stepson Antonio. Its modern editor, Guido Arbizzoni, convincingly suggests that the dialogue is supposed to take place in December 1462,[39] though in this month Battista was not at home discussing literature, but visiting her husband's encampment near Pietracuta, more than thirty miles away, where he was engaged in his bitter war with Sigismondo Malatesta. This visit suggests that her principal concern at the time was not classical studies, but starting another baby: if Federico could not come to Urbino, she would have to go to him, as she had done in the previous year.

Filetico's dialogue averts its eyes from such gritty realities; he is concerned only with the life of the mind. The dedicatee is not Battista, but Ottaviano Ubaldini, whom he evidently regards as his patron. The first day's discussions begin with a review of the Cicero-based education Battista and Costanzo had received in Pesaro when Filetico was teaching them together, from 1458 to 1459. Benedetto Reguardati da Norcia's letters to Bianca Maria Visconti reported that Battista was immersing herself in the works of Cicero, so this evidently reflects reality. It seems, though, that without Filetico at his side, Costanzo's learning has ground to a halt, which of course is a dig at fellow humanist Porcellio Pandoni, who had taken over from Filetico as Costanzo's teacher in Pesaro. Humanists were intensely mutually competitive, and so Filetico is taking the opportunity to talk down a potential rival. 'Battista' speaks in praise of learning and, in particular, voices Filetico's own view of the importance of studying Greek and declares her interest in learning about classical metre, which suggests that she wrote Latin poetry. She may well have done: in a marginal note to his elegy on her death, Filetico says she wrote epigrams, and translated the Greek rhetor Isocrates, and another writer credits her with a poem on St Jerome, but none of this writing has survived.[40] 'Battista''s defence of Greek, and 'Costanzo''s argument that it isn't worth the effort, reflects an acrimonious debate between rival humanists at the time, in which Filetico was a major spokesman for the pro-Greek party.[41] Ottaviano and Federico were both pro-Greek. Though Federico's own Greek was probably fairly rudimentary, he encouraged all his sons, and perhaps his daughters, to master the language.

The dialogue showcases Battista's intellectual brilliance and eloquence at the expense of Costanzo, which, of course, flatters Filetico himself as a teacher. Later in the day, talk turns to Cicero's biography, his complex personality, and his various works. Cicero is presented as a heroic character, whose fame has gone down in posterity not merely because of his eloquence, but also on account of his magnanimity, justice, patriotism, courage, military genius, temperance, and love for his wife. This is clearly a way of presenting Cicero that makes him into an avatar of Federico da Montefeltro. Additionally, stress is laid on the fact that Cicero's wife Terentia acted as a proxy for her husband when he was in exile in Greece, which made her a useful role model for condottiere women ruling as proxies for their husbands.

Days two and three are devoted to a discussion of Cicero's *Stoic Paradoxes*, which Battista has been studying with Filetico. Costanzo hasn't read the work, so Battista is able to demonstrate her superior learning to her brother. The second book of Filetico's dialogue explores the precise nature of the paradoxes and contrasts the Stoics with other major philosophical schools. Battista is the main speaker, and Filetico keeps himself in the background, asking questions, which she answers. When Battista declares her passion for rhetoric, which is challenged by Filetico in Socratic style, she defends herself with spirit, and when Filetico in turn declares his love for philosophy, she goes on the attack. Antonio comes in, a good little boy (aged ten or so), and recites the lessons he has learned. Battista is thus presented as a true humanist and fully formed scholar, capable of constructing and defending her own arguments; Costanzo is lazy, or badly taught, and parroting received wisdom of an old-fashioned kind (from Filetico's point of view); while Antonio is at the first stage of learning, where rote education is appropriate.

In his dialogue, Filetico twice makes explicit reference to Battista as an active proxy ruler. At the beginning of day two, she discusses receiving petitioners in Federico's absence, and at the end of the same day she brings the session to a close, excusing herself from the debate because she has to go and meet a legation from the kingdom of Naples: 'Thank you, for now I understand something I didn't know before. But, if you don't mind, let us put an end to the conversation for today. I must give an audience to the king's ambassadors who, as you know, arrived late yesterday evening.'[42] Filetico then pokes fun at himself, since the 'Filetico' of the dialogue is obtuse to this pretty plain statement that she is a busy woman with other things to do, and starts a rant about the awfulness of one of the other humanists around the court (probably Porcellio, because he was prominent in the anti-Greek party), trying to get her to agree with him. She shuts him down good-humouredly, and the day's discussion comes to an end.

Another reference to the historical context of this dialogue is interesting. We are told that Ottaviano had planned to join in the debate, but was unable to do so because Federico was besieging Fano, which was being held by Roberto Malatesta on his father's behalf, and had asked him to prepare a bombard for use against Malatesta's troops (this would date the dialogue to June–September 1463, so Filetico is evidently being purposely vague about the time frame). These great guns could be annihilating if they could be got to the right place, so presumably Ottaviano is busy organizing the lifting of one of the Urbino bombards onto a gun carriage, and rounding up dozens of draught animals from local farmers. As we have seen, the gun itself would need at least forty pairs of oxen or buffalo to move it, and since bombards fired balls that might weigh 300 lb or more, there would also have to be an ammunition train,

1. The Palace at Urbino.

2. Duke and Duchess preside over an ideal landscape: Piero della Francesca's double portrait of Federico and Battista, his second wife.

3. Federico reading, with the young Guidobaldo by his side, probably by Joos van Wassenhove.

4. Piero della Francesca, *Brera Madonna*. Federico kneels before the Virgin and a host of saints.

5. *opposite* The fortress of San Leo: its conquest was one of Federico's most notable early victories.

6. Bonifacio Bembo, double portrait of Francesco Sforza and his wife Bianca Maria Visconti.

7. Domenico Roselli's low-relief putti, dancing in the Hall of Angels, one of the reception rooms in the duke's suite.

8. Death mask of Battista Sforza, now in the Louvre: the source for all other representations of her.

9. Piero della Francesca's portrait of Sigismondo Malatesta, aged around forty-six.

10. *below* Fresco of Urbino from the 'Gallery of Maps' in the Vatican, based on drawings by the geographer Ignazio Danti, and painted between 1580 and 1583.

VRBINVM

11. Giorgio Vasari's portrait of Lorenzo de' Medici, surrounded by artefacts chosen to 'illustrate the great qualities of this extremely rare, very unique citizen'.

12. Intarsia in Federico's *studiolo*: Federico himself stands, robed for an evening of study, and books are piled up in a cupboard.

plus a squadron of masons, engineers, ox-leaders and sufficient manpower to carry out the heavy lifting required. Battista's immediate response is to declare her own readiness to assist Ottaviano in any way possible, followed up by an enquiry into the origins of the term 'bombarda', which of course is not classical Latin, but kept the Greek-loving Filetico and Battista happy, since it derives from the Greek 'bombos', meaning 'boom'.[43] We know that Federico did in fact use heavy artillery against Fano, because he blew the top off the Arch of Augustus, which remains one of the sights of the city. Filetico's text reminds us of two things: first, that there was a war on, and second, that Battista was prepared to involve herself with any and all aspects of ruling Urbino.

This is backed up by Gaugello Gaugelli, a Montefeltro court poet who comments admiringly that Battista turned up in person late in the siege of Fano, on 25 September 1463.

> This lady was so spirited she came to the battlefield out of the
> desire to watch that fighting which was happening so grandly.

He even suggests that she made herself useful:

> She saw all the skirmishing, who was dead, who was wounded,
> and she saw who fled and who was taken prisoner.[44]

She was notably observant, and had an excellent memory, so she may have had a role to play. However, it seems likely that she really took this tremendous risk because Fano was a long siege, and she was still trying to conceive, so once again her only option was to come and share her husband's tent. She was successful in this instance: Giovanna, future ancestress of the della Rovere dukes of Urbino, was born in 1464; her name suggests that Federico still remembered his foster mother, Giovanna degli Alidosi.

Interestingly, Filetico's dialogue offers Battista a gentle corrective to her assumption of 'feminine modesty' on the grounds that a woman in her position needed to be able to look squarely at facts. The context is a discussion of Cicero's feud with Clodius.

According to Plutarch's *Life of Cicero*, Cicero was a chief witness at Clodius's trial after the latter had been accused of cross-dressing in order to infiltrate an all-women religious ceremony, in the hopes of seducing Julius Caesar's wife Pompeia. Clodius has gone down in history as someone who scorned the laws of God and man; there are therefore echoes here of Federico's feud with Sigismondo, who was similarly accused of atheism and sexual crimes. Costanzo asks why the two men hated each other, and Battista tells him it was because Cicero truthfully said Clodius had visited him on a day when he had sworn blind in court that he had been a long way from Rome. Costanzo understandably says he doesn't understand, and Battista says she doesn't want to go into details. He replies, quite acutely, 'It seems to me that it has to do with some indecency' and his sister snaps that he should read Plutarch if he really wants to know. Instead, he asks Filetico, who opens his mouth to reply, beginning 'Pompeia…', when he is silenced before he could go on with, perhaps, 'was having an affair with Clodius…':

> Battista: 'I don't want you to say any more!'

> Filetico: 'But for the love of God, you can discuss these things without blemishing your own virtue or modesty! But you, my queen, permit only things that honour women; therefore, Costanzo, I will explain things to you in greater detail at some other time.'[45]

He seems to be implying that a woman in Battista's position simply could not afford to play the blushing damsel – especially since she had obviously *read* Plutarch, and knew there was something to blush about.

There is no evidence that this work ever existed other than in a single fair copy. Bruni's *On the Study of Letters*, addressed to Battista's great-grandmother Battista Montefeltro, but so widely circulated that it was actually issued as a printed book around 1470, is concerned to protect the chastity of the female reader, who is mostly to read Christian writers and a carefully curated selection of classical authors, avoiding satirists and comic poets who are liable to discuss indecent topics. Filetico, though, tells Battista that within the four walls of the palace at Urbino, she is free to think about whatever needs to be thought about; she is a responsible adult. This is really very unusual advice to a woman of the fifteenth century.

Bernardo Tasso, father of the epic poet Torquato, joined the court at Urbino a century later, in 1559, and spent the next three years there working on an epic poem of his own, the *Amadigi*, a version of the Spanish chivalric romance *Amadís de Gaula*. He read sections of this work in progress to the then duchess, Vittoria Farnese, and her ladies. In Canto 44, his heroine experiences a vision of notable women of the future, which includes a handsome compliment to Battista's learning that complements Filetico's pen portrait:

> The Former, who seems to have before her Demosthenes and Plato, and who can also read Plotinus,
> bears comparison with Cicero in eloquence and knowledge.
> She will be the wife of another unconquered champion,
> Federico, Duke of old Urbino.[46]

Since he was writing a century after the event, we cannot know what this is based on, but it is a good fit with Filetico, since it suggests that she favoured the Greek orator Demosthenes and the philosopher Plato, and also read the extremely difficult Christian Neoplatonist Plotinus. This suggests that, as Ottaviano and Federico certainly did, she may have taken an interest in Neoplatonism and hermetic writings. But she was also noted for her eloquence in Latin.

One thing that it is strange to realize is that when the learned Battista was at Urbino, there wasn't much of a book collection, and no library as such. When Federico came to power, the book collection he inherited was tiny, comprising fewer than a hundred volumes, and while it contained some literature, notably Dante and Petrarch, mostly the books were on practical topics such as law and horse-breeding. The books seem to have been kept in 'the lord's storeroom', or *guardaroba*, where precious items were kept under lock and key. Federico started to collect books in his twenties, since the first volumes dedicated to him date from the 1450s, and he already had the poet Angelo Galli as his secretary. But from around 1460, the year he married Battista, he became more organized and methodical in his collecting, perhaps actively encouraged by her intellectual gifts and enthusiasm for reading. Through the 1460s, after the defeat of Sigismondo Malatesta, he became increasingly wealthy, and thus able to indulge in book purchasing. In 1467, for example, the Duke of Milan and the League made him their captain-general, with pay of 60,000 ducats a year in peace, or 80,000 in war.

Once he could afford it, he began collaborating with the Florentine book-purveyor Vespasiano da Bisticci.[47] The first books Federico bought from him were in the style Vespasiano had developed for books commissioned by the Medici, with decorative borders on the frontispiece pages and the internal initials '*a bianchi girari*' (in white vine), interlacing white tendrils against a coloured background. His Latin translation of Xenophon's *Education of Cyrus*, for instance (Urb. Lat. 410), must be a Vespasiano book that came into the library relatively early. It has a white vine title page, with a flattering miniature in which Federico, on horseback and wearing his red beretta, is riding up to greet the great Persian king Cyrus, seated on his throne. His coat of arms at the bottom of the page is flanked by the letters Fe: Co: Ur:, so he was still count, not duke, when it was illuminated.

Federico's Virgil (Urb. Lat. 350) is particularly interesting. It was probably written by a Florentine scribe who was active *c.* 1445–60, so it looks as if it was bought second-hand. It was a big handsome book, decorated with white vine, with little vignettes illustrating the start of each section. He must have commissioned decoration to be added, since his arms and C.F. (*Comes Federicus*) appear on the bottom margin of the second page. Battista could have enjoyed the book in this form, but after he became duke in 1474, he commissioned another round of very splendid decoration for it.[48]

There are relatively few 'C.F.' books in the collection. There are also no books with ownership indications that they were commissioned either by, or for, Battista herself, though a few of Ottaviano Ubaldini's books entered the library. If Battista brought her own books to Urbino, a Cicero, Plato, or Plotinus, they have been lost. Books had to be very decorative and very choice to enter the library, as Federico came to conceive it, though, as we now know, there was a sub-library in 'the lord's storeroom' where lurked books unsuitable for display, because they were printed, or simply not pretty, and her personal books may have ended up there.[49] These 'ugly' books would eventually have been dispersed, since they were not part of the library as such. There is no reason to think that a Renaissance ruler would necessarily value a book merely for its associations. Federico's lack of sentimentality is suggested by the fact that the spaces he had shared with Battista were obliterated, like the house he grew up in: the duke's and duchess's rooms in the palace were built after her death, and the palace at Gubbio she had loved was given back to the comune in 1474, swapped for a more prestigious building.

Battista had limited leisure for reading and relaxation. Year on year, she gave birth to daughter after daughter, Sabadini says nine in all, other writers say eight,[50] though only six of them lived to adult years. The strain on her, physically and mentally, as well as on the marriage, must have been terrible. Few Italian noblewomen breastfed their own children, which helps to explain why the intervals between births were so short.[51] The extent of Battista's desperation to conceive a son is revealed by the fact that she several times joined Federico when he was on campaign, as we saw when she visited him during the siege of Fano. These hazardous travels were almost certainly undertaken at points when she judged that she was sufficiently recovered from her last pregnancy to try yet again for a boy.

The daughters, meanwhile, were not neglected. She liked to see them prettily dressed, and they lived in her apartments in the Palazzetto della Iole with a swarm of ladies-in-waiting, wet-nurses, servants and governesses.[52] The most important of these was Pentasilea Baglione, an effective and reliable woman who took over the household when Battista died.[53] The only men allowed into this female domain were tutors, Federico himself, and Ottaviano. The daughters were confirmed by the Greek scholar Cardinal Bessarion when he came to Urbino in 1472, which may suggest that they, like the women of their maternal lineage, were being taught Greek. The humanist Lilio Tifernate of Città di Castello claimed in a manuscript dated 7 October 1476 that he was teaching Antonio, Guidobaldo, Gentile (the illegitimate daughter) and the second daughter, Giovanna; the oldest, Elisabetta, had married Roberto Malatesta in 1475.[54] Giovanni Maria Filelfo (1426–80), the son of Francesco, seems to have entered Federico's service in 1476, mainly to discuss philosophy with the duke, though perhaps also teaching Latin grammar to Guidobaldo and his two youngest sisters. Certainly, Agnesina, the youngest, received a humanist education, since she handed it on to her own child, Vittoria Colonna, the friend of Michelangelo, who became perhaps the most famous woman poet in early sixteenth-century Italy, the product of a maternal lineage that, by then, had been Latin-literate and humanistically educated for six consecutive generations.

Battista and Federico were very much a ruling couple. We know from Ser Guerriero de' Berni of Gubbio that they made official visits as a pair (and Battista sometimes made official visits alone).[55] She was completely trusted to act as her husband's proxy, and in a letter to Cristoforo Landino, sometime after her death, Federico wrote, 'nothing was more intimate and more loving than the friendship in which Battista and I were joined'.[56] But while she enjoyed an unusual amount of authority, autonomy and respect for a woman of her time, the relationship was not an equal one. One piece of evidence for this is that, though she was well known to be highly educated – more so than Federico – only one humanist, Porcellio Pandoni, dedicates work to her (he wrote poems to all members of the family),[57] while Federico received dozens of dedications from the 1440s onwards. Even Filetico's *Iocundissimae disputationes* is dedicated to Ottaviano Ubaldini, not Battista, although she is its subject. What this suggests is that she was not in a position to reward writers or to commission work: humanists followed the money.

One public action that is unequivocally associable with Battista is the foundation of the Urbino Monte di Pietà in 1468. The Jewish population of Italy expanded through the fifteenth century, partly because of an influx of Jews fleeing persecution in the Christian kingdoms of Spain. Urbino certainly had a Jewish community. But the involvement of the Jews with moneylending provoked both a backlash from Franciscan preachers and a positive development: Christian banks called Monte di Pietà. These were established as a charitable venture on a non-profit basis, and were to be set up in each town to provide funds for lending to the poor in small amounts without charging interest. The first Monte di Pietà opened in Ascoli Piceno in 1458, and the original charter of the Urbino Monte was signed in the name of Pope Paul II, on 6 April 1468, by Battista Sforza.

Battista, having been pregnant most of the time since her marriage in 1460, was finally rewarded on 24 January 1472, when she gave birth to the longed-for boy in the summer palace at Gubbio, which seems to have been where she preferred to lie in, perhaps because it was more restful than the bustling main court at Urbino, with its almost continuous building works. Sabadino says she was well enough after the birth to go to church and thank God.[58] The child was baptized in the cathedral of Gubbio by the bishop, Antonio de'Severi, and named Guido Paolo Ubaldo, though he never seems to have used Paolo. The name given to the child links Guido, the first name of his grandfather Guidantonio, and Ubaldo, the name of the saintly twelfth-century bishop who was patron of Gubbio, so it looks as if she and Federico may have thought that St Ubaldo had helped to confer male gender on the last of Battista's children.

Federico decreed civic rejoicing on a large scale. However, it is worth observing that when the fabulously learned Cardinal Bessarion paid a state visit in April to baptize three-month-old Guidobaldo and confirm his sisters, the Greek-loving Battista – who had also been baptized by him and who would in ordinary circumstances have surely been pleased to welcome him, and perhaps to offer a formal oration – seems to have been absent. She is not mentioned in accounts of Bessarion's visit, so one wonders if she had regained full health. Perhaps Ottaviano, also a friend of Bessarion's, who had welcomed at least one Greek humanist to Urbino, did the honours.[59]

Federico himself was otherwise engaged. He had just been temporarily recruited by Lorenzo de' Medici to deal with a crisis. Florence claimed hegemony over smaller towns in its hinterland, claims that were sometimes contested. The mountaintop town of Volterra, south-west of Florence, was one such, nominally independent, but acknowledging Florentine authority. Part of its territory was an unfarmable volcanic badland, which was collective property, and contained valuable minerals such as sulphur. A group of speculators took a five-year lease of part of this inhospitable terrain, using capital from several Florentine companies, including the Medici bank, and in 1470 discovered a rich deposit of alum, which is valuable because it is essential for fixing dye in cloth, particularly woollens. Fine fabrics were a major Florentine industry, so this was important. The speculators were able to undercut the price fixed by what had up till then been the only source of alum in Italy, the papal mine at Tolfa. But some of the Volterrans' fellow citizens were furious because they were extracting wealth from what was publicly owned land, and attacked the mineworks, so at this point the Florentine investors appealed to their own government. Lorenzo de' Medici, who was *de facto* leader of Florence, held the

Tolfa monopoly, so he was concerned to protect his own wealth. He argued to the signoria that the Volterrans had revolted and were injuring Florentine citizens, and persuaded them to let him hire Federico da Montefeltro with a sizeable army, perhaps as many as 12,000 men, to bring them to heel.

Federico assembled his army at Mazzolla, four miles from Volterra, and let them think about it for a while, sending ambassadors to the city to spread alarm and despondency. The Volterrans, thoroughly frightened, started to fortify their citadel, and hired a thousand mercenaries, all they could afford. Federico then set about a leisurely siege, and after three weeks, with the aid of the military engineer Gentile Veterani and the ballistics expert Scirro Scirri, he got bombards into position and holed the city wall.[60] At that point, the mercenaries employed by the Volterrans decided they were going to lose; they realized they were stuck on the wrong side, and that there was not the slightest advantage to themselves in defending the city to the last. Meanwhile, a lot of diplomacy was going on, and on 18 June 1472 the Volterrans surrendered on terms very favourable to Florence, with the stipulation that life and property would be spared, and no reprisals taken for recent events. But before the negotiations were complete, some of the mercenaries the Volterrans themselves had employed opened the gates and invited the Florentine army to join them in sacking the city.

It was very difficult for commanders to control troops who weren't given occasional licence for murder, rape and theft, since their pay was often in arrears, especially if they had just endured the boredom and physical hardship of a longish siege. But the convention was that the commander could call time and move in to restore order with his own *casa*, or household troops.[61] Federico allowed his men twelve hours of terror (Santi says twenty-two), though he moved to prevent the looting of churches, and hanged a Venetian and a Sienese whom he found amassing a collection of church silver. Otherwise, the mercenaries attempted to extract as much as they could from the Volterrans in this limited time; breaking open homes, collecting Volterrans' portable valuables, raping anyone they fancied, or simply indulging themselves in licensed cruelty. Writers have tended to assume that Federico spent this day of mayhem trying to mitigate the effect on the civilian population, because he was a civilized and humanist prince. Santi's 'Rhymed Chronicle' proudly asserts:

> He nothing brought away but honour bright
> Which every other treasure far outshines.[62]

Carlo Grossi, in *On the Illustrious Men of Urbino* (1819), writes that all the duke took from Volterra was a Hebrew Bible of unusual beauty, 'an innocent monument of his triumph', but the truth is far more brutal.[63] Federico was not a figure of romance, and had no aspirations in that direction. In actual fact, he joined in the looting: the proof is to be found in his library, which contains the collection of Hebrew books amassed by a rich Jewish merchant of Volterra, Menahem ben Aharon da Volterra, including a beautiful thirteenth-century Old Testament.[64] On that night of grief, 18 June 1472, Menahem lost his son as well as his Torah. By the time the 'old index' of Federico's library was written, between 1487 and 1498, it contained eighty-three Hebrew manuscripts. Thirty-two of these contain explicit ownership or purchase notes linking them with Menahem da Volterra, and there are reasons to suggest that another eight of Federico's books were originally his. Was it just serendipity that led Federico to find a valuable library in the shrieking chaos of the sack of Volterra? Or did he know it was there? Because Federico was so successful in curating his reputation, his historians, from his contemporary Santi onwards, have been reluctant to believe that he ever acted like an ordinary captain of mercenaries, but the evidence of the library is against them. A fourteenth-century bronze music stand in the Urbino Duomo, which may be English, is also thought to have come from Volterra.[65]

From the point of view of the Volterrans, the sack was a disaster; from the point of view of Florence, it was in some danger of being seen as a public relations disaster. The Florentine Tomasso Soderini warned Lorenzo de' Medici, 'better a lean truce than a fat victory', and after the event said sadly that he thought Volterra had been lost, not won.[66] Many Florentines were inclined to blame Lorenzo for the way things turned out; so it was therefore events in Volterra in 1472 that set in motion the attempt to unseat the Medici, known as the Pazzi conspiracy, six years later. At the time, however, Lorenzo was a direct beneficiary of Federico's actions, because of his alum monopoly and his connections with the Florentine textile trade. He was delighted and, on his say-so, the sack was treated as a triumph, the suppression of a rebellion, which in point of fact it wasn't.

Delighted by the territorial and financial implications of the victory, Lorenzo, the signoria and the majority of the Florentines celebrated the victory with something like a classical triumph towards the end of June. Federico was received with the honour due to a man who had secured an important income stream for the Medici. He was met outside the gates, and cheering crowds escorted him to the Piazza della Signoria through streets hung with tapestry and brocade. There he was welcomed by the signoria, who were drawn up in the piazza, with a complimentary oration delivered by no less a figure than Bartolomeo Scala, humanist and chancellor of the Florentine Republic. At the public banquet that followed, Federico was given a fine horse with splendid trappings, and told that a silver parade helmet worth 500 ducats had been commissioned for him from the sculptor Antonio del Pollaiuolo, decorated with jewels and gold, with a crest showing Hercules trampling on a griffin (the badge of Volterra). Pollaiuolo brought it to Urbino the following year, and it was doubtless an extremely splendid object. They also made him a personal gift of the Villa di Rusciano, recently restructured by Filippo Brunelleschi, as his official residence when he visited Florence.[67] But once the festivities were over, he was heading for Urbino to receive his own people's congratulations when he received news that had him spurring for home as fast as horses could carry him.

The indomitable Battista was definitely back in Urbino when she heard the news of Federico's Florentine triumph, because she and Ottaviano Ubaldini decided to go and meet him at Gubbio, a journey of about forty miles in the heat of July, in the course of which she probably contracted pneumonia. Her father, writing with the news, said her symptoms were fever and a headache. Renaissance writers were convinced of the deadly effects of imbibing very cold water: for instance, Louis X of France is said to have died from gulping cold water after playing tennis. At some point, the party stopped to fish, and Battista slaked her thirst from a mountain stream. When she subsequently fell sick, contemporaries blamed the water. But pneumonia is often the final blow to someone whose health is already compromised for some reason.[68] Perhaps, as her strength ebbed away, classically educated Battista called to mind the bleak words of Euripides' Medea: 'I'd three times sooner go to war than suffer childbirth once.'

She died on 6 July 1472, aged only twenty-six. Federico was with her, and according to Gaugello Gaugelli's poem on Battista's life and death, so were Ottaviano Ubaldini, her brother Costanzo, and Federico's son Antonio, who had perhaps been with him on the Florentine campaign.[69] A letter from Federico to the magistrates of Siena gives some details. 'My wife Battista having sickened on Tuesday last, with fever and headache, our Lord God has taken unto himself her soul at four o'clock tonight, after she had received the sacraments with the utmost devotion, leaving me as afflicted, desolate, and unhappy as anyone can be in this world... I arrived but this morning, and found her in a happy frame of mind.'[70] In another letter, to Sixtus IV, he acknowledges the importance of their partnership, saying, 'she was the beloved consort of my fortunes, and the lightener of my labours both privately in the home and in public life. No greater misfortune could have befallen me.'[71]

A death mask was taken, and a terracotta cast from it survives, now in the Louvre.[72] She looks heartbreakingly young, but she has the sharp nose and sunken features of the 'Hippocratic face', which the great Greek physician observed centuries before: '[If the patient's facial] appearance may be described thus: the nose sharp, the eyes sunken, the temples fallen in… it must be realized that this sign portends death.'[73] She is not in the least serene; she looks as if she fought hard for every last breath.

Battista's body was carried to Urbino and buried in the common grave of the convent of Santa Chiara, where her grandmother was still abbess, dressed in the habit of a Franciscan tertiary, by her own choice. If this suggests a simple and austere ceremony, it misleads. The funeral, on 17 August, was the most magnificent event that had ever taken place in Urbino. This reflects Federico's very obvious and genuine grief, but it also reflects his instinct for spectacle. He wrote a lot of letters in the days after her death, telling people when the funeral was going to be – more than forty days after his wife's death, to give important people time to rearrange their diaries. Volterra had raised his professional standing, and while he would infinitely rather have had his wife, since he did not, he used her obsequies to consolidate his newly elevated status, which explains why his historians, from Paltroni onwards, itemize the guest list. There were thirty-eight envoys from all the powers of Italy, from the pope and the Duke of Milan down; everyone except representatives from Venice and Siena, who were kept away by bad weather. There were 316 foreign notables at the funeral, and 308 ecclesiastics, with Cardinal Orsini at their head.

The funeral oration was given by Giannantonio Campano, a talented Neapolitan humanist, who had been a protégé of both Cardinal Bessarion and Pius II, two men very important to Federico. Funeral orations were very much a humanist genre; dozens survive, all of them stressing that virtuous actions flow from a thorough training in the humanities. What was relatively unusual, though, was that this was an oration praising a woman for exhibiting manly virtues – above all, eloquence: Campano praised both the little Latin speech she delivered aged four and the speech she had given before Pius II, stressing that the pope was convinced women were unjustly denied a humanist education. A paragon such as Battista could govern properly when her husband was away, because her education, combined with her native character, gave her the manly virtue of practical wisdom, without robbing her of the feminine virtues of modesty, chastity and compassion.[74] This speech circulated in manuscript (several copies survive), and it was printed four years later at Cagli, at a press sponsored by Ottaviano Ubaldini, a further advertisement of her greatness, and hence, of Federico's.

In several accounts of Battista's life and death, contemporaries praise her willingness to make a selfless sacrifice of her life in order to ensure the continuity of the dynasty.[75] This led to the creation and circulation of the sort of mythic narrative more usually associated with the birth of a saint or a legendary hero. According to the story, she went to the Montefeltro summer palace at Gubbio with Federico in April 1471. There, she prayed fervently for help in conceiving a boy. She fell asleep, and dreamt of a tall tree whose branches extended to the sky. She was lifted up over the tree and gave birth to a beautiful male phoenix, who stayed there with her for thirty-six days before it opened its wings, flew towards the sun, and disappeared. Nine months after this experience, she gave birth to Guidobaldo.

But there are problems with this story: the 'vision' isn't exactly coherent. The tall tree may symbolize the Montefeltro line, drawing on the medieval iconography of the Tree of Jesse, a symbolic tree or vine originating with Jesse, its spreading branches representing the genealogy of Christ. It is the idea of ramification that matters, that the lineage of Federico will multiply into the future, just as multiple branches emerge from one tree trunk, and multiple twigs from each branch. Additionally, there may be a learned reference: in Donatus's fourth-century life of Virgil, his mother dreams of a great tree that towers up to heaven and becomes covered with flowers and fruit, a symbol of his undying fame.[76] The phoenix is a symbol of resurrection, and so, presumably, of the resurrection of the Montefeltro line. It's also, among other things, a metaphor for someone's uniquely glorious character, and it is a bird; and *uccello* is an Italian slang word for a penis. But the question is, is this a narrative that was circulating shortly after the birth of Guidobaldo, or not? Because the fact that the phoenix vanishes after thirty-six days has to mean something. Guidobaldo lived for thirty-six *years*. We might see here the tossing together, after Guidobaldo's death, of an obscure legend about Virgil and the symbolic representation of his short life, in which case the hand that did the tossing is probably that of Ludovico Odasio, Guidobaldo's learned tutor, who also wrote his funeral speech, and first told the story. Did he originate it? If he did, it therefore post-dates the death of Guidobaldo, and tells us nothing about the aftermath of his birth.[77]

Following her sadly premature death, Battista was something of a model for women who came after her. As we have seen, Giovanni Sabadini degli Arienti includes her in his 1483 list of new-style politically active wives. But he wasn't the only one. A little earlier, in 1479, Antonio Cornazzano, a poet and courtier who was initially stationed at Francesco Sforza and Bianca Maria Visconti's court in Milan, produced a laudatory and instructive 'mirror for princes', which was unusual in being a 'mirror for a princess', since it was written for Eleonora of Aragon in the year in which she temporarily ruled Ferrara, *c.* 1478–9.[78] His text offers both male and female examples of individual princely virtues, both theological and cardinal. Battista Sforza is included as exemplifying the princely quality of prudence. Other remarkable female contemporaries are also presented for Eleonora's consideration: Bianca Maria d'Este (1440–1506) and Ippolita Maria Sforza (1446–84).[79] What this reveals is that these effective and dynamic women not only showed the way to the next generation, they also smoothed the path, since female rule, and female participation in public life, came to seem less and less exceptional. On the title page of the presentation copy of Cornazzano's work, Eleonora is shown in profile, and the hand of God is reaching down to her with a golden sceptre, which she grasps in her right hand. There could be no clearer statement that he is arguing that her authority was deemed absolutely in accordance with the divine will, and was not a challenge to the rightful order of society.

We can see the next generation acting on this bold notion that female rule is sometimes legitimate. In Pesaro, after the death of Battista's brother, Costanzo Sforza, in 1484, his wife, Camilla Marzano d'Aragona, who was Eleonora d'Aragona's first cousin as well as Battista's sister-in-law, ruled together with her husband's illegitimate son, Giovanni Sforza. Camilla's co-investiture as papal vicar by Sixtus IV was exceptional, and a testament to her personal qualities, since Giovanni was sixteen when his father died, an age when he would have been considered adult. She did not step down until Giovanni married Maddalena Gonzaga in 1489, and thus had an intelligent woman at his side. Interestingly, Camilla had adopted the name by which she is known. She was born Cubella, a name entirely without historical resonance, but at the time of her marriage to Costanzo in 1475 decided to go by Camilla, the name of the virgin warrior queen who is an important minor character in Virgil's *Aeneid*. The choice of name suggests that she had not the slightest intention of going through her life with eyes cast down, being meek, mild, and subservient.

7

Magnificence
1472–1482

Once Battista's funeral was over, Federico entered the strange new world of the griever. Porcellio Pandoni, one of the court humanists, caught something of the dreariness of the mourning palace in his *Feltria*.

> On first returning to his home, he surveys the empty halls
> And soon seeks to withdraw, with the windows closed, as is the
>   custom,
> He sat, dressed in black, in grief and tears.
> Companions come in in their weeds, and lesser servants,
> And the tablecloths are black, and black are the furnishings
> And the unhappy bedchamber is entirely veiled in black.[1]

Federico himself wrote bleakly to the Doge of Venice, Niccolò Tron, 'I can do nothing but suffer acutely.'[2]

His next move was wholly uncharacteristic. He stayed at home. For the next two years, he did not chase after a condotta, but sat in Urbino with his infant son and Ottaviano Ubaldini. Consequently, his historians, who are inclined to focus on battles and public achievements, edit out this period; so much so that Paltroni telescopes it entirely and says that Battista died in 1474.

He had estates in the territory of his state, while every town made him an annual grant, so from these sources there was more than sufficient for everyday administration and living expenses, though not for extravagance.[3]

What, then, was Federico doing – apart, that is, from mourning with the utmost sincerity? Grievers now tend to be advised not to make sudden decisions in the aftermath of personal tragedy, but life in fifteenth-century Italy was fast and hard. People were generally encouraged to imagine their baby/spouse/parent had been lovingly received by angels and conducted into the celestial court, and to get on with begetting another baby, remarrying, or dealing with the estate, as the case may be. The dukes of Urbino generally responded to the loss of a wife by remarrying within the year.

One decision Federico certainly made was not to remarry. An ambassador from the Gonzagas suggested that he might consider marrying one of the not very attractive daughters of the King of Naples, and was told that he would consider no such thing.[4] But from how he proceeded after the summer of 1472, it is possible to suggest that he made some other decisions. Reviewing the situation, he had the legitimate son he had longed for since the 1440s, and he had earned a good deal of money. A conservative estimate of his income, beyond what he required to run his state, from 1468 until his death, apart from this two-year sabbatical, is the enormous sum of 50,000 ducats a year, at a time when the total revenues (not profits) of merchants, bishops and cardinals were rarely 20,000 ducats a year.[5] What with the lands that came with Gentile da Brancaleoni and subsequent territorial gains, mostly at the expense of the Malatesti, he had tripled the size of his territory. The son, in the charge of the sterling Pentasilea Baglioni, appeared to be a healthy baby, and thriving. It was therefore sensible to proceed on the assumption that Guidobaldo would live to grow up. However, on the downside, Federico was fifty years old, and had developed a number of chronic health issues, including gout. Eventually he would go back to work, which meant risking his life every time he took a condotta. While it looked as if Guidobaldo would survive to adulthood, it was only too likely that he himself wouldn't live to see it.

But another of his major assets was his brother Ottaviano Ubaldini. Ottaviano's only child, Bernardino, had died along with Federico's own Buonconte after the ill-starred trip to Naples in 1458. There was no risk, therefore, of him setting Guidobaldo aside in favour of offspring of his own. He could be trusted as a regent, and since his life was far less physically dangerous than Federico's, the chances were that he would be around to guide a young heir's steps, should that become necessary.

From Federico's point of view, the really important thing was to safeguard, as far as humanly possible, his son's future, and with it, his own status as the founder of a dynasty. Guidobaldo's existence fundamentally changed his attitude to Urbino itself. Everything about his attitude to ruling had been provisional, until he had a legitimate son, and even after that, until he became a duke. With Guidobaldo in the nursery, the money he had amassed as a condottiere had a new and glorious purpose, because he could afford to look to the future. He approached the safeguarding of Guidobaldo in a way that speaks volumes about the culture of Renaissance Italy: he decided to become glorious. He would make his palace the wonder of Italy, he would fashion himself as a philosopher king, and he would associate Guidobaldo with himself. He had spent money on the palace, and on books, while Battista was alive, but only to quite a modest extent. Now he could create a legacy, because there was a second generation to leave it to.

It was only after 1474 that Federico became the Federico we know. His new ambition was to make Urbino uniquely splendid, in which he was successful. His building, his art commissions and his library all entered a new phase of splendour, supported with massive investment, and occupying almost his entire attention. Precious possessions and magnificent buildings had become a defining marker of princely status throughout Europe, but this proposition could be reversed: to be magnificent is to assert princely status. Giovanni Santi writes of Federico's growing passion for building in the last ten years of his life, declaring that there were 130 constructions in progress simultaneously. Among other projects, he ordered the rebuilding of the Urbino Duomo, probably as a thank-offering for the birth of a son, and made plans for a mausoleum. It all suggests a man in a tremendous hurry.

One of the witnesses to Federico's temperament and personality in the 1470s is a very learned, Oxford-educated Franciscan. The Montefeltri had strong connections with the Franciscan order, and Giorgio Benigno Salviati (born Juraj Dragišić), from Srebrenica in Bosnia, came into Federico's orbit because he had been connected with Cardinal Bessarion around 1470. He was invited to Urbino in 1472, and stayed until 1482, the year of Federico's death. His dialogue *Fridericus, On the Prince of the Kingdom of the Soul* was written during his years at Urbino, and is dedicated to Federico's heir, Guidobaldo. The two speakers in the dialogue are Fridericus, arguing for the superiority of the will, and his close friend Octavianus (Ottaviano Ubaldini), who argues for the superiority of the intellect. Salviati is here making his own important contribution to fifteenth-century discussions of the dignity of man. The work concludes with Octavianus' praises of Fridericus, comparing him with Alexander the Great (educated by Aristotle and world conqueror) and Julius Caesar (distinguished man of letters and conqueror of Gaul), but above all, with the mythological figure of Hermes Trismegistus. In 1460, the Florentine Marsilio Ficino had developed the idea of the writings attributed to Hermes as a missing link between Christianity and pagan philosophy, so this was cutting-edge Renaissance thought: Ottaviano's comparison of Federico to Hermes Trismegistus must reflect his own well-attested interest in hermetic philosophy. The positions of Fridericus and Octavianus have a relation to the historical characters of Federico and Ottaviano, since Federico's career as condottiere and dynast was fundamentally dependent on the steady exercise of will, whereas Ottaviano, the more educated of the two, was applying his intelligence to the practical problems of building a palace, overseeing other works, and running the state.[6]

Another highly intellectual recruit to the Urbino court was a man called Lilio Tifernate. He had been a protégé of Cardinal Bessarion's, and after the cardinal's death, which also occurred in 1472, he came to the court of Urbino. He is documented there in 1476, but may have arrived earlier. Fluent in Greek as well as Latin, he translated a Middle Platonist work, Philo of Alexandria's first-century *De Gigantibus*, which he dedicated to Federico, and also acted as a teacher of Federico's children, both girls and boys.[7]

Federico's last ten years coincided with the pontificate of Sixtus IV. Relations between the two of them got off to a good start. Sixtus had been born Francesco della Rovere, and rose to be general of the Franciscan order. Federico, like his father, had been a great patron of the Franciscans; so they were old friends when Sixtus became pope. Just as, in Guidantonio's time, the Colonna pope Martin V had put Colonnas in every position of advantage he could, Sixtus proceeded to fill any available appointment with a della Rovere. The fallout from his nepotistic policies included a reshuffling of Italian politics, which put a north-Italian coalition of Florence, Milan and Venice on one side, and Rome and Naples on the other. Both sides were keen to recruit Federico, who had become a considerable force in Italian politics as a diplomat and guarantor of the peace in Italy. In particular, Sixtus IV and Ferrante of Naples were keen to keep him on side, and dispensed honours accordingly. In the early summer of 1474, Federico, after his two-year sabbatical, went to Naples to discuss renewing his condotta. There he was surprised by King Ferrante with a glittering ceremony in front of the whole court, inducting him into the Order of the Ermine.

Ever since Philip the Good of Burgundy had thought up the Order of the Golden Fleece, and started inducting important foreigners into it, other rulers had entirely seen the point of developing chivalric orders of their own and using them as an aid to diplomacy. A whole series of knightly orders were founded between 1430 and 1470, demonstrating that chivalry remained a far from negligible aspect of Renaissance culture. Federico's induction took place during High Mass; after the Gospel reading, he and Ferrante's son, Federico of Aragon, were arrayed in mantles of scarlet satin lined with ermine, open at the right side like an antique Roman military cloak, as worn by Justinian in the famous sixth-century mosaics at Ravenna. After the sermon, they knelt at the high altar and each received a golden collar with a pendant ermine studded with jewels. Antonio, who had accompanied Federico, was knighted by Ferrante, and given a golden chain. In September, Federico had a chance to offer his thanks when Federico of Aragon visited Urbino en route to Burgundy, where he was wooing Mary, daughter of Charles the Bold. He was lavishly welcomed, and the versatile Giovanni Santi produced an allegorical representation, 'Love at the Tribunal of Chastity' (and also designed costumes and special effects), which was performed in his honour.[8] The performance included a celebrated Burgundian rondeau for three voices sung by Chastity, beginning 'J'ay pris amour', with two cupids on either side of her singing soprano and tenor. She also sang a canzone, 'gens cors': this was a performance in very much a Burgundian or French taste.[9]

Then, in August 1474, Federico went to Rome, with an escort of 2,000 knights, where Sixtus proposed, finally, to make him Duke of Urbino. Again during a High Mass, he was first dubbed a Knight of St Peter, and then invested with a ducal robe, a golden chain, sceptre and cap. He was also made gonfaloniere, or standard-bearer, of the Church, and general of the new Neapolitan-Roman League. The day after, his daughter Giovanna was married to Giovanni della Rovere, thus binding Federico tightly into Sixtus's della Rovere kin group, since Giovanni was a favoured nephew of the pope.

Also that August, in distant England, Federico was unanimously elected into another chivalric order, the Order of the Garter. King

Edward IV, aware of Federico's high standing with the new pope, thought this a good investment, in case he ever needed a friend at the papal court; the quid pro quo was that Federico became spokesman for English matters to the Holy See. A little later in the year, he was presented with his Garter and other accoutrements by the English ambassador in yet another ceremonial, held at the abbey of Grottaferrata, and attended by King Ferrante and two cardinals: Giuliano della Rovere, another of the pope's favourite nephews (the future Pope Julius II), and Rodrigo Borgia, also a future pope. Previous Italian Garter knights had been Alfonso I of Naples (1450), Ferrante and Francesco Sforza, both in 1463. In the 1460s, these men were Federico's employers, not his equals. Induction into the Order of the Garter symbolized a huge change of status for him.

Federico had always craved honours and recognition, for his standing to be ratified, and he took all this intensely seriously. In the massive programme of building and manuscript commissioning at Urbino that followed on these honours, we see an endless proliferation of Fe:Dux, or F:D, standing for Federico Dux, of ermines, the gold collar of the Order of the Ermine, and English Garters, together with a revised coat of arms now including a central stripe featuring the papal crossed keys and tiara, representing his status as gonfaloniere. They are carved all over the palace buildings, and represented again and again in his illuminated books. The Ermine, Garter, and the papal gonfalon were awards granted by what Federico considered legitimate authorities. It is revealing of Federico's mentality that the magnificent Pollaiuolo parade helmet given him by the Florentines is not included among his honours, because there is no representation of it anywhere. He seems to have thought that a gift from self-made men such as the Medici, however illustrious, conveyed no permanent elevation of status, whereas, in his eyes, honours from superiors were meaningful, and a source of real pride.

The condotta that Federico signed in 1474–8 yielded him 40,000 ducats a year in time of peace, 70,000 in time of war.[10] With that sort of money at his disposal, and Ottaviano at his side to keep the projects moving forward when he was otherwise engaged, he was well able to embark on an accelerated campaign of glorification, described in the chapters that follow. The style of his commissions changed noticeably. The new books he commissioned after 1474 were much gaudier, decorated with brightly coloured floral motifs. They also now tended to have a decoration, often circular, on the page opposite the frontispiece, framing the title or a description, and these pages almost always feature his *imprese* or his honours. Similarly, the new work on the palace was far more sumptuous than in the previous phase of building.

The Burgundian dukes set a standard of magnificence for the courts of Europe in the second half of the fifteenth century, and among their court offices was that of poet-chronicler. Federico was increasingly seen to be in that sort of league, since Francesco Filelfo, a most distinguished humanist, came forward with a Latin *Commentary on the Life and Deeds of Federico Count of Urbino* in 1475/6, which chronicled his career to 1461. Subsequently, Filelfo's son Giovanni Maria Filelfo wrote an epic poem, *Martias*, suggesting that Federico was the son of Mars, god of war himself (thus neatly sidestepping rumours about the identity of his earthly father); Naldo Naldi wrote *Volterrais*, on the siege of Volterra; Giovanni Santi, courtier, theatrical designer, painter and popular poet, began his Italian *Rhymed Chronicle*, which he finished in 1487; and Pierantonio Paltroni, who had known Federico since his teens, wrote a *Commentary*, which went up to 1473. Porcellio Pandoni, meanwhile, completed his *Feltria*, commissioned in 1461. Thus, to the best of his ability, Federico fixed his own image in history.

One of the most remarkable witnesses to Federico's new idea of himself appears in a list of the members of his household, which is undated but must relate to his life after 1474: 'keeper of the camel-leopard' – that is, of a giraffe. This is even more extraordinary than it seems at first glance. In 46 BC, Julius Caesar paraded a giraffe through the streets of Rome, the first ever seen in Italy, which was duly noticed by Pliny the Elder. Otherwise, the next giraffe recorded in Italy was a present made to Lorenzo de' Medici in 1487, a gift from the Sultan of Egypt. But it seems as if Federico had one, or hoped to have one, around 1478. The association with Julius Caesar made the animal particularly appropriate as a symbol of military power. As to where it might have come from, Bernardino Baldi (writing in 1604) tells us that 'Uzun Hasan, mighty King of Persia, who sent a mission of ambassadors to the Christian rulers, ordered them especially on his behalf to visit [Federico] and present to him very rich gifts, which they did with diligence'.[11] The Shahanshah Uzun Hasan, who died in 1478, seems like the most likely donor of an exotic Eastern animal. In any case, the possession of such a gentle giant, if it actually arrived, would have been a status symbol that put him on a par with the greatest men in Italy.[12]

Meanwhile, an important initiative of Ottaviano's in the 1470s was to bring printing to the Marche. Federico personally preferred large and beautiful manuscripts, but all over Italy, scholars and intellectuals were excited by the possibilities of printing. Ottaviano sponsored the first printing press in the Marche in Cagli in 1475, that of Robertus de Fano and Bernardinus de Bergamo, under the direction of the scholar Lorenzo Astemio, who later (after Federico's death in 1482) became a ducal librarian. Their first venture was humanist, Maffeo Vegio's essay on the death of Astyanax, an episode from Homer's *Iliad*. Another was of the most direct concern to the ducal household, since it was an edition of Campano's funeral oration for Battista Sforza, which came out on 1 March 1476, making this account of her multiple merits far more widely accessible. The press also issued a book on safeguarding oneself against the plague, and, again with Astemio's assistance, they produced a book on grammar, Servio Mauro Onorato's *Libellus de ultimis syllabis*, which includes a letter to Ottaviano Ubaldini making it clear that he had lent the printers money. Printing became increasingly important in the region: after Federico's death, in the 1490s, Heinrich of Cologne started up a press in Urbino itself, and there were several important printing initiatives in the time of the first della Rovere dukes, which will be discussed in another chapter.

Vespasiano da Bisticci has left a picture of Federico's way of life after the great rebuilding of the palace, whenever he was at leisure. 'In summer he would ride out from Urbino at dawn with four or six horsemen and one or two servants, unarmed, at his stirrup and go forth three or four miles, returning when other folk were rising from bed. When they dismounted it would be the hour of Mass. In order that his rule might be conjoined with religion, [Federico] was before all things most devout and observant in his religious duties; for without this, and without a good example to others by his life, his rule would never have endured. Every morning with his household, and with whatever townsfolk might wish, he heard the sermon, and after this the mass.' Vespasiano is not entirely clear where this Mass took place. His phrasing gives a slight impression of townspeople joining him in the palace, but it only acquired a chapel in the final phase of building, a tiny structure that could only hold ten or twelve at the most and, moreover, was part of the duke's private apartments.[13] What he must mean is that after his morning ride, Federico went into the Duomo, adjacent to the palace, to which he had a private entrance.

Afterwards, Federico would 'go into a garden with the doors open and give audience to all who wished, till the hour of repast. When the Duke had sat down the doors would be left open, so that all might enter, and he never ate except the hall were full.' Someone read to him during dinner; spiritual reading of some kind if it was Lent, and otherwise Livy's *Roman Histories*, in Latin. There was nothing epicurean about his tastes. Because of his tendency to gout, he had to be rather careful. He ate 'plain food and no sweetmeats, and drank no wine save that made from such fruits as cherries, pomegranates or apples... he fasted according to all vigils ordered by the Church, without exception'. Every day, without fail, bread and wine were distributed to those in need.

Although the palace staff ran to some five hundred individuals, life there was very orderly. 'At all hours of the day, even during meals, the duke was accessible to provide counsel. He liked not that anyone should ever address him on behalf of any of [his subjects], seeing that everyone could speak to him at any hour of the day… There were few whose business could not be dispatched on the same day.' The service of meals was an orderly ballet of carvers, stewards, waiters, and servants with water and towels for hand-washing. 'Anyone who wished to address him might do so either between the courses or after the meal, and a judge of appeal, a very distinguished man, would lay before him, one by one, the causes before the court which he would determine, speaking in Latin.' The palace was also perhaps the most hygienic building in Europe. The *De Ordine et Officij*, an official register of procedures at the Ducal Palace, indicates that all the people who came into the palace, from Urbino citizens to food handlers and grooms, were bound by rigorous standards of cleanliness. The entire palace was cleaned regularly. Beggars were not allowed into the heart of the building, because they were dirty – Federico sent almoners to meet the poor in peripheral areas of the palace. Members of his court were constantly reminded to clean their nails, to refrain from scratching themselves in public, and to wash to prevent body odour. Hands were washed both before and after a meal, and a barber-surgeon and doctor were kept in attendance.[14]

Music was a particular pleasure for Federico and his household. The proliferation of musical instruments in the intarsia of the two *studioli* is one indication of this: they include three different portative organs, a fiddle, two lutes, a rebec, a harp and a cittern. Another is the number of musicians listed in the *Ordine et officij*: singers, who could also play stringed instruments, a good organist, and pipe players.[15] Vespasiano tells us that Federico liked stringed instruments best, and didn't much enjoy louder music, so the four

trumpeters and three drummers listed may have been expected to
follow him to war. The notes of 'J'ay pris amour', which had been
sung to Federico of Aragon, are shown in an open music book in
the intarsia of the Urbino *studiolo*, and a Latin motet on Federico
himself, perhaps by Johannes Tinctoris, appears in another, and
begins 'He waged war, and cultivated the Muses'.[16] A music book
depicted in the intarsia in Gubbio once said 'Rosa Bella', the title
of a fifteenth-century Venetian ballade. There was a text of it in a
book in Federico's library.[17]

Vespasiano continues, 'In summer, after rising from table and
giving audience to all who desired, he went into his closet to attend
to his affairs and to listen to readings, according to the season. At
vespers he went forth again to give audience.' He accepted a number
of foster children, the sons of other condottieri who were placed
with him to learn their trade, just as he had himself been taught by
Gianfrancesco Gonzaga in Mantua. In the early evening, he would
visit his cousin Elisabetta, abbess of Santa Chiara, or the convent of
St Francis, where in a large meadow he would observe 'while thirty
or forty of his young men, after stripping to their doublets, would
throw the lance. When [the Duke] marked a want of dexterity in
running or catching, [he] would reprove them, in order that they
might do better. During these exercises anyone might address him;
indeed he was there for this end as well as for any other. About the
hour of supper the Duke would bid the youths put on their clothes',
and they would all return to the palace to dine. After the evening
meal, Federico would challenge the youths under his tutelage to
rise early for exercises the following morning, and if there were
no further requests for his counsel, 'he would go with the leading
nobles and gentlemen into his closet and talk freely with them'.
Afterwards, the duke would go to an observatory (the duke's loggia
entered from the *studiolo*) to view the stars before retiring.

His life was not always that serene. In late November 1477,
Federico was in San Marino. According to Giovanni Santi, the
duke and his entourage had gone up to the loggia of the building

they were staying in, presumably to admire the view. Looking out over the hills of the Marche, Federico fell into reminiscing about past victories, and in particular his defeat of Sigismondo Malatesta in the 1460s. He must have been striding about, excited by his memories, because he suddenly put his weight on a decayed plank, and fell through the floor. The only other account of the incident says that he was on his way to bed after dinner and fell through the stairs.[18] The basic fact of falling through wooden planking and landing on the floor below is common to the two accounts. This could theoretically have been an enemy stratagem, though there would have been absolutely no way of ensuring that it was Federico and not one of his companions who stood on the weak, or weakened, spot, and on the whole, it seems more likely to have been bad luck. It was very bad luck, though. He fractured his left ankle, and lacerated the leg. The injury went septic, and doctors had to drain pus from it at least five times. This was a devastating injury for a fighting man, and there must have been an element of sheer chagrin in knowing that, after surviving dozens of battles, he had jeopardized his career and possibly his life and his legacy, merely by not looking where he was going. Apart from his constitutional problems such as gout, Federico's injuries are linked with uncharacteristic moments of impulsiveness.

It was not the best of times for such an injury. The Italian peninsula was fairly peaceful for a couple of years after 1474, and Federico was able to spend a lot of time at home supervising his projects and enjoying the exemplary régime set out by Vespasiano da Bisticci. However, on 26 December 1476, Galeazzo Maria Sforza, son and successor of Federico's old friend Francesco, was assassinated in Milan. His wife Bona was a princess of the house of Savoy, not a condottiere's daughter, and she had neither the education nor the personal qualities necessary to take charge on behalf of their son Gian Galeazzo, then aged seven, so she was rapidly stripped of all but notional power. Eventually, Galeazzo's brother Ludovico 'il Moro' seized control, theoretically as 'regent', and Gian Galeazzo never got to rule. But in the immediate aftermath of the assassination, the question of who would prevail was not so obvious, and for a time the chancellor, Cicco Simonetta, was able to hold the balance of power on behalf of Bona and the legitimate heir, and exile the rival claimants. Federico was kept up to speed with these developments in Milanese politics by Simonetta, who was an old friend, and sent him news in cipher. Watching the swirling political currents round the vulnerable young Gian Galeazzo must surely have had a special resonance for Federico, whose own son was then a child of four.

Both Federico and Simonetta sensed that Lorenzo de' Medici was looking for advantage in this situation, and making friendly overtures to Ludovico Sforza, then living in exile in Pisa. Federico advised the chancellor that, in the circumstances, he had better drop the traditional alliance between Milan and Florence, and side with Ferrante of Naples – who was allied with Sixtus IV.[19] His distrust of Lorenzo, who had loaded him with honours after the siege of Volterra, was probably compounded by the fact that, in the intervening years, their own relationship had become increasingly tense, and Lorenzo had refused to pay Federico some back wages that were owed. The Florentines often found it hard to come up with the moneys they had promised to condottieri.[20] Sixtus IV, meanwhile, indicated his hostility to Lorenzo by transferring the papal bank account from the Medici to another Florentine banking family, the Pazzi. A conspiracy was launched in the spring of 1477: Sixtus was pressing for régime change in Florence, while piously insisting that nobody was to be killed; though it was perfectly obvious that only assassination would be an effective way of removing Lorenzo de' Medici from the political scene.[21] Federico's standpoint as a loyal supporter of the pope is suggested by the fact that in August 1477, before his unfortunate accident, Federico was employed in besieging Carlo of Montone, an ally of Lorenzo's who had rebelled against Sixtus IV. It took him eight weeks to conquer Montone, north of Perugia, so it was presumably in the aftermath of this that he took a little holiday in San Marino.

Lorenzo was increasingly concerned that the pope was trying to destroy him, and certain that Federico was in league with Sixtus IV, which he was. From a remarkable coded letter, which was deciphered in 2001 by Marcello Simonetta, it is clear that Federico was not just fully aware of the conspiracy, but part of it. Once action in Florence began, he was to be in position to lead a detachment of troops to seize the city, with his illegitimate son Antonio, who had taken a condotta as captain of the Sienese army, bringing up additional forces from Siena to secure it. There had already been a quid pro quo: Sixtus IV had sent Federico's legitimate son, Guidobaldo, a thick gold chain. Federico had him painted wearing it around March 1478, from which we can see that it is identical to the thick gold chains worn by the pope's secular nephews in the well-known painting of Sixtus and family by Melozzo da Forlì. So it was not merely a valuable ornament, it was a chain of office, and, given to a child, it was a direct indication that Sixtus was prepared to recognize the legitimacy of the Montefeltro dynasty. For such a prize, Federico was prepared to commit himself to this enterprise, even though he was still profoundly disabled.

On 26 April 1478, the Medici brothers, among many others, went to the Duomo to hear Mass. A group of assassins struck while the priests were singing the Agnus Dei, and Giuliano, the younger of the Medici brothers, was successfully felled; Lorenzo, however, reacted in time, and received only a light neck wound before leaping for the safety of the sacristy. Complete chaos ensued, until it became known that Lorenzo had survived. The citizens rallied to the Medici, and such conspirators as could be identified were hung out of the windows of the Palazzo Vecchio, including the Archbishop of Pisa, Francesco Salviati.

In the aftermath, Federico sent a convoluted letter to Lorenzo, which essentially advises him to take no further action. He also wrote to Cicco Simonetta in Milan, distancing himself from the Pazzi, and hinting that Lorenzo had brought the situation on himself by his disrespect for the pope's authority. He also said that, given that Ferrante and Sixtus were his employers, even if he had got wind of the conspiracy (which he did not directly admit) he would have considered that he owed it to them to keep silent. Both the Florentines and the Milanese accepted this, though doubtless with mental reservations. Though the Count of Montesecco, who had been arrested after the plot, implicated Federico in his written confession, when the Florentine chancery published the document later in the summer, they censored the passages that mentioned him. Federico was just a bit too important in Italian politics to embarrass: if his involvement was not generally known, he would be able to switch sides without losing face. This turned out to be prescient of them.[22]

During the cold war that followed, in which Sixtus excommunicated the Florentines and the Florentines attacked the pope as 'Vicar of the Devil', Federico had a specific and personal embarrassment to deal with. He had invested several thousand florins in having a spectacularly gorgeous Bible made for him by Vespasiano da Bisticci's workshop, and volume two was completed on 12 June 1478. He couldn't bear the thought of losing this immensely costly book, and so had to swallow his pride and write to Lorenzo humbly asking if it could be forwarded. Lorenzo obliged.

Federico, meanwhile, was planning for war, but when active hostilities between Sixtus IV and the Medici began in July 1478, he was still unable to ride. Yet he was captain-general of the papal forces, and he would have to take the field. He had a special saddle made, constructed normally on the right side, but with a brace on the left to support his left leg extended in front of him. His horse was led about daily in public, wearing this contraption, whether Federico was riding it or not, in order to show that he fully intended to keep his promise to lead his own troops in person. This was a desperate measure; a Florentine agent reported to Lorenzo de' Medici that, while he had seen Federico confidently riding around Urbino with his left leg stuck out, the duke had been unable to suppress gasps of pain as he dismounted.[23]

Some of the clearest evidence for Federico's use of guns is in this campaign of 1478, when his resources included five monstrous and temperamental siege bombards. They had individual names, such as The Cruel, The Desperate and The Ram. The biggest was in two parts, a 9-foot-long barrel weighing 14,000 lb (6,350 kg) and a train half as long, weighing 11,000 lb (5,000 kg). It had been cast by a bell-maker, Pietro of Siena, Siena being a principal source of expertise in this field, and fired stone cannonballs weighing 370–380 lb.[24] Bombards could be massively destructive weapons, but actually getting them to justify the incredible amount of trouble they caused was a job to break a soldier's heart. Federico wrote to Siena from camp on 14 July 1478, in a tone of suppressed fury, that the powder he had with him turned out to be not fit for purpose; and on 12 August, he asked for two barrels of nitre to improve it – as commander, he had to be, or employ, a competent chemist. A third problem was the balls; in the same week, he asked Siena to send any balls they had, even ones that were too big, since they could be cut down – a long job, but not as long as quarrying stone and carving them from scratch.[25]

The first point when the bombards came in useful was in attacking the castle of Sansavino, not far from Siena. He paraded their presence in front of the castle walls, and obtained a general ceasefire for eight days, during which time he ostentatiously received money and ammunition from Rome, and a detachment of crossbowmen from Urbino. The captain of Sansavino opened the gates to him without a shot being fired, which, given Federico's private fears about his gunpowder, may have been just as well. But clearly, bombards had their uses; and Federico, as he had shown at Volterra, was a master of the art of psychological warfare, and simply frightening the opposition into surrender. He went on to seize the other key Florentine fortresses, Poggio Imperiale and Colle Val d'Elsa, the last of which did require weeks of actual bombardment before it fell on 13 November.

With victory thus in sight, Federico changed tack in the most astonishing fashion. He strongly advised Ferrante's young heir Alfonso, who was in charge of the Aragonese troops, *not* to tackle Florence itself. On one level, this was shrewd and sensible: when challenged back in April, the Florentines had rallied round the Medici. They hadn't taken the chance to push out an unpopular ruling family, quite the opposite. Ultimately, Federico seems to have thought that it would not be possible to hold Florence if the citizens thought of their conquerors not as liberators, but as an invading army of occupation. And he remembered Volterra: how on earth could they prevent the Neapolitan troops from sacking Florence, something that would provoke international outcry and permanently tarnish his reputation? But he must have been only too well aware that Sixtus, wholly committed to extending the temporal territories of the papacy, would regard this as betrayal. Even so, Federico was not prepared blindly to support policies he considered short-sighted, something that had got him into trouble with previous popes, particularly Paul II. For example, after the death of Federico's ancient enemy Sigismondo Malatesta, Paul II had tried to reclaim Rimini for the Papal States. Federico thought, however, as he apparently did in the case of Lorenzo de' Medici, that the annihilation of the Malatesti was not in the interest of the Marche as a whole. He assisted Sigismondo's son Roberto in besieging Rimini, and was in command of the force that attacked and defeated the papal army on 30 August 1469. Three hundred dead were left on the field, and the episode cast a long shadow over his relations with the papacy.[26]

We have to conclude that, despite Federico's famous loyalty to his employers, he did not consider himself merely a tool. He did not follow orders blindly. In 1478, Federico thought that the best outcome for everybody (including himself) would be a restored balance of power, with the Milanese power struggle resolved, and a diminished Florence. This seemed increasingly on the cards, because on 7 September 1479, Ludovico Sforza, the late duke's brother, had secretly entered the Sforza castle in Milan, and Bona

Sforza had had the extreme political unwisdom to let him back into the city. Since it was the interim government of Cicco Simonetta that had been Lorenzo's ally, the young Medici now found himself completely friendless; and he was also losing control of his own city, mostly because the continued papal excommunication was having a dire effect on trade. In autumn 1479, Lorenzo sent a secret ambassador to Federico, asking for help, and Federico advised him to go to Naples and plead his case to Ferrante. This he did, and in March 1480, peace was declared.

On 18 December 1479, Federico went to the thermal springs at Viterbo, hoping for a cure for his injured leg, which was still giving him a lot of trouble. The mineral-rich water at Viterbo is hot and sulphurous, so he will have sat in it, soaking. Whether it helped with the leg or not, it will have eased other chronic aches and pains. He will also have had a significant easement to his spirits when, just after Christmas, a Blessed Sword and Hat arrived from the pope, one of the highest honours he could offer a layman. These were given to monarchs who had been active in the defence of Christendom, and were blessed by him on Christmas Eve. Sixtus had previously given swords and hats to Philibert, Duke of Savoy and Alfonso, Duke of Calabria; and in 1481, he also gave them to Edward IV of England.

The hat was a showier affair than Federico's usual beretta. Although there are no extant examples from the fifteenth century, a sword and hat survive from 1582, which were given by Gregory XIII to Ferdinand of the Tyrol. The crown was a stiff, high, crimson velvet cylinder, domed at the top, with a brim turned up all round. Two lappets, like those of a bishop's mitre, hung down at the back. A haloed dove, symbolizing the Holy Spirit, was embroidered in goldwork and pearls on the right-hand side of the cylinder. On the top centre of the hat was a shining sun from which alternately straight and wavy rays descended, also embroidered in gold. The sword was a standard weapon, but had been given silver hilts and an elaborate scabbard.[27]

The implication of this gift was that Federico was a true Knight of St Peter and warrior on behalf of the Catholic Church. Unfortunately, by the spring of 1480, Sixtus had found out about the deal struck between the Florentines and Ferrante. He suspected, rightly, that Federico had a hand in it, and was furious. Informants suggested that Sixtus was so angry he was contemplating having Federico assassinated.[28] What this suggests is that Federico's commitment to the balance of power in Italy was a genuine one. The last thing he wanted to do was to offend the pope, but in this instance, he seems to have tried to act for the general good of Italy.

In March 1482, there was an incident that reveals how much his relationship with the pope meant to him, and casts an interesting sidelight on his decision to act for the common good in preventing the sack of Florence. His ambassador to Rome, Piero Felici, was expelled from the palaces of both Sixtus IV and his nephew Girolamo Riario, on humiliating terms, as a token of the della Roveres' anger. The ever attentive calligrapher/spy Matteo Contugi reported the outburst that followed. Federico lamented,

> Now, by God, we are plunged into the greatest enmity with
> Count Girolamo! The last straw was that the holy Pope built a
> very worthy hall in which he had all the popes painted, and in
> the spot he reserved for himself he wanted to be portrayed with a
> huge gonfalone in his hand, and also with myself, portrayed as if
> I were receiving the gonfalone from his hand. The Count has
> ordered the master painters not to do it until further notice![29]

This revealing speech relates to one of Sixtus's most enduring legacies, the Sistine Chapel. In March 1482, the Life of Christ and Life of Moses cycles on the walls were almost finished, as were the portraits of martyred popes at the level of the windows (Michelangelo's ceiling and Last Judgement were added in the sixteenth century). The end wall was still blank, and Federico seems to have convinced himself that he would feature on it. As a fantasy, this provides an insight into his deepest longings: the papal gonfalon meant a great deal to him, and he had clearly come to hope that his image would be fixed for all time as the virtuous knight fighting on behalf of Christendom. In the event, Perugino painted an Assumption of the Virgin above a kneeling portrait of Sixtus IV, decoration that was subsequently swept away in favour of Michelangelo's masterpiece.

Fortunately for Federico, there were external forces in play. The conquest of Constantinople by the Ottoman Turks in 1453 had brought a flood of refugee Greek scholars and their books to Renaissance Italy, and by 1480 the Turks were ready to bring war to Italy itself. A force of nearly 20,000 Turks commanded by Gedik Ahmed Pasha launched an attack on the southern tip of the Italian mainland and captured the city of Otranto. This may be relevant to the fact that in December 1480, Sixtus absolved the Florentine republic and received it back into the Church. In April 1481 Sixtus IV called for an Italian crusade to liberate Otranto, and forces raised by Ferrante of Naples and Matthias Corvinus of Hungary besieged the city in May 1481. The Turks surrendered in August and left Otranto in September 1481, having occupied the city for a little over a year. While they had been successfully ousted on this occasion, the Christian powers could not ignore the possibility that they might return more effectively, perhaps even mount an attack on Rome itself, though the implicit message that Christians would be better to patch up their mutual quarrels was not always heeded. Meanwhile, Lorenzo and Federico exchanged friendly letters, and in November Federico paid an extremely secret visit to Florence, which was nonetheless observed by Contugi.[30]

One of Sixtus's more contumacious nephews, Girolamo Riario, was particularly disturbed by this rapprochement. He had had every hope that, if the glorious conquest of Florence had taken place, he would have been made its prefect. Sixtus and the della Rovere clan therefore turned against Federico, and decided he was unreliable. When his condotta with the pope ran out in March 1482, it was not renewed.

Federico set store by his name, which yielded a useful pun: 'fede', faith, 'rico', rich. In fact the name is German and means 'peaceful ruler', and came into the family because of their early connection with the Hohenstaufen emperors. Nonetheless, he was known to like the way it emphasized his strongest selling point, which was loyalty. For example, the intarsia decoration of the Urbino *studiolo* includes the letters F E D E, found on the four visible facets of an octagonal inkwell. The Florentine Neoplatonist Marsilio Ficino played up to his liking for puns on his name, claiming that the gods had styled him both 'Fideregum' (by the faith of kings) because of his kingly faith, and a duke 'Orbinatum', or born for the world, in the Apology to his translation of Plato's *De regno*, which he dedicated to Federico on 6 January 1482.[31]

Sixtus's resentment against Ferrante, as well as Federico, provoked a realignment. Federico was offered a new condotta by a completely new coalition: Lorenzo de' Medici, Ludovico Sforza, nominally ruling Milan on behalf of his young nephew, and Ferrante of Naples. On 17 April 1481, Federico signed it. He was to provide 600 men-at-arms and 562 infantry, with 165,000 golden ducats of pay. In peace, he was to have 65,000 ducats, and keep 300 men-at-arms and 371 infantry.[32] Sixtus therefore allied himself with the Venetians, Girolamo Riario now turned his attention to Ferrara, and Federico found himself once again at war. The Venetian forces bearing down on Ferrara were led by a noted condottiere, Roberto Sanseverino, and the papal forces by the same Roberto Malatesta whom Federico had restored to his father's throne, the new captain of the Church in Federico's place. The ruler of Ferrara was Ercole d'Este, married to Ferrante's daughter, Eleonora of Aragon. Battle was joined over a long hot summer on swampy ground, and by late August 1482, Federico was seriously ill with malaria.

Around the beginning of September, he was persuaded to turn over control of the army to Giulio Orsini, and was taken to the garden room of the Este castle in Ferrara for nursing. He was visited there by his son Antonio. Antonio had been legitimized in 1454, subject to the prior claims of a son born in wedlock (giving him the same status Federico had had as a child), and on a variety of occasions he can be seen acting as his father's lieutenant: notably, he was with Federico on the trip to Naples in 1474. But he was clearly thought of as a fallback: when he left camp at Ladino, where he was serving with the Florentine contingent, and hastened to his dying father's bedside, he may have hoped that Federico would prefer a thirty-two-year-old son with military experience over a ten-year-old, and name him as heir. But Federico tore a strip off him and ordered him back to his post.

On 28 August, the Neapolitans, with whom Federico was allied, had been defeated by Roberto Malatesta, who was leading the Venetian forces. Though Roberto was married to Federico's daughter Elisabetta, their condotte put them on opposite sides. It was not a good time to be lying in bed stewing with fever, since the defeat of the Neapolitan army left the way open for Roberto to invade Urbino. Federico was sufficiently worried by this possibility that, though he was unable to get up, let alone ride a horse, he ordered a litter and began heading for his home territories. But his attendants became so concerned by his condition that they turned back, and he died in the Castello Estense in Ferrara on 10 September. Federico was only sixty. He had cheated death many times from the age of eleven onwards, and his body was covered in scars, but it was malaria that finally conquered his iron constitution. What he could not know is that Roberto had also been stricken by fever, and would die at Rome some ten hours later. Federico himself must have died in a state of overwhelming anxiety about the future of his dukedom.

His half-sister Violante, who by then was the abbess of Corpus Domini in Ferrara, left her convent to be with him in his last hours; while doubtless she was orchestrating his spiritual care, praying, and offering what spiritual consolation she could, the fact that he had not left a written will meant that it was also vitally important that responsible people should be at his bedside waiting to catch his final words. These were recorded by his secretary, but the presence of Abbess Violante as a witness added credibility. It seems rather strange that so meticulous a man had not made a will, but in any case, his final disposition was to name ten-year-old Guidobaldo as his heir, to be succeeded, if he died, by Ottaviano, naming Antonio as only the third in line.

As Violante kept her vigil by the bedside of a dying man, watching as 'the light of Italy' guttered out, what was she thinking about? Christian duty, family honour, personal affection? Only the first and second, surely. Their lives had only overlapped in Urbino for about five years; in that time, a careful mother would surely have kept her daughters apart from her husband's bastard son, known as a womanizer, and anyway, he was frequently away fighting. Whatever she may or may not have felt about her brother Oddantonio, who was probably not the monster history has made of him, she can hardly have forgotten the night she and her sisters spent clutching one another in terror, listening to his dying screams and wondering if assassins would burst through their door. She had been so frightened at the time that she made a vow of chastity to the Virgin if she survived the night.[33] Federico had personally treated her very shabbily. He had thrown her out of Urbino, usurped her legitimate right to rule, and taken advantage of the deaths of her father and brother to cheat her of her legitimate dowry of Montefeltro lands, which must have caused a good deal of anguish and heartache and humiliation back in the day. But back in the day was a long time ago. She was genuinely religious, and she had been a nun and a widow for seventeen years. Her husband, Malatesta Novello, had been, like Federico, passionate about books. When the marriage proved childless, he poured his wealth into a library, gifting it to the people of Cesena, where, amazingly, it still is. Perhaps this gave her a certain sympathy with the man who lay dying beside her. As a servant of God, it was her duty to forgive. But also, he had made the Montefeltro dynasty so glorious that it was famous throughout Italy, as it had never been before. So she perhaps forgave him as a good Christian, and also as a daughter of the Montefeltri.

Once he lay dead, she wrote a letter to young Guidobaldo, formally notifying him of his father's death and, interestingly, pleading that, as duke, he should take the name of Guidantonio, her father's and, officially, Federico's. What she says is that if he takes the name, he will become 'wholly our father'.[34] This seems to be another instance of the Montefeltro tendency to use nostalgia as a tool of statecraft. Federico himself had embarked on his rule promising a return to the good old days and the good old ways of Guidantonio, and in this new emergency, it seems as if she thought it might help, even though after an interval of more than forty years, there would be few who remembered the old duke. She was also, of course, remembering the Urbino she had last seen in 1446, and since she was an enclosed nun, she was probably quite unaware of Federico's indelible stamping of his own identity and agendas on his city.[35]

The other person who was bereaved that night was Federico's daughter Elisabetta, wife of Roberto Malatesta. Her story starkly illustrates the importance of bearing a male child. She was Federico's oldest surviving legitimate daughter. Though, as Roberto's wife, she had ruled on his behalf when he was absent on campaign, the only child of the marriage was a girl. But Roberto had had a long-term mistress, Elisabetta Aldovrandini, a woman of family and not a floozy, who had given him sons.[36] Elisabetta Malatesta made the grimly practical decision that the optimal resolution of this situation for the good of everyone was for her to withdraw from Rimini, leaving its government in the hands of her rival, because the other Elisabetta was acting in the interests of Roberto's male children.[37] She accordingly retired to the convent of Santa Chiara in Urbino, where she took the veil as Suor Chiara.[38] Like her father, she consoled herself for her misfortunes with architecture, and spent her fortune on getting Francesco di Giorgio to remodel the convent.[39] Her daughter Battista's fate is unknown, but she probably went into Santa Chiara with her mother.

After the first stages of embalming had been performed, a sad contingent of Urbinate set forth to take Federico's body home. The coffin was covered with black satin, and carried to Forlì on the back of a mule, where it was met by a deputy of Girolamo Riario's and virtually the entire clerisy of the town. Though Riario had been bitterly angry over Federico's preventing him from seizing Florence, his body was thus honoured on account of his past service to the Church, his status as gonfaloniere, and perhaps with a sense that crowing over the dead was unlikely to do anyone any good.

The next day, in torrential rain, the coffin was loaded back onto the mule and the cortège wound up to Urbino, pausing for the night at Sassocorvaro. A procession of notables led by Ottaviano Ubaldini, in black cloaks, met the coffin a mile outside the city, and ushered Federico back to his palace. There, the embalming process was completed, and the corpse laid to rest in state, dressed in a red cloak, probably that of the Order of the Ermine, and his beretta, with his sword by his side. We know these details because his successor, Francesco Maria della Rovere, opened his coffin in 1512. His secretary, Urbano Urbani, left an eyewitness account: 'and I saw your body, just as good as ever it was, wearing your bonnet, dressed in your hose and mantle of crimson'.[40] The body was presumably laid in one of the rooms in the palace, so the people could file through and pay their respects. Ultimately, he would be taken to San Bernardino, but this was not yet built, and the Duomo was also under construction, since Federico had ordered it rebuilt after the birth of Guidobaldo, and the work was not complete. He was therefore given temporary burial in San Donato, a mile or so outside the city walls, alongside his forefathers, Guido il Vecchio and Guidantonio.

Francesco di Giorgio had designed a mausoleum for him, a classically inspired centrally planned monument, which was initially intended to stand in the middle of the Cortile del Pasquino. After the birth of his son, a personal mausoleum was no longer relevant, since he hoped to be the founder of a dynasty: he therefore revised his intentions and directed the construction of a different kind of memorial, a church that could serve as a ducal family monument. He and Guidobaldo were buried there.

As the news went around, Italy's chroniclers were unanimous that a great man had died. A Venetian, thus a man from a city with no great reason to love Federico, Fra Girolamo Maria, sums him up as follows: 'he was a most virtuous man. Educated, a genuine lover of religion and all good conduct, and possessing all the good qualities a true duke needs to have.'[41] He was universally respected and admired, and contemporaries considered that he had played his part admirably. What would happen next rested in the hands of Ottaviano Ubaldini.

When Federico died, there was still one panel to be completed in his *studiolo* at Gubbio. The design was revised, probably by Ottaviano: a round, polished steel mirror hangs, with G*BA*LDO*DX written on its frame. And a manuscript of the *Aeneid* stands open on a lectern. The text is legible, and the passage on view is the death of Pallas, of whom Jupiter says:

> Every man's last day is fixed.
> Lifetimes are brief, and not to be regained
> For all mankind. But by their deeds to make
> Their fame last: that is labour for the brave.

PART II

Federico's Legacy

8

The Palace at Urbino

The context of Federico's palace building is the redefinition of magnificence, which took place during his lifetime. One of the Greek works that was rediscovered in the Renaissance was Aristotle's *Nicomachean Ethics*, in which, among much else, the philosopher states: 'The magnificent man is an artist in expenditure: he can discern what is suitable, and spend great sums with good taste... Moreover he will spend gladly and lavishly, since nice calculation is shabby; and he will think how he can carry out his project most nobly and splendidly... It is also characteristic of the magnificent man to furnish his house in a manner suitable to his wealth, since a fine house is a sort of distinction; and to prefer spending on permanent objects, because these are the most noble.'[1]

Apart from in Venice, where patrician families had already started building palaces on the Grand Canal by the time Federico first visited, aged eleven, in 1433, Cosimo de' Medici was the only man in Italy who was spending very large sums of money on building projects between 1436 and 1450. In the fourteenth century, if new buildings were needed, they were financed through state or guild funds. Public opinion in Italy in the first half of the fifteenth century was still that the creation of ostentatious personal monuments was inappropriate. By 1450, a major change had taken place. Under the influence of Aristotle, it was now not only thought that noblemen could legitimately patronize architecture, but that this was actually a duty accruing to superior status.[2] The obvious irony of this as far as Cosimo de' Medici is concerned is that Florence was a republic, and in fact he was turning this proposition on its head. The Medici did not become dukes of Florence until 1530. It was by creating ostentatious personal monuments that Cosimo could make himself and his family something other than successful bankers and leading citizens. Pius II notes in his *Commentaries* that some Florentines were highly suspicious of Cosimo's architectural patronage, for precisely this reason.[3] But Leon Battista Alberti observes the new two-way link between greatness and architectural patronage in *On the Art of Building*, writing: 'since we all agree that we should endeavour to leave a reputation behind us… for this reason we erect great structures, so that our posterity may suppose us to have been great persons.'[4]

The condottiere princes looked and learned. Ludovico Gonzaga began building in 1450. Similarly, Federico, who never forgot that his half-brother, Oddantonio, had been Duke of Urbino while he himself was only a count, began to rebuild his palace as an ostentatious personal monument, in order to send out a message to contemporaries about the security and magnificence of his rule, his religious devotion, and his humanist training. The author of *De Ordine et Officij* completely accepts that magnificence is an expression of regality. He discusses the decoration of the palace in the chapters that address table service and guest housing, declaring that guest rooms should be splendidly decorated and furnished with honour, and also argues that the care of the signore's objects, all of which were splendid and conveyed a sense of authority, is of great importance to the *famiglia* 'because the dignity of the signore manifests itself in all that is seen'. Federico spent 200,000 ducats on building his palace, and 50,000 ducats on furnishing it, at a time when contemporary noblemen's houses in Mantua ranged in value from 1,000 to 2,500 ducats.[5] His profit from condotte between 1451 and 1482 has been estimated at 875,000 ducats, mostly earned in the last fourteen years or so of his career.[6]

His (official) father and grandfather had also been builders, albeit on a much smaller scale. Count Antonio bought the old town hall of Urbino in 1392, and around 1434 his son Guidantonio enlarged and redecorated it.[7] They disposed of the previous Montefeltro residence to a relative, Antonio di Niccolò da Montefeltro, who rebelled against Federico two years into his reign. After his execution, this palace was confiscated and sold to the Bonaventura family, and, under the name of the Palazzo Bonaventura, it is now home to the central library, archives and administration of the University of Urbino.[8]

The two-storey brick building of the previous counts was swallowed up in the first phase of Federico's building campaigns. We have some information about what it was like from documents of before 1444 that specify precisely where they were signed, which was either in an audience hall referred to as the 'ostrich room', or in a first-floor 'studiolo'.[9] We now know from material discovered in spoil heaps that the 'ostrich room' was decorated with Count Guidobaldo's *impresa*, an ostrich holding an iron arrow-point with a motto in German that means 'I can digest anything', while upstairs, one room was decorated with a repeating pattern of crowned black Montefeltro eagles, and another room had a repeating pattern of leafy branches and Guidantonio's monogram. One was probably the *studiolo*, the other perhaps a bedroom.[10] Guidantonio's personal style therefore was to surround himself with highly self-referential imagery, something that is imitated by Federico. On the night he was killed, Oddantonio received his assassins in his private apartment upstairs, so he must have been murdered in the *studiolo*, and thrown out of its window.[11]

Federico seized power in 1444, and the consensus of contemporaries is that the palace we know today was begun somewhere between 1463 and 1466, twenty years later. It looks as if the new walls started going up in the 1460s. Thus Federico must actually have lived in the old palace of Guidantonio during his first marriage, to Gentile Brancaleoni. It was only once he was established and wealthy that he initiated the much more ambitious structure that would bring him fame. As Giovanni Santi puts it, 'from there, the Count, burning with ardent love and with a high heart, began to build a great palace in Urbino, a construction not human but divine and, although of this world, it was distinguished from the earthly, according to what everyone said, by a beauty superior to anything that could be'.[12]

The new palace was begun shortly before Federico made a prestigious second marriage to the niece of the Duke of Milan, Battista Sforza. Phase one was creating the Palazzetto della Iole, which obliterated the old palace and constituted an ambitious restatement of the kind of man he was. Janez Höfler, the most recent historian of the evolution of the palace, attributes the design of the Palazzetto della Iole to the architects Pasquino da Montepulciano and Michele di Giovanni da Fiesole.[13] It consists of the continuous row of seven rooms that run the entire length of the eastern side of the Cortile d'Onore, with the rooms beneath. There were only three decorated rooms in this new palace: the Sala della Iole, the largest, its fine fireplace decorated with spontaneous and graceful relief sculptures, including caryatids of Hercules and Iole on either side of the fireplace opening, which were originally gilded; the Sala dell'Alcova, which contains Federico's remarkable bed, a polychrome wood room-within-a-room decorated by Fra' Carnevale; and the Sala degli Affreschi. The last of these was frescoed by Giovanni Boccati. The vault was painted with fictive damask, as were the walls, with, standing in front of them, giant figures of warriors. Beneath the dado were coats of arms. The decorative scheme is now in very poor condition, though sections of it are still legible.[14] The décor of the Sala degli Affreschi suggests that it was the room used for public audiences before the Throne Room was built. Battista's quarters would have been within this palazzetto, and after the final enlargement of the palace in the 1470s, the ducal children and their attendants continued to live there.

In the second half of the 1460s, Federico embarked upon the further expansion of his palace with the aid of the architect Luciano Laurana, who hailed from La Vrana on the Dalmatian coast. He was sent by Alfonso of Naples to Federico's court in 1465. The work was under way by 1466, since an eighteenth-century inventory of dated administrative record books (the books themselves are now lost) include one that records work on the 'Casa Nuova del Signore' in 1466–7, and another that relates to building work in 1467–9.[15] In June 1468 a patent was issued to 'Maestro Laurana from Dalmatia' as engineer and overseer of the scheme to beautify the city (not merely the palace) of Urbino. It opens: 'We deem as worthy of honour and commendation men gifted with ingenuity and remarkable skills, and particularly those which have always been prized by both the Ancients and the Moderns, as has been the skill of architecture, founded upon the arts of arithmetic and geometry, which are the foremost of the seven liberal arts because they depend upon exact certainty, and by us much esteemed and honoured.'

The second phase of work was therefore directed by Laurana, acting as Federico's principal lieutenant. The building was extended north to link up with another medieval building, the Castellare beside the Duomo, which was at an angle to the main structure, while wings were extended from the Palazzetto della Iole, which eventually became one side of a square surrounding a courtyard.

Vespasiano da Bisticci emphasizes Federico's educated patronage of architecture, and there can be no doubt that he had very clear ideas of what he wanted, even if the achievement of his ends was left to engineering specialists: 'as to architecture, it may be said that no one of his age, high or low, knew it so thoroughly... though he had his architects about him, he always first realized the design and then explained the proportions and all else'.[16] This phase was critical, since by the end of 1472 the main structure from the ground floor up, including the articulation of the rooms within the larger plan, the design of the courtyards, the garden and the façades, was in place. One of the few guides to the dating of different areas of the palace is that Federico was made a duke in 1474. Before that, his title was 'count'. The initials F C (Federicus Comes) are found around the Cortile d'Onore, on both floors, including the Throne Room; in his own suite and its loggia, in the rooms and loggias below that apartment, and on the little balcony overlooking the hanging garden. F C also appears on the door leading into the Sala degli Angeli. This tells us that these rooms were built before 1474.

The first phase of ornamentation was also completed under Laurana. For this aspect of the project, he turned to Tuscan artists, or artists working in a Tuscan style, to produce elegant but understated limestone doorcases, window surrounds, fireplaces, and other decorative low-relief carving. This must relate to how Federico saw himself at the time, carefully positioning himself as a successful man, without appearing boastful or excessive. Bernardino Baldi, writing in the 1580s, observes that the walls were plain white – the frescoed Throne Room of the first phase of building was an experiment not repeated, though the rooms would have been full of colourful painted furnishings. Additionally, during this phase of development, Federico began to commission intarsia doors for his new staterooms. In 1472, when he was besieging Volterra, Federico had had the assistance of Francesco de Giovane, who was an expert on military fortifications. In his civilian life, however, he was also the head of a major Florentine workshop creating intarsia work and architectural woodcarving, and he may well have been called upon.

The final phase of work, which began in 1474 and continued until Federico's death in 1482, left the Palazzo largely as it is today, a legacy of glory intended to shed a protective golden glow over his young son. In the last building phase, two architects are documented in Urbino, or employed by Federico: Baccio Pontelli and Francesco di Giorgio Martini. Pontelli came to Urbino in 1479, after spending three years working on a programme of intarsia for the Duomo of Pisa. However, he was not merely a decorator, since after the death of Federico in 1482 he left Urbino for Rome, where he entered the service of Sixtus IV as an architect and military engineer. He is named as sole architect of the Ducal Palace in an inscription of 1577, placed by his grandson, Francesco Fazino, above the door to a chapel in the church of San Domenico in Urbino, to which his tomb was relocated in that year. In this, Fazino says, 'he designed a palace which was the most beautiful of the buildings in the region by his art, and oversaw the construction'.[17] As Dr Johnson said, 'in lapidary inscriptions a man is not upon oath', and family pride has obviously led to overstatement, since most of the palace was in existence by 1474, but the inscription does suggest that Pontelli's contribution was substantial. He perhaps oversaw the completion of the *torricini* (the famous slender towers of the Ducal Palace), building the loggias, the completion of decoration in the courtyard, the ground-floor chapel and temple of the Muses, the library, and the hanging garden on the first floor.

The garden was much admired. Its design prefigures the pleasure gardens of the sixteenth century. Baldi indicates that it was intended as a 'green room', with a central fountain that could be turned on when required, and four formal beds with scented herbs, jasmine and citrus. This organization is typical of fifteenth-century gardens, but its most remarkable feature was the rectangular piercings in the wall, which frame long views out over the hills of the Marche, contrasting with the well-disciplined interior space. Since the garden was dismantled in favour of a lead roof in the eighteenth century, there is no direct information about its original planting. The architecture was restored in several phases from 1919 onwards, and it has been replanted several times, most recently in 2018. The palace at Gubbio also had a 'giardinetto' with a fountain by 1494, and another hanging garden was made at the convent of Santa Chiara, which has now also been restored.[18]

Francesco di Giorgio Martini served Federico for some ten years as architect, designer and engineer. He had entered Federico's service by May 1477, when he was charged with the decoration of the ducal apartments in Gubbio, and was a consultant on the new bastion at Costacciaro, which defended Federico's border with Perugia.[19] However, while di Giorgio's life is reasonably well documented, no evidence survives to link his name to the main building of the Ducal Palace in Urbino. In his treatise on military architecture, di Giorgio refers only to his work on the stables, though in another passage he notes that he was extensively employed by Federico, who commissioned 136 'structures' from him.

In Urbino, Francesco di Giorgio's work was related to the lowest layers of the expanded palace. To create the vast foundations that house the service areas, enormous quantities of soil were moved out beyond the city wall. A huge substructure, a wall with seven masonry vaults called the Risciolo, was created as foundation for a new marketplace outside the old walls, the Mercatale. Francesco also built very extensive stables, the Data, incorporating one of the towers of the old city wall and lying against the existing perimeter wall. The survey of the city walls drawn in 1502 by Leonardo da Vinci for Cesare Borgia makes it evident that the Data was part of the existing defensive border at the time. The tower was reconstructed so as to allow space for a wide spiral ramp, one of di Giorgio's trademarks, which made a direct connection between the palace and the Mercatale, but was also defensive.[20] He also built the basement bathing complex and kitchens.[21] This complex was begun in 1480 and completed after the death of Federico da Montefeltro. It is also probable that, in consultation with Federico, he helped to articulate the decorative scheme for the newer rooms.

Federico's commissions after 1474 show his desire to display his new ducal status and increased wealth by means of a vastly expanded and much more elaborately serviced structure, inscriptions, rich and exquisite ceilings, superb tapestries and, overall, a far more Burgundian aesthetic than he had employed hitherto, appropriate to his elevation. The friezes in the loggia of the piano nobile, which display his new insignia, the Garter, the Ermine, and his new coat of arms, and therefore post-date 1474, are far more ornate and deeply cut than the work done under Laurana.

Thus the overall picture that emerges is of a continuous process of building from the mid-1460s on for twenty years, in which new directions were taken periodically as Federico's circumstances changed and he needed his surroundings to evolve accordingly. In Alberti's view, 'the magnificence of a building should be adapted to the dignity of the owner'.[22] The peculiar quality of the palace at Urbino derives from the interplay between the large areas that, to our eye, express an elegant minimalism, but to a fifteenth-century viewer perhaps expressed the carefully calibrated dignity of a successful condottiere with the rank of count. While many details are disputed, we might envisage the palace built by Laurana for Count Federico as a large two-storey structure beside the Duomo. The *torricini* were there, but as buttresses, securing the back of the building to the steep western slope of the hill. As the restoration work of 1968–73 revealed, the loggias were an afterthought. No accommodation was made for them when the wall was constructed: they were inserted subsequently, anchored with transverse oak beams and iron trusses.[23] After all, why would Federico have wanted a 'frontispiece' for what is actually the back of the building?

In fact, the famous west façade is dependent for its stunning effect on the engineering work that was undertaken in the final stages of Federico's building campaign, and therefore relate to Federico's sense of his new magnificence. At some point, he and his architects realized that once the Mercatale, supported by the giant vaults of the Risciolo, had been conceived, with the great bulk of the spiral ramp linking the two, if the twin *torricini* were linked by elegant loggias, they would produce a remarkable visual coup de théâtre, rising clifflike over these great works of engineering, as indeed they do. The structure as we have it expresses the confident greatness of a duke and a Knight of the Garter, a dignity that put him on an equal footing with kings.

At Urbino, we are told by Vespasiano da Bisticci, the palace doors normally stood open from dawn to dusk, and citizens were admitted – though to carefully defined public areas only. The vestibule and courtyard, the main stair, the *sala* and *salotto* on the piano nobile, were freely accessible, with the added bonus that as they entered the building, visitors could stick their heads in the door of the ducal library, though we know that actual access to the books was strictly controlled. A series of ducal audience chambers on the piano nobile, entered both from the public parts of the palace and the duke's private apartments, allowed access to Federico himself for more privileged visitors. His apartments consisted of his bedroom, a *guardaroba*, or storage room for valuable items, his personal loggia, and his *studiolo*. There was a small audience room, the same size as his bedroom, with doors to his bedroom and to the *studiolo*, and a somewhat larger room, the Sala degli Angeli, which had doors leading to his bedroom and the small audience room. The Throne Room, which could be entered from the Sala degli Angeli, and which took up one whole side of the grand courtyard, was the largest room in the palace. It is clear how this space could be used to articulate the duke's interactions with visitors: the Throne Room could be used to emphasize ducal grandeur to large numbers, the Sala degli Angeli to receive smaller numbers of more important people, and the small reception room would be used for very important visitors. Only an exceptionally favoured one or two would enter the tiny and intimate space of the *studiolo*, which has a footprint of less than 15 square metres.

The palace at Urbino is metonymic for the duke himself: the duke was simple and unaffected, the palace was open. Leon Battista Alberti, whom Federico greatly admired, declares in his architectural treatise, *On the Art of Building*, that a wise ruler builds a palace in the middle of the town, where it would be accessible to the citizens. A tyrant, on the other hand, builds a fortress, walled off and inaccessible. The distinction is eloquently expressed by contrasting the palace at Urbino with the grim keep of Sigismondo Malatesta. The Urbinate citizens had access to the entrance, staircase, corridor and portico. But of course, everything beyond that was private, and Federico was a secret man. Unlike his della Rovere successors, who wrote quite extensively, Federico preferred to leave literary composition to the professionals, apart from letters and dispatches. He did, however, leave a little treatise on code-writing, *De furtivis litteris*, which may tell us something about him.[24]

The walls of the palace that face the piazza are known as the *facciata ad ali*. A continuous stone bench runs along it. Originally, carved stone reliefs were set in a row at the back of the bench representing machines of war, presented like *imprese* or emblems. Carved by Ambrogio Barocci da Milano, the designs were principally taken from the sketchbooks of Francesco di Giorgio. By incorporating these images into the palace façade, at the interface of public and private, the duke and his architects reminded the citizens of the basis of their prosperity. The reliefs, like the bench, extended on to the east façade. They were removed during a round of restoration in 1756, and are now displayed inside the palace.

The bench is a feature that Federico may have borrowed from Pius II's Palazzo Piccolomini at Pienza. Early Renaissance cities, or even particular palaces, that include such benches often seek to portray either the ruler or the head of the family as available and interested in the problems of the citizens. They function as a visual reminder of kindly and paternal rule; citizens could sink down on them, take the weight off their feet and chat, and they somehow imply that the duke, in his unassuming way, might come out and sit down with you to ask about the harvest. Given Federico's cautiousness about infection, which may have stemmed from the abscess on the jaw that almost killed him aged eleven, it is unlikely that he made a habit of this, but the possibility remained.[25]

Other rooms on the ground floor, apart from the library, included guest quarters, several audience chambers, and a pair of *tempietti*, very small, private and intimate spaces. One of the little temples is a Christian chapel, the other celebrates humanism, and was decorated with paintings of Apollo, Pallas and the Muses, as Bernardino Baldi mentions in his description of the structure. The two little rooms are next to one another, halfway between the *torricini*. The pairing of these *tempietti* with the *torricini* symbolizes the interplay between humanism, based as it was in classical thought, and Christian theology, or the opposition between the *vita activa* and *vita contemplativa*. This suite of rooms, directly underneath Federico's apartments, may have been used by Ottaviano Ubaldini, who is named in an inscription on the Capella, which states that he obtained from Sixtus IV the extension of the forty-day indulgence that was gained from visiting the patriarchal churches of Rome to visitors to the chapel. Alternatively, some contemporary palaces, including Pius II's palace at Pienza and Paul II's palace in Rome, have two sets of apartments, cooler ground-floor rooms for summer use, and heated rooms on the first floor, for winter.[26] The work on the *tempietti* post-dates the work on the ducal *studiolo*, which would be appropriate given that Ottaviano was second in command, if they are his.

In the last years of Federico's reign, after the palace had assumed its final form, a distinguished visitor's experience of the palazzo was carefully controlled. The *studiolo* was the most 'private' of the spaces within the palace and entering into it was a symbol of trust and privilege, which would certainly have been taken as a great honour. It is also a culmination of two routes through the palace that play with dualities: active and contemplative, Christian and humanist, as Maria Grazia Pernis has argued. Viewed from outside, Federico's private quarters are marked out by the two slender towers, the *torricini*, with the three tiers of loggias on the west front. The highest one is part of the ducal suite, his personal lookout point.

The route for distinguished guests starts from the open piazza between the entrance to the palace and the Duomo, goes through the Cortile d'Onore, up the ceremonial staircase to the Throne Room and into the Sala della Udienza. The other route was Federico's own, passing from the basement stables to the bathroom and then up to the *studiolo* and his private balcony.[27] In 1480, Francesco di Giorgio Martini built him a classically inspired bathing complex with a *caldarium*, *frigidarium*, and a complicated hydraulic system that allowed water to flow from the *neviera*, which stored the run-off from winter snow and rain, directly into the bath. The filtered drinking water was a separate system. The stables adjoin the north-western *torricino*, and the bath-house was opposite. This meant that in the last two years of his life, at any rate, he could return from a journey, leave his horse with the grooms, and bathe before entering the main areas of the palace. Once bathed, Federico could then climb his private staircase in one of the *torricini* to his private apartments two floors above. This bathing complex not only met his physical needs and provided a site for a kind of ritual cleansing, but also underscored the association between Federico and the glory of classical antiquity.

When Federico went up to his private rooms, they gave him sharply contrasted spatial experiences: above all, the passage from the intimate interior of the *studiolo*, a place for reflection, to the extensive view over his domain from the loggia, the inward and outward life held in balance. The heart of the ducal apartments is the *studiolo*, with its doors to the *guardaroba* and the smallest audience room. The *studiolo* is a tiny room, very high – 5 metres – with an elaborate coffered ceiling. The lower half of the walls were covered in intarsia work, with, above it, two rows of paintings depicting great men: poets, philosophers, teachers and popes. The magnificence of the decoration, and the ducal insignia represented in it, indicate that the decoration of this complex was in process after Federico became duke in 1474. An inscription in Roman capitals runs round the *studiolo*, just below the ceiling, which gives its completion date, as well as Federico's styles and titles: FEDERICUS · MONFELTRIUS · DUX · URBINI · MONTISFERETRI · AC · DURANTIS · COMES · SERENISSIMI · REGIS · SICILIAE · CAPITANEUS · GENERALIS

· SANCTAEQUE · ROMANAE · ECCLESIAE · GONFALONERIUS ·
MCCCCLXXVI. (Federico da Montefeltro, Duke of Urbino, Count
of San Leo and Castel Durante, captain general of the Most Serene
King of Sicily, gonfaloniere of the Holy Roman Church, 1476.) As
Dora Thornton says in her book devoted to the Renaissance study-
room: by 1470, 'to own a study was to lay claim to the civility,
polite manners and educated tastes which came to define the ruling
élite in the Italian renaissance'.[28] The decoration of such a room
expressed its owner's sophistication and the qualities he possessed,
or aspired to: it was intended to be read as a personal statement.

It is not clear who conceived the decorative programme of
the *studiolo*: Luciano Laurana left the court in July of 1472, three
weeks after the death of Battista, to join the service of the Sforza
family in Pesaro and that of the King of Naples. It may have been
modelled on the lost *studiolo* of Leonello d'Este at Palazzo Belfiore,
which was designed by the humanist Guarino Guarini of Verona
in 1447, since we know that this had intarsia decorations and a
cycle of paintings dedicated to the Nine Muses.[29] Federico himself
was probably at least partially responsible. Intarsia work was highly
fashionable by the 1470s. As Vasari notes, the architect Filippo
Brunelleschi, who was interested in both intarsia and perspective
studies, had created a fashion for using the medium to display a
mastery of geometric perspective some years previously.[30]

The intarsia panels represent fictive cupboards full of precious
possessions, books, musical and scientific instruments, and
random treasures, depicted at life size, and playing games with
perspective – for example, the necks of musical instruments that
'project' from the flat surface seem to move as you walk past them.
Fabio Benzi suggests that a series of artists worked on the design
and execution of the intarsia work, including Giuliano Maiano
of Florence, Francesco di Giorgio Martini, and Baccio Pontelli,
who studied alongside Maiano in the workshop of Giuliano da
Sangallo.[31] Drawings for certain panels were solicited from artists,
notably Botticelli. The almost life-sized half-length portraits seem

to have been largely the work of Joos van Wassenhove, perhaps with later repainting by Pedro Berruguete.

Two major themes in the *studiolo* are the balance between the *vita activa* and *vita contemplativa*, and the celebration of virtue and learning. The north wall represents thinkers, or the power of thinking, both pagan and Christian: Plato and Aristotle, Ptolemy and Boethius, and Doctors of the Church. On the left of the east wall, a cupboard – *armamentum* in Latin – contains Federico's armour, a symbol of the active life. On the right is a fictional study with a lectern, symbol of contemplation; in the centre, we look out over a wide landscape to an ideal city. A pet squirrel (it is wearing a collar) sits up between the pillars, nibbling a nut; because of the squirrel's habit of storing up food for the winter, the little animal symbolizes prudent rulership. The Latin word Petrarch uses to describe his study is *armariolum*, from *armarium*, Latin for a bookcase. On this wall, the fictive *armariolum*, with its lectern and books, and the armour (Latin *arma*) stored in an *armamentum* are linked by an underlying etymological connection to equate the ways in which Federico 'arms' himself for physical and intellectual battle in order to remain the worthy lord of the rolling countryside presented in the middle panel.

The items in the cupboards suggest its owner's concerns and activities: inkwells and paper, for when he sits and writes, an armillary sphere and astrolabe, suggesting that when he stepped out of the *studiolo* onto his balcony last thing at night, he was studying the stars. The astrolabe is a representation of an actual instrument made by Abu Bakr ibn Yusuf of Marrakesh around 1200, which was given to Cardinal Bessarion in 1462, and by him to Federico.[32] We also know that Federico (or the enthusiastic astrologer Ottaviano) had another astrolabe made, because it had '1462 Urbini' engraved on it. It survived to the mid-1970s, but was then stolen from the Musée Départmental in Moulins in east-central France.[33] A mechanical clock is also represented in the intarsia; a rare possession in the fifteenth century. There are of course many books depicted: a Bible, Cicero and Seneca, Homer and Virgil, and the medieval theologian Duns Scotus. The precious objects depicted may have been kept in the *studiolo* itself. When the antiquarian Bernardino Baldi described the palace at Urbino in 1587, he referred to various items of furniture in the *studiolo* – two chests and two cabinets, as well as benches and an intarsia table – so the room must have been rather crowded.[34] Alternatively, the treasures were kept in the *guardaroba* (storeroom), another part of Federico's suite, which is also where he seems to have kept his books before the great library was built.

The *studiolo* is a very masculine space. The only female presences are the Theological Virtues, Faith, Hope and Charity. The contemplation it embodies is rigorous study: philosophical, mathematical, religious or musical. Emblems of leisure and pleasure are not included. Federico himself appears in an intarsia portrait, wearing robes and holding a spear, point down, a token of peace. His costume is suitable for an evening's contemplation, as we learn from a letter that Niccolò Machiavelli wrote in 1513: 'when the night arrives, I return home, and enter into my studiolum; and on the threshold I take off that everyday costume, and put on royal and curial vests; and thus I enter into the ancient courts of those ancient men'.[35] Federico also specifically links the *studiolo* portraits to his own self-fashioning, because each one once had an identifying inscription indicating what the subject meant to him personally: they were transcribed by a visitor in 1592. Federico is the grammatical subject of every single sentence.[36] For example, 'to Vittorino da Feltre, most saintly of teachers, for humanistic culture transmitted by his writings and by his example, Federico places this'.

The *studiolo* is not exactly a private study. Certainly, it could be, and doubtless was, used as one. But it represents who Federico was (or what he wished to be seen as); what he thought about, his honours, his power, his political associations, and his private life as a scholar, while alluding to his public life as statesman and soldier.

Christiane Hessler has also suggested that it specifically represents him as a widower.[37] This all strongly suggests that the programmatic self-representation of the intarsias was fundamentally aimed at privileged guests. Access to private apartments was a basic tool of early modern statecraft. A conversation in the *studiolo* allowed the duke to impress his personality and achievements on his interlocutor without any need to boast or show off: the room did all that for him.

The *studiolo* remained intact until 1631, when, on the death of the last duke, the palace contents reverted to the Holy See. Though the intarsia panels stayed in place, the paintings were removed at this point and given by Urban VIII to his nephew, Cardinal Antonio Barberini, witnessed by a chirograph dated 17 January 1632. Some have since been returned, though others are now in the Louvre. There is a second *studiolo* at the palace of Gubbio, a strong indication that Gubbio was very much a second home to Federico. It was begun after 1474, and not completed until shortly after Federico's death. It was taken out in the nineteenth century, and is now at the Metropolitan Museum in New York.

Vasari notes that intarsia had gone out of fashion by the time he was writing, because it was 'time thrown away in vain… since it is a work that soon becomes black… and is also of short duration because of worms and fire'.[38] However, the Urbino intarsias are in a miraculous state of preservation. They were taken down twice in the course of the twentieth century. The first time, for safety's sake, was at the onset of the Second World War, by the Bolognese intarsia master Enrico Bernardi, who studied them carefully. Both the intarsias and the coffered ceiling were dismantled again for cleaning and restoration in 1969 as part of the great Urbino restoration project. The ceiling was restored by Silvestro Castellani, and the intarsias by Otello Caprara.[39]

It was the Urbino palace, above all Federico's other works, that captured the imagination of contemporaries. Baccio Pontelli, who was involved in the completion of the building, wrote from

Urbino on 18 June 1481 to Lorenzo de' Medici, dispatching, at his request, detailed plans of the palace, which indicated every room, its measurements and decoration. Lorenzo claimed that he frequently read Alberti's theoretical treatise, and presumably was eager to study what might be termed its finest practical achievement, and what was accordingly the ideal princely habitation. Similarly, before embarking on his vast extension to the palace at Mantua, the 'Nova Domus', Federico Gonzaga asked for designs of the palace from Federico himself, and also consulted Francesco di Giorgio in 1481 about how he had managed to construct chimneys that didn't smoke.[40]

The interior decoration, with its carved grotesques based on a study of antique models such as the recently rediscovered 'Domus Aurea' in Rome, set the fashion, and was copied as early as the 1480s in Santa Maria dei Miracoli, Venice.[41] Federico's commissions also set fashions. The theme of portraits of famous men, used in the décor of the *studiolo*, was frequently reused through the sixteenth century. Additionally, Piero della Francesca's famous portraits of the duke and his wife seem to have been the model for those of Giovanni II Bentivoglio of Bologna and his wife, probably painted by Ercole de' Roberti, and many other double portraits.

The miracle of the palace's survival arises from a potent combination of neglect and action. In the first place, because they moved the centre of the duchy to Pesaro, the della Rovere dukes left Federico's palace almost unaltered, except for adding a top storey designed by Bartolomeo Genga. Because Pesaro was of more use to the della Rovere than Urbino, there are few baroque interventions in Urbino apart from the Porta Valbona, and a round of redecoration in 1548 in preparation for Guidobaldo II's second marriage, to Vittoria Farnese. Additionally, the birth in 1605 of Federico Ubaldo della Rovere brought the ducal family back to Urbino for a big dynastic celebration, which must have caused some tidying up, at the very least. In 1700, the election of an Urbinate of antiquarian tendencies as Pope Clement XI gave rise to another round of repairs.

Thus, when a major programme of restoration was undertaken after 1968, the structure had had enough basic care in the intervening five centuries that the timeless palace we know today could be recalled to life.

IDEAL CITIES

The idea of Urbino and the idea of the ideal city are closely linked. According to Baldassare Castiglione, the palace of Urbino was itself an ideal city:

> Among his other commendable enterprises, Duke Federico built on the rugged site of Urbino a palace which many believe to be the most beautiful in all Italy, and he furnished it so well and appropriately that it seemed more like a city than a mere palace.[42]

In his palace, particularly in the *studiolo*, Federico represents himself as an ideal ruler, presiding over an ideal city. Though 'Urbino' does not mean 'little city', to a fifteenth-century Italian it probably sounded as if it did, suggesting the idea of a microcosm. The design of Federico's palace, and the life that was lived there, with its scrupulous attention to order and hygiene, embodies an almost modernist idea of creating virtue through architecture.

A variety of architectural perspective paintings are associable with Urbino; in particular, three idealized cityscapes now in Urbino, Baltimore and Berlin. The classicizing buildings that fill the panels conform to the kind of strict perspective system also visible in both Piero della Francesca's *Flagellation of Christ* and in the design of Federico's *studioli* in Urbino and Gubbio. These paintings of classicizing architecture contain almost no human figures: the Berlin one, with an arch at either end and a view through a loggia, curiously resembles a Renaissance Italian

'Annunciation' from which the Angel Gabriel and the Virgin are mysteriously absent.

Federico's contemporary Lorenzo de' Medici recognized pictures of this type as a known category of domestic painting:

> Three things in my judgment are called for for a perfect work of painting, namely, a good support, a wall or cloth or whatever it may be, on which the paint is applied; a master who is very good both in drawing and in colour; and besides this, that the matters painted be, in their own nature, attractive and pleasant to the eyes, for even if the painting were very good, what is painted might be of a kind that would not be in harmony with the nature of the person who is to see it. For some people take pleasure in things such as animals or greenery or dances or similar merrymaking, others would like to see battles either on land or on the sea, and similar martial wild things, still others landscapes, buildings, and foreshortenings and proportions of perspective.[43]

The creation of these pictures ties in both with Renaissance fascination with architecture in classicizing styles, since all the buildings in these panels are 'after the antique', and with the Renaissance fascination with perspective: they feature a single, central vanishing point, and the structures are arranged so as to draw attention to this fact. The first perspective paintings known were made by the Florentine architect Brunelleschi, and the theme was taken up by Masaccio. Vasari describes a much-admired 'Annunciation' painted for San Niccolò in Florence, in which 'there were a house and many columns, admirably painted in perspective... so managed that the colonnade gradually recedes from view in a manner which proves Masaccio's knowledge of perspective'.[44] All these early paintings are lost.

Federico da Montefeltro's interests included both architecture and mathematics, and he seems to have taken pleasure in perspectives, and in thinking about perspective. He owned Piero della Francesca's treatise on perspective, and hosted Leon Battista Alberti in Urbino in 1469. Alberti was both a student of antique architecture, the practical adviser to Nicholas V on restoring outstanding monuments in Rome, and an architect himself. Since Cristoforo Landini creates a dialogue between Alberti, Federico and Lorenzo de' Medici in his 1475 *Disputationes Camaldulenses*, in which they converse on civic virtue, his regard for Alberti must have been well known. Vespasiano da Bisticci says of Federico, 'as to architecture, it may be said that no one of his age, high or low, knew it so thoroughly... he was a skilled geometrician and arithmetician'.[45] He adds that among the learned men of the court in the 1480s was Paul of Middelburg, an internationally respected mathematician and astronomer, and notes that Federico had Paul read over books about mathematics with him. Federico himself wrote to Laurana that mathematics and geometry were 'the most important of the liberal arts, for their being based on scientific truth, and the very foundation of architecture'.[46]

Guidobaldo, his son, was also seriously interested in mathematics. Fra Luca Pacioli, who also wrote on perspective, seems to have taught him, and certainly dedicated his *Summa de Arithmetica* to him in 1494.

We know that perspective drawings were in the palace in the time of Federico. The Urbino historian Bernardino Baldi wrote in 1587 that there were perspectives in the palace drawn by the architect Luciano Laurana: 'certain panels, in which there were various scenes drawn with rules of perspective and coloured, which one cannot doubt are his, and there is his name written with other things with characters in the Slavonic language'.[47] One of them may be the perspective panel that is in Urbino now, since there are indecipherable inscriptions in the pediments of the two palaces to left and right. Another perspective was described in the 1582 inventory as three braccie long and one and a half high (thus a different size from any of the pictures we still have), mounted over the door of the duke's bedroom. The 1599 inventory mentions 'a long painting of a perspective, old but beautiful, by the hand of Fra Carnevale'.[48] An Urbinese painter called Giovanni

Francesco Micalori noted that he saw two other perspectives by Fra Carnevale in 1670.[49] Fra Carnevale was working for Federico, producing architectural drawings and painting Federico's bed-alcove, in the 1450s, and he is known to have been interested in perspective.

The theme of the ideal city reappears in the marquetry decoration of the palace, especially in the doors of the ducal apartment, and on furniture. In the Urbino *studiolo*, a panel depicts a bowl of fruit standing on the floor of a loggia, with a squirrel nibbling at a stolen item. The scene is framed by two pillars, and the view is across a floor with the perspective emphasized by darker lines of stone, to an arch flanked by two superimposed pilasters. Beyond is an ideal landscape. The arch and pilasters is a motif typical of Francesco di Giorgio, who used it at the entrance portal to the spiral ramp that leads up to Federico's castle, and he is certainly responsible for designing the intarsia panels in Gubbio. The design has also been attributed to Botticelli.[50] The whole project of the intarsia panels plays games with perspective, because the illusion is completely dependent on it: there is a single central vanishing point for each wall, but also a separate viewpoint in front of each fictive cupboard. One indication of this is that both sets of intarsias include a '*mazzocchio*', a polyhedral torus that apparently represents a sort of doughnut-shaped inner piece used to support the shape of a hat – a *mazzochio* was repeatedly represented both by Uccello and by Piero della Francesca as a test of skill in rendering perspective.[51]

Adjoining the *studiolo* is Federico's *guardaroba*, where his most valuable possessions were kept. This has two sets of inlaid wood doors decorated with views of ideal cities. The Sala degli Angeli, which adjoins the bedroom and served as an audience chamber, also has intarsia doors. One has figures of Hercules and Mars, but the second is yet another view of an ideal city. All of this suggests that the palace at Urbino was a place where the ideal was realized as far as was humanly possible.

9

Gubbio & Beyond:
Other Architectural Projects

Federico undertook architectural projects all over his territories. He built up his cultural profile in the region with spectacular architectural commissions including *rocce* (outposts or armed forts), a number of religious buildings, particularly in Urbino itself, and ducal palaces in Gubbio and Castel Durante (Urbania). He also created suitable homes in Sassocorvaro and Mercatello for his brother Ottaviano Ubaldini. These monuments reflected his personal magnificence, which grew in stature in concrete cultural and material terms.

Gubbio was Federico's first home, since he was born there, and throughout his adult life it was his secondary or summer palace. The oldest buildings in Gubbio were along the ridge of the hillside up which the city now extends. In the twelfth century, the city walls were extended and neighbourhoods expanded to fill the space they bounded. Like most Italian cities, it was divided into quarters, San Pietro, Sant'Andrea, San Giuliano and San Martino, and the medieval centre was constructed. An aqueduct was built to provide the growing city with a stable water supply. This was always a major issue for Italian hill towns, because if hostile forces could interrupt the water supply, during a siege, for example, the citizens might be forced to surrender. Even in the earliest building phases of the structure that became Federico's palace, fourteenth-century craftsmen included a simple hydraulic system to bring water from the main supply route, which could be stored in a cistern in the basement.

Although Gubbio remained autonomous and self-governing, by about 1400 the Montefeltro counts had, by mutual agreement, come to act as its protectors. In recognition of this, a house was assigned for the family's use, which was in the town, near the bishop's residence. There are a number of references in Guidantonio's time to his occupation of 'the usual residence'. Federico visited Gubbio shortly after succeeding his half-brother, in August 1444. He agreed a variety of administrative matters with the comune, and the resulting document declared that he and his family could stay 'at the expense of the comune in the place of their usual residence', with the same privileges as before. Around the time of his marriage to Battista Sforza, Federico began to feel the need of larger and more prestigious quarters. By 1464, he was given the use of a large city building, no longer extant, known as the Old Palace (Palatium Vetus). This palace was of particular importance to Federico from 1468 to 1472, when building work in Urbino was at its height, since he and Battista could entertain honoured guests there in peace and quiet. They hosted Alfonso of Calabria at Gubbio in 1468, and Borso d'Este of Ferrara in 1471. In 1473, another state reception was held at Gubbio to welcome Cardinal Pietro Riario, one of the nephews of Sixtus IV, the new papal legate to Italy.[1] Battista Sforza was particularly fond of Gubbio. Most of her children were born there, including Guidobaldo, and she died there in 1472.

After his great access of wealth and status in 1474, Federico decided he needed a palace that would overlook the city. He gave the Palatium Vetus back to the comune, and was permitted to take over the fourteenth-century Palazzo della Guardia and remodel it for his own use. During the last years of Federico's reign, this palace was again central to the cultural life of the court, as a retreat, and a place where honoured guests could be entertained.[2] From 1474 to 1477, it was restored and enlarged under the supervision of Francesco di Giorgio Martini. Far less elaborate than the Urbino palace, it began as a simple three-storey rectangular structure, with crenellations. Most of the ground floor is occupied by a large hall, useful for large-scale entertainment, dancing or performances. A smaller audience chamber adjoins this. Martini turned the building into a square surrounding a courtyard. He copied some details, such as the composite capitals, from Laurana's work on the main palace at Urbino. The palace was elegant, with blue and gold coffered ceilings and elaborately carved fireplaces with details picked out in blue and gold, few of which are still in situ. On the whole, apart from fireplaces, principal doorcases, intarsia doors and the intarsia in the *studiolo*, the Gubbio palace was decorated with paint rather than with relief carving. The duke's bedroom was given a frieze with gold letters on blue, and another frieze on purple (*damaschino*), painted by Bernardino Nanni; the contract for this work survives. A description of the room made in 1660 mentions panels with gilding and all the duke's devices, perhaps identifiable with Nanni's 'purple frieze', and an inscription giving all his titles.[3] The palace was equipped with a *studiolo*, like the palace at Urbino, and, though much smaller, followed a similar layout.

The next duchess, Elisabetta Gonzaga, wife of Guidobaldo, Federico's son and successor, also liked Gubbio, and entertained her sister-in-law and friend Isabella d'Este there. After spending Easter 1494 there, Isabella wrote, 'the palace is furnished magnificently, besides being so beautiful and so well located that I don't think I ever saw anything I liked better. It is built high above the city and the plain, and has a small garden with a delightful fountain.'[4] Gubbio suffered heavily during Cesare Borgia's usurpation of the duchy during Guidobaldo's reign. The town was twice occupied by Borgia soldiers, and the palace was sacked, presumably losing all its movable furniture. It became a sad place, and when Guidobaldo was succeeded by Francesco Maria della Rovere in 1508, the town fell into provincial obscurity, as the ducal court moved to Pesaro. Unlike the Ducal Palace in Urbino, it was allowed to fall into disrepair. When the Urbino historian James Dennistoun visited in 1843, he found the palace closed up and inaccessible. An Italian acquaintance who had been able to get in to see it told him that the coffered ceilings were decaying, though the *studiolo* was still intact.[5] In 1870, the Balducci family, who owned the palace, began negotiations to sell the intarsias, and they were bought by Prince Filippo Massimo Lancellotti in 1874. He intended to install them in a belvedere, but he received a visit from the police, who told him that because the building was a scheduled national monument, the panels had been illegally removed. The legal wrangle rumbled on, so the panels were stored in the attic of the Villa Lancellotti at Frascati until 1937, when the dealer Adolfo Loewi got to hear of them, and eventually sold them to the Metropolitan Museum in New York in 1941.

Castel Durante was another town important to the Montefeltri, but still more to the Della Rovere dukes. It was first known as Castel delle Ripe, a free comune of the Guelph party. It was destroyed by the Ghibellines in 1277, and seven years later rebuilt by a Provençal, Guillaume Durand, in 1284, who rechristened it Castel Durante. Later it was ruled by the Brancaleoni family, and acquired by Federico through his marriage with Gentile, last of the Brancaleoni line. The ducal palace at Castel Durante was another summer residence for the Montefeltri, and Federico laid out a *bosco*, or deer park, there, because game was plentiful in the area. The palace was most probably constructed between 1477 and 1501, when Martini was in the employment of the first two dukes of Urbino. A Martinian core remains, including one of his trademark spiral ramps, which originally linked all the floors of the structure. At the ducal palaces in both Urbino and Castel Durante, the ramp climbed from cellar level through all the floors of the building. Since a horse cannot negotiate stairs but can walk up a ramp, the ramp allowed heavy items to be moved up to the top floors of the palace by horsepower. The most striking façade faces the river, with an overhanging loggia stretching between two cylindrical towers. The della Rovere dukes became particularly attached to this residence, and it was considerably altered to their requirements in the sixteenth century by Bartolomeo Genga. The last Duke of Urbino, Francesco Maria II, lived an increasingly reclusive life there from 1606 to his death in 1631, and is buried there.

The first defensive structure that Francesco di Giorgio Martini built for Federico was Costacciaro, which guarded the border with Perugia. This was similar to the new fortifications at Volterra, which were raised under the supervision, and apparently to the design, of Federico, who had destroyed the old defences. With his extensive experience of blowing holes in city walls with big guns, he was aware that effective defence needed new types of fortification. The Volterra bastion was square in plan with low walls, an escarpment and massive cylindrical towers of the same height at the corners, creating an uninterrupted horizontal plane all around the perimeter that was wide and solid enough for heavy bombards to be trundled about. It drew on the design of the Malatesta bastions at Fano and Rimini, well known to Federico. This suggests that di Giorgio, whose previous experience was mostly in hydraulics, achieved his innovations as a military architect in close collaboration with his client.[6]

Care and attention was also lavished on the two palazzi of Ottaviano Ubaldini at Sassocorvaro and Mercatello. A papal bull of 1474 indicates that control of the *rocca* of Sassocorvaro was granted to Ottaviano Ubaldini, and a new bastion was built by Francesco di Giorgio. The attribution of the *rocca* to di Giorgio is on stylistic grounds, but is generally accepted. The construction was extremely protracted, since the building was not actually completed till the late sixteenth century.[7] It featured what seems to be the first of Martini's spiral ramps, winding up through the heart of the fortress as its principal stair, with a well at the bottom of the central light shaft so that water could be drawn up to any level of the building. The *rocca* combined defensibility with internal living spaces appropriate to a nobleman such as Ottaviano.[8] During Ottaviano's time in Milan he became interested in the study of astrology, which seems to have influenced the design of the *rocca*: it has the shape of a tortoise, an animal that symbolized excellence in the language of alchemy and also represented defensive impregnability. The pattern of the stones in the cortile also reflects Ottaviano's astrological interests, as some of the stones were laid in the form of circles and stars. However, Michela Liotta has observed that the castle was actually rather vulnerable, because it was endangered by the hill overshadowing the town and because the slits are wrongly positioned for defensive fire.[9] This may be because it was one of the first of di Giorgio's military commissions not to be directly supervised by Federico da Montefeltro, and since Ottaviano knew more about astrology than ballistics, it reflects its architect's inexperience.

Fossombrone belonged to the Malatesta family until 1446, when Galeazzo Malatesta was persuaded to sell the lordship to Federico for 13,000 ducats, and it was also one of the vicariates that Nicholas V similarly sold him when he confirmed Federico as papal vicar over the Montefeltro in return for 12,000 gold ducats in 1447. However, from 1447 until 1462, during Federico's long feud with Sigismondo Malatesta, actual control of the city continued to fluctuate until, in 1462, Sigismondo Malatesta surrendered to Montefeltro forces in Fano. Federico claimed a complete victory and took control of all the contested lands, including Fossombrone. The earliest settlement there, the *cittadella*, was, like that of Gubbio, located along the top of the hillside following the Via Flaminia. It expanded down the hillside until, by the sixteenth century, it reached the river Metauro. The little that remains of the Roman origins, and the heart of the Malatesta town, is the *castello* at the top of the hill, overlooking the river basin. This dates to the thirteenth century and was renovated by the Malatesti in

1444, just before Federico laid siege to the town, and then again, after the site was in Montefeltro hands, by Francesco di Giorgio Martini sometime after 1477. In addition to his work on the *castello*, Federico renovated the court residence, later called the Corte Alta, which, like the palace at Gubbio, is halfway down the hillside, between the *cittadella* and the river Metauro, and created a deer park.[10] Guidobaldo I and Elisabetta Gonzaga were particularly fond of the Corte Alta, and remodelled it as a pleasure palace with a large hall that could be used as a theatre, and laid out gardens there.

San Leo had both an actual and a symbolic importance to the Montefeltri. It is situated on a remarkably steep mountain on the eastern side of the valley of the river Marecchia, since antiquity the site of a path through the Apeninnes that eventually became a road. The Romans built a temple to Jupiter Feretrius to celebrate their victory over the Gauls at Clastidium in 222 BC, which had allowed them to conquer Milan, a site that was repurposed for the cathedral. 'Feretrius' probably means 'striker' (of the enemy): Consul Marcus Claudius Marcellus, who had commanded the Roman forces at Clastidium, donated the *spolia opima* (armour and clothes) of Viridomarus, leader of the Gauls, to the temple. Montefeltro, the name of the region and of the Montefeltri, seems to derive from Mons of [Jupiter] Feretrius. The Montefeltri certainly believed that it did. One of the oldest family *imprese* is an eagle, which is both a reference to their Ghibelline heritage and an attribute of Jupiter. The site itself embodies Montefeltro regional planning and architecture.

A fortress was built at the top of the mountain in the fifteenth century, but the great importance of this tiny town is that it was the first episcopal see of the whole of Montefeltro from the seventh century. Pieve di Santa Maria Assunta was first built in the early fourth century by Saint Leo, a stonecutter from Dalmatia, who founded the first Christian community in the Marche. In 882 the original church was incorporated into a larger one, which eventually collapsed because of an earthquake and was rebuilt in the eleventh century.

The cathedral is situated opposite Pieve di Santa Maria Assunta and is gigantic relative to the size of the town. It was built in 1173 on the site of an older church. Like Pieve di Santa Maria Assunta, part of the building stands directly on the rock, without foundations. Both churches have side entrances because their façades are on the edge of a precipice. The masons (probably from Lombardy) did their best to decorate the façades, in particular that of the cathedral, even though they could only be seen by locations down in the valley. Today the diocese includes the territory of the Republic of San Marino and it has three cathedrals (at San Leo, at San Marino and at Pennabilli, in the upper Marecchia valley). The cathedral and the bell tower are now isolated, but in the Middle Ages they were part of a complex of religious buildings, including the bishop's palace, a house for the canons, and hostels for pilgrims.

In the late fourteenth century, the Malatesti acquired San Leo and strengthened its medieval castle by adding square towers to it. In 1441, Federico, then aged nineteen, contrived to seize the castle and the town. After 1475, he commissioned Francesco di Giorgio to modify and strengthen the *rocca* San Leo to make it capable of withstanding cannon fire. As at Sassocorvaro, the *rocca* integrates the functions of a palace within the framework of a fortress and exhibits architectural features characteristic of his work. His solution to the problem of defending against artillery fire was to use ravelins and bastions. For San Leo, he designed two imposing round bastions, which could withstand the impact of cannon fire, and, by projecting from the walls, allowed the defenders to fire on their assailants from a side position (flanking or enfilade fire).[11] Between 1497 and 1521, three successive popes (Alexander VI, Julius II, and Leo X) tried to turn Montefeltro and San Leo into a fiefdom for their relatives. In 1516, in the pontificate of the Medici pope Leo X, the Florentines conquered the fortress of San Leo and the event was regarded as such a military achievement that in 1557 it was celebrated by Giorgio Vasari in a large fresco at the Palazzo Vecchio in Florence, in a hall dedicated to Pope Leo X.

One interesting commission Federico entrusted to Francesco di Giorgio is the Palazzo Salvatico at Milan. This was given to Federico by Galeazzo Maria Sforza in 1468, but redesigned by Francesco di Giorgio. It had previously been the residence of one of the duke's mistresses, Elisabetta da Robecco, and had been overhauled for her use by Francesco Solari. Francesco di Giorgio gave it an atrium, in the antique Roman manner, an intervention perhaps intended to demonstrate Federico's sophisticated humanist taste, and also his status.[12] Vitruvius, author of the most important book on architecture to survive from classical antiquity, was clear that an atrium conveyed status: 'For men of rank who, from holding offices and magistracies, have social obligations to their fellow-citizens... most spacious atriums... appropriate to their dignity [must be constructed].'[13]

The della Rovere dukes were also patrons of architecture. Their commissions include a chapel in the Basilica of the Holy House in Loreto, a very popular pilgrimage destination, by the great Urbinate *stuccatore*, Federico Brandani, who worked on several of their palaces, including the palace at Urbino. Brandani also created the famous presepio in the church of San Giuseppe in Urbino, with its dozens of life-sized stucco figures adoring the Christ Child.[14] One of the della Rovere projects, which was of the greatest importance to them, was the Villa Imperiale in Pesaro. The Montefeltro family never owned a seaport, but Federico's marriage to Battista in 1460 allied him with the Sforzas, and Battista's father, Alessandro, controlled the port city of Pesaro. The modern co-capital (with Urbino) of the Marche, Pesaro commands the mouth of the river Foglia, which runs through the northern sections of the Montefeltro to the Adriatic.

The first castle at the site was begun in 1452 by Alessandro Sforza, to honour the Holy Roman Emperor Frederick III, who visited the city, and construction continued until 1469. After various changes of ruler in the intervening decades, Pesaro was assigned to Francesco Maria I della Rovere in 1513, and it, rather than Urbino, became the principal ducal seat, due to its great advantages in terms of communications. The Palazzo Ducale in the town was not big enough for lavish entertaining, and there was no space to extend it, so Francesco Maria commissioned the painter and architect Girolamo Genga to build a country villa beside the Sforza castle as a suitable place in which to entertain their many distinguished guests. It was constructed between 1529 and 1538, and his wife, Eleonora Gonzaga, made herself principally responsible for overseeing the work.[15] In 1635, the villa became Medici property when Vittoria della Rovere married Ferdinando II. It gradually fell into disrepair, but in 1763 it was put in the custody of the Camera Apostolica of the Catholic Church, and in 1777 it was ceded by Pope Pius VI to Prince Orazio Albani, brother of the former pope, Clement XI, and father of Cardinal Alessandro Albani, who began its refurbishment. In the nineteenth century, many of the frescoes were restored by Giuseppe Gennari, though much of this work was removed again during a round of restoration in the 1970s.

The Villa Imperiale was surrounded by a *bosco*, an informal plantation of trees, but within it featured intricate, terraced gardens in the new style of the sixteenth century. There is a hanging garden at roof level, and a mezzanine one constructed on top of a *nymphaeum* looking onto the inner courtyard.[16] A number of major Mannerist painters were employed on the interior frescos, including Dosso and Battista Dossi, Camillo Mantovano, Raffaellino del Colle, Bronzino and Francesco Menzocchi. Topics include the Labours of Hercules and the story of the Rovere family, and there is a Hall of Calumny, its principal decoration being a version of the legendary Greek painting *The Calumny of Apelles*. Some rooms are decorated with caryatids, amorini, and trompe l'oeil vistas, and others with grotesques.[17] The Villa Miralfiore at Pesaro, another della Rovere palace, acquired by

Guidobaldo II in 1559, also had elaborate formal gardens, six compartments bordered with box hedges, and bronze statues of monkeys – *singeries* were already considered stylish, especially in contexts such as pleasure grounds, and many Italian gardens have grotesque statues of some kind.[18] Both these gardens have been carefully restored.

10

Federico as Patron
of the Arts

Federico's art patronage is one of the most important aspects of his achievement, though detailed evidence of its precise nature is rather scanty. Most of the Montefeltro chancery accounts, where we would find information about Federico's art, architectural commissions and building projects, together with what they cost, were destroyed in the nineteenth century, which is unfortunate, because there are some major unanswered questions, especially with respect to his patronage of Piero della Francesca. What little we know about how much Federico actually spent, when, and on what, has to be pieced together from surviving records in other archives.

A Ferrarese poet, Lodovico Carbone, wrote, 'the merits of princes are reflected in the talents of their subjects'.[1] The image of Federico, and the splendours of his palaces, were envisaged by contemporaries as collaborations between the *ingegno*, or creative talent (it is a word much used by humanists), of Federico, as patron, and that of the many artists he employed. His indirect impact on the history of art is suggested by the fact that two of the leading artists of the High Renaissance in Rome, Raphael and Donato Bramante, the architect of St Peter's, Rome, were raised and trained in his Urbino. Federico also brought a variety of artists to his city, such as Piero della Francesca from Borgo Sansepolcro and Joos van Wassenhove from Ghent, as well as architects and sculptors, including Luciano Laurana from Dalmatia and Francesco di Giorgio Martini from Siena. He also employed natives of Urbino: Raphael's father, Giovanni Santi, who had moved to the city as a young man, Bartolomeo di Giovanni Corradini, and perhaps Melozzo da Forlì. A surprising number of High Renaissance architects began as painters, and passed through Urbino, where they were influenced by Federico's passionate interest in geometry and perspective, including di Giorgio, Bramante, and Raphael.[2]

Giovanni Santi was employed by Federico in a variety of capacities, as painter and creator (both text and design) of court masques, and after the duke's death he wrote a rhymed chronicle celebrating Federico's life for his heir, Guidobaldo. Raphael received his first training in his father's workshop.[3] Santi sometimes worked with Evangelista da Pian di Meleto, who also collaborated with Raphael himself on the altarpiece of San Nicola da Tolentino for the church of Sant'Agostino in Città di Castello.[4] This suggests that, despite the city's small size, Urbino supported at least one workshop, in which painters might either work independently or collaborate on larger projects, such as the cycle of pictures for the Temple of the Muses in Federico's palace. Other artists associated with Santi are Bartolomeo di Maestro Gentile and Timoteo Viti: the latter took over from Santi as court painter to Guidobaldo. According to Vasari, Raphael himself helped his father with work on the palace while still a child (he was only eleven when his father died).[5] Santi's workshop continued to function after his own death, since Raphael took control of it in 1500, when he was seventeen. The architect-painter Girolamo Genga, a friend and contemporary of Raphael's, is also associated with this group of painters.

Bartolomeo di Giovanni Corradini is one of the earliest painters to be associated with Federico and his projects. He went to Florence as a young man to pursue a career in art, and joined the studio of

Filippo Lippi, the favourite painter of Cosimo de' Medici, which meant that he was in a position to establish contacts with many Florentine artists.[6] In 1445/6, he was one of Lippi's assistants on the major *Coronation of the Virgin*, which he painted for the Benedictine convent of Sant'Ambrogio, a painting greatly admired by contemporaries. It is now in the Uffizi. Corradini took holy orders around 1449, and became known as Fra Carnevale, which probably implies not dissipation but its precise opposite: he had said 'farewell to meat' and become a strict vegetarian. After he returned to Urbino, he became a friar in the convent of San Domenico, just opposite the Ducal Palace. Federico would employ him as both artist and architect. Fra Carnevale's interest in perspective suggests that he was influenced by Piero della Francesca, whom he may have encountered either in Florence or in Urbino.

In 1449–51, Fra Carnevale is mentioned in the account books of Maso di Bartolomeo, the most important bronze sculptor in Florence after Donatello's departure from that city in 1444. The devout citizens of Urbino wanted an improved façade for their Dominican monastery church, San Domenico, which, since he was a Dominican, was Fra Carnevale's own house. He did the necessary design work, and invited Maso and his workshop to Urbino. It is worth noticing that the very fine portal that was produced was sponsored by the citizens, and not by Federico, whose response to the presence of Maso in his city was to commission from him not artworks, but armaments: bombards and *cerbottane* (primitive handguns). In the mid-fifteenth century, the same man might well cast bronzes, or bells, or cannon, depending on his clients' needs. Federico's spending was strictly practical at this stage of his career. He had inherited an empty treasury from his extravagant predecessor in 1444, and somehow found the money to buy Fossombrone for 13,000 ducats in the same year. In September 1447, it cost him 12,000 ducats to make his peace with the pope. Thus the Federico of 1449 did not yet have money to spare for art.[7]

The painting and sculpture commissioned by Federico includes some of the most famous masterpieces of early Renaissance art, above all, works by Piero della Francesca, but for the first thirty years of his reign, there is little evidence for art patronage other than decoration within the palace, notably a room painted in fresco, and architectural carvings in relief in several of the public rooms. The research of Maria Giannatiempo López suggests that Federico inherited highly decorated rooms in the old Montefeltro palace: colourful illusionistic frescos of wood panelling or tapestries, adorned with mottos and heraldic symbols, from the late Gothic workshops of Salimbeni and Antonio Alberti.[8] One of his early commissions, the Sala degli Affreschi in the Palazzetto della Iole, painted by Giovanni Boccati, suggests continuity with the taste of the décor he inherited. It is now in poor condition, but it seems to have featured notable warriors in fantastic, classicizing armour, and may have been modelled on the series of outsized standing heroes in the 'Corridoio' of the Palazzo Trinci at Foligno,[9] the now-lost frescos of 'Illustrious Men' commissioned by Robert, King of Naples for the Sala dei Baroni in Castel Nuovo, designed by Giotto *c.* 1330, which Federico would certainly have seen, or Andrea del Castagno's 'Illustrious People' series in the Villa Carducci at Legnaia. Pasquale Rotondi observes that 'the spirit which enlivens these frescoes is in harmony with that particular climate of taste prevailing at Urbino a little before 1466'. The giant figures stand on a fictive platform, with a fictive curtain of pomegranate-patterned damask hanging behind them. They include Mucius Scaevola and Horatius Cocles, from Livy's Roman history, but most are unidentifiable. The heroes were probably drawn from a variety of sources: figures such as Gideon and Joshua, Alexander, Charlemagne, Arthur and Lancelot. Beneath a dado are painted coats of arms.[10] When Federico received guests in this room, it must have seemed as if the great warriors of antiquity were looking down on them.

One feature of the palace décor which may be assumed is brightly painted *cassoni*, large storage chests. They were commissioned in pairs, and were important luxury items made for, and owned by, women: a new bride would bring at least one pair of them to her marital home and store her clothes and personal possessions in them. The grandest ones were often decorated with mythological scenes particularly appropriate to women, such as the story of Dido, or Susanna and the Elders.[11] Many Renaissance Italian paintings began life as part of a *cassone* or other furniture, even works by artists of the stature of Botticelli, who painted a suite of paintings of the life of Esther for a pair of *cassoni*. Two *cassoni* (not a pair) survive from the palace at Urbino, one (in a private collection) decorated with three roundels containing the familiar profiles of Federico and Ottaviano Ubaldini with a Montefeltro eagle in the centre, and so made either for Battista Sforza or for Federico himself. The other, gaily decorated with Montefeltro and Gonzaga family emblems, was probably made for the wedding of Guidobaldo with Elisabetta Gonzaga in 1488.[12] Gentile Brancaleoni will have brought at least one pair of *cassoni* filled with her belongings when she and Federico moved to Urbino from Mercatello, as will Battista Sforza when she came to Urbino from Pesaro.[13]

One painting that is known to have been made for Federico in the 1450s is a '*spalliera*' panel. *Spalliere* were decorative wall-mounted panels, often sited behind a *cassone* or as the headboard of a bed, and generally wider than they were tall. They were a common feature of elegant households in fifteenth-century northern Italy. '*Spalla*' means shoulder, and the panels were attached to the wall at eye or shoulder level above pieces of furniture such as chests and daybeds in bedchambers and studies.

This particular *spalliera* is unusually long, nearly seven feet, and was painted by Giovanni di Francesco.[14] It is described in an Urbino inventory of 1631.[15] Perhaps it hung over two smallish *cassoni* placed side by side, like the pair of storage chests in the background of Titian's 'Venus of Urbino'. It features two hunting scenes: on the left, commoners hunting a boar on foot, with dogs, with a bridge in the middle and a view of the walls of Florence behind it. On the right, aristocrats on horseback are deer-hunting, and a man on a grey horse is just about to lance their catch. Though, like all the other nobles, he is blond, since he wears a red captain's beretta he is the leader of the hunt and might be taken to represent Federico. The vegetation underfoot is represented in minute detail, and the effect is very much that of a verdure tapestry. One very curious feature is that there is a definite effort to represent the passage of time: the deer hunt is happening in the afternoon, the sun is setting in the middle of the panel, and the commoners are hunting the boar in early evening. The picture suggests that in the 1450s, Federico's taste was still late Gothic. He may well have had other *spalliere* decorating his walls, now lost, or not identified as possessing an Urbino connection. An earlier inventory, made in 1599, refers to 'an old picture of a hunt', which may be the Giovanni di Francesco, or alternatively Paolo Uccello's well-known picture, now in the Ashmolean Museum in Oxford, which could well have been made for the palace at Urbino, since the artist worked in the town on at least one occasion. Federico built hunting lodges at both Castel Durante and Fossombrone, so hunting was very much part of the culture of his court.[16]

Other domestic furnishings were also often decoratively painted in the fifteenth century. Vasari, looking back from the standpoint of the mid-sixteenth century, says of the mid-fifteenth, 'they painted... not only the chests, but the wall panels, the cornices which ran round the room, and other ornaments for the room, which in those times one used to use magnificently, as one can see in infinite examples throughout the city'.[17] A notable survival of this kind of applied art in Urbino itself is the bed-alcove that Fra Carnevale painted for Federico in the 1450s. This room within a room, which contained his bed, features Doric columns, trees covered in ripe quinces, and panels imitating luxurious polychrome marbles. The interior ceiling is a fictive brocade, with trompe l'oeil hangings on the inner walls (also a feature of Giovanni Boccati's work in the Sala degli Affreschi). The use of paint to simulate more luxurious and expensive materials suggests something about

Federico: at this stage of life, he could not afford tapestries and brocade, but his taste ran that way, so he did the best he could for the time being. It also suggests a strong appreciation of trompe l'oeil effects, which later featured so largely in the intarsia woodwork of his palaces.

Portrait medallions were very popular among Renaissance rulers from the 1440s, as an easy way of disseminating their image: Federico sent a medal by Pisanello as a gift to Alfonso of Aragon as early as 1442, though he did not commission one of his own at that time.[18] His earliest known portrait medal is by Paolo de Ragusa, the only image of Federico before his nose was damaged in 1450. It must have been made to celebrate his association with Alfonso of Aragon, since the reverse declares him to be 'Regius Capitaneus Generalis' (royal captain-general), over an ermine, Alfonso's badge. The condotta was not signed until 2 October, 1551, but the medal is evidence that agreement had been reached by 1450.[19] A later medal by Clemente da Urbino, perhaps from 1468, depicts him in elaborate parade armour with astrological symbols, and a captain's beretta. The inscription on the front describes him as a second Caesar and Scipio, echoing the language of Virgil's *Aeneid*. On the reverse, the Montefeltro eagle balances a beam with a sword and cuirass on one side and a *scopetta* with an olive branch on the other. Since this device originated with the Sforzas, it references Battista. In the centre is the globe of the world, and at the top, three stars, with the astrological signs for Mars, Venus and Jupiter, so the armour stands for both Federico and Mars, the globe for Jupiter, or rule, and the *scopetta* for both Battista and Venus. A long inscription reads: 'the fierce Mars and Venus, in conjunction with the might of the thunderer [Jupiter], unite to give you dominions and influence your destiny'. This image was probably designed by Ottaviano Ubaldini, who was an expert astrologer.

One possible exception to Federico's apparent lack of interest in commissioning paintings in the first three decades of his reign needs to be considered: his patronage of Piero della Francesca. The

enigmatic *Flagellation of Christ* is regularly assigned a date before
1472; most critics now hover between 1455 and 1472.[20] There is no
documentation for the picture before 1717, when it is listed among
the possessions of the 'old sacristy' of the Urbino Duomo. In 1744
it was described as 'The Flagellation of Our Lord Jesus Christ,
with the Figures and the Portraits of Duke Guidobaldo and Oddo
Antonio'.[21] While it could conceivably have been paid for by
Federico, it looks as if it was commissioned for the Duomo rather
than for the palace. Alternatively, Carlo Bertelli has suggested
that there are reasons to think it was actually commissioned by a
Malatesta patron (Piero also worked for Sigismondo Malatesta),
and subsequently brought to Urbino.[22] As he says, one possible
person who might have done this is Federico's daughter Elisabetta,
widow of Sigismondo's son Roberto Malatesta, who could have
brought it with her when she came back to Urbino in 1482 and
retired into the convent of Santa Chiara.

From its first appearance in the Duomo inventory, critics have
been attracted by the historicist explanation for the three curious
figures in the right foreground: that the barefoot, blond youth
represents Oddantonio, who was killed in 1444, while the older
men to either side are either his father and grandfather or his
'Evil Counsellors'. The association between the blond youth and
Oddantonio was established as early as the sixteenth century, since
his image was used as the basis for a fancy portrait of the first duke
ordered by Francesco Maria II della Rovere in 1581.

More recently, other explanations have been proposed. The
picture might be an allegory: the three men represent three non-
Christian faiths, oriental or Jewish, Greek paganism, and European
heresy, united by the condemnation of the Church. Or its meaning
may be political: according to this interpretation, the bearded man
is the Byzantine emperor John VIII Palaiologos and the third man
Count Guidantonio da Montefeltro, who met at the 1439 Council
of Florence, while the painting as a whole represents the suffering
of the oriental Christians under the menace of the Turks.[23] The

seated man on the far left watching the flagellation, while one must assume him to be Pontius Pilate, is represented as John VIII Palaiologos, identified as such by his unusual hat, which has this form in a medal of the emperor by Pisanello; again, there is no consensus as to what Piero can have meant by linking Pontius Pilate and John VIII in this way.

A completely different interpretation, suggested by the distinguished art historian and Renaissance specialist John Pope-Hennessy, is that it represents a famous nightmare experienced by St Jerome, in which a heavenly judge accused him of preferring Cicero to the Bible, and he was punished with a beating.[24] The three figures at the front might thus be an angel, representing the word of God, perhaps between the Greeks (Aristotle, in medieval manuscripts, is usually represented wearing a turban) and the Latins. As Pope-Hennessy observes, this interpretation is strengthened by a picture of *The Dream of St Jerome* by Matteo di Giovanni, born in Borgo Sansepolcro fifteen years after Piero, which was painted for a Sienese church dedicated to Jerome in 1476 (now in the Art Institute, Chicago); as in Piero's picture, the floor emphasizes perspective and features bands of pale lime-stone separated by squares of brick, and classicizing architecture. Reading left to right, the Chicago picture offers a man seated on a throne, two servants beating Jerome, who wears only a loincloth, and two well-dressed onlookers who calmly survey the scene.[25] It is a far less complex painting, but it might suggest that Piero is drawing on an established iconography, especially since, as Pope-Hennessy also observes, there is an earlier version of *The Dream of St Jerome* by Sano di Pietro painted in Siena in 1444 (now in the Louvre), which shares the same formal features, and also explains why Piero's composition includes onlookers: an adjacent panel depicts Sulpicius Severus and a friend experiencing a vision of St Jerome and is set in the same pictorial space. But clearly, a painting offering this much scope for interpretation is never going to yield to a 'decoding' that is universally acceptable.

Another picture that is sometimes dated to the late 1450s is Piero della Francesca's *Brera Madonna*. The painting has always attracted attention for its symmetry, with all the perspective lines converging directly on the head of the Virgin, and for the odd relationship between Federico, staring straight ahead, hands joined in prayer, and the Holy Conversation behind him (and, since he lacked a right eye, completely invisible to him). The line made by his arm continues the diagonal of the sprawling body of the Christ Child, making a strong visual link between them. Jane Bridgeman has suggested that the painting was commissioned as a thank-offering after his recovery from a near fatal illness and his appointment as captain-general of Naples in 1454, because, as she observes, this is consistent with the date of the armour. The image depicts him kneeling, facing across to a void where one might expect a reciprocally kneeling wife, but his first wife died in 1457 and he did not marry Battista until 1460. Bridgeman therefore suggests that the picture dates to 1457/9.[26] But part of the overall context for weighing up probabilities is this: Federico, who was still comparatively poor, was not investing heavily in the patronage of religious buildings in the 1450s, let alone in art, so why would he commission a large altarpiece? Piero della Francesca was an expensive artist. He charged the Augustinian friars of Borgo Sansepolcro 320 florins for a polyptych of St Augustine in 1454.[27] In the 1450s, this would have been a considerable investment for Federico, whose significant accumulation of wealth dates from the mid-1460s onwards.

All the datings for this important painting have some kind of problem. Art historical consensus dates the painting to 1472–4, after the death of Battista, and before a marble medallion portrait of Federico, one of a pair now on the inner façade of San Francesco in Mercatello sul Metauro, for which the upper portion of Piero's figure, including the bent-out shoulder piece and bolted screw, clearly served as a model. The medallion is dated by a dedicatory inscription to October 1474.[28] Cecil Clough, however, has suggested that the altarpiece was painted after Federico's death in 1482, and that Piero reproduced the duke's features from his earlier cartoon for the portrait diptych (John Shearman has in fact demonstrated that this was indeed the case).[29] This would explain why the praying hands were painted by someone else, perhaps the Spaniard Pedro Berruguete, since hands do not feature in the diptych, and Piero therefore did not have a drawing of them to work from. In this view, the picture would have been commissioned not by Federico, but by Ottaviano Ubaldini, which might account for why the Garter and Ermine insignia and other items Federico set great store by are not included. This would also explain why the most prominent saint on the right of the Madonna is John the Baptist, the name saint of Battista Sforza; the blank space opposite Federico thus becomes a portrait of an absence.

Federico left instructions on his deathbed for building a Franciscan church dedicated to San Bernardino of Siena, and directed that he should be buried there. Ottaviano fulfilled this direction. The Madonna seems to have hung over the high altar, since its presence is indicated in a sketch of the east end from 1525 attributed to Baldassare Peruzzi, which also shows a doorway to the right leading into Federico's mausoleum.[30] Was the painting made for San Domenico, as a combination altarpiece and commemoration of Federico, who was not buried in as grand a style as one might have expected? The money from Federico's condotte had dried up, so Ottaviano had to be careful not to overspend. A painting was very much less costly than a mortuary chapel or grand tomb; similarly, the fourteenth-century condottiere Sir John Hawkwood was commemorated in Florence by a fresco by Paolo Uccello rather than a marble tomb because the money ran out. Since there had to be some kind of painting over the high altar, it could usefully serve two purposes. Federico's embalmed body rested in a tomb beside the main altar of San Bernardino, dressed in a cloak of scarlet satin. We know this because it was opened by

Francesco Maria I della Rovere, and the body remained exposed for a century, since Bernardino Baldi saw it there in 1603.[31]

Thus it seems very possible that this portrait is not a statement by Federico but a commemoration of him, informed by an aesthetic and sense of priorities that are not those of Federico himself.[32] It is worth noticing that the duke has laid down his baton, his steel gauntlets and his helmet at the feet of the Virgin, in a symbolic farewell to arms. Since Giovanni Santi used the painting as a model for his altarpiece in the mausoleum of the Counts of Oliva in 1489, it seems highly likely that this *Madonna* was perceived by contemporaries as commemorative.[33] The armour is Federico's own: this is evident from the way it is rounded out at the top of the back to accommodate his 'dowager's hump'. One explanation for how this is compatible with the evidence of the Mercatello relief is to suggest that the sculpture is not based on the painting; rather, both relief and altarpiece are based on Piero's detailed life drawing of Federico's profile, which also underlies his portrait in the Montefeltro Diptych. Piero's first thought for the diptych could have been to represent Federico in armour (just as, in Clemente da Urbino's medal, he appears in armour and wearing his beretta), later revised to the familiar red tunic. As Joanna Woods-Marsden has observed, condottiere princes are frequently portrayed in armour, particularly in their medals.[34] If so, Piero would presumably have preferred to work up his figure using the same suit of armour.

While it is quite possible that neither the *Flagellation* nor Piero's *Madonna of Senigallia* (a gift, some have suggested, from Federico to his daughter Giovanna on the occasion of her marriage to Giovanni della Rovere) were actually commissioned by him, Piero seems to have painted a lost portrait of Federico himself in 1465/6.[35] Giovanni Andrea Ferabò, a Veronese Carmelite humanist, was in Urbino that year and mentions a portrait of Federico by Piero in a poem that plays with the idea of the 'speaking likeness', 'The Likeness of the Prince painted by Pietro of Borgo addresses the Prince himself'.[36] This ends,

> Piero has given me nerves and flesh and bone
> But thou, Prince, hast supplied me with a soul from thy divinity
> Therefore, I live, and speak and have movement of myself
> Thus does the glory of both king and artist excel.

Thus, it seems that Pietro's hand supplies the representative skill, but the sheer greatness of his subject has somehow animated it with a soul.[37] This poem may relate loosely to one of Martial's epigrams, on a painting of Marcus Antonius Primus: 'Would that art could paint his character and mind! No painting in all the world would be more beautiful.'[38]

The commissions that are definitely Federico's own are highly purposeful, either personifications (Muses, Liberal Arts, Famous Men) intended to complete a decorative scheme in which paintings play a part, or they are portraits, and rather specific ones at that. They seem to be entirely about himself and his dynastic ambitions. Some of his contemporaries displayed portraits of friends (or enemies): Lorenzo de' Medici kept portraits of Galeazzo Sforza and his own murdered brother, Giuliano, in his bedroom,[39] and several of Isabella d'Este's friends had her portrait.[40] A painter called Niccolò d'Alemagna gave Borso d'Este a Flemish-style double portrait of Francesco Sforza and Bianca Maria Visconti, 'opening like a book and with a gilded frame', possibly the surviving double portrait of the couple.[41] Federico, by contrast, seems to have wanted only dynastic or fancy portraits. He was not a connoisseur of painting as such. None of the pictures that were certainly his commissions were created purely for their own sake, and it is far from clear that he had a very advanced sense that one artist might be significantly better than another, since he was quite happy to have one painter overpaint another's work (for example, Pedro Berruguete revising several of Joos van Wassenhove's 'Famous Men', discussed below). His portraits relate to his curation of his own image as a dynast. All his other commissions are what interior decorators call 'furniture pictures', by which they usually mean pleasant but undistinguished artworks hung to contribute to an overall effect. In the context of the Montefeltro palace, the standard of the art was high, but pictures were part of ensembles such as the *studiolo*, not the centre of attention.

It's important to observe which likenesses we do and don't have. There are no known portraits of his sons Buonconte and Antonio, and there is no known image of Federico's first wife, Gentile, even though he was clearly fond of her. We know of none made of his second wife, Battista, during her lifetime except the portrait included in the Sforza triptych, which was commissioned by her father, Alessandro – both Piero della Francesca's profile in the Montefeltro Diptych and Laurana's sculpted bust are based on her death mask. Nor did he commission portraits of his daughters. Federico's obsessive insistence on his own portraits and the tokens of his success, together with the images of his heir that he repeatedly commissioned, does not read as confidence. Throughout his life, he set enormous store by marks of other people's regard for him. It was evidently highly significant to him that he was adopted into the Compagnia della Calze during his brief sojourn in Venice, aged only eleven: this was the first time he had achieved recognition on his own merits, outside the family. He used the elegantly waving 'flames of love' of the Compagnia as a personal badge for the rest of his life.[42] When he was invested with the Order of the Garter and the Order of the Ermine in 1474 by Edward IV of England and Ferdinand of Aragon respectively, garters and ermines proliferated, carved on his walls, featured in the intarsia of his *studioli*, painted in his manuscripts. After 1474, he had his eagle's-beak profile reproduced again and again: painted by Piero della Francesca and Joos van Wassenhove, drawn in many of his manuscripts, sculptured in stone (in relief, not in the round), facing his brother Ottaviano, in the intarsia of his *studiolo*, and among the crowd in a bronze relief *Deposition* sculpted by Francesco di Giorgio Martini. His image is un-idealized: his facial warts, the scar on his jaw from his childhood abscess, his wrinkles and sagging skin are carefully delineated in a parade of veracity: a representation of a plain man with nothing to hide, though Joanna Woods-Marsden observes that, despite showing 'warts and all', the Federico depicted by Piero della Francesca is nobler, his nose more aquiline, his chin less double, and his flesh firmer than the Federico of Joos van Wassenhove, and his majestic bearing and dominating presence is emphasized.[43]

Additionally, unlike his half-brothers or his sisters, Guidobaldo features again and again in paintings made during his father's lifetime. He first appears as a babe in arms in van Wassenhove's *Institution of the Eucharist*, and as a young child he stands beside his father in two other paintings. In a painting perhaps for the Urbino *studiolo*, and probably by Joos van Wassenhove, Federico is depicted reading Gregory the Great's *Moralia in Job*. This is no ordinary 'scholar in his study' picture, but a rather complex statement. Federico is wearing full armour to indicate his warrior status; his honours are visible, the collar of the Order of the Ermine round his neck, and the Garter clasped round his left calf, with the foot thrust forward so it is very noticeable. His sword crosses with his commander's baton, a subtle indication that he is a warrior for Christ. An exotic cap decorated with pearls rests on a high shelf; it is either a gift from the Shah of Persia, or from the pope. Little blond Guidobaldo is represented as a prince; he clasps a sceptre, and wears a necklace of huge pearls, and a pearl-bordered belt.[44] The portrait is a statement about power, prestige, wealth, scholarly interests and, above all, a secure male lineage.

The child Guidobaldo is also depicted alone in a portrait by Bartolomeo della Gatta, executed in spring 1478, when the child was six. The portrait is revealing in many ways: he is shown in profile, wearing a red robe, with a red ducal cap, thus echoing the famous portrait of his father by Piero della Francesca in which, similarly, Federico wears a plain red robe and red captain's beretta. But the child Guidobaldo is also conspicuously wearing a thick gold chain, a gift from Pope Sixtus IV. Both he and his father were delighted with this handsome ornament, which, apart from its value, carried a clear message that Sixtus, who had conferred the dukedom on Federico in 1474, recognized the boy as his heir. Federico knew full well that as a professional soldier, he could be killed at any time; he was in fact only sixty when he died, though not in battle but from fever. The portraits he commissioned thus represent two things: a purposeful stamping of his own image as duke on the imagination of his own times and, as far as possible, that of posterity, and giving what help and protection he could to the child he sired aged fifty by ensuring that the memory of his own achievements would remain lively, and associating the boy with himself.

Three more commissions from around 1480 place father and son together. The portal leading into the Throne Room of the Ducal Palace was decorated with elaborate carvings in relief in the later 1470s, which include profile portraits of Federico and Guidobaldo on the architrave of the door.[45] At about the same time, Federico also associates his son with himself in a bronze relief he commissioned from Francesco di Giorgio for the Confraternity of Santa Croce, which includes portraits of himself, Guidobaldo and Ottaviano Ubaldini kneeling at the foot of the cross. And in another painting, probably by Joos van Wassenhove, they are together, listening to an oration in Latin made before the duke between the autumn of 1477 and the spring of 1478 by Antonio Patrignone near Ascoli Piceno. Federico wears a red ducal hat and the insignia of the order of the Garter, and Guidobaldo once more stands beside him, bejewelled and richly dressed in cloth of gold.

Battista Sforza was also co-opted into this dynastic image-making, most famously in Piero's Montefeltro Diptych, which was made after her death, but before 1474. Again, this may relate to Guidobaldo as much as herself, since having an impeccable mother was as important to the image of Guidobaldo that Federico was constructing as having a glorious father. Battista's manifold virtues demonstrated that his noble heritage came from both sides. But also, the art theorist Leon Battista Alberti claimed that portraiture

13. One of several perspective paintings of an ideal city owned by Federico, who was interested in perspective: the painter is unknown.

14. The courtyard of Federico's ducal palace at Gubbio, acquired in 1474 and remodelled by Francesco di Giorgio Martini.

15. Federico's 'alcova', or bedroom, with trompe l'oeil decorations by Fra Carnevale. His various *imprese* are depicted on the heads of the columns.

16. Piero della Francesca's enigmatic and much discussed *Flagellation*: who are the three men prominent in the foreground, and who is being beaten?

17. Luciano Laurana's coolly dignified posthumous portrait bust of Battista Sforza, based on her death mask. It was probably originally painted in lifelike colours.

18. Federico, with the attributes of a man of war, and Ottaviano Ubaldini della Carda, humanist and man of peace, possibly by Francesco di Giorgio Martini.

19. Joos van Wassenhove, a man, perhaps Costanzo Sforza, kneeling before a personified 'Music'.

20. *opposite* One of the 'Troy Tapestries' woven in Tournai: Andromache and Priam admire Hector as he rides to war.

Andromata la mort hector doubtans · Que une loge une hourgeno/plourer
en pnta en grans pleurs les enfans · En luy priant e men Jour non aller ·
la bataille hector se fist armer · Et non obstant et acheual monta ·
top priant le conftrait retourner · Par la prie quil print dandromata ·

21. Federico's illustrated Dante, Urb. Lat. 365, with his garter, coat of arms and collar interspersed among 'white vine' decoration and vignettes from the poet's narrative.

22. The medal Elisabetta Gonzaga commissioned in 1495 from Adriano de' Maestri, conveying both her loyalty to her husband, and her longing to conceive an heir.

23. *opposite* Guidobaldo, perhaps by Raphael, painted two years before his early death, when he was already a very sick man.

24. *overleaf* A new generation: Vittore Carpaccio's *Young Knight* wears Montefeltro black and gold, and an ermine lurks by his foot: he may be Francesco Maria della Rovere.

made the absent present and brought the dead to life, and Federico may have taken a melancholy pleasure in these images.[46] He also commissioned a portrait bust by Francesco Laurana, possibly the brother of his architect Luciano Laurana, which was based on her death mask. He encountered Laurana's beautiful and refined portraits in the round either via recommendation from Luciano, or via his visits to the kingdom of Naples, since the sculptor had been working on busts of female relatives of King Ferrante in the early 1470s. The bust and its pedestal are cut from a single piece of stone, and the inscription is remarkable: DIVA BAPTISTA SFORTIA VRB RG. 'Diva' means 'divine'; it frequently appears on Roman imperial portraits, indicating posthumous deification, and was, rather inappropriately, adopted by the Christian princes of the Renaissance. Pisanello's portrait medals of the 1440s often use 'divus/diva'. But 'Urb. Rg.' might be short for Urbinae regnatrix (ruler) or regina (queen). The divine Battista Sforza, Queen of Urbino – who in her lifetime had been the wife of a relatively humble count. This must be another back-projection of Federico's newly acquired status.[47] The bust seems originally to have been polychrome, like Laurana's bust of Eleonora of Aragon, which retains much of its original painted surface, including gilding and individually pressed wax flowers adorning the headdress.

There are other portraits of Battista based on her death mask: two low-relief busts in profile, one by Francesco di Giorgio Martini, which seems taken directly from the death mask, and one by Domenico Roselli, now in Pesaro, which is more probably based on Piero della Francesca's diptych. Additionally, a high-relief Madonna and Child, also by Domenico Roselli, gives the Virgin features that strongly resemble those of Laurana's bust of Battista, rather different from his usual Madonna type. The Christ Child is clutching up his shirt in his left hand, revealing his genitals, an unusual gesture, which presumably reflects Federico's anxious focus on the very precious boy baby in his own nursery.

Piero della Francesca's double portrait of Battista and Federico must surely be one of the most discussed paintings in the whole field of Renaissance Italian art. Owing to the long Roman and Byzantine tradition of profile coin portraits, the profile had strong associations with antiquity, and consequently with the idea of a commemoration that would last for all time. Pisanello's introduction of portrait medals emulating Roman coins into Renaissance court culture profoundly influenced portraiture conventions in the courts of condottiere rulers such as the Montefeltri, Sforza, Malatasti and Gonzaga. The profile pose favoured by the emperors for their coinage carried dynastic and political significance for the condottieri, because it connoted both magnificence and legitimate governance. Additionally, women donors had also long preferred to be represented in profile, kneeling at the margins or in the side wings of the pictures they commissioned. Since it was widely considered improper for a woman to lock gazes with anyone but her husband, profile, in which the gaze was averted completely, marked a woman as virtuous.[48]

Federico, as is well known, had a special reason for wanting to be represented in left profile only, since he had lost his right eye, but even without this disfigurement he would probably have chosen this format. Around 1455, Francesco Sforza had commissioned a double ruler portrait of himself and Bianca Maria Visconti, tentatively attributed to Bonifacio Bembo (fl. 1447–78) and now housed at the Pinacoteca di Brera. This seems to have set a fashion among condottiere princes: Baldessare d'Este painted Ercole d'Este and his wife Eleonora of Aragon, each kneeling in profile in front of a doorcase, in 1473. Duke Ercole wears a captain's beretta and sumptuous golden robes.[49] Around the same time, in Lombardy, Zanetto Bugatto painted profile portraits of Galeazzo Maria Sforza and Bona of Savoy. Baldassare d'Este also painted a head-and-shoulders profile portrait of Ercole's predecessor, Borso d'Este, in a beretta, and other beretta-wearing condottiere not now identifiable. As already discussed, Piero della Francesca seems to have made a 'Condottiere Prince Portrait' of this type for Federico in 1465/6.

The Duke of Milan had been an important patron for Federico in his younger days, and was certainly a major role model. Bianca Maria had taken the motherless Battista and Costanzo into her care, and was the living woman who most effectively embodied the idea of a wife as half of a ruling conjugal pair when Battista was growing up. The Urbino panel, then, probably took its inspiration from the Sforza double portrait. Francesco is shown wearing a captain's red beretta, which has seen better days, though he is clad in fine brocade. Bianca Maria displays gem-embroidered borders on her magnificent garments, many pearls, and has her hair caught up in a jewelled net. They both have a mild, neutral expression. One unusual aspect of this painting is that Bianca Maria has a double chin and is no longer youthful (she would have been about thirty), since surviving likenesses of fifteenth-century Italian women almost exclusively portray them in nubile adolescence.[50] This in itself suggests that her value is not entirely dependent on her beauty. Because Battista died aged only twenty-six, it was possible for Piero della Francesca to represent her as untouched by age, with a smoothly waxen pallor. The serene landscape behind Battista and Federico speaks of the peace enjoyed by a country living under a wise ruler; the van Eyckian sense of depth and distance also illustrates the interplay of Flemish and Italian influence in Urbino. It is a version of the landscape Federico would have seen from his loggia: the area round Urbino was much more richly wooded in the fifteenth century than it is today.[51]

What is unique about these two paintings is that they are double-sided: on the reverse, Battista and Federico ride in classical/Petrarchan triumph, with a continuous landscape scrolling behind them both. Classical descriptions of Roman triumphs fascinated Renaissance princes (Mantegna's *Triumphs of Caesar* is the best-known witness to this). In Piero's pictures, Latin inscriptions beneath read 'this illustrious hero is celebrated for the fame of his prowess. Carried in signal triumph, and worthy of the sceptre that he wields, he is equal to the greatest captains' and 'she preserved modesty in prosperous fortune, her fame flew on all men's lips, she was adorned by the praises of her great husband's deeds'. Battista's inscription is in the past tense, indicating that she was no longer alive, and represents her entirely as a reflection of her husband, conforming her to feminine stereotypes in a way that was not characteristic of her actual life.

Federico is represented in armour, stretching out his commander's baton in a gesture of active rulership, with Fame or Victory standing behind him, crowning him with laurel. The Four Cardinal Virtues, Justice, Prudence, Fortitude and Temperance, ride with him. His chariot is pulled by white horses. The annals of ancient Rome did not offer a feminine version of a triumph, but Petrarch's *Trionfi* offers a Triumph of Modesty, which serves as a starting point for the triumph of Battista. Her chariot is pulled by unicorns, as in Petrarch's poem (and also, the Triumph of [virtuous] Love in an intarsia door panel in the Sala della Iole),[52] and she is reading a small book, probably a Book of Hours, to emphasize her Christian devotion. She is accompanied by at least two of the Theological Virtues, Faith and Charity, while the woman in white, standing beside her, may be the third, Hope. There is also a woman in grey, painted from the back, who might be meant for St Clare or a Clarissan nun more generally, since Battista had been buried, at her request, in the common tomb of the Clarissans at Santa Chiara.[53] Thus Federico embodies the virtues suitable to a man engaged in the *vita activa*, and Battista, the virtues of the *vita contemplativa*, suitable for a woman.

The diptych was an intimate object. In its original form, it seems to have been hinged together like a book, like the lost double portrait of Francesco Sforza and his wife owned by Borso d'Este, which may have been the model.[54] It has been suggested by Joanna Woods-Marsden that Battista's Triumph was the 'front cover', which may explain why the inscription is so focused on Federico, the portraits were inside, and Federico's Triumph was the 'back cover'. It was probably not on permanent display, but brought out in special circumstances to show an important visitor, along with classical coins and statuettes and suchlike personal treasures.

There is a curious kinship between the diptych and a much less famous artwork, an architectural lunette from the late fifteenth century that was once positioned over the upper loggia of the Ducal Palace in Urbino, and is thought to have been the work of Francesco di Giorgio Martini or Domenico Roselli.[55] It is carved in low relief with Federico and Ottaviano, who are facing one another, looking into each other's eyes, smiling slightly; they would seem to be standing about a foot apart, because they are intimates. Behind Federico is a fantastical helmet, and a Roman military standard topped with a small model citadel. Behind Ottaviano are two bound books, one open, one closed, and an olive branch. As with the diptych, Federico claims the *vita activa*, military triumphs and building castles. Ottaviano is the man of peace, the humanist, so his is the *vita contemplativa*. While Ottaviano and Battista enjoyed quite different types of relationship with Federico, they were both his partners, and this image reflects a united face of co-rulership in a similar way, as do the two other relief portraits of Federico and Ottaviano at Mercatello.

The Montefeltro Diptych is an indication that Federico had begun to spend substantial sums of money on art after 1474. However, Piero della Francesca aside, relatively few of the duke's commissions in the last ten years of his life went to Italians. Since we tend to think of fifteenth-century Italy as the cradle of the new, it is easy for us to overlook how much it was borrowing from Flanders. But the condottiere princes bought Flemish tapestries and other luxury goods, and they wholeheartedly admired the jewelled brilliance of the paintings of Jan van Eyck and other Flemish masters of oil painting. One of van Eyck's most famous paintings shows the marriage of an Italian merchant, Giovanni Arnolfini, and several of his major paintings were exported to Italy, where they exercised considerable influence on Italian artists.[56] Alfonso of Naples owned a triptych by van Eyck, which had been brought to Italy around 1444 by Battista di Giorgio Lomellini, a Genoese with commercial interests in Bruges. Another triptych by van Eyck, painted in 1437, carries the arms and portrait of another Genoese, Michele Giustiniani; it is now in Dresden.[57]

Italians also started to commission paintings in northern Europe. In 1451 the church of Santa Maria della Carità bought an altarpiece from one 'Piero from the Low Countries', which cost them 100 ducats, a quarter of which was the cost of shipping it from Flanders. Filarete took note of this painting in his *Treatise on Architecture*, and recommended Francesco Sforza to seek good painters from northern Europe. Rogier van der Weyden was himself enticed over the Alps to paint panels for the Medici and Este, while one of the first major Flemish paintings to arrive in Florence was the Portinari Altarpiece for the hospital of Santa Maria Nuova, now in the Uffizi, commissioned from Hugo van der Goes in 1477–8, just about the time when Federico was spending serious money on painting. It was sponsored by Tommaso Portinari, who had lived in Bruges for forty years as a representative of the Medici bank.

Federico was thus in line with contemporary Italian taste when he recruited Joos van Wassenhove. As Marina Belozerskaya has pointed out, Renaissance Italian fascination with Flemish art (and artefacts) has been thoroughly obscured by a tradition of art criticism that starts with Florence, the revival of ancient glories through the mediation of Florentines, and Giorgio Vasari's *Lives of the Painters*, written for Cosimo I de' Medici of Florence, which privileges Italian creations, and Florence in particular, over artwork from other parts of Europe.[58] As a result, in the words of Patricia Rubin, 'central Italy continues to be studied as the site and centre of the renaissance of the arts, despite repeated attempts to dislodge it from its place at the summit of achievement'.[59]

To Vasari, Jan van Eyck was the first northern painter of international renown, and he and Rogier van der Weyden are often admitted to Italian artistic pantheons, as if they were honorary Italians; they are the only foreigners mentioned by Giovanni Santi, for instance.[60] One of the first attempts at art criticism is a chapter on painters in the treatise *On Illustrious Men*, written in 1456 by an Italian humanist, Bartolomeo Facio. He singles out two Italians, Gentile da Fabriano and Pisanello, and two Flemings, Jan van Eyck and Rogier van der Weyden, as the greatest masters of the art of painting, and tells us that his knowledge of van Eyck's work is based on a painting, or paintings, owned by Ottaviano Ubaldini. His description is worth quoting, since the picture is lost.[61]

> There are also fine paintings of his in the possession of that distinguished man, Ottaviano della Carda: women of uncommon beauty emerging from the bath, the more intimate parts of the body being with excellent modesty veiled in fine linen, and of one of them he has shown only the face and breast but has then represented the hind parts of her body in a mirror painted on the wall opposite, so that you may see her back as well as her breast. In the same picture there is a lantern in the bath chamber, just like one lit, and an old woman seemingly sweating, a puppy lapping up water, and also horses, minute figures of men, mountains, groves, hamlets and castles carried out with such skill you would believe one was fifty miles distant from another. But almost nothing is more wonderful in this work than the mirror painted in the picture, in which you see whatever is represented as in a real mirror. He is said to have done many other works, but of these I have been able to obtain no complete knowledge.

Facio worked for Alfonso of Naples, one of Federico's principal employers, so he had many opportunities to visit Urbino.[62] He refers to 'paintings', plural, but describes only one. We might envisage a work something like Albrecht Dürer's well-known 1496 drawing of women bathing together, but with typical van Eyck touches.[63] Facio's description seizes on features familiar to us from the surviving works of van Eyck: the exquisite miniature landscapes glimpsed through a window, as in the *Madonna with Chancellor Rolin*, the mirror, an effect the painter uses in the Arnolfini portrait, and an uncommon ability to represent light emanating from a source. In this context, the mirror symbolizes virtue and purity, while the dog represents fidelity. The beautiful naked Eve in the Ghent Altarpiece suggests that van Eyck would have been more than capable of tackling female nudes, though none is known to survive. Various bathing scenes were licensed by the Bible, such as Bathsheba being spied on by King David, Susanna spied on by the Elders, and Judith preparing for her encounter with Holofernes. Van Eyck is known to have painted a nude of Judith taking a sponge-bath, attended by her maid,[64] but there is no known copy or drawing of his 'Women Bathing'.

Giorgio Vasari knew this painting, and was under the impression that it had belonged to Federico, so wherever the painting had got to by the sixteenth century, it must have had an Urbino provenance. Additionally, it would have been easy to assume that every fifteenth-century artwork of quality in Urbino belonged to the great duke.[65] In fact, Ottaviano's ownership of the van Eyck, and perhaps his commission of the *Brera Madonna* from Piero della Francesca, suggests that he was far more of a connoisseur of art than his brother. Federico was not eagerly collecting pictures for their aesthetic qualities. He wanted art that would reflect his personal agendas, and it was Burgundian style that most answered his needs, because it was the Burgundian dukes who had most successfully used art to project, justify and cement their ambitions in the eyes of subjects and enemies alike. The Burgundian court favoured intrinsically precious objects – tapestries, gold, silverware and illuminated manuscripts – over paintings, though they valued portraits and, to some extent, devotional subjects.[66] But so did rich Italians: when Isabella d'Este made her will, she left her intaglios, agate and jasper vases and antique sculptures to her children, while her favourite ladies-in-waiting were each allowed to choose a picture.[67]

Federico's priorities seem to have been similar. He owned 16,000 ducats' worth of 'wonderful jewels' in later life.[68] Doubtless on special occasions, Battista displayed splendid ornaments, as, clearly, did the young Guidobaldo, but the term '*gioie*' also covered the sort of small precious objects coveted by Renaissance princes and shown off in their *studioli*: agate cups mounted in silver gilt and gems, costly toys of enamelled gold, classical intaglios, items that were testimonies to wealth, power and taste. This is how Lorenzo de' Medici showed off his collections to Giovanni of Aragon in 1480: 'Then we returned to the little loggia opening off the study. And there on a table, he had brought his jewels... vases, cups, hard-stone coffers mounted with gold, of various stones, jasper and others. There was a crystal beaker mounted with a lid and a silver foot, which was studded with pearls, rubies, diamonds, and other stones.'[69] It is easy to imagine Federico doing the same. Some of his jewels may survive as part of the great Medici collections, having been taken to Florence with other movables after 1631.

The aesthetics of magnificence set a high value on art created with precious materials: jewels, gold and silk. Flemish masters used the medium of oil to create optical illusions of sumptuousness, representing the effect of light on various textures, sparkling glass or gleaming silk, or the glow of light on a wall. As Facio's essay suggests, this fascinated Italian contemporaries. According to Vespasiano da Bisticci, Federico took the unusual step of sending for a Flemish painter of his own, Joos van Wassenhove, because he preferred oil painting to the Italian tempera technique: '[Federico da Montefeltro] was much interested in painting, and because he could not find in Italy painters in oil to suit his taste he sent to Flanders and brought thence a master who did at Urbino many very stately pictures, especially in Federico's study, where were represented philosophers, poets and doctors of the Church, rendered with wondrous art.'[70] In fact, both Flemish and Italian artists used combinations of oil glazes, resins and tempera, but to very different effect: as Ernst Gombrich pointed out, the Flemings were primarily concerned to describe sumptuous surfaces, while Italians were much more focused on perspective, and used light as an instrument to render three-dimensional form.[71] The point is that for the kind of man Federico was, and what he wanted to achieve with his art patronage, his heart was set on a Flemish painter. He also wanted someone who would work to direction, and fast: Piero della Francesca, the best-regarded contemporary painter in the Marche, was notoriously slow. Both the altarpiece and the portraits were painted very quickly. In both cases, the poplar panels, unevenly planed and with numerous knots, were prepared with an insubstantial ground. Paint layers for the portraits are few and thin, and craquelure suggests rapid application and insufficient drying time.[72]

Joos van Wassenhove has left some faint traces in the historical record. He was admitted to the Antwerp guild of painters in 1460 and to that of Ghent in October 1464. In the latter city he was friendly with the young Hugo van der Goes, because he was one of his two guarantors when Hugo was admitted to the guild in May 1467. He is last documented in Ghent on 19 January 1469 when he and Hugo van der Goes stood surety together for the Scottish illuminator Sanders Bening,[73] and he seems to have reached Italy by 1471, when he was commissioned to paint a large *St Mark the Evangelist* for the church of San Marco in Rome (in tempera).[74]

Joos and Federico may have met at the papal court, since Federico was frequently employed by Sixtus IV, but the first work the painter did in Urbino was not commissioned by Federico, so he may have arrived in Urbino independently, whereupon Federico realized that he was potentially useful. Van Wassenhove is first recorded in Urbino working on an altarpiece for the church of the Confraternity of Corpus Domini, the most important lay religious organization in the town. This was in the Piazza di Pian di Mercato (now the Piazza della Repubblica) and was demolished in 1705. The Confraternity had been looking for a painter for years. Fra Carnevale was offered the commission in 1456, but turned it down. They commissioned a predella from Paolo Uccello, executed between 1465 and 1468, but he was apparently not considered as the artist of the main panel.[75] Piero della Francesca came to have a look in 1469, but the commission did not go ahead.[76] The name of Joos van Wassenhove first appears in the confraternity's documents on 12 February 1473. A year and a half later, on 25 October 1474, he received final payment for 'his work in painting the picture for the fraternity'.[77] His fee was 250 gold florins.

The Institution of the Eucharist was not a commission by Federico, but he did contribute a rather parsimonious fifteen florins to the cost, and he intervened in the design.[78] At the centre of the picture, Christ gives holy communion to his apostles, a conflation of the Last Supper as described in the Gospels, where Christ took bread, broke it and shared it out, with the solemn rites of celebration of the Mass as performed in fifteenth-century Italy. The subject was of obvious relevance to a confraternity devoted to the body of Christ. But behind and on the right, there is a group in contemporary dress: Federico himself, shown, as always, in profile, wearing a red beretta and touching the sleeve of a bearded man. The art historian Marilyn Lavin has suggested that this individual represents Dr Isaac, an ambassador from the Shahanshah of Persia who visited Urbino. He was a Spanish Jew by origin and a recent convert to Catholicism. As a converted Jew, he would have a particular resonance in this picture, which shows the moment of the institution of Catholic Christianity, since communion is being received by the apostles, who were converted Jews. She has also suggested that the other men in the group are Ottaviano Ubaldini and, behind him, Costanzo Sforza, Battista Sforza's brother.[79] Federico delicately touches the arm of Isaac, who raises his hand to his heart to indicate how deeply moved he is, while Ottaviano marks with his fingers the points made during Christ's discourse. The gesture indicates someone making, or following, an argument.[80] Looking on from a distance is a crowned baby, who must be Guidobaldo, held by a woman.

Da Bisticci assigns the twenty-eight three-quarter-length paintings of famous men that were in the Urbino *studiolo* to Joos van Wassenhove. These were originally painted upon large panels, with at least two figures to a panel, though they have since been divided into single portraits. Many of them have been returned to the *studiolo*, though some found their way to the Louvre. This substantial commission was undertaken between 1474 and 1476. To judge by the way the light falls on each figure, they were probably arranged as follows: Plato and Aristotle above St Gregory and St Jerome on the west wall; Ptolemy and Boethius above St Ambrose and St Augustine and Cicero and Seneca above Moses and King Solomon on the north wall; Homer and Virgil above St Thomas Aquinas and Duns Scotus and Euclid and Vittorino da Feltre above Pope Pius II and Cardinal Bessarion on the east wall; and Solon and Bartolo Sentinati above Albertus Magnus and Pope Sixtus IV and Hippocrates and Pietro D'Abano above Dante and Petrarch on the east wall.[81] This arrangement gives classical sages in the top tier, and Christians in the lower tier. Philosophers and Christian thinkers go together, Ptolemy and Boethius are linked as scientists, Cicero and Seneca as eloquent moralists. Solon and Bartolo Sentinati are both lawgivers, Hippocrates and Pietro D'Abano both doctors. The writings of all of these individuals are extensively represented in Federico's library. Other arrangements have been proposed, but we know that Isabella d'Este insisted that the direction of the light in pictures for her *studiolo* should be determined by the natural light in the room, and it is likely that Federico and his painter observed the same principle.[82]

Humanists such as Lombardo della Seta, Poggio Bracciolini and Alberti observed that it was a Roman custom to put portraits of famous men in libraries. The earliest known Renaissance study with a decorative programme depicting famous writers was that of Pope Nicholas V in the Vatican (no longer extant), where the intarsia was surmounted by frescoed portraits of writers, both pagan and Christian.[83] One possible model that van Wassenhove may have drawn on for his Famous Men is the series of oak busts in the choir stalls at Ulm, carved in 1469–74 by Jörg Syrlin the Elder, which represent half-length figures from the Old and

New Testaments together with classical worthies, extending both laterally and vertically within a linked architectural framework. The route from the Netherlands to Italy led through Ulm, and the church was one of the most admired in Europe, so it is more than likely that van Wassenhove had seen these figures.[84] For the Old Testament figures, he drew on an established iconography, but the ancient Greeks, with their beards and exotic clothing, derive from Netherlandic depictions of prophets, while the Romans are clean-shaven and in more ordinary dress. Both Vittorino da Feltre and Sixtus IV are probably based on portrait medals. One trick used in the portraits of Aristotle, Boethius, Homer and Virgil, the space-defining motif of extending a hand, fingers first, was perhaps borrowed from Piero della Francesca, who employs it quite frequently, since he also worked at Urbino, and there is every reason to think that van Wassenhove was aware of his paintings.

Despite Vespasiano da Bisticci, the attribution of these pictures has been questioned. In 1604, Pablo de Céspedes wrote that a Spanish artist had painted the Urbino 'Famous Men'. A Spanish painter called Pedro is referred to in a 1477 account book of the Urbino Confraternity of Santa Maria della Misericordia (as 'Pietro Spagnuolo, pittore') Several words in Castilian are painted on the open book held by the figure of Albertus Magnus, which does suggest the involvement of a Spaniard. This person has been identified as Pedro Berruguete; and it is now suggested that he finished the pictures, though Joos was primarily responsible.[85] There is some reworking by a second hand, particularly of Aristotle, Vittorino da Feltre and Sixtus IV, who were almost completely repainted. Two of the three were personally known to Federico, suggesting that improved likenesses came to hand at a time when Joos was no longer available, or otherwise engaged. The second painter also added ducal insignia, such as the Order of the Garter, to the panels.[86]

Another cycle of pictures that also seems to be by Joos may have been made for the *studiolo* at Gubbio, or perhaps hung in the ducal library. Two survive, and two were destroyed during the Second World War, though there are black and white photographs, but there must originally have been seven, since they represent the Liberal Arts as female personifications, with Federico and his associates kneeling before them. In the two lost paintings, the identity of Federico's Art is unclear, though his interests might suggest Geometry (there seem to be some regular solids in a niche beside her), and Ottaviano Ubaldini, with his astrological interests, kneels in front of Astronomy. The two surviving Arts are Rhetoric, with a young man who may be Ferrante of Naples, and Music, with a still younger man who appears to be Federico's late wife's brother, Costanzo Sforza. The other three pictures, for which there is no evidence, perhaps featured Guidobaldo, one or two of Federico's sons-in-law, or his other son Antonio, with Logic, Arithmetic and Grammar.

The Temple of the Muses on the first floor was another highly decorated little room. It once had intarsias (completely lost), and panels representing the nine Muses, Apollo and Pallas, as we know from Baldi's description made in 1587.[87] Pallas, Euterpe and Urania have disappeared, but the other eight pictures are in the Galleria Corsini in Florence. The structure of the tiny Tempietto and its adjoining rooms was apparently complete by 1480; the paintings, by Giovanni Santi and Evangelista di Pian di Meleto, were probably begun shortly after this date, though the cycle remained incomplete and Timoteo Viti finished the work in the 1510s. This is the oldest representation of the Muses as a group of musicians in a courtly context, and is further evidence for Federico's love of music. Like the *studiolo* – and the other *studiolo* in Gubbio – this was a little room like a jewel box, with intarsias and pictures forming a rich decorative ensemble together with a polychrome coffered ceiling, further evidence for Federico's taste for lavish and spectacular effects.

Paintings, fine furnishings and intarsias were not the only art forms admired in the fifteenth century. Federico began collecting tapestries when he was still a count. Gaugello Gaugelli, in *Il Pellegrino*, a poem he dedicated to Federico in 1464, describes the palace as it then was (the Iole wing) as 'entirely covered in tapestries' (*tucte coperte de panni de raçça*).[88] Quite probably, the commission of Federico's that was most admired by contemporaries was his set of Troy tapestries, bought in 1476 after he became duke, which is no longer extant. Isabella D'Este, visiting Urbino for Easter in the days of Guidobaldo, was deeply impressed to find that there were enough tapestries to cover all the walls of the state apartments; at her own palace in Mantua, they had to be hastily moved ahead of the guests as they went from room to room.[89] His eleven-piece set of the History of Troy was purchased in July 1476 for the eye-watering sum of 2,557 ducats and 19 bolognini from Jean Grenier, of the famous Grenier family of tapestry merchants in Tournai, who were the most famous suppliers of tapestry in late fifteenth-century Europe. The History of Troy designs were among the most sought-after of all tapestries. Scot McKendrick has estimated that as many as nine sets may have been woven,[90] and their buyers included Henry VII, King of England, Matthias Corvinus, King of Hungary, and Ludovico 'il Moro', Duke of Milan, suggesting that they were among the most prestigious possessions it was possible to acquire, a statement of magnificence for rulers all across Europe. The first set was made for Charles the Bold, Duke of Burgundy, and presented to him in 1472, so by 1476 Federico could certainly have known of the Greniers' reputation as the best '*tapissiers*' in Europe, and that Troy was in fashion, either through the Netherlandish craftsmen in his employ, or through direct contact with the Burgundian court, since Agostino Fregoso, who in 1476 married Federico's illegitimate daughter Gentile, had before that recently served in the army of Charles the Bold.[91]

These were vast artworks; each of the eleven hangings was about 4.8 metres high and 9–10 metres long, so the eleven together were about 105 metres long, with a surface area of about half a kilometre.[92] They narrated the story of the Trojan War from the

Mission of Antenor to the Fall of Troy, transforming the ancient tale into a Burgundian chivalric romance. There were legends explaining the action in French verses at the top, and Latin legends at the bottom.[93]

Tapestries were only hung on special occasions, so as not to wear them out; and on ordinary days, plain or frescoed walls sufficed. Our perception of the Ducal Palace is that it was relatively austere inside, with plain white walls relieved only by wonderful intarsia work on doors, and delicate relief sculpture on pale limestone doorcases, fireplaces and other architectural elements. This has to be considered in the context of a realization that the Iole fireplace, and perhaps other internal stonework, was gilded,[94] there would have been painted furniture and *spalliere*, and when Federico was showing off his palace on festival days, the plain white walls of the palace came alive with blazing colour, shimmering with multicoloured textiles. While Bernardino Baldi notes that the walls were plain white, the reason he gives is that wall decorations 'would be useless, [as] the walls of the palace are dressed, according to the seasons, either with tapestries or with embossed leather'.[95] Porcellio Pandoni's poem *Feltria* (after 1472) gives an idea of how Federico wished his palace to be perceived, since he commissioned the poem. Clearly, elegant minimalism was not the effect intended. Pandoni says:

> Here there are a thousand windows, and a thousand doors,
> which lead to the inside of a magnificent house, like the Cretan
> labyrinth, carved with great art. You see doorposts and lintels
> of Parian marble; there are innumerable halls, refulgent with
> marble and gold.[96]

The Troy tapestries were woven in wool and silk, perhaps including gold and silver threads, and brilliantly coloured. The effect, terms of scale, design, visual richness and technical refinement alike must have been amazing. They were very much admired by contemporaries: Giannantonio Campano, who had written the funeral oration for Battista Sforza, wrote a short poem on them, *De Aulaeis* (On Tapestry), addressed to the duke, which evoked their spectacular appearance, 'refulgent with red and gold'.[97] Part of the reason why there's a gap between our own perceptions and Renaissance taste is that few surviving tapestries have anything like their original colour, though a surviving Trojan War tapestry now in the Metropolitan Museum in New York is blazing blue and red, which were probably the dominant colours in Federico's set. For the most part, tapestries are now khaki and beige hangings in the great museums of the world. One tends to quicken one's pace, heading for the picture galleries, or the café. Another factor that makes them seem lifeless is that they are still: when they were hanging on hooks in a fifteenth-century palace, they would have shivered a little with passing currents of air, making the faces come alive, while the gold threads would glitter in the light of fire or candles.

In their own time, nothing said wealth, power and privilege like a collection of tapestries, which is why Federico was buying them before he started to spend money on paintings. As Marina Belozerskaya observes, 'frescoes were mundane compared with tapestries. They were what remained on the walls when tapestries were not superimposed on them.'[98] Apart from anything else, it was immediately obvious to contemporaries that they were fabulously expensive, which gave them social cachet. Raphael was paid 1,000 ducats to produce his cartoons for the Acts of the Apostles tapestries commissioned by Leo X, but the weaver was paid 15,000 ducats. It was rumoured that the enormous cost of the tapestries was defrayed by raiding funds collected for the crusade against the Turks and the rebuilding of St Peter's. According to Antonio de Beatis, who visited the workshop where they were being made, they cost 2,000 ducats apiece.[99]

Unlike paintings, which have turned out to be remarkably durable, technical aspects of tapestry production have militated against their long-term survival. Iron mordants were used to fix dark colours, and these tend to corrode over time, silver threads tarnish, while many natural dyes are light-sensitive. Also, these immensely heavy fabrics could be damaged both by use and disuse. While they were hanging on walls, they might sag or even rip under their own weight, and they were vulnerable to damage from sunlight. If they were put away, they might deteriorate through poor storage, whether from damp, mildew or the attentions of mice, and they also suffered from being taken up and down too often.[100] But if treated with care, they remained covetable objects for decades, if not centuries. The local writer Antonio di Francesco Nuti da Mercatello, in a poem on Federico written in 1480, which includes a detailed description of the Ducal Palace, describes the Troy tapestries in the Throne Room, where, he says, they were 'often' displayed: 'Often in the sala you see adornment / Of tapestries, none more beautiful.'[101] In 1566, nearly a hundred years after their acquisition, Federico da Montefeltro's biographer Gallo Galli was still describing the Troy tapestries as 'very beautiful and lovely work', and guessing that they had cost 10,000 ducats.[102] Tapestries were, above all, portable magnificence, so they could be lent out. In 1490, Federico's Troy tapestries were lent to Francesco Gonzaga to decorate the palace at Mantua for his wedding to Isabella d'Este. They were among the treasures of Urbino looted by Cesare Borgia in 1502 and the only items specifically mentioned during his abject interview with the recently restored Guidobaldo da Montefeltro at Rome in December 1503. But their final appearance is in the inventory of 25 June 1631, taken shortly after the death of Francesco Maria II della Rovere, by which time they had done a good 165 years of service, and were worn out: 'in poor condition and torn'.[103]

Vespasiano da Bisticci also records that Federico actually started a tapestry workshop in the 1470s: 'he also brought in Flemish tapestry weavers who wrought a noble set for an apartment, worked with gold and silk mixed with woollen thread, in such fashion as no brush could have rendered. He also caused other decorations to be wrought by these masters.'[104] This description suggests that to a fifteenth-century eye, tapestry was better than painting. According to a list of Federico's household, there were five of these weavers.[105] It is noticeable that they post-date his acquisition of the ducal title, since an inventory of the Urbino palace made on 28 April 1631 lists tapestries with Federico's arms and the letters F and D.[106] These must have been made by his own weavers, and perhaps some of the verdures that are also mentioned were their work. It seems likely that as well as embarking on new projects, the weavers also had the job of keeping the Troy tapestries in good shape, repairing minor damage as it occurred before it got any worse.

There is little evidence for Federico's investment in antiques, despite the fact that Castiglione says 'he adorned [his palace]… with countless antique statues of marble and bronze'.[107] Buying antiques was something of a craze in fifteenth-century Italy, and considered both intellectually and socially prestigious: thus Castiglione asserts their presence in the perfect palace, whether they were there or not. As early as 1471, Pope Sixtus IV donated a collection of antique bronze statues that had previously been in the Lateran Palace (the She-Wolf, the Spinarius, the Camillus and the colossal head of Constantine, with his hand and globe) to the people of Rome, and housed them on the Capitol. The first person to hold an exhibition of antique statues was Julius II, and the papal collection became famous. However, it seems on the whole unlikely that Federico was a major investor.[108] There was a papal embargo on exporting antiquities from Rome, the best source of supply. To get hold of good statues, a collector needed to call in favours, and it seems unlikely that Federico would have squandered the goodwill of his patrons on anything so frivolous. We do know that in 1474, the poet Pandoni sent him an antique head of Minerva. According to the poem Pandoni wrote about it, Federico had it mounted below the Montefeltro eagle (also associated with Jupiter) that surmounted the carved coat of arms over the main entry to his palace, hardly the action of a connoisseur.[109] But there was also a fine Roman statue of Venus in the palace by 1502, provenance unknown, because it was coveted, and eventually acquired, by Isabella d'Este, whose taste was refined.[110]

One type of art commission that was important to Federico was low-relief decorative sculpture for doorcases and fireplaces in his properties, reflecting the practical orientation of his art patronage. Vespasiano da Bisticci says, 'as to sculpture, he had great knowledge, and he took much thought as to the work which he had made for his palace, employing the first masters of the time'.[111] He says nothing about collecting antiques. Even in the 1460s, Michele di Giovanni, 'il Greco', was carving delicate reliefs in the Palazzetto della Iole. One of the most interesting of these is the chimneypiece in the Sala della Iole, attributed by Rotondi to Michele di Giovanni and Pasquino da Montepulciano. The principal decoration, apart from the Hercules and Iole caryatids, is a frieze representing a Bacchic procession, in which several of the figures are directly based on figures from an antique Roman sarcophagus with reliefs of the 'Triumphal Procession of Bacchus and Ariadne', discovered near the church of Santa Maria Maggiore in Rome, and now in the British Museum. Several artists made drawings of all or part of the design from the 1420s onwards, which were then copied by other artists: this suggests that Federico's sculptors were keenly looking out for the latest and best models for their work.[112] In the 1470s, another round of sculpture was commissioned from Francesco di Giorgio Martini, Domenico Roselli and Ambrogio Barocci. The palace wall facing the piazza was lined with stone benches whose backs were carved with Machines of War, mostly from designs by Francesco di Giorgio, executed by Ambrogio Barocci (they have since been moved inside).

Overall, Federico's art commissions suggest a highly intelligent appreciation of the social functions of art: the expression of magnificence, dynastic image-making, and the creation of statements about oneself. His approach seems essentially practical; as with his architectural projects or the books in the library, he had an idea of what he wanted to achieve, and put together a team of people capable of realizing his vision: in the *studioli*, for example, highly competent men with different skills worked together, painters, intarsia makers, carpenters, calligraphers. The creation of a book involved a calligrapher, at least one painter, and a binder. There is no reason to think that Federico thought of a painter such as Joos van Wassenhove as being in a different category from an intarsia maker such as Baccio Pontelli. Few fifteenth-century Italian painters were in a position to dictate terms to their clients. Most were highly versatile craftsmen – Francesco di Giorgio Martini trained as a painter, but spent most of his career as an architect. Pontelli started out as an intarsia maker, and ended up an engineer. What Federico needed was not masterpieces, but competent work that would form part of a complex ensemble. Therefore Joos van Wassenhove was of more real use to him than Piero della Francesca.

11

Urbino:
The Ducal Library

In Renaissance Italy, a ruler's grasp on his territories was strengthened if he could demonstrate his fitness to rule by his *virtù*: his humanist education, moral character and wisdom. For such men, a library was not a private indulgence, it was a public statement. Thus the mid-fifteenth century was an age of great princely libraries. Collectors such as the Aragonese kings of Naples and the Sforzas in Milan amassed stately collections of beautiful manuscripts – a swansong for the age of handwritten books. The value of these books, in their own time, was colossal. Ferrante of Naples raised enough capital by pawning 266 books from the royal library with the Pandolfini bank in Florence in 1481 to finance his siege of Otranto after it was captured by the Turks.

Most of these libraries lasted a generation or so and were dispersed, but the library at Urbino is a magnificent exception.[1] From its beginnings in 1468, it continued to grow for a century and a half, and contemporaries considered it a tremendous achievement. By the time Duke Federico died in 1482, he owned almost 1,100 volumes, which the Florentine bookseller Vespasiano da Bisticci estimated as worth 30,000 ducats – since it was da Bisticci who had sold the duke most of the books in the first place, his estimate is worth something.[2] The Urbino library building itself survives, and though the collection is no longer housed there, the books have by no means been scattered to the four winds. Most of the manuscripts from the main library have been kept together and now form Classis Urbinese in the Biblioteca Apostolica in the Vatican, while a substantial number of the printed books amassed by later dukes, particularly Francesco Maria II della Rovere, are in the Biblioteca Alessandrina, the library of the university of La Sapienza in Rome.

There are different kinds of great library. The Renaissance was a great age of recovering and editing classical texts, but the Urbino library reflects other concerns. A scholar's library was a recognizable phenomenon in the Italy of Federico da Montefeltro. Contemporary humanists such as Coluccio Salutati and Poggio Bracciolini were already out searching for forgotten texts. In 1451, for example, the scholar-pope Nicholas V charged his agent Enoch of Ascoli with scouring the monastic libraries of Germany in search of ancient texts that 'have been lost by fault of earlier ages'.[3] Why this was a sensible mission is that in the course of the ninth century, the emperor Charlemagne and his heirs had sponsored a tremendous initiative of recovering and copying ancient texts, and many of these books survived in ancient monasteries. But these were not the kind of books that Federico wanted to collect. The only Latin book in the Urbino library that is an important witness to a classical text is the earliest known copy of the only surviving Roman cookery book, Apicius' *De Re Coquinaria*. It was certainly in Federico's library, since it is in the catalogue compiled in 1482–7,[4] but the reason for its presence there is probably that it is a spectacular copy written at Tours towards the middle of the ninth century as a present for the Carolingian emperor Charles the Bald. The frontispiece is written in gold ink on purple, and it has an illuminated contents page, so it is self-evidently an aristocrat's book of its day. Federico also owned a handsome gospel-book, which had belonged to another Carolingian emperor, Lothar, probably for the same reason; it has incipit pages and first initials finely drawn in gold ink over red under-drawing.[5] These are magnates' books; they are academics' books only by the accident of their extreme age.

Apart from the Apicius, which he probably acquired for its beauty, Federico was not part of the Renaissance scholarly enterprise of recovery, nor did he share its values. He was a reader and bibliophile, not a scholar, and his book collection reflected his needs and, above all, his social status. It was a concrete demonstration of his magnificence and his cultural credentials. Professional soldiers who had also received a humanist education, such as Duke Federico and his contemporary Ludovico Gonzaga at Mantua, were very much aware that cultivating the arts at their respective courts would enhance their reputation among their contemporaries just as much as their skill in warfare, and would actively support their claim to rule. Much of the wealth acquired by Federico through his exercise of his professional talents as a condottiere was therefore spent on books for his library, but rather than sending envoys off to source six-hundred-year-old manuscripts, Duke Federico turned to Vespasiano da Bisticci, the premier book dealer in Florence, which was then the centre of the manuscripts trade in Italy. Vespasiano sold second-hand manuscripts, but he also kept a stock of new manuscripts of texts that he knew were in demand. For princely patrons like Federico, he employed an atelier of scribes and illuminators, so he could arrange for bespoke manuscripts of works he didn't keep in stock, or for particularly beautiful copies of common texts. Some 85 per cent of the manuscripts from Urbino were written specially for the library, and are calligraphically elegant, with lavish painted illuminated borders and initial letters, or even illustrations. Many of them also feature the duke's coat of arms or a portrait, or a special inscription: Urb. Lat. 1192, for example, a volume of poems by the Urbino scribe/librarian Federico Veterani, has Federico's distinctive profile portrait in a roundel at the bottom of the second page, while Pietro Acciaioli's history of the wars with Rimini shows him as a captain on horseback (Urb. Lat. 883). So does the Urbino copy of Poggio Bracciolini's *Florentine History* (Urb. Lat. 491). The books he acquired ready-made or inherited are often made more glorious with frontispieces, and/or with decorations, called *anteporti*, on the verso of the first page. These tend to be circular, usually a crown of laurel or floral branches enclosing the title, often with Federico's emblems or crest included in the design.[6]

Marcella Peruzzi observes acutely that there is a certain vulgarity about Federico's commissions: the earliest books he ordered from Florence have classic humanist 'white vine' decoration, but as time goes on, the decoration becomes increasingly extravagant and multicoloured, and more and more inclined to include his *imprese*, his orders, and his portrait, the so-familiar coin-like profile. His books affirm and celebrate him to an extent that makes very clear that he is using his commissions to put over a message about his personal glory, legitimizing the status as a princely figure that he only in fact achieved in the last eight years of his life – precisely the period when he was investing lavishly in his library.[7]

The plan for the contents of the Urbino library was based on that drawn up in the 1440s by Tommaso Parentucelli, the future Pope Nicholas V, for the library Cosimo de' Medici created at San Marco in Florence, which was the first public library in the history of Europe.[8] The core of the collection dates to a relatively concentrated period of time comprising the last fifteen years of Federico's reign. He was very much involved with the project, and so it reflects his values. Overall, Marcella Peruzzi has shown that about a third of Federico's collection was classical and a quarter theological; the remainder was about half and half medieval texts and works by contemporary humanists.[9] Some of the books in the library directly reflect his interests and concerns: he was a great patron of architecture, and so it is hardly surprising that he owned the classic works on architecture, Vitruvius and Serlio, as well as books on the subject by recent authors. Treatises by Piero della Francesca and Francesco di Giorgio were shelved alongside Leon Battista Alberti. The fact that the two great masters of perspective, Paolo Uccello and Piero della Francesca, were both employed by him suggests the centrality of science, mathematics and architecture to the cultural climate of the court. There is also a tranche of books that relate to the technical aspects of warfare, such as fortifications and mining, relevant to a professional soldier. But according to Angelo Longi, who spent several years at the court of Urbino,[10] much of Federico's reading time was actually devoted to theology and the Church Fathers; in support of this, the volume he is perusing in his portrait with young Guidobaldo has been identified from its size, shape and binding (red silk with silver clasps) as the Urbino copy of Pope Gregory the Great's *Moralia in Job*.[11]

There are also numerous books in the library that bear witness to his activities as a patron of learning and scholarship, since they are dedicated by grateful contemporaries.[12] They include, for example, Porcellio Pandoni's *Feltria*, a poem in nine volumes on the glories of the Montefeltri; Latin verse from Giovanni Battista Cantalicio, 'On the deeds of the unconquered Federico';[13] a commentary on the Latin language from the distinguished grammarian Niccolò Perotti, who had, like Federico, been educated by Vittorino da Feltre; and a good deal of other verse, both Latin and Italian. Federico's successors also received tributes of a similar kind, witnesses to a steady commitment to patronage of scholars and writers. One of the most interesting is Torquato Tasso's autograph first draft of the beginning of his *Gerusalemme* (Urb. Lat. 413), which he gave to Guidobaldo II.

In da Bisticci's memoirs, he praises the duke's library for both its completeness and its beauty. 'A short time before the Duke went to Ferrara it chanced that I was in Urbino with His Lordship, and I had with me the catalogues of the principal Italian libraries: of the papal library, of those of S. Marco at Florence, of Pavia, and even of that of the University of Oxford, which I had procured from England.' He claims that Duke Federico's library was more complete than any of them, which is most unlikely to have been true, but since he was the principal source that the duke had turned to for his books, it was very much in his interests to say so.

He also stresses the sheer attractiveness of the books at Urbino. 'In this library all the books as superlatively good, and written with the pen, and had there been one printed volume it would have been ashamed in such company. They were beautifully illuminated and written on parchment.' In fact, Federico did own printed books; there are fifty-one of them in the 'old catalogue' (Indice Vecchio), made by the librarian Agapito around 1487. However, there are also references in this catalogue to 'the other library'. It seems that besides the beautiful books in the grand saloon, there was a secondary collection of books that were useful but not worthy of display, or perhaps waiting to be copied by one of the professional illuminators, or disbound. After Federico's death, some or all of this beta collection was amalgamated with the fine codices in the main library, and so they appear in Agapito's catalogue.[14]

This emphasis on the physical beauty of books is typical of noble collectors in Renaissance Italy, with their predilection for splendid materials, virtuoso workmanship and high decorative value. Some aristocratic Renaissance patrons preferred manuscripts, or would only buy print copies if the text was very special – for example, printed on vellum (Isabella d'Este, *arbitrix elegantarium* and Marchioness of Mantua, was a book-buyer of this type).[15] There are indications that Federico did value manuscripts over printed books, notably his copy of Francesco Berlinghieri's *Septe Giornate della Geographia*, which was printed in Florence in 1482. Since it had thirty-one double folio engraved maps, the print edition was an extremely impressive object in itself. Some copies of the print edition were further decorated with hand-drawn illuminations; and these were bought by, among others, the kings of Hungary and Naples, and the Ottoman Sultan, Bayezid. However, there are also two entirely manuscript copies, lavishly illustrated, one of which was commissioned by Lorenzo de' Medici, the other by Federico da Montefeltro – who unfortunately died before it was finished, so it ended up being presented to young Guidobaldo instead.[16] Federico's copy is still further personalized by a drawing of Volterra, a small and unimportant city, but included in this special copy because Federico himself had been at the head of the victorious Florentine army, which took it in 1472.[17]

An indication of what Italian dukes wanted from books is provided by Borso d'Este of Ferrara's illuminated Bible. This had more than 600 leaves, and cost twice as much to make as the famous frescoes of the seasons in Palazzo Schifanoia in Ferrara, which was another of his commissions.[18] It accompanied him on state visits, suggesting that exquisite manuscripts of this kind functioned as portable magnificence, like tapestries, which were routinely carted from palace to palace by late medieval and Renaissance rulers.[19] Borso d'Este's Bible was completely unsuitable for reading; it was for admiring, a witness to its owner's piety and sophisticated taste. Unsurprisingly, Duke Federico, whose requirements were similar, also commissioned a huge illuminated Bible in two volumes (now Urb. Lat. 1–2), written by the Florentine calligrapher Hugo de' Comminellis, under the auspices of Vespasiano. The illuminations were by the most important Florentine miniaturists of the 1470s under the direction of Francesco d'Antonio del Chierico.[20] The Pazzi conspiracy of 1478, in which Lorenzo de' Medici nearly lost his life, led to cooling relations between Federico and Lorenzo, since the latter suspected (correctly) that Federico had a hand in it. Though Vespasiano continued to work for Federico until his death, because of the changed political circumstances Federico became wary of being entirely dependent on Florence for books, and directed his artistic patronage elsewhere, using miniaturists from Ferrara and the Po Valley.[21]

His beautiful gospel book, accordingly, was not created by Florentine artists. Instead, it was written by Matteo Contugi da Volterra, and illuminated by the Ferrarese Guglielmo Giraldi.

Another book similarly created by Contugi and Giraldi is his magnificent Dante, Urb. Lat. 365, made in 1478.[22] It has 110 illustrations, and in the full-page illumination at the beginning of *Purgatorio* on f. 97r, Federico's monogram, arms, and collar of the Order of the Garter are depicted in a roundel at the bottom of the page, while two putti are holding the unfurled Garter itself swagged over the top of the main panel. He was intensely proud of his Garter, which also features in the intarsia panels of his *studiolo*; and the presence of these personal insignia on the page suggests how directly a book of this kind contributed to his dignity. One thing the duke seems never to have realized is that Matteo Contugi, as well as writing a beautiful hand, was also a spy for the Gonzaga, for whom he had worked extensively.[23]

Apart from Giraldi, other important northern illuminators who worked on the library include Franco dei Russi, whose career had started some thirty years earlier with his work on the great Bible of Borso d'Este. Many of Federico's manuscripts were illuminated by identifiable artists such as the Florentines Francesco d'Antonio del Chierico and Francesco Rosselli. There is also evidence that illuminators actually moved to Urbino, where they were sure of steady work: Giraldi, for example, moved to Urbino from Ferrara to work on the Dante, and so did some Florentines.

Federico took pains to acquire luxury manuscripts, as well as commissioning them: the emperor Lothar's gospel book was the earliest that he owned, but he also treasured an exquisite and luxurious breviary, which contains the earliest known work of the famous French miniaturist Jean Pucelle, and was made in 1318–20 for Blanche of France, daughter of Philip V, who had become a Franciscan nun. Nathalie Roman, who has studied this manuscript, suggests that Duke Federico acquired it from his patron, King Alfonso of Aragon, whom he served as a condottiere.[24] As Cecil Clough has observed, 'Federico's relationship with the kings of Naples was remarkable for the length of time that it endured, as well as for friendly relations between patron and client throughout.'[25]

An armorial bearing with a crowned shield on f. 24v suggests that the book found its way to the Aragonese court, since the shield carries the arms of Violante de Bar, descended from the French royal family, quartered with those of Jean I of Aragon, whom she married in 1380.[26]

Federico had little time to spend on cultivating humanists, since his condotte took him away from Urbino for months at a time. Fortunately, he was good at delegating. It was his brother, Ottaviano Ubaldini della Carda, who dedicated himself to the delicate process of building up the library by developing relationships and exchanges with humanists. For instance, the humanist and poet Giorgio Merula wrote to his friend Piattino, hesitating about whether it was worth his while to dedicate his commentary on Juvenal's satires to Duke Federico; Piattino responded, saying that he had broached the question with Ottaviano, who approved, so he should go ahead (the work was duly presented, and the presentation copy is Urb. Lat. 663).[27]

While the Latin library is more remarkable for its spectacular beauty and elegance than for its contribution to knowledge, the duke's Greek books are rather different. This is because he was able to buy a substantial number of books that had been collected by a notable Greek scholar of the previous generation, the Florentine noble Palla Strozzi, who died in 1462. Strozzi left some of his books to his natural heirs, but also gave some of them to the Benedictine monks of Santa Giustina in Padua, who started selling them off, just at the point when Duke Federico was beginning to collect.[28] One of Strozzi's most treasured Greek books was a thirteenth-century copy of one of the greatest of all geographical works, Ptolemy's *Cosmography*, with twenty-six coloured maps, which the scholar Manuel Chrysoloras had brought to Italy in 1397. This came, via the monks of Santa Giustina, to the library at Urbino, where it was considered so precious it was kept in a cedar-wood box: it is now Urb. Graec. 82.[29] Others of Strozzi's books that came to Urbino included tenth-century copies of the *Roman*

History of Dionysius of Halicarnassus, works by the philosopher Dio Chrysostom, and the oldest copy in Italy of Theophrastus's seminal work on botany (Urb. Graec. 105, 124, 61). The duke also commissioned a beautiful copy of the Latin translation of Theophrastus, Urb. Lat. 250, which he himself would certainly have found more accessible than the Greek original. Federico read and wrote Latin with ease. He was highly intelligent, and he had attended Vittorino da Feltre's famous school, though only from 1434 to 1437. By the end of that year he had embarked, aged fifteen, on his career as a professional soldier. How much Greek Vittorino managed to cram into his head in the time is a question, though, clearly, Federico respected the study of Greek, encouraged his sons to take it seriously, and himself worked on Aristotle with the help of a scholar who could translate as they went along.

One of the more notably scholarly inputs to the library's Greek collection came through Federico's friendship with the immensely learned Greek Cardinal Bessarion, a lifelong book collector, who was, among other achievements, responsible for reintroducing the study of Plato to the Western world. It is not known when and where the two men met, but sometime in the 1450s Bessarion was in Urbino, where he baptized the duke's middle son, Antonio. We know this, because Bessarion gave the child a copy of the *Iliad* (Urb. Graec. 137), with an affectionate Latin inscription: 'Bessarion gives this book to his godson, so that when he begins to learn Greek, he can imbibe the greatest of poets from his earliest years.' A few years later, in the first half of 1456, apparently with some help from Federico, Bessarion received the great abbey of Santa Croce at Fonte Avellana, in Montefeltro territory, *in commendam* (meaning that he drew an income from it, but was not required to supervise it). That same year, Federico's oldest son, Buonconte, showed off his Latin and Greek by writing to the cardinal in both languages, inviting him to Urbino to become his confirmation godfather, an invitation Bessarion enthusiastically accepted. In fact, Bessarion stood as godfather to all three of Federico's sons, and took a genuine interest in their education, particularly their Greek studies.[30]

Bessarion had only just missed becoming pope in 1455; while the cardinal and Federico were clearly bound by mutual liking and common interests, since Urbino was part of the Papal States, it was very much in Federico's interest to be on friendly terms with a man who might well ascend to the chair of St Peter next time round. And conversely, especially after the fall of Constantinople in 1453, Bessarion's long-term political and cultural goal of strengthening the links between Eastern and Western Christendom were advanced by encouraging the heirs of Italian princes to study Greek.

The extent of Bessarion's faith and trust in Federico can be seen in the fact that, in 1472, having been sent to France as papal legate, he left his library in store at Urbino. For nearly two years, thirty chests of Greek books, including texts previously inaccessible to Italian scholars, were stored in the cloister of Santa Chiara close by the Ducal Palace. The presence of these chests in Urbino from 1472 to 1474 coincides with the beginning of the formation of the ducal library. Since the Urbino library had a Greek secretary, as long as they remained in Urbino, these books were available as copy-texts.

The library also contained some more exotic volumes, notably about eighty books in Hebrew, half of them Federico's spoils from the siege of Volterra. Federico was keen to learn new things, and two Arabic manuscripts reflect this. A Sicilian Jewish convert to Christianity, Guglielmo Raimondo Moncada, also known as Flavius Mithridates, translated parts of the Koran and Arab astrological texts at the duke's request. Urb. Lat. 1384 is a fascinating manuscript containing parallel text of several Arabic works, with Moncada's Latin translation.[31]

The location of the library within the palace is highly significant. The main door led from the courtyard, so Federico chose to locate his library on the ground floor of his residence, implying accessibility and a semi-public character for the collection. This reflects the fact that part of the purpose of a library was to display the owner's piety, wealth and scholarly disposition – the virtues that made him an ideal ruler. Visitors to the palace could easily enter and be shown round, and invited to admire the marvellous and beautiful books it contained. With so many illustrated codices in the collection, even visitors without a humanist education would find there was plenty to admire, and the sheer value of the collection would have been obvious to all.[32] The presiding *bibliotecario* was encouraged to exercise discretion, and size up his visitors' importance and likely level of sophistication: 'when ignorant or merely curious persons wish to see them, a glance is sufficient unless it is someone of considerable influence'. For visitors of high status, he was to handle the books himself, and keep them away from perhaps grubby fingers, but to show and explain them, emphasizing their value and beauty and the elegance of the handwriting, though keeping a sharp eye out for any attempt to steal individual leaves.[33] From about 1476 to 1480, this librarian was Lorenzo Abstemio, who was succeeded by Agapito, a Greek.

The physical organization of the books of the library at the time of Duke Federico's death is revealed by a poem by Federico Veterani, who worked for the library for many years, which was inscribed above the door in capitals:

SI CVPIS HIC POSITI QVONAM SINT ORDINE LIBRI
DISCERE, QVI TRANSIS, CARMINA PAVCA LEGE.
DEXTERA SACRORVM, IVRISQVE VOLVMINA SERVAT,
PHILOSOPHOS, PHYSICOS, NEC GEOMETER ABEST.
QVICQVID COSMOGRAPHI, QVICQVID SCRIPSERE POETAE,
HISTORICIQVE OMNES DAT TIBI LAEVA MANVS.[34]

'Visitor, if you want to understand what order the books are in, read this short poem. The right hand side serves for sacred writing and the volumes of the law, philosophers, doctors and geometers are also there. The left hand side gives all the writings of the geographers, the poets, and historians.'

Thus we can see that on entering the library, visitors would find Bibles, books of hours and so forth, plus Gregory, Jerome and Augustine, Justinian's *Digest* and its commentaries, Plato, Aristotle and Euclid on the shelves to their right, while Ptolemy, Virgil and Livy were on the left.[35] The great room is empty now, but it still has its original ceiling. An eagle, a Montefeltro badge, is displayed in the centre, with the letters F. D., Federigo Dux. It is surrounded by golden rays, and all over the ceiling little golden flames wiggle away from this refulgent centre. These are 'flames of love', the symbol of the Compagnia della Calza, an order of knights based in Venice, of which Federico had been made a member when he was eleven. Little flames like this often feature in Renaissance pictures of Pentecost, representing the inspiration of the Holy Spirit descending on the apostles. The resemblance is doubtless intentional, since divine wisdom was embodied in the books along the walls, but it is Federico, as patron of learning, who is the centre and inspiration.

The room had a table at the centre, and benches for scholars; to one end there was another table covered by a rug, probably for the staff to use, from whence they could exercise discreet supervision, find books for readers, or show people round.[36] The library was not shelved in the way we take for granted, since the manuscripts were mostly bound either in coloured velvet or in leather, and some of the bindings were decorated with filigree silver-work. Da Bisticci comments on the duke's attention to costly fine bindings: 'he began, as it has already been said, with the Bible, the most important [text] of all, and it is said that he had it covered with gold brocade. Then he had [the works of] each of the Church Doctors bound in crimson and decorated with silver.' Velvet, brocade and, even more, silver filigree would be extremely vulnerable to damage if the volumes routinely rubbed against each other. In fact, there were eight book cupboards, four down each of the long walls, each with seven shelves, on which the books were arranged in three or four piles according to their dimensions, not unlike the fictive books piled up in cupboards represented in the *studiolo*, though one suspects that the real ones were stored more tidily, with due care for their bindings. Another cupboard in the middle of the rear wall was modelled on a triumphal arch. Red underdrawings, executed by Francesco di Giorgio, are visible on the library walls, which record the original design and placement of these cupboards.[37] We know that one particularly valued manuscript, Ptolemy's *Geography*, was kept in a cedar-wood box, and other notably precious books might also have been similarly stored, the Renaissance equivalents of a modern librarian's Solander boxes.[38] Otherwise, the room contained an eagle lectern for public readings, tripods with copper braziers for heating the room, and three ladders.[39]

Part of the duty of the librarians, Abstemio, or later, Agapito, was to look after the books, but they were also scholars.[40] They were expected to identify gaps in the collection and source suitable copies, and copyists. After 1480, many manuscripts were written locally: it was often possible to borrow a rare book, copy it, and return it.[41] Especially after Florentine illuminators were attracted to Urbino by the prospect of steady work, Abstemio and Agapito seem to have been increasingly inclined to create books in their own workshop. One of the copyists working in Urbino itself was a man called Federico Veterani, who eventually took over as librarian *c.* 1520. He claimed that he had copied about sixty manuscripts for the library between about 1468 and 1482, in a precise humanist hand: twenty-nine of these still survive.[42] Sometimes he took his text from a printed book: the source of the Urbino copy of Sallust's history, which Veterani wrote in 1478/82 (Urb. Lat. 411), is the edition printed at Mantua by Johann Schallus in 1476–8, which was perhaps owned by Federico, and stored in the *guardaroba*. Veterani's manuscripts are lavishly ornamented with capitals and borders, very attractive to look at, but on closer inspection turn out to be riddled with errors. Though he could read Latin well, Federico does not seem to have been concerned about this. When the Florentine humanist and brilliant classical scholar Angelo Poliziano visited the library, his overall comment on the collection was that the standard of copying was poor, though he was pleased to be able to make a correction in the text of Juvenal from Federico's ninth-century Carolingian copy: it's now not considered to be a very important one, but it was better than any version available to Poliziano.[43]

Though Guidobaldo was only ten when his father died, he received a sound humanist education, supervised by his uncle Ottaviano Ubaldini, and once he reached adult years, he began adding to the library, though not very extensively, since his failing health meant that the principal source of the ducal income, condotte, dried up. When Ottaviano died in 1498, some of his books were absorbed into the Urbino library. He had had far more leisure to cultivate his scholarly tastes than had Duke Federico, and some of his manuscripts are exceptional, notably a collection of Solomonic texts, the present-day Urb. Lat. 548.

The first major setback to the library's development came in 1502–4, when Urbino was briefly conquered by Cesare Borgia. His soldiers stripped precious bindings from the books, and also stole some of them. When Duke Guidobaldo regained his kingdom, he found the remains of his library in fifty-nine cases stored in Forlì. About fifty manuscripts were missing, though in the years that followed a few of these were recovered. But Federico's spectacular copy of Petrarch, illuminated by Bartolomeo della Gatta of Umbria, is now in the Biblioteca Nacional, Madrid,[44] and there are stray volumes in other major libraries. A note by Leonardo da Vinci records that he researched where the library's copy of Archimedes, an author of particular interest to him, had got to: 'Archimedes in its entirety is at the home of the brothers of Monsignor di Sant'Augusta in Rome; he affirms that he has given it to his brother who lives in Sardinia. The works were before in the library of the Duke of Urbino; they were taken away in the time of Duke Valentino' (Cesare Borgia).[45] The manuscripts that went missing were replaced, for the most part, with printed books, indicating changed ducal priorities, perhaps the changing status of printing, and also the new duke's need to economize. In 1512, Francesco Maria della Rovere, Guidobaldo's successor, was granted the fiefdom of Pesaro, which had previously come under the rule of Giovanni Sforza, and as a result he acquired some of Sforza's books, which he added to the library. But another setback occurred in about 1516, when Francesco Maria della Rovere was forced to flee from Urbino. During this emergency, library treasures were deposited with the nuns of Santa Chiara in Urbino. When peace was restored, probably in 1520, the collection was returned again to the library building.

All the dukes valued the library, and continued to build the collection, but it was the first and last of them whose achievements as collectors were outstanding. The last duke was Francesco Maria II della Rovere, who died in 1631. He was a considerable scholar, and devoted himself to books. Owing to the vast expansion of European printing through the sixteenth century, it was very much easier for him to buy books. By 1631, there were two collections, a library of some 1,800 manuscripts, and tens of thousands of printed books. In 1613, Francesco Maria II acquired the autograph draft of the Urbino scholar Polydore Vergil's *History of England*, Urb. Lat. 497–8, a gift from Marcantonio Vergili Battiferri, the author's great-nephew.[46] Another acquisition of his that is of outstanding importance is the unique manuscript copy of Leonardo da Vinci's *Paragone*, an essay comparing the twin arts of painting and sculpture.[47] The manuscript, titled 'Libro di Pittura di M. Leonardo da Vinci, Pittore et Scultore Fiorentino', is a compilation made from da Vinci's original texts: internal evidence suggests that it was an attempt, soon after Leonardo's death, to make a selection from his various manuscripts for publication, though it did not actually reach print until the twentieth century.

In later life, Francesco Maria II preferred Castel Durante (present-day Urbania) to Urbino. However, he decided not to export Federico's book collection and risk denaturing it. Instead, he created a new library in Castel Durante.[48] He built an annex to the ducal palace at Castel Durante between 1607 and 1609 in order to house it. The furnishings of this library survive, and are now permanently in New York, 7 East 95th Street. They were designed by a young architect from Pesaro, Nicola Sabbatini (1574–1654), who would go on to become a theatrical designer, and the author of the most famous book on stage design of the early baroque, *How to Make Sets and Machinery for the Theatre*, published in 1638.[49] The shelving of the library is his first known project, and has an interesting history. After the books were moved to Rome in 1657, the library stood empty for years, and around 1870 Sabbatini's shelves were removed. The building itself was demolished in 1955; the shelves, however, had been sold as architectural salvage. In 1915 they were shipped to New York for use in the townhouse that Egisto Fabbri, a wealthy Italian-born banker and entrepreneur, was building for his brother Ernesto Fabbri and sister-in-law, Edith Shepard Vanderbilt Fabbri, where they remain to this day.

Since Francesco Maria II died childless, the duchy reverted to the Papal States in 1631. The library, however, was the duke's personal property, and he directed in his will that the city of Urbino was to have the manuscripts, while Castel Durante was to retain the printed books. However, in 1658, the rapacious collector Fabio Chigi, by then Pope Alexander VII, overrode his wishes and persuaded the citizens of Urbania to part with their books for 10,000 scudi, a very modest sum, because they would fill his own new library building, the Biblioteca Alessandrina, the library of the papal university, the Sapienza. In the course of January 1667, 13,0000 volumes were packed up and sent to Rome on the backs of eighty mules. At the same time, he moved the library of Duke Federico to the Vatican.[50] While high-handed, these were probably fortunate interventions, since, as a result, both collections survive substantially intact.

PART III

The Duchy after Federico

12

Guidobaldo

Like both his parents, Guidobaldo was not permitted much in the way of childhood. If we can believe Joos van Wassenhove's painting, he was expected to be able to sit through a lecture in Latin at the age of six or so without disgracing himself. The most constant presences in his young life were Pentasilea Baglioni, his foster mother; Ottaviano Ubaldini, his uncle; and his tutors, the first of whom seem to have been Lilio Tifernate and Giovanni Maria Filelfo. In 1482, the year of his father's death, the distinguished humanist Ludovico Odasio of Padua was called to Urbino as his principal teacher. Odasio pronounced Federico's funeral oration, and in the fullness of time would do the same by his former pupil.[1]

Ducal heirs have a tendency to be paragons of all the virtues, at least as far as written testimony is concerned, funeral orations above all. Odasio's description of Guidobaldo is duly hyperbolic, but suggests that the boy's temperament leant more towards Ottaviano than Federico. He was an apt pupil, and completely mastered Greek as well as Latin. This is confirmed by Pietro Bembo, who was impressed by the depth of his learning. As a boy, he particularly enjoyed poetry, but as he matured he started to prefer philosophy and ethics, and was also interested in geography. He had a good memory.[2] He was also taught how to ride and fight, in the expectation that he, like his father, would bring wealth to Urbino as a condottiere.

The situation he and Ottaviano faced after Federico's death was not an easy one. Despite their earlier ties of friendship, Federico had died fighting against Sixtus IV, so the pope was not likely to view his heir with much sympathy. Lorenzo de' Medici actually owed Federico a good deal, but was not very likely to acknowledge as much, in the circumstances. The Malatesti of Rimini, at least, were not in a position to take advantage, since Roberto Malatesta died on the same night as Federico, and his illegitimate son Pandolfo was only seven, even younger than Guidobaldo.

Guidobaldo was invested with his dukedom on 17 September 1482, and proceeded to tour Gubbio and other principal towns, receiving the homage of his subjects, and making a good impression wherever he went. He was a long-nosed, solemn-faced child, with a thick mop of blond hair, which later darkened to brown, and if we can believe Bartolomeo della Gatta, he had heavy-lidded eyes that gave him a rather sleepy expression. His education, like his mother's, had laid stress on public speaking, so even aged ten he could react appropriately to loyal addresses and speeches of welcome.

News even more welcome came from the coalition of Naples, Florence and Milan, in whose service Federico had died: they transferred Federico's condotta to his son. Meanwhile, little Pandolfo Malatesta in Rimini was similarly invested with his father's status as captain of the Venetian and papal forces. Since the war was a stalemate, this was a temporary measure. Sixtus IV sought a reconciliation with Ferrante of Naples, and they signed a peace treaty on 6 January 1483. The Venetians were not best pleased, but a further peace treaty signed between Venice and Milan the following year brought hostilities to an end, with some gains to the Venetian Republic. Sixtus IV died in August 1484, shortly after receiving the news, and was succeeded by Giovanni Battista Cibo, who took the name of Innocent VIII.

Guidobaldo received another condotta from the new pope, who had quarrelled with Ferrante of Naples. Urbinate troops were sent to Innocent's assistance, but the first time they went forth led by Guidobaldo himself was in 1488, when he was fifteen. At this time also, letters from the papal court started to be addressed to Guidobaldo himself rather than to Ottaviano, so he had evidently come of age.

One interesting document gives a suggestion of life at the palace early in the reign of Guidobaldo, which continued to be lived with the grave decorum instituted by Federico. There was evidently no risk of Guidobaldo repeating the mistakes of Oddantonio. All court officials had to be competent, to be clean in their ways, and wash their hands frequently. Anyone who developed bad breath had to report to a doctor. Food was simple, even at the duke's table, and Guidobaldo's only vice, if you can call it that, seems to have been a marked liking for fruit.[3]

Inevitably, Guidobaldo married young. He had been betrothed to Ferrante's daughter Lucrezia of Aragon since 1474. Ferrante had agreed to the match when bestowing the Order of the Ermine on Federico. In the 1480s, Guidobaldo looked like less of a prospect for an Aragonese princess, even an illegitimate one, and the engagement fizzled out. Lucrezia married Onorato III, prince of Altamura, and Ottaviano looked elsewhere. He chose a girl from another condottiere lineage, Elisabetta Gonzaga, youngest sister of Francesco, Marquis of Mantua. The Gonzagas were a clever family, but not a beautiful one, though Elisabetta seems to have been one of the more attractive of the girls. Like all Gonzaga women, she had been given an excellent education. She studied with Antonio da Verona and with the leading humanist Giovanni Maria Filelfo until his death in 1480, and thereafter with Columbino da Verona. Her manners and virtues were widely praised. She was a year older than Guidobaldo, having been born on 9 February 1471.

In the same negotiations, her sister Maddalena was betrothed to Giovanni Sforza, lord of Pesaro, who had succeeded Guidobaldo's uncle Costanzo Sforza in 1483, co-ruling with his stepmother Camilla d'Aragona. The winter journey through the Montefeltro hills to Urbino was cold and uncomfortable, and Elisabetta was homesick. Aristocratic marriages tended to take place in the run-up to Lent, to save money, since the preparations doubled as carnival celebrations, though this could be hard on the bride. However, she was heartily welcomed. In a letter to Francesco Gonzaga, Benedetto Capilupo, who was a member of her entourage, describes being received by a series of allegorical pageants and other entertainments as they passed through the various towns of Guidobaldo's territory. For example, they were met by a magnificent triumphal pageant at Castel Durante (modern Urbania): twelve life-size temporary triumphal arches, two of them with fountains spouting water. Actors dressed as Scipio, Caesar and the deceased Federico rode in a triumphal cart driven by centurions, and Federico was flanked by an angel and a sibyl.[4] Elisabetta's future intimate friend Emilia Pia, married to Federico's illegitimate son Antonio, was among the people who came out to welcome her.

Guidobaldo and Elisabetta were married on 11 February 1488 in the church of San Francesco in Urbino. The festivities were crowned with a dramatic poem by Raphael's father, Giovanni Santi, in which all the gods and goddesses of Olympus came down to welcome the new bride; she describes all this in her letters home. She arrived with a sumptuous wardrobe, a settlement of 26,000 ducats, and an additional dowry of jewels, gold and silverware.[5] She owned a necklace with thirteen diamonds, fourteen rubies, and fifty-two pearls; a pendant with a sapphire and a large pearl; a choker with seventeen balas rubies and fifty-one pearls; three brooches with diamonds, rubies and large pearls; and a collection of 300 small pearls and 500 large ones to be used to ornament future dresses. A *cassone* now in the Victoria and Albert Museum is probably one of her wedding chests, since it has the arms of Gonzaga impaled with Montefeltro as well as various family devices. Elisabetta enjoyed hunting, so the young couple paid visits to the deer parks at Fossombrone and Castel Durante. She was a girl of cheerful and sanguine temperament, more outgoing than the rather grave Guidobaldo, who seems to have been somewhat oppressed by the weight of expectations placed on him from birth.

As it turned out, the new young duchess needed all the cheerfulness she could muster. Despite their long honeymoon, and a learned intervention from Ottaviano Ubaldini, who produced an astrological argument for the most auspicious date on which to consummate the marriage, it turned out that Guidobaldo was unable to consummate it at all. Pietro Bembo's *Dialogue* on the duke and duchess, composed *c.* 1509–10, declared, 'the lord Guidobaldo either through a physical defect of nature, or as people believed, impeded by the magical arts of his uncle Ottaviano, who desired the kingdom and was extremely skilled in all science, was never able at any time of his life to have carnal knowledge of a woman or to consummate his marriage'.[6] The Venetian diarist Marin Sanudo noted in 1502 that Elisabetta Gonzaga had confided in him, and commented that she had come to think of Guidobaldo as a brother.[7] In the circumstances, the bawdy jokes and comments a Renaissance bride would face – openly expressed wishes to see her dresses getting tighter and so forth – must have been hard to put up with. It cannot have helped that her sister Maddalena, who lived near enough to visit, fell pregnant after two months of marriage, but died in childbirth in 1490, having survived less than a year of married life. However, also in 1490, Giovanni della Rovere and his wife, Guidobaldo's sister Giovanna, produced a healthy son, whom they named Francesco Maria, a name most probably dictated by their devotion to the Franciscan order. In default of a natural heir, this child, Federico's grandson, would eventually be adopted by Guidobaldo and his virgin bride.

One person who must have taken a keen interest in the succession question is the young duke's illegitimate half-brother,

Antonio, since he seems to have put himself hopefully forward when Federico was on his deathbed. He more or less disappears from the historical record after 1482, apart from the fact that in 1487 he married Emilia Pio di Carpi, the daughter of a minor nobleman, who would become Elisabetta Gonzaga's closest friend in Urbino. She was another literate humanist, who had studied with Giovanni della Porta, and wrote good Latin.[8] But Antonio was no more successful than Guidobaldo in leaving an heir. The ducal couple might well have turned to his family if he had had a son, since he carried the Montefeltro name, but he was unsuccessful even as a dynast. Though Antonio received condotte in his father's lifetime (he was fighting for the Sienese in 1478, and as a subordinate to Federico in 1482), there is no indication that he carved out an independent career for himself, which may explain why his father took rather a dim view of him. He fades out of history as an inglorious also-ran, and he died at Gubbio in 1500.

Guidobaldo's problem actually seems to have been early-onset gout rather than sorcery. Gout is a hereditary condition, and Federico had been afflicted by it in his day. Antonio was also a sufferer. It predisposes the sufferer to erectile dysfunction, which seems to have been the first symptom Guidobaldo experienced. The first major attack came in 1493, the second when he was on a condotta in 1499. Thereafter, the attacks got worse and more frequent until by 1507 he was bed-bound, and he died in 1508. There is a portrait, uncertainly attributed to Raphael, that shows him pale and tired-looking, dated to 1506, when he was already very ill. Two doctors, who examined this painting with diagnostics in mind, thought they saw uric acid deposits in the whites of both eyes.[9] The education and the training in statecraft and the art of war were thus made useless by a disastrous genetic heritage.

Bembo also says that Guidobaldo was a virgin when he married, and attributes this to Ottaviano's malign influence. It seems perfectly possible that the black legend of Federico's predecessor, the profligate Oddantonio, may have caused Ottaviano to discourage his young ward from sexual experiment; but in any case, the life of the court was conducted with strict decorum: it was not the kind of place where young courtiers romped with the maidservants. The suspicion of Ottaviano voiced here as common gossip probably had as its immediate cause the latter's learned fussing about with horoscopes. Also probably contributory is that Ottaviano had the unenviable task of sweeping up after the high-spending reign of Federico, which in its last decade had been glorious as never before. He must have cut unnecessary expenditures, dismissed servants, turned a deaf ear to ingenious humanists and driven hard bargains, in the knowledge that the money flowing into the duchy would reduce and reduce until Guidobaldo proved himself. The palace must have started looking rather worn and shabby: an inventory made around 1494 notes that two chairs in Guidobaldo's own room had tattered covers.[10] It would be very easy to think that Ottaviano was letting everything go out of jealousy and spite, not out of loyalty. Similarly, discouraging Guidobaldo from possibly complicating the succession by begetting bastards seems, from this distance, simple prudence. After all, since the boy was only sixteen when he married, he was not being asked for heroic self-restraint. That he was not capable of rising to the challenge at all was a disaster nobody could have anticipated.

In 1492, Innocent VIII died, and was succeeded by one of the most notorious of all Renaissance popes, Alexander VI, born Rodrigo Borgia, a Spaniard. He was not the first Borgia pope, since his uncle had held the papal see in the 1450s as Callixtus III. In the intervening forty years, Rodrigo had embedded himself deep in Vatican power structures, and made a great deal of money. Ottaviano Ubaldini apparently commented, 'Judas sold Christ for thirty denarii. This man would sell him for twenty-nine.'[11] He also took several mistresses, and was quite unabashed about his unofficial family, or families: he was the father of eight or possibly nine children, by three different mothers. After the initial bout of bellicosity that had caused Innocent to retain Guidobaldo, the pope had lived up to his name and refrained from further war-making, so Italy had been fairly peaceful for a few years. Under Alexander VI, that would change. He made his son Juan Duke of Gandia, and carved out fiefs for Juan and his brother Jofré from the Papal States and the kingdom of Naples. This inevitably brought him into conflict with Ferrante of Naples, as did the fact that Ferrante had backed Sixtus IV's nephew Giuliano della Rovere when the papacy became vacant.

Ferrante allied himself with Florence, Milan and Venice, giving Alexander enemies both to his north and his south. He therefore looked outside Italy for help, to Charles VII of France, whom he hoped would deal with Ferrante for him. The Aragonese kings of Naples had seized control of southern Italy after the death of Joanna, last ruler of the Angevin dynasty, which had preceded them, but the French kings continued to think they had a superior claim. Charles could therefore be tempted into intervening in Italian politics. Another factor was that Ludovico 'il Moro' Sforza could be tempted to break with the other northern Italian powers because he had set aside the rightful ruler, his nephew Gian Galeazzo. He was desperate for legitimation, which he thought could be achieved with the help of the French king. Ferrante died in January 1494, succeeded by his son Alfonso II, and the French sensed advantage. Charles crossed the Alps with 25,000 men, and joined Ludovico in Milan. Alexander was forced to come to terms with Charles, who passed through the Papal States and conquered Naples with surprising ease. Italy was plunged into a new series of wars – which would last into the 1560s – and lost its independence, which it did not regain until the Risorgimento of the nineteenth century. The new Duke of Urbino could play no very active part in these developments. By the time the French conquered Naples, he was getting too ill to fight.

One excitement in the Urbino of 1495 was that Adriano de' Maestri, a well-known sculptor and medal-maker, visited the city. In a letter to her brother written in May that year, Elisabetta

Gonzaga heartily recommended him, saying that he had made some beautiful medals during a three-month stay at Urbino, and had also been amusing to have about because he wrote sonnets and was a good lyre player. Since he subsequently moved to Mantua, the recommendation was taken up. While in Urbino, he made a medal of Elisabetta, in left profile, with her hair pulled back and tied into a long bag called a *coazzone*. An embroidered coif covers the back of her head and ends in the *coazzone*, which is secured by a jewelled headband called a *lenza*. This hairstyle was very fashionable in the early 1490s. The reverse, as always with medals, is enigmatic. A nude woman lies supine with only a scarf protecting her modesty. She holds a bridle in her left hand, a symbol of restraint and discipline, while a source of fire, perhaps the sun, blazes away above her. This seems to allude to the myth of Danaë, seduced by Zeus in the form of a shower of gold. The motto is 'this you might call fleeting fortune'.[12] The figure is a piece of learned antiquarianism, because it is modelled on the semi-nude figure of the Vestal Virgin Rhea Silvia, mother of Romulus and Remus, as she appears on a Roman sarcophagus that was then in the church of St John Lateran in Rome. The flame-like appearance of the shower of gold evokes the flames that are a frequent Montefeltro device.

In the fifteenth century, Danaë was considered a type of the Virgin Mary, and so the medal must allude to Elisabetta's combination of frustration at her childlessness and loyalty to her husband. Rhea was similarly a virgin, impregnated by the god Mars. It seems to say that although she would not break her marriage vows (symbolized by the bridle), if, like the Virgin Mary, Rhea or Danaë, Elisabetta became mysteriously pregnant through the action of a god, she would eagerly embrace this.[13] Bembo describes Elisabetta as 'golden virgin', perhaps because he was familiar with this medal.[14] Emilia Pia also commissioned one. The reverse shows a tall thin pyramid, based on the pyramid-mausoleum of Gaius Cestius, a Roman landmark, with a funerary urn on top of it, and the motto 'to chaste ashes', meaning that she would remain faithful to her husband until her dying day. Neither Antonio nor Guidobaldo seem to have commissioned medals from Adriano. The only medal known for Guidobaldo is one that shows him as a young boy, probably cast to celebrate his becoming duke, aged ten.

It has been suggested that a painting also dating from around 1496 might possibly be a portrait of Guidobaldo before his health failed. The name of Jacopo de' Barbari, a collaborator of Leonardo da Vinci, appears in a *cartellino* on the table, so the painting is probably his. The principal subject is Fra Luca Pacioli, a distinguished mathematician whose book *Summary of arithmetic, geometry, proportions and proportionality* was published in 1494 and much used by artists interested in perspective, including Leonardo. It was dedicated to Guidobaldo, who, like his father, was interested in mathematics; he was also the dedicatee of Piero della Francesca's *On the Five Regular Solids*, and the competing 1505 and 1509 printed editions of Euclid.[15] A well-dressed young man stands at Fra Luca's side, who could be Guidobaldo, though his hair seems to be chestnut and wavy, and in all other representations of the duke, it is straight. He has a long nose, but otherwise looks very different from the thin, tired, hollow-eyed young man with lank brown locks depicted in 1506. If it is the young duke, who was described by contemporaries as very handsome, then illness and suffering wrought a terrible transformation in his appearance. However, there is nothing to indicate that it is him, no Montefeltro insignia or emblems, and Nick Mackinnon has suggested that it in fact represents the long-nosed and curly-haired Albrecht Dürer, a keen student of perspective who travelled in Italy.[16] Pacioli is in the act of explaining Euclid's *Elements* XIV.8, with a copy of the 1482 edition of Euclid open at Book XIII.12.[17] They are standing in front of a table filled with geometrical tools: slate, chalk, compass, a dodecahedron model. A glass model of a regular solid called a rhombicuboctahedron, half-filled with water, is suspended from the ceiling. The painting was in Urbino by 1582, since it is described by the Urbino historian Bernardino Baldi (he does not suggest that the student is a portrait of Guidobaldo).

> In the wardrobe of our most serene princes of Urbino is conserved, by the hand of Pietro de Franceschi, Pacioli's countryman and excellent painter and perspective expert, a naturalistic portrait of this friar, his book, the Summa arithmetica, in front of him and several fictive crystals in the form of regular solids suspended from up high; from the lines, reflections, and shadows of these crystals one discovers how accomplished a painter Piero was.[18]

The association of Piero with Pacioli is a natural assumption since they both came from Borgo Sansepolcro.

Another side of the intellectual life of the court is shown by the early career of the humanist Polydore Vergil. He was probably in the duke's service before 1498, since in the dedication of his *Proverbiorum Libellus* (April 1498) he styles himself Guidobaldo's client. His earliest known work was an edition of Niccolò Perotti's *Cornucopia*, a commentary on Martial, from a manuscript in Federico's library. His second book, *On Those Who Invent Things* (*De Inventoribus Rerum*), was dedicated to Guidobaldo's tutor, Lodovico Odasio, in August 1499, and again made extensive use of the ducal library. The book broke new ground in its rationalistic approach to origins, and proved immensely popular. He transferred to papal service at some point before 1502, since he appears in England that year as the deputy of Cardinal Adriano Castelli, collecting the papal tax known as 'Peter's Pence'. He settled in England, where, as an Italian humanist, he found himself welcome at the court of Henry VII, and was thus a link between the Urbino and English courts. With the king's encouragement, he began an English history: the first draft of this, written 1512–13 in Polydore's own italic hand, was presented to Francesco Maria della Rovere II in 1613 by Marcantonio Vergilio-Battiferri, a great-nephew of the author.[19]

In 1496, Guidobaldo was still trying to fight as a condottiere, despite his poor health. He was hired by Alexander VI, who had picked a fight with the Orsini, an old Roman family with extensive landholdings that would come in useful for dowering his own children. He raised an army led by his son the Duke of Gandia, supported by Guidobaldo and Fabrizio Colonna. The campaign opened in October 1496, and for three months fighting continued with no clear benefit to either side. Guidobaldo received a gunshot wound. In January, he was pursuing the Orsini's forces in the direction of Viterbo when they were successfully ambushed: their artillery train was captured, and so was Guidobaldo. He was taken to Soriano, an Orsini castle, while negotiations were opened. He was not released until his duchess produced a ransom of 30,000 ducats, raised by the sale of her jewellery and contributions from leading citizens of Urbino.[20]

In 1498, Guidobaldo recouped some of his losses with a condotta of 20,000 scudi to fight on behalf of Venice, which was supporting Pisa in a small war with the Florentines. He went into winter quarters in Bibbiena, and was cut off and besieged by the enemy forces. His health gave way under the strain, and in the middle of February, Paolo Vitelli, commander of the Florentine army, gave him free passage home to Urbino as an act of charity. One positive outcome of this rather miserable episode is that he got to know Cardinal Giuliano della Rovere, who was, by temperament, a warrior rather than a man of God, and had sat through the siege of Bibbiena with him. Guidobaldo shared his worries about the succession to Urbino with the cardinal, who suggested that the answer was to adopt his nephew, Francesco Maria della Rovere, who was the cardinal's nephew also.

That summer, he visited Venice, as Marino Sanudo noted in his diary: 'a handsome man, dressed in black after the French fashion, as were all his attendants, on account of the death of his uncle Ottaviano Ubaldini, who had long governed both the state and the duke'.[21] He was given a condotta worth 27,000 ducats, but with the understanding that he would no longer lead his forces in person. Sanudo notes that he did not dance at a ball given in his honour, which suggests that his health was broken.

A sense of grim desperation hangs over the dukedom of Guidobaldo. He had the willpower to be a good duke, evident from the courage with which he took on condotte even while his health was giving out. He was virtuous, he had an appropriate education, and a loyal and intelligent wife, but in a world where a duke had to be a man of action, he was forced into a role for which he was physically unsuited. And his inability to beget a son was even more of a problem than it had been for his father, since for Federico, illegitimate sons and a string of legitimate daughters bore witness to his potency. The complete absence of any heir of Guidobaldo's body, legitimate or otherwise, began to attract attention from predators, in particular Pope Alexander VI and his children.

Another major festivity took place in Urbino in January 1501, the arrival of the pope's daughter Lucrezia Borgia, on her way to marry Alfonso d'Este, Duke of Ferrara (her third husband). She brought 2,000 attendants and 150 horses, and the entertainment cost Guidobaldo about 8,000 ducats he could ill afford. In November, Giovanni della Rovere, Prefect of Rome, died, and Francesco Maria, then twelve, was brought to Urbino, while his mother was left to rule Senigallia on his behalf. Alexander VI confirmed him in his father's title of Prefect of Rome. Meanwhile, Duchess Elisabetta was travelling. Having attended Lucrezia to her new home in Ferrara, she, her close friend and sister-in-law Isabella d'Este, and Emilia Pia, who had recently lost her husband, all went to Venice for an informal visit. After Venice, they went to Verona, and then back with Isabella to her palace in Mantua.

Guidobaldo received a surprise gift early in 1502 from Lucrezia's brother Cesare: one of Michelangelo's earliest known sculptures, his celebrated forgery, the 'Sleeping Cupid', whose first purchaser believed it was a genuine Roman antique. He returned it to the dealer, Baldassare del Milanese, when he realized his error;

and while Michelangelo shot to fame on the basis of the story, Baldassare resold it, as a modern piece, to Cesare, who gave it to Guidobaldo.[22] Cesare had not the slightest interest in the arts, so this, like Lucrezia's visit and the favour shown to Elisabetta Gonzaga, looks like part of a Borgia charm offensive.

Guidobaldo would have been wise to suspect that he was being set up, since only weeks later he appeared in Mantua, a desperate, penniless fugitive with nothing but the clothes he stood up in. He was in exile. Alexander VI had been thinking for a while how to create a suitably lavish endowment for his son Cesare, and decided that the way to do it was to build him a power base in the Marche as Duke of Romagna. The fact that this would result in the permanent alienation of most of the Papal States and impoverish the popes of the future doesn't seem to have bothered Alexander, who was more concerned with providing for his family than with the fortunes of the papacy. In 1500, Cesare began the overthrow of the semi-independent papal vicars of the Romagna. He took Pesaro without a shot being fired, and in Rimini, Sigismondo's grandson, 'Pandolfaccio' (Bad Pandolfo) Malatesta had made himself so loathed that his people abandoned him before Cesare even appeared. With the excuse that Camerino was defying his authority, Cesare asked permission from Guidobaldo to send his artillery through the duchy, since it was an easier road than the direct one to Camerino. Having secured Guidobaldo's consent, he sent 2,000 men from his main army in a forced march up the Via Flaminia, while some of his Romagnol troops were sent to converge on Urbino from the opposite direction, and achieved a complete tactical surprise.[23] Guidobaldo managed to escape, and got himself to Mantua after a difficult and devious journey, hotly pursued by Borgia partisans. At one point, his chamberlain deliberately fell behind and let himself be captured, pretending to be the duke, which bought him some time. As Guidobaldo wrote from Mantua to Cardinal Giuliano della Rovere on 28 June, 'I have saved nothing but my life, a doublet and a shirt.' At the time, he knew nothing about what had happened to Francesco Maria, who had taken a different route out of Urbino, so he was worried sick, but in fact the boy was also safe. Guidobaldo and Elisabetta then made their way to Venice, where they were given a palazzo and thirty pounds of gold a month as a pension.

Alexander VI made it known that Guidobaldo was impotent, in the hope that he would agree to annul the marriage and accept a cardinal's hat and a pension in exchange for his duchy, thus legitimizing Cesare's usurpation, while Elisabetta could be found another husband. He announced this as a done deal in Rome on 20 August 1502, presumably hoping that the embarrassment would make the ducal pair fall into line with his intentions: 'The pontiff is content to annul the marriage of the duke due to his impotence, and make him a cardinal. The wife is giving herself to a baron in France.'[24] But Guidobaldo refused, and Elisabetta was firm in her loyalty, for which she was greatly admired.[25]

Meanwhile, in Urbino, Cesare continued to hold the city. He took the precaution of invading the convent of Santa Chiara and kidnapping Guidobaldo's sister, the former Elisabetta Malatesta, as a hostage. Several of his captains then conspired with Guidobaldo to help him retake the city, which he succeeded in doing in October, and in the exchange of prisoners that followed, Elisabetta was allowed to return to her convent. However, in December, Cesare convinced his captains to rejoin him and regained control of the city. He did not forgive or forget, however. According to the chronicler Paolo Giovio, Cesare deceived the men into believing he bore them no ill will for their temporary change of allegiance, then captured them and imprisoned them in Senigallia – and had them garrotted on 1 January 1503.[26] He also rounded up the silver, tapestry, books and valuables from the palace at Urbino, and carted them off to his fortress at Forlì. Marino Sanudo reckoned the total value of the duke's movable possessions was 150,000 ducats, and the transport of goods reportedly employed 180 pack mules per day for an entire month.

After his failure, Guidobaldo then returned miserably to Venice, and the life of a pensioner. Despite her long and close friendship with Elisabetta Gonzaga, Isabella d'Este was sufficiently unscrupulous to write immediately to her cardinal brother Ippolito asking him to intercede with Cesare to let her have Michelangelo's Cupid, and a statue of Venus that she also coveted. She received them in July.[27] On 31 January 1503, Timoteo Viti, the principal Montefeltro court painter (a position he obtained after the death of Raphael's father, Giovanni Santi, in 1494), was paid to paint Cesare Borgia's coat of arms on the palace of the priors and the city gate.[28] But the young Borgia did not enjoy his conquest for long. On 18 August 1503, both Alexander VI and Cesare went down with malarial fever in Rome. Alexander died, and Cesare was so ill he was incapable of taking immediate action to secure his position. Since the Borgias were widely loathed, his downfall was therefore only a matter of time. The family were powerful enough in Rome to secure the election of a pro-Borgia pope, who took the title of Pius III, but unfortunately for Cesare he died after a mere twenty-six days. The next time round, the cardinals elected Giuliano della Rovere, the 'Warrior Pope', Julius II, inveterate enemy of the Borgias, and partisan of Guidobaldo on account of their common nephew, Francesco Maria della Rovere.

When Guidobaldo got the news, he set out to reclaim his duchy, with the power of Venice and the goodwill of the pope behind him. Elisabetta, left behind in Venice, went into the signoria on 10 October to make a formal speech of thanks, and spoke to them again on 15 November, the day before she left for home.[29] Cesare lost control of his cities in the Romagna while he was sweating out his fever in the Borgia stronghold in Nepi. Weeks later, he returned to lead the papal armies, but his duchy of Romagna was falling to pieces. Julius II imprisoned him at Ostia in November, and before the end of 1503, Guidobaldo had reclaimed the entire duchy of Urbino. Cesare was a spent force; he was sent to a Spanish prison, escaped, and died in an ambush in 1507, aged thirty-one.

In November 1503, Guidobaldo was in Rome sorting out the details of his reinstatement with Julius II. There he met up with his heir, Francesco Maria della Rovere. Guidobaldo was named gonfaloniere of the Church, with a year's pay of 7,000 ducats, paid in advance. He also acquired a new follower, Baldassare Castiglione. Castiglione had been a courtier in Mantua, serving Francesco Gonzaga, and had met the Montefeltri while they were there. By mutual agreement, he transferred his service to the Duke and Duchess of Urbino. His first service was going to London as proxy for the duke, who, like his father, had been invested with the Order of the Garter by Henry VII: the reason, almost certainly, was that Guidobaldo was known to be a protégé of the new della Rovere pope, and Henry, like Edward IV, when he conferred the same honour on Federico, thought he would be a useful advocate at the papal court. He took a variety of presents with him, horses and falcons for the king, and the first painting by Raphael ever to reach England, a St George and the Dragon. The painting was probably given to Sir Gilbert Talbot by Castiglione on his way to London via Calais, where Talbot was Lord Deputy, in recognition of Talbot's role as the Garter Knight sent to Rome in 1504 to invest Guidobaldo as a Knight of the Order of the Garter. It was inherited by the Herbert family, probably when the third Earl of Pembroke married Mary Talbot, since the fourth earl owned it in the 1620s, and swopped it with Charles I for a book of drawings by Holbein.[30] This suggests the different priorities of the England of 1500 and 1600: in Henry VII's day, Italian horses were deemed much more valuable and interesting than Italian pictures. It was only in the seventeenth century that English priorities changed.

On 2 December 1503, Julius II held an audience with Guidobaldo and Cesare in order to negotiate the return of Urbino's looted treasures and library. According to an anonymous chronicler, Cesare threw himself at Guidobaldo's feet, begged for mercy, and blamed his father, Pope Alexander.[31] Almost everything was returned, except for stuff that had found its way into soldiers' knapsacks (which is why, for example, Federico's magnificent copy of Petrarch's *Trionfi* is in the Biblioteca Nacional in Madrid), and the famous Troy tapestries, which he had given to Georges d'Amboise, from whom they had to be retrieved. That same day, Duchess Elisabetta Gonzaga returned to Urbino from exile with her family in Mantua. One wonders quite how her cupidinous sister-in-law had explained away the appearance of the Roman Venus, a statue Elisabetta would have known well, and the Michelangelo sleeping cupid, in her own *studiolo* – she never did give them back.

The Mantuan ambassador reported that a thanksgiving Mass was celebrated in the cathedral: 'Bishop Arrivabene came before everyone, adorned ecclesiastically. He took Our Lady Duchess by the hand and went to kneel before the high altar, where all the clergy was, and they began to sing Te Deum Laudamus.'[32] While Castiglione was in England, Guidobaldo and his heir made their way home and found Elisabetta and Emilia Pia established there. His restoration was also celebrated with a play that crowed over their fallen enemies; *The Comedy of Pope Alexander VI*. The anonymous dramatist presented the various plots of the Borgias to overthrow the duchy, concluding with the death of the pope, and Guidobaldo's triumphal return.[33]

Meanwhile, Francesco Maria's mother, Giovanna della Rovere, went to Rome. She arrived there on 18 March 1504. She had gone to press the claim of Francesco Maria to be heir to the duchy of Urbino. Though this was his own intention, Julius II disliked being pressured. She was still governing Senigallia on her son's behalf, though when he came of age, Julius insisted that she step down, calling her an insolent fool: it sounds as if her nagging had annoyed him considerably.[34]

One indication of the impact of Cesare's usurpation is that books lost from the library were not replaced by expensive fine manuscripts, but by printed volumes. This partly reflects financial retrenchment, but also the fact that the status of print was changing and printed books were becoming much more widespread. Urbino even acquired a press of its own in the 1490s, run by a German, Heinrich of Cologne. Other towns in the dukedom also developed presses in this period. Among the most interesting ventures are the Hebrew publishing house of Gershom Soncino, who printed in Pesaro from 1507 to 1520, and the press of Gregorius de Gregoriis, a Venetian, which was established at Fano, and printed the first ever book in Arabic characters using movable type.[35] Ottaviano Petrucci, who was born at Fossombrone and educated at Urbino, went to Venice and developed a much-improved methodology for printing music. In 1498 he petitioned the doge for the exclusive right to print music for the next twenty years. This was probably granted, since no examples of printed music from other Venetian printers are known before 1520. Once the twenty years were up, he returned to Fossombrone, where he received the patronage of Francesco Maria I della Rovere. This was an important development, since the effective printing of music made it vastly easier for musical fashions to travel around Europe, leading to the Franco-Flemish polyphonic style becoming an international musical language, and contributing to the increasing importance of music as an art form in the sixteenth century.

Another remarkable talent who was born in Urbino in this period is Raphael, the son of the courtier Giovanni Santi, also a painter – and author of a lengthy chronicle of Guidobaldo's father. His son's first documented work dates from 1501, for a church in Città de Castello, near Urbino. He moved around northern Italy for some years, absorbing influences. The ducal family were early patrons: Federico's daughter Giovanna della Rovere wrote a letter of recommendation for him to the gonfaloniere of Florence, dated October 1504: 'The bearer of this will be found to be Raphael, painter of Urbino, who, being greatly gifted in his profession has determined to spend some time in Florence to study. And because his father was most worthy and I was very attached to him, and the son is a sensible and well-mannered young man, on both accounts, I bear him great love…'[36] He moved to Rome in 1508, and worked there for the rest of his short life. Before he did so, Guidobaldo and Elisabetta sat for their portraits around 1505/6. Both portraits are frontal. Conventions had changed since the 1480s, and profiles were no longer *de rigueur*, though facing straight forwards was an unusual choice. Elisabetta's gown is in the heraldic colours of the Montefeltri, black velvet with gold stripes. A headband is visible, so she was probably still wearing her back hair in a *coazzone*. Though she faces forward, her eyes are cast down, so she does not engage with the viewer's gaze. The strangest aspect of the portrait is that the band is ornamented with a small black scorpion, perhaps of enamelled gold, since it is holding a gem in its claws. According to the theory developed by Ptolemy, and widely circulated through the Middle Ages, that each astrological sign governed a particular part of the body, Scorpio is associated with the genitalia, suggesting that Elisabetta, who was only in her early thirties, was still hoping against hope.[37] Another curious feature of the portraits is that Elisabetta was portrayed in front of a mountainous landscape, and Guidobaldo in an interior; a reversal of the usual association of women with inner, men with outer, life, and perhaps an acknowledgement of Guidobaldo's invalidism. A third possible Raphael from around this time, known as *Young Man with an Apple*, is probably a portrait of Francesco Maria della Rovere, aged fifteen to sixteen. He is posed against an ideal landscape and richly dressed, but apart from the apple, there are no props to suggest anything about the young man's character or preoccupations.[38]

A painting by Timoteo Viti, commissioned by Giovanni Arrivabene, bishop of Urbino, for his burial chapel in 1504, is a pictorial witness to the trauma of Cesare Borgia's usurpation. Arrivabene died shortly after the restoration, and left instructions for the building of the chapel and its altarpiece in his will, asking the duchess to act as his executor. The theme of this painting is unusual: it shows St Thomas à Becket and St Martin of Tours seated together, with two donors, one of them the bishop himself, and the other probably his nephew and heir, Giacomo Arrivabene.[39]

He presumably chose St Thomas because the saint had famously defied Henry II of England, and Arrivabene wished to draw a parallel with his own resistance to the rule of Cesare Borgia. He chose St Martin to accompany him, because the principal Borgia emblem was a bull, and St Martin is one of very few saints who can in any way be associated with disciplining cattle, one of his miracles being the exorcism of a demon from a cow.

After all this, life in Urbino, under the powerful protection of Julius II, settled down again. It is these few years that are the scene for Castiglione's *Book of the Courtier*; its backdrop, a peaceful domestic life with a group of congenial friends, and a semi-invalid duke. Castiglione created his first evocation of Urbino in a pastoral eclogue, *Tirsi,* performed during Carnival in 1506, which was a tremendous success.[40] He tells us that the idea for the *Courtier* came to him when he was still living in Urbino in the service of Francesco Maria della Rovere, after Guidobaldo's death. He wrote the first draft in odd moments between 1508 and 1516, and finished it when he was at home with his wife in 1516–18. He might have gone on tinkering with it indefinitely, but according to his preface he lent a draft to Vittoria Colonna, who was not only an admired poet but Battista Sforza's granddaughter and Guidobaldo's niece, and discovered that she was having copies made and circulating them. In order to keep control over his own text, he was forced to publish a final revised version.

The Courtier is profoundly a book about nostalgia. As its modern English translator says, 'when *The Courtier* was finally published… the world of ideas and institutions which it idealised was, as far as Italy was concerned, and as Castiglione well knew, buried in the past'.[41] The nostalgic tone of Castiglione's dialogue is set by its opening, in which he reflects on the dramatis personae who have since died: 'what should not be recounted without tears is that the Duchess herself is dead; and if I am so distraught through the loss of all the noble friends I have mentioned that I seem to be living in a desert of solitude and misery, it is no wonder that my grief over

her death is more bitter still'.[42] His evocation of the past is linked
with a visit from Julius II. The pope and his entourage stayed at
Urbino for several days in September 1506, en route to Bologna,
and again on 3 March 1507, on his way back to Rome. On both
occasions, the duke and duchess went to great lengths to receive
him with suitable magnificence. The palace was a little shabby:
it was almost a quarter of a century since the death of Federico,
and in the meantime it had suffered from the rapacity of Cesare
Borgia, so Elisabetta borrowed luxury furnishings from her brother
Francesco Gonzaga and her sister-in-law Isabella d'Este.[43]

She also summoned Pietro Bembo, an elegant young Venetian
man of letters (and future cardinal) who was living as a rather
ornamental hermit at her expense in a tenth-century monastery
on Mount Catria, between Gubbio and Urbino, while waiting for
some kind of employment to turn up. He was delighted to come
and entertain the honoured guests, because he was angling for
church patronage. He features extensively in Castiglione's dialogue,
and he would stay in Urbino until 1511.[44] This visit of the pope's
was a huge diplomatic success. In 1507, both King Ferdinand of
Spain (who was then in Naples) and the Holy Roman Emperor
Maximilian contemplated trips to Urbino as a result of what they
had heard about the beauty of the Ducal Palace and the cordiality
of the hospitality.[45] Julius's second visit was brief, because he wanted
to get back to Rome by Palm Sunday, 28 March, but after he had
left, some members of the papal court remained for an informal
stay. This is the period Castiglione writes about.[46]

The world the book describes is one where women have a very
prominent place. Because Duke Guidobaldo went to bed immediately after dinner, the court assembled for the evening in the Sala
delle Veglie – the sitting room of the duchess's suite, which had
been created by Federico, though never used by Battista Sforza
– where Elisabetta, supported by Emilia Pia, took charge of the
evening's entertainment. It is Castiglione who says that the palace
was the most beautiful in Italy, and it is also he who describes

Federico as 'in his day the light of Italy'.[47] His dialogue recreates a world of elegance and sophistication, of a life lived in an almost perfectly civilized place. He thus floods his recollections with a rosy, golden light, but it was not always quite that much fun at the time. The early sixteenth century was a period of retrenchment, when construction was suspended on the Ducal Palace and artistic commissions were reduced. In many letters he wrote to his mother while he was serving Guidobaldo, Castiglione complains that his salary is in arrears. The members of the party were not clients of Guidobaldo, but exiles, such as Giuliano de' Medici, who had been ejected from Florence in 1494, and the Fregoso of Genoa, the children of Federico's illegitimate daughter, or men who were seeking ecclesiastical patronage, such as Bembo, who were hoping to impress the papal contingent.[48]

The Courtier reached print in 1528, and was a tremendous success. Peter Burke found 153 editions before 1850, in many languages.[49] The first English translation is that of Sir Thomas Hoby, published in 1561, which gave a significant boost to Italian studies in England. The book was eagerly read as a guide to real elegance and how to achieve it, so the Urbino Castiglione describes thus became a benchmark of European civilization. In Thomas Sackville's commendatory poem attached to Hoby's translation, Federico da Montefeltro and Baldassare Castiglione are counterposed as equivalent, because one made the palace, and the other populated it.

> The Prince he raiseth houge and mightie walles,
> Castilio frames a wight of noble fame:
> The kinge with gorgeous Tyssue claddes his halles,
> The Count with golden vertue deckes the same

In England, where nobody but the traveller William Thomas had seen the palace at Urbino, it was words that counted above all, since all the readers could go on was description.

Urbino continued to resonate as a distillation of the Renaissance

spirit centuries later, in the poetry of W. B. Yeats. In 'The People',
he writes

> And you know well how great the longing has been,
> Where every day my footfall should have lit
> In the green shadow of Ferrara wall;
> Or climbed among the images of the past —
> The unperturbed and courtly images —
> Evening and morning, the steep street of Urbino
> To where the Duchess and her people talked
> The stately midnight through until they stood
> In their great window looking at the dawn.

This is the image with which *The Book of the Courtier* itself
ends, the party having talked, unawares, all night, until the sun
rose over Mount Catria and peeped through the shutters of the
duchess's room.[50]

Yeats often refers to Castiglione's work, in both prose and verse.
The aristocratic society gathered at Urbino meant a great deal to
him, since he saw it as a symbol of the interrelation of aristocracy
and art, the development of refined and educated taste in both
the producers and consumers of literature. Art 'approved before
all men those that talked or wrestled or tilted under the walls of
Urbino, or sat in those great window seats discussing all things,
with love ever in their thought, when the wise Duchess ordered
all, and the Lady Emilia gave the theme', and he admired the
courtiers' art, which conceals art.[51] In the final book of 'A Vision',
he represents Urbino as both the Ideal City of Italian perspective
paintings and an ideal pastoral landscape, or paradise: 'of what else
did Bembo think when he cried, "would that I were a shepherd
that I might look daily down on Urbino"?'[52]

Meanwhile, Francesco Maria della Rovere was growing up.
He was sixteen in the year of *The Courtier*, in which he figures.
When Julius II left Urbino in September 1506, he was going to
Bologna to eject the Bentivoglio, who were its unofficial rulers,
and reassert his authority over the city. Guidobaldo and Francesco

Maria went with him. Guidobaldo's debility prevented him from active fighting, though he still held the title of captain-general, so operational command of the papal army at Bologna was given to Francesco Gonzaga, his friend and brother-in-law. But for the first time, the young Prefect of Rome, Francesco Maria della Rovere, was commanding a company of men-at-arms. He had accompanied Guidobaldo on at least one previous campaign, but the Bologna expedition was his first experience of personal leadership.[53]

In 1510, Vittore Carpaccio painted *Young Knight in a Landscape*, now in the Thyssen-Bornemisza National Museum in Madrid, which may be a portrait of Francesco Maria, aged twenty, the year of his marriage. The central figure is in full armour, with his hand on the hilt of his sword, and his brown hair is in a long bob, like the hair of Raphael's *Young Man with an Apple*. An ermine, that familiar Montefeltro emblem, lurks in the grass by his right foot. A figure, perhaps another representation of the same young man, rides out on a warhorse from the gates of a palace, wearing Montefeltro black and gold.

It is just as well that Francesco Maria was prepared to assume an adult role, because Guidobaldo was fading out. One of his last effective actions was to found a university. The University of Urbino grew out of the Collegio dei Dottori (doctors of law), which was already active around the middle of the fifteenth century, in his father's time, and authorized to act as an appeal court for suits involving the duchy of Urbino. At his request, this college was officially recognized in a papal bull of 1507, issued by Julius II, and entrusted with the administration of penal and civil law throughout the duchy. He also established what would become the Officina degli strumenti scientifici (Office of Scientific Instruments), an important centre for practical scientific learning down to the age of Galileo.

While this was the small beginnings of an institution that flourishes to this day, other Urbinate were having a tough time, including the duke. Drought set in in the Marche: it is said that no rain or snow fell between September 1506 and January 1508, except for a few April showers. Fountains failed and springs dried up, and wheat had to be ground by hand because no water was running through the mills. December 1507 was unnaturally warm, but this reversed in January to freezing cold. In his weakened state, Guidobaldo found these see-sawing temperatures very difficult to endure, and had himself carried to Fossombrone, which had the best climate of any city in his domain. But when the severe cold returned again in April, it became clear that he was dying. Elisabetta and Emilia, Francesco Maria, Castiglione and Ottaviano Fregoso, who all feature in *The Courtier*, were with him to say farewell.

Fregoso wrote a letter to the pope, which was read out in Rome, describing Guidobaldo's final illness, the actions taken to secure an orderly succession, and his quiet death surrounded by his court, with the duchess holding his hand, followed by Elisabetta's wild grief. His body was carried to Urbino, where the will was read on the following day, and the new duke, Francesco Maria I, rode in cavalcade through the city, showing himself to the people. The duchess was still prostrate, lying on the floor of their bedroom by the marriage bed, dressed in black, her face veiled, in a sunless, airless room, lit by a single torch. Delegations came to express their sympathy and greet the new duke, while a catafalque with the body of Guidobaldo, dressed in a black damask doublet with crimson hose and the mantle of the Garter, stood in the centre of the great hall of the castle, surrounded by countless candles. He was buried in San Bernardino with his father, a son of whom so much had once been hoped; a good, affable, learned and talented man, loved by his wife and his people, and yet the physical frailty that denied him the chance to seek wealth as a condottiere, together with his inability to beget an heir, casts a pall of failure over the twenty-six years of his ducal reign.

13

Francesco Maria
della Rovere

Francesco Maria was another young duke when his predecessor died, but not a child duke. Since he was born in 1490, he was eighteen at the time, fully adult by the standards of his age and milieu. He had been carefully educated, mainly at the hands of Antonio Crastini, a philosopher and theologian who later became Bishop of Cagli,[1] and Guidobaldo's own tutor Ludovico Odasio, who remained at the court, also taught him. However, his own tastes didn't lie in the direction of abstract studies, nor was he humanistically inclined: when the Venetians honoured him with a Latin oration in 1524, the diarist Marin Sanudo noticed that he didn't understand it.[2] His ambitions were military, and he asked for nothing more than to pursue the career he had already begun, and make money. He does not seem to have been a complex man, and though he was tied to the party of the Church by traditional allegiance, he was rather too straightforward to cope effectively with the devious and wily popes of early sixteenth-century Italy. He was also a della Rovere by nature as well as name. It was said of his uncle Giuliano, who became Pope Julius II, 'anything he has been thinking of overnight has to be carried out immediately the next morning and he insists on doing everything himself. It is almost impossible to describe how strong and violent and difficult to manage he is.'[3] Francesco Maria was a man of the same type. He had an extraordinary career, marked by tremendous reversals of fortune, mostly resulting from the sudden, early deaths of either friends or enemies.

By the time Francesco Maria became duke, his experience of the world was quite extensive, and, like Federico, he had had to learn how to live by his wits at the age of only twelve. When Guidobaldo was exiled by Cesare Borgia in 1502, one of his many causes of anguish and anxiety was that he had no idea what had happened to his adopted heir. But Francesco Maria had been both crafty and cautious beyond his years. Having initially escaped to Bologna, he realized that Giovanni Bentivoglio, the unofficial ruler of that city, had it in mind to sell him to Cesare Borgia, so he slipped out and made his way to Genoa. He then went down the beautiful Ligurian coast to Savona, where his uncle Giuliano della Rovere, still a mere cardinal, was living in a splendid palazzo, occupying his time by making it even more splendid, and keeping a careful distance from the Borgias in Rome. Concerned, for his nephew's sake and his own, that the arrival of Francesco Maria might bring the Borgias down on them in Savona, he sent the boy across the border into France. Like many senior churchmen of his day, Giuliano was an unabashed pluralist, and among other titles he was Archbishop of Avignon, a city that was not only 250 miles away but in another country. So he sent Francesco Maria to his palace at Avignon, from whence letters of recommendation could be sent to the French king, Louis XII.

Louis received the boy in his court at Lyon, where he continued his education, particularly in horsemanship and other military skills, and acquired excellent French. He became page of honour to the young Gaston de Foix, Duke of Nemours, who would become one of the famous commanders of his generation before his early death at the age of twenty-two.[4] Francesco Maria made such a good impression that he was inducted into the French king's chivalric order, the Order of St Michael, aged only thirteen. He stayed in France until summoned back by Giuliano after he became Pope Julius II, and travelled to Rome with his della Rovere cousin, Galeotto Franciotti, whom Julius had nominated to the cardinalate in his own place. They arrived in Rome on 2 March 1504, where he was reunited with Guidobaldo.

When they returned to the Marche, he was welcomed at Senigallia, his father's old fief, where his mother had been holding the fort. On 18 September, they travelled to Urbino, where he was invested with the dukedom in reversion, a prudent gesture given Guidobaldo's uncertain health. At about the same time, a marriage was arranged for him with Eleonora Gonzaga, oldest daughter of Francesco, Marquis of Mantua and Isabella d'Este, and therefore niece of Elisabetta Gonzaga, then Duchess of Urbino. Elisabetta was very fond of her brother and his wife, to whom she sent many affectionate letters in the course of her life, so she was delighted by the prospect of welcoming her niece to Urbino. The engagement was announced in January 1505, but the marriage was postponed for four years, since the bride was still only twelve. John Shearman has suggested that a portrait of a young girl, which he attributes to Raphael, is a picture of her as she looked at the time of her betrothal.[5]

The young duke-in-waiting was hot-tempered, but no libertine. A major scandal that erupted in October 1507, reported by an anonymous Urbinate diarist, suggests that he was, if anything, inclined to be puritanical. His sister Maria had come to live in Urbino with her son after Guidobaldo's reinstatement, because her husband, Venanzio Varano, and their two other sons had been murdered by Cesare Borgia. Also at the court was a retainer of Guidobaldo's called Giovanni Andrea, who was both handsome and likeable. Maria fell in love with him, and there was an affair. Francesco Maria sent for the man one Saturday evening, and when he entered his chamber, leaped on him and stabbed him twenty-four times. He also sent out a servant to murder a servant of his sister, who was rumoured to be their go-between. The body was carried to the cathedral, where a funeral mass was said on Sunday, and he was buried according to his rank.[6] In terms of a fifteenth-century honour culture, Francesco Maria was more or less within his rights, but the ruthless brutality of his response to this blot on the family honour says something important about him. The della Roveres were a choleric family – Julius II would become famous for his epic rages – and the young man seems to have tended to this side of his heritage, rather than the cautious and prudent Montefeltri. After all, there was no reason why the situation could not have been quietly resolved by a marriage between a man of rank and status and a young widow of good family. Also, Francesco Maria's murderous assault must have very much upset his patron, Guidobaldo, since he valued Giovanni Andrea, but clearly his heir thought of the business only as it related to himself and his family pride.

Fortunately, the duchess Elisabetta and Francesco Maria were fond of each other. Once she had pulled herself together from the first shattering grief of her widowhood, she acted as regent in the early days after Guidobaldo's death, but even after she stepped down, she continued to help her adopted son however she could, and to live at the court, where she was treated with respect and consideration. The wedding of Eleonora Gonzaga and Francesco Maria took place in Mantua in February 1509, and the celebrations were tremendous. The works were undertaken by the principal Montefeltro court painter, Timoteo Viti, and Girolamo Genga, another Urbino painter/architect with a flair for theatricals who had helped design the decorations for Guidobaldo's funeral. According to Vasari, the chief decorations along the route of the entry procession were 'triumphal arches, resembling those of the ancients' and he also noted that comedies were presented.[7] The marriage thus got off to an excellent start, and the young bride was universally pronounced very attractive, sweet-natured and clever. The honeymoon, however, was fairly short. Julius II ordered

Francesco Maria to lead the papal army in Romagna, where he succeeded in imposing the pope's authority on Brisighella, Ravenna and Rimini.

One serious problem that arose from this short campaign was that Francesco Maria fell foul of the Cardinal of Pavia, whom Julius had put into Bologna as papal legate after ousting Giovanni Bentivoglio from the city in 1507. The cardinal, Francesco Alidosi, was a firm favourite of the pope's, but regarded by everyone else as a man completely devoid of principle. Pietro Bembo said of him, 'Faith meant nothing to him, nor religion, nor trustworthiness, nor shame, and there was nothing in him that was holy.'[8] He governed Bologna with notorious cruelty and made difficulties for Francesco Maria wherever possible. As the nephew of his only patron, Francesco Maria provoked the cardinal's resentment, since Alidosi perceived the young Duke of Urbino as a natural rival.

One minor mystery relates to Francesco Maria's being unanimously chosen, as Guidobaldo and Federico had been before him, as a Knight of the Garter in May 1509. Henry VIII, who had succeeded to the English throne on 21 April, aged seventeen, failed to confirm the appointment for reasons that are now obscure – most probably because the young king, though still very much a Catholic, did not understand how having an Italian advocate at the papal court might be useful to him.[9]

Once the Romagna campaign was concluded, Francesco Maria collected his new duchess from Urbino and took her to Rome, where they were greeted with a tournament in the Piazza Navona and a masque. They spent the winter in Rome. In April 1510, the Bolognese were dismayed to find that Julius had reinstated Alidosi as their papal legate, since they were convinced he had been treacherously engaged with the French during Francesco Maria's campaign in Romagna. Francesco Maria and Eleonora returned to Urbino in May, but he left again shortly afterwards to lead the pope's armies against Ferrara. This campaign did not go particularly well, and Julius II travelled north to look into things for himself. On 7 October, he arrived at Modena, where he found that the citizens were convinced that Alidosi was about to betray them to the French, and directed that Francesco Maria should have the cardinal captured, handcuffed and led back to Bologna escorted by 150 horsemen to stand trial for high treason. However, Julius, having listened to Alidosi's explanations, ruled in his favour and reinstated him in Bologna, which was bad news for Francesco Maria. Three weeks later he once more accused the cardinal of treasonous dealings with the French, who were then advancing on Bologna, and once more went unheeded.

In May 1511, when Julius II left Bologna for Ravenna, the citizens revolted against the rule of Alidosi, who escaped from the city in disguise. Francesco Maria abandoned the situation as hopeless, and, like Julius, retreated towards Romagna, while the French entered Bologna in triumph. Alidosi, meanwhile, went straight to Ravenna to give his own version of events, and convinced Julius that the blame for the disaster fell squarely on Francesco Maria. When he, in turn, arrived in Ravenna, and sought an audience with Julius, he was blamed and berated by his uncle. They were not alone: Francesco Maria had taken an entourage of eight. Nobody of any importance went anywhere without a following. Having been angrily dismissed, Francesco Maria and his men, furious and dismayed, left the pope's audience chamber, and came face to face with Cardinal Alidosi, primly mounted on a mule, coming to have supper with Julius and a few friends.

The cardinal saluted him casually, and Francesco Maria went berserk. He threw himself at Alidosi and, according to one account, stabbed him so fiercely that he skewered him to his saddle. Some of his followers then piled in. Other versions say that it was the followers who started it, and it was a man called Filippo Doria who actually ended the wretched cardinal's life.[10] The scene must have been intensely confusing, and it would all have been over in seconds. The murder of his sister's lover in 1507 had been an ominous indication that Francesco Maria had something of Julius's own choleric temper, and responded to insult with uncontrollable rage. He had been very severely provoked by Alidosi, who was almost certainly the traitor Francesco thought him, but cutting the man down outside the pope's very door was not an insult that the famously pugnacious Julius could be expected to forget or forgive.

Francesco Maria then ran for Urbino to await events. These included the arrival of his firstborn, a boy called Federico, who was to die at the age of two months. Julius, meanwhile, declared war on France, suspended Francesco Maria from all his dignities, and summoned him to stand trial in Rome. His defence lawyer, Filippo Beraldo, rather than seeking to palliate his offence, went on the attack, and painted a picture of Alidosi as a traitor to Italy and the papacy, and a human being so loathsome that Francesco Maria had been an instrument in the hand of God. Before any conclusion was reached, Julius collapsed with fever, and the trial was suspended. He refused to eat anything but fruit, and grew weaker and weaker.

Francesco Maria effectively resumed his authority during this interlude, suggesting that the feeling of the court must have been sympathetic to him. With rather uncharacteristic subtlety, he asked one of Julius's old enemies, the Cardinal of San Giorgio, to take the dying old man the Last Rites. Since any movement of the Blessed Sacrament in Renaissance Rome involved a procession, candles and, frequently, a choir, this was not merely a question of a cleric slipping into the pope's bedroom carrying a pyx and a chrismatory, but of the dramatic arrival of a cardinal in robe and stole accompanied by a sizeable supporting cast amid clouds of incense. This gave Julius such a fright that he sat up in bed, and said he thought he could manage an egg. Francesco Maria's care for his uncle during this illness touched Julius's heart, and he absolved him of his crime. However, the duke thought it would be safer to insist that the process for murder should be resumed, and duly, the trial was brought to a somewhat artificial end on 9 December by a consistorial bull absolving him of the charges of murder and treason.

In the course of the year that followed, Francesco Maria was once more commander-in-chief of the armies of the Church, and both the Holy Roman Emperor and the King of France were successfully ejected from Italy. Milan was restored to Massimiliano Sforza, son of the usurper Ludovico 'il Moro', and the Medici returned to Florence. An important upshot, as far as Francesco Maria was concerned, is that Julius gave him Pesaro and its territories. The last of the Pesaro Sforzas had been Galeazzo, illegitimate uncle of the last heir, Costanzo II, acting as his regent. The child died aged two in 1512, so Galeazzo went on ruling by common consent but without authority. While the people of Pesaro had been attached to the Sforzas, they greatly preferred the della Roveres to rule by a papal legate. By an odd irony of history, one of the condottiere captains Francesco Maria inherited from the Sforza régime was one Theodore Palaiologos, who claimed to be descended from the Palaeologues, the final dynasty of Byzantine emperors, who had gone into exile after the fall of Constantinople in 1453.

One notable cultural event of 1513, which must be linked with the removal of the shadow hanging over Francesca Maria's career, is that on 6 February, a play called *La Calandria* by Bernardo Dovizi da Bibbiena was staged in the Ducal Palace at Urbino, in the theatre room on the ground floor, as part of Carnival celebrations. It was one of two plays performed that Carnival,[11] and the famous Trojan War tapestries were hung for the performance. This was one of the first new Italian comedies, and had a plot roughly based on one of Plautus's Roman plays, *Menaechmi*, a comedy about mistaken identity. Bibbiena was intending to produce the play himself but in January he was summoned to Florence by Giovanni de' Medici (whose secretary he was) to meet the Spanish viceroy. His friend Castiglione took over as producer, and consequently wrote a long letter to Ludovico Canossa (another friend who, like Bibbiena, appears in *The Courtier*) telling him all about it.[12] The characters of *La Calandria* include twins, a brother, and a sister who is pretending to be a boy; it is the first known play to use this device, so familiar from Shakespeare's *Twelfth Night*. The set depicted an ideal version of the city of Rome, illusionistically painted by Girolamo Genga, one of the first sets obeying the rules of perspective in Renaissance scene painting, so the performance broke new ground in all directions. While there is no record of Genga's set, a drawing survives of Baldassare Peruzzi's design, also in perspective, for a restaging of the play at Rome in 1515.[13]

On 21 February 1513, Julius II died, and Giovanni de' Medici, second son of Lorenzo, was chosen as the new pope, taking the name Leo X. Francesco Maria attended the solemn installation in the Vatican, dressed entirely in black velvet and satin to indicate mourning for his uncle as well as respect for the new incumbent. He was confirmed in his various dignities and retained as captain-general of the Church for another year, and returned to Urbino. However, like most Renaissance popes, Leo regarded his position as an opportunity to extend the power, wealth and influence of his family, the Medici. The dukes of Urbino had benefited handsomely from this tendency under the della Rovere popes Sixtus IV and Julius II, but they were not connected by birth or marriage with the Medici, so they stood to lose out under the new régime.

The first sign of serious trouble was that Leo stood Francesco Maria down as captain-general of the Church, and gave the position to his own younger brother, Giuliano de Medici, an old friend of Francesco Maria's who had spent a good deal of time at Urbino after the Medici were exiled from Florence in 1494 – he features in *The Courtier*. He was hardly in a position to refuse the honour his brother had conferred, but he made a detour to Gubbio in the course of a journey to France, where he was to marry Filiberta of Savoy, in order to apologize to Francesco Maria in person and assure him of lifelong friendship. Francesco Maria accepted the olive branch and, with it, a subordinate position.

Unluckily, in sixteenth-century Italy, lifelong friendship didn't always mean long-lasting friendship. On 17 March 1516, four weeks after his marriage in Paris, Giuliano died suddenly, and Francesco

Maria no longer had an ally at the Medici court. Leo's territorial ambitions were refocused on his nephew Lorenzo, son of his oldest brother, Pietro, whom he made captain-general of the Church. In this capacity, Lorenzo summoned Francesco Maria and his troops to join him in Lombardy. The latter refused, because he strongly suspected that he was being summoned in order to be assassinated, which may well have been the case. The pope chose to interpret this as an act of rebellion, but rather than going to Rome, Francesco Maria garrisoned Urbino, Pesaro and the old fortress of San Leo, and sat tight in his duchy. The dowager, Elisabetta Gonzaga, went to Rome in his stead, to try her considerable powers of eloquence, but was quite unable to secure any concessions: Leo told her he would listen to nothing until Francesco Maria appeared in person to give an account of himself. It was unsurprising that her pleas fell on deaf ears, since Leo had just taken out a loan of 800,000 ducats to pay for a war.[14] When Francesco Maria understandably failed to trust himself to the dubious mercies of the papal court, he was excommunicated. Leo conferred the dukedom of Urbino on his nephew Lorenzo, and put pressure on the king of Naples to confiscate Sora, Francesco Maria's patrimonial territories in the south of Italy. He also made Lorenzo Prefect of Rome, by way of adding insult to injury.

Three different armies now converged on the dukedom. Francesco Maria, seeing the hopelessness of the situation, authorized the surrender of all of his citadels except Urbino, Pesaro, San Leo and Maiuolo, while he sent frantically for assistance and found nobody was prepared to help him. The fact that he now held Pesaro saved him, since it is coastal and has a harbour: at the end of May, he sent his wife and baby son and the dowager duchess off to their relations at Mantua in a convoy of six or eight ships laden with all the movable wealth he could lay hands on. It was possible to sail to Mantua in vessels with a shallow draught, such as galleys. Though it is inland, its river, the Mincio, is a tributary of the mighty Po. A bird's-eye view of Mantua made in 1628 shows a wharf by the palace and vessels of some size moving to and fro.[15] Francesco Maria then directed his commander at Urbino to surrender, escaped in disguise, and followed his family to Mantua, though he did not join them at the palace, but stayed in hiding, and put out a story that he had fled to France: Pesaro withstood a siege for eight days to cover his retreat before capitulating and asking for terms.

Towards the end of the year, Francesco Maria gathered together an army of mercenaries, paid for with borrowed money and the sale of his wife's jewellery and valuables. Silver was melted down: Eleonora tried to rescue two silver basins in antique style because they had been designed by Raphael, and were very lovely, suggesting that he give them to Isabella d'Este instead (she must have hoped that the latter would give him at least their value by weight in return).[16] The duke's great problem was time, since his resources were very limited. An inconclusive war was waged over the course of the winter, since the Medici were equally aware that delay was their greatest asset. Lorenzo at one point was almost killed by a bullet that grazed his skull, but made a good recovery. After eight months, Francesco Maria was forced to give up and crawl back to discreet exile in Mantua. Lorenzo, meanwhile, left the dukedom to look after itself, and returned to the papal court. In the spring of 1518, he travelled to the Loire Valley in France, where he married Madeleine de la Tour d'Auvergne, daughter of Count John III of Auvergne. Their marriage – part of an alliance between François I of France and Lorenzo's uncle, Pope Leo X – was celebrated in a ceremony of great splendour in the Château d'Amboise. Their daughter was born a year later and named Catherine – she would grow up to become the Queen of France. But Duchess Madeleine died of puerperal fever, and just six days after his wife, Lorenzo also died, apparently from the effects of general debauchery.

Federigo Gonzaga, the Duke of Mantua, was named captain-general of the Church in Lorenzo's stead, at which point Francesco

Maria became an embarrassment to him. He was good enough to keep the Urbino ladies at Mantua, living very discreetly, and Francesco Maria must have been able to pay conjugal visits from time to time, because children were born in 1515, 1516, 1518 and 1521, none of whom lived to celebrate their third birthday, which must have added considerably to the dismalness and anxiety of the duchesses' lives. Francesco Maria was given some support from the French king, to whom he offered his services as a soldier, but left him in a huff and retired to Lonno, on Lake Garda.

But on 1 December 1521, Leo X was found dead in bed. Francesco Maria promptly rallied all the support he could, and headed for his duchy. There was still a Medici cardinal in play, Giulio, so the outcome of this gambit was far from certain, but to everyone's surprise, when the cardinals met in conclave, they elected a compromise candidate, a mild-mannered Fleming who had nothing to do with Italian politics, who took the name of Hadrian VI. The new pope only ruled for twenty months, but during his brief reign he saw no particular difficulty in lifting the excommunication from Francesco Maria, and in 1523 the two duchesses returned after their seven-year exile, though to Pesaro rather than Urbino.

Eleonora celebrated her husband's reinstatement by commissioning the della Rovere court painter and architect Girolamo Genga to create the Villa Imperiale at Pesaro as an elegant 'Villa di Delizia' where they could entertain, between 1523 and 1538. A Latin inscription on a frieze round the outside of the building reads: 'For Francesco Maria Duke of the Metaurian States on his return from the wars, Eleonora his wife has built the villa for his diversion.'[17] She later commissioned further refurbishment by Pietro Bembo, and the interior is lavishly decorated with wall and ceiling paintings by Girolamo Genga, Raffaellino del Colle, and Dosso Dossi, among others.[18] The Welsh traveller William Thomas, who saw it in the 1540s, soon after its completion, actually preferred it to the palace at Urbino.[19]

> The Dukes palaice is a verie faire house, but not so excellent as
> the Conte Baldasar in his Courtisane doeth commende it…
> Amongest other this Dukes father builded an house within a mile
> of Pesaro, called Imperiale, whiche in mine opinion is one of the
> best devised litle thynges that may lightly be founde. It standeth
> on the syde of an hyll, and hath prospect bothe to the citee and
> to all the valey, it hath many fine little chambers, goodly open
> vaultes, and excellent faire fountaines. But that whiche most of all
> pleased myne eye, was that being of a great height, you may out of
> the highest gardeine ryde about on the toppe of the house, which
> is very faire paved with bricke, and railed on bothe sides with fine
> pillers and railes of white marble.[20]

The della Roveres also refurbished the palace at Pesaro, again with
the help of Genga, and lived there with considerable elegance.
Theatrical performances apparently took place in the ducal palace at
Pesaro during the winter months. A variety of manuscript play-texts
are preserved in the Urbino library, one of which, *Herode insano*,
by the Urbinate poet and playwright Marco Montano, specifically
states that it was performed for Francesco Maria II.[21] The ceiling of
the great hall imitates Federico's palace, in that the compartments
of the ceiling hold the della Roveres' various *imprese*, the oak tree,
the ermine, and an inclined palm tree, which was the traditional
emblem for anyone who had suffered adversity and overcome it.
These also appear on internal lintels and chimney pieces, just as
Federico had ordered at Urbino. The palaces in Pesaro were almost
too successful. Pesaro was handily on the coast road and on the
way to Loreto, much visited by pilgrims. It was much easier to get
to than Urbino, so the duke and duchess received many highly
distinguished – and consequently expensive – guests.[22]

Since he was no longer fighting for the Church, the reinstated
duke went into service with the signoria of Venice. He was soon
called to action, because the French king, François I, suddenly
marched across the Alps and seized Milan. Francesco Maria was
sent to guard the Venetian border. He therefore took no part in the

battle of Pavia, fought on 24 February 1525, a terrible defeat for the French, which left François himself a prisoner and Charles V, the Holy Roman Emperor, the ruler of Lombardy, Burgundy, Spain, Austria and the Two Sicilies.

After the brief reign of Hadrian VI, Cardinal Giulio de' Medici became Clement VII. He was the son of Giuliano de' Medici, younger brother of Lorenzo, who had been assassinated in the Pazzi conspiracy of 1478 with which Federico da Montefeltro had been much involved. Giuliano's mistress, Fioretta Gorini, was seven months pregnant when her lover was killed, and in due course gave birth to Giulio, who was adopted by his uncle Lorenzo.[23] Clement VII was generally regarded as capable and industrious, but his policies inadvertently led to the biggest single disaster to befall sixteenth-century Italy, with some unfortunate assistance from Francesco Maria, who continued to be captain-general of the Venetian forces.

Concerned at the disproportionate power now wielded by Charles V, Clement formed the League of Cognac in 1526, ratified with a treaty signed by the pope, Henry VIII of England, François I, and the rulers of Florence, Venice and Milan, which pledged them to fight against the Emperor, and he made Francesco Maria its captain. One of the first results of the formation of the League was that Francesco Sforza was besieged in Milan by an imperial army. The relieving army moved remarkably slowly, partly because the various commanders were arguing with each other. They attacked the siege lines on 6 July 1526, and failed to break through to Milan. Francesco Maria decided to wait for expected Swiss reinforcements: he planned to attack again on 25 July, but by then, Sforza had been forced to surrender, so Francesco Maria took his troops to besiege Cremona, which was more successful. He then blockaded Milan, but had to withdraw late in the year. His next venture was to try and head off 14,000 German landsknechts (mercenaries), who had come into Italy under the command of Georg von Frundsberg. Though he managed to meet them in battle, he was unable actually to turn them back, and von Frundsberg was able to join up with the main Imperial army, under Charles, Duke of Bourbon.

By 1527 the Venetians had completely ceased to trust Pope Clement, and ordered Francesco Maria to limit his actions to the defence of Venetian territory. As captain of the League, he was supposed to do what he could to defend Florence, but as Venetian commander, his priorities were quite different: as he subsequently explained, 'we will do all we can to protect the territories of the Florentines and the pope, but always with the preservation of the Venetian state in mind, which depends on the intactness of our army'.[24] The Venetians had a real need to be cautious. Their land territories had suffered terribly since 1509 – a chronicler in Vicenza observed that there had been thirty-seven régime changes between 1509 and 1517, which, as he said himself, might almost have seemed funny were it not so tragic. Meanwhile, their maritime empire was being threatened by the Turkish navy.[25] No wonder they were insistent that their commander must not squander resources.

When the undisciplined, unpaid, and substantially Protestant Imperial army began to move south towards Rome under the Duke of Bourbon, Francesco Maria shadowed it at a safe distance. As Shaw and Mallett observe, justly, though he and the League have been heavily criticized for not attempting to stop the Imperial army, 'it is from the perspective of hindsight that their failings loom so large. They could not anticipate that the great city of Rome would fall to the assault of a mutinous army, in a single day.'[26] Because what happened was that, on the morning of 6 May, while the besiegers were attacking the city walls, Bourbon was felled by a lucky shot, but shortly afterwards the leaderless Imperial army broke into the city, scaling the walls of the Borgo under the cover of mist, which prevented marksmen in Castel Sant'Angelo from seeing what they were doing. The pope, who had been in St Peter's when they started coming over the wall, fled to Hadrian's mausoleum, which had been converted into a papal fortress, the Castel Sant'Angelo, with as many people as possible, about three thousand of them. Luckily for him, Pope Nicholas III had connected the castle to St Peter's Basilica by a covered fortified corridor, called the Passetto di Borgo.

Meanwhile, the soldiers of the Imperial army found themselves in one of the richest cities in the world, with no effective opposition. They began an orgy of rape and looting, breaking into the homes of the wealthy and torturing them to get them to reveal hidden treasure. Their depredation continued unopposed, since Francesco Maria, in charge of the League's troops, does not seem to have felt any sense of urgency. He absolutely failed to rise to the occasion. Concerned that his own forces were not going to be adequate, he demanded 15,000 Swiss mercenaries, 10,000 other troops, with forty cannon and enough money to pay them all properly, before he was prepared to move, arguing that the Castel Sant'Angelo was provisioned for three months, so there would be plenty of time. Given the scale of the disaster, with thousands of masterless and uncontrollable landsknechts rioting through the city, he obviously had a point, but it seems extraordinary that the fate of the civilian population, the rape of the treasures of Rome, and even the profanation of the relics of the saints, don't appear to have concerned him.[27] To this day, graffiti praising Luther are scratched into the frescoes of the Vatican.

On 5 June, after the sack had gone on for a month, the pope signed surrender terms: a safe conduct to Naples, with security for the personal property in the Castel, in return for an enormous ransom, 150,000 scudi and the surrender of the Castel, Civitavecchia, Ostia and Civita Castellana. Stephen Gardiner, Bishop of Winchester, visited him in his exile and reported his abject state, without so much as a tapestry to his name: 'before reaching his privy chamber, we passed three chambers all naked and unhanged, the roofs fallen down, and as we can guess, 30 persons, riff raff and other, standing in the chamber for a garnishment'. He reckoned that the furniture in the pope's bedchamber, bed and all, was worth less than twenty nobles.[28]

Meanwhile, summer arrived, and the streets of Rome were choked with unburied corpses, which generated plague and typhoid fever. Some of the Imperial soldiers, who had become a completely undisciplined rabble, actually abandoned the city of their own accord. One subsequent estimate of the damage was four to six thousand Romans murdered, while thirty thousand or more died of disease or starvation; two million ducats' worth of goods pillaged or destroyed, and as much again extorted in ransoms, plus the utter humiliation of the pope.

In the aftermath of the sack, questions were inevitably asked, and Francesco Maria defended himself as best he could. The only possible defence, however, was his dual loyalty. His reputation abruptly sank, at home and abroad. In May of that year, Eleonora and her surviving child, Guidobaldo, had gone to Venice, and by the end of June they were being treated not as guests, but as hostages. However, his avoidance of combat was fundamentally in the interests of Venice, if not of Italy or the Church, so Francesco Maria was reinstated in the Venetians' good graces some months later. He was received civilly by the signoria in the following spring, and presented with a palazzo in Venice.[29] But his reputation had suffered and he was somewhat under-unemployed between 1530 and 1533, so he took to authorship, dictating rambling thoughts about military tactics. His book was published in Ferrara in 1583.[30]

One instance of papal nepotism on the part of Clement VII is worth noting. Though the Medici had led Florence for generations, they had done so as the first citizens of a republic. Under Clement, this would change. When the Medici were restored to power in Florence in 1530, he elevated his family into a dukedom, and chose Alessandro de' Medici as Florence's first hereditary monarch in 1531. The young man's mother was a black servant, Simonetta da Collevecchio. He had been officially recognized as the son of Lorenzo II de' Medici, though it was widely rumoured that Clement was his actual father. Thus Alessandro de' Medici became the first mixed-race European head of state, though not for long, since he was assassinated in 1537 and succeeded by Cosimo, from a junior branch of the family.

Another event of 1527 was of particular importance to the della Roveres. In the neighbouring fiefdom of Camerino, Count Giovanni Maria Varano died of the plague, leaving a four-year-old girl, Giulia, as his heir. The city was promptly sacked by Sciarra Colonna and the late duke's widow, Caterina Cibo, took refuge in the citadel with her little daughter and sent a message to Francesco Maria, asking for his help and promising him her daughter's hand for his heir. Francesco Maria was sitting about in Umbria doing nothing, while the negotiations for the release of Clement VII from Castel Sant'Angelo were going on, so he sent troops to her aid. Caterina was the niece of Leo X, so this was doing a signal favour to a Medici connection: on the back of it, Francesco Maria applied formally for papal sanction for a marriage between Giulia and his son Guidobaldo, but was put off on grounds of the girl's extreme youth.

Agnolo Bronzino's portrait of Guidobaldo II della Rovere was painted between April 1531 and April 1532, since the subject is specifically described as eighteen years old. Francesco Maria, accompanied by his wife, the duchess Eleonora, was away from the duchy at the time, inspecting the Venetian troops in northern Italy. Guidobaldo was acting as regent; he had recently received a small military command and salary of his own from Venice, and it was the first time he had been left in charge. He insisted on being painted wearing an elegant, brand-new dark green and gold Milanese suit of armour. In his *Life of Pontormo*, Giorgio Vasari mentions that Bronzino was kept hanging about in Pesaro and unable to return to Florence because he had to wait for the arrival of this harness.[31] The helmet carries a Greek inscription, which translates as 'It will certainly be as I have decided', which, together with his martial trappings and direct gaze, indicate the sitter's determination to be fully in control of his own destiny. His unusually large and prominent codpiece suggests that he is pointedly distinguishing himself from the unhappy and impotent Guidobaldo I. He is caressing an enormous mastiff dog, an accoutrement of nobility, as aristocratic an animal as the hound in Titian's portrait of Charles V. This assertion of self-will is highly relevant, because in 1532 relations between Guidobaldo II and his father, Francesco Maria, were extremely strained. Guidobaldo had fallen in love with Clarice Orsini, daughter of a noble Roman family. Francesco Maria objected vehemently: on social grounds, because the Orsini were inferiors; on eugenic grounds, because Clarice's father was generally considered quite mad; and on practical grounds, because if Guidobaldo took the child Giulia Varano as his wife, he would add Camerino to their territory. But Guidobaldo continued to defy his father, who threatened to disinherit him.[32]

In March 1533, his mother, Eleonora, gave birth to a second son, Giulio, and Guidobaldo realized that if he annoyed his father sufficiently, he could make good on his threat. No more is heard of the beautiful Clarice, and the following year, after the Medici pope Clement VII died on 25 September, and the new pope was widely tipped to be Alessandro Farnese, another man with a son he was anxious to promote, Pier Luigi, Guidobaldo accepted being packed off to Camerino to marry Giulia before the election took place, so that technically they could say there had been no pope to ask permission from. He did so on 12 October 1534, the day after Alessandro Farnese became Paul III, and on his father's instructions, consummated the marriage, even though his bride was only eleven. This was not according to custom, when the bride was pre-pubescent, but the pope had the power to annul a marriage as long as it remained unconsummated.

The most remarkable aspect of the last years of Francesco Maria is the amount of money he spent on pictures. Like Federico, he confirmed his magnificence by patronage, once he felt financially secure. In 1536, he commissioned portraits of himself and his wife from Titian, the leading painter of Venice. Like his son, he chose to be painted in armour, in a suit made by the famous armourer

Kolman Helmschmid of Augsburg.[33] Titian borrowed it in order to paint it, and by June that year the duke was worrying about getting it back. He was then forty-six. The purpose of the painting is evidently to represent him as a success, and it forms a sort of visual *curriculum vitae*. He holds the baton of command of Venice, with the lion of St Mark in a roundel. The golden baton of the papacy and the silver baton of Florence, which he had carried in the past (only for a year, in the case of Florence), are on a shelf behind him. The companion portrait of Eleonora Gonzaga shows her seated in three-quarters profile, wearing Montefeltro black and gold, richly bejewelled, and holding a *zibellino*, a fashionable accessory of the time: a sable pelt with a gold head.[34] An open window shows the landscape of the Marche behind her, perhaps in a nod to the double portrait of Federico and Battista. On a table by the window are a sleeping lapdog, representing fidelity, and a clock. Chamber clocks were a distinctive product of Urbino, and those of the Barocci family were particularly famous, but it also symbolizes her patient waiting for her husband to return from his campaigns. Such clocks were much prized possessions: Titian includes a Barocci clock in no fewer than six paintings.[35] Francesco Maria also gave Titian another commission around this time. The painter had produced a series of pictures of beauties around 1515–20, which seem to have caught Francesco Maria's eye: 'Tell Titian we want him to finish the portrait of a woman in a blue dress and make sure that she is presented in beautiful form.'[36] The identity of the sitter seems to have been unimportant to him, but he had obviously noticed that Titian excelled in representing lovely women. The blue of the dress was very expensive lapis lazuli, so the colour called attention to the painting as an object of value and not just an objet d'art.

A liking for Titian was something that Francesco Maria and his son, Guidobaldo, had in common. When Vasari visited Urbino in 1548, he saw a substantial collection of the painter's works. In 1538, Guidobaldo bought another picture by Titian, the famous

Venus of Urbino. He wrote to his agent on 9 March 1538 that he was extremely anxious to take possession of two paintings that were then in Titian's studio, a portrait of himself and a 'picture of a nude woman'. Unfortunately, he was rather short of funds, so he asked his mother to lend him some money. She wrote to her son on 14 April that she was having the portrait sent to him, though three days earlier it had been described as unfinished. On 1 May, Guidobaldo was still trying to get his nude, and afraid that Titian might sell to someone else.

The key to the della Roveres' eagerness to own this Venus is probably that it is a painting about licit – i.e. marital – sexuality. The dog sleeping on the bed is an emblem of fidelity, like the almost identical dog in Titian's portrait of Eleonora Gonzaga. Venus meets the viewer's gaze, but it is only the approach of a husband that would leave the dog slumbering on. In the background, a woman rummages in one of a pair of painted *cassone*, items that a bride brought to her marriage. This all suggests that the Venus's frank eroticism relates to a domestic and social context. In 1538, Guidobaldo's young wife, Giulia Varano, was fifteen. The relationship had begun terrifyingly for her: one wonders whether Guidobaldo's determination to acquire the painting, and his mother's willingness to finance it, suggests that when Giulia reached puberty and marital relations began properly, things did not go well because she was sexually traumatized. This painting, in the context of Guidobaldo's actual marriage, might be thought of as there to teach her that sexual relations are legitimate and even pleasurable. Thus once again, despite the virility Guidobaldo boasts in his portrait by Bronzino, the succession was in trouble.

Francesco Maria continued to be held in esteem as a general, since he was made commander of land forces for the Holy League against the Turks in 1538. But he was taken ill in Venice on 20 September, and had himself taken by sea to Pesaro, where his constitution began to fail, and he died on the 22nd. His death was ascribed to poison, though there seems no particular reason to believe this: his Mantuan barber confessed under torture that he had dropped a poisoned lotion in the duke's ear, which may be the story that originated the plot of the 'Murder of Gonzago' play in *Hamlet*. The wretched barber may have confessed simply to end his agonies, but contemporaries pointed their fingers at a Gonzaga, Luigi, Marchese di Castelgoffredo, and his ally Cesare Fregoso as the instigators, since they were known enemies of Francesco Maria.[37] One problem with this story is that Francesco Maria was ailing before he got back to Pesaro and the dubious ministrations of his barber, and another is that given the perfectly extraordinary Renaissance beliefs about effective poisons (marinaded spiders and the like), even if the barber did attempt to poison the wretched duke, he probably did little actual harm.[38]

MAJOLICA

Majolica is the most typical high-quality ceramic of Renaissance Italy. It was used for dishes, bowls and jugs, for sculpture, most notably by Luca della Robbia, and for floor and ceiling tiles. The distinctive milky glaze of majolica ware was achieved by adding tin oxide, which made the glaze opaque, to a mixture of potash, sands and lead oxide. Tin, however, was not mined in Italy. It was an expensive import, and thus majolica was much more expensive than ordinary pottery. The tin-glazed surface was smooth and shiny but not brilliant. The glaze was liquefied with water and, probably, a little gum arabic as a binder, into which the clay objects were dipped. When thoroughly dry, the surface was ready to be painted. One reason majolica was much admired, apart from its beauty, was the technical virtuosity involved in painting the unfired vessels. The pigments used were dry powdery metal oxides mixed with a little water and perhaps gum arabic. Since the unfired glaze acted like blotting paper, sucking up the pigment, it was hard for the painter to keep his design under control.

At the beginning of the fifteenth century, only a few colours had been developed: manganese purplish-brown, copper green, and cobalt blue. Between 1430 and 1460, a whole range of new colours was developed, allowing for much more naturalistic effects: antimony yellow and an orange made with antimony and iron. True reds were always difficult. There were also iridescent lustre colours, ruby red, pink, yellow and reddish brown, made by a technique borrowed from the Islamic world. The lustre colours seem to have been the speciality of several workshops in Deruta and of Maestro Giorgio and his descendants in Gubbio. Once colour became more important in majolica decoration, sixteenth-century producers began to apply a second, clear glaze to their wares, after painting, which produced a brilliantly shiny surface and enhanced the decorative effect.

The main centre of majolica production in the fifteenth century was Florence. Before the turn of the sixteenth century, fine majolicas were made in many parts of Italy, but after that the process became rather a speciality of the Marche. Exquisite objects were made in Forlì, Cafaggiolo, Castel Durante and Urbino. Majolica had a last flowering at Urbino in the last third of the sixteenth century, but by 1600 production had declined owing to economic constraints, although the so-called bianchi di Faenza, lightly decorated white wares made in Faenza, continued the tradition of new designs and fine workmanship.[39]

For important commissions, sources of design were either new drawings incorporating the arms and insignia of the client for one-off pieces, or prints and other available drawings that were often repeated in an early form of mass production for a larger popular market. One plate, possibly made in Gubbio or Deruta, must date before the death of Guidobaldo I, since it has the post-1474 Montefeltro coat of arms. A large trencher now in the Victoria and Albert Museum must have been made after Francesco Maria was designated heir, but before Guidobaldo died, since it has the arms of della Rovere impaled with Montefeltro in a central disc with, round it, two bands of grotesque decoration that recall the decorative borders of contemporary deluxe manuscripts.

Majolica was a status symbol. When Lodovico Podocataro, secretary to Pope Alexander VI, was made a cardinal in 1500, he sent to Francesco Garducci in Urbino and ordered a service of ninety-one pieces decorated with his arms, stipulating that it had to be completed within two months. Displaying these pieces to his guests was a visible and unmistakable token that he had 'arrived'.[40] Vasari tells us that the della Roveres used majolica as a diplomatic weapon: for example, Guidobaldo II ordered the painter Battista Franco to make a series of drawings of episodes from the Trojan War around 1545.

> The duke thought that Franco's designs would be a success if executed by those who made excellent pottery at Castel Durante... [he] sent a double service of this ware to the Holy Roman Emperor Charles V and a service to cardinal Alessandro Farnese, brother of Signora Vittoria [Guidobaldo's second wife].[41]

The della Rovere dukes of course commissioned items of this much sought-after ware to decorate their own palaces. They were still commissioning majolica at the end of the century, since a plate survives that must have been made to celebrate the wedding of Francesco Maria II and Livia della Rovere in 1599.

One major development in Urbino majolica was the creation not of grotesques or bands of decoration, but full-blown painterly scenes drawn from art and literature, '*istoriato*' or story-telling majolica, like the Trojan War ware designed by Battista Franco. This new style seems to have been introduced by Orazio Fontana, who migrated to Urbino from Castel Durante and specialized in unusually shaped vessels. The single most famous majolica painter of all is the slightly later 'Nicola da Urbino', who has been described as 'the Raphael of majolica painting',[42] and was active in the 1520s and 1530s. He drew on engravings and drawings for his own *istoriato* pieces, which feature scenes from classical mythology and sometimes the Bible, naturalistically coloured. Such pieces were too precious for use. They were designed for display in cabinets or cupboards, though perhaps at the grandest meals they might be set on the tables to hold fruit or sweetmeats. Nicola was responsible for one of the most prestigious majolica commissions ever undertaken, a set of dishes made for Isabella d'Este. There is no documentary evidence relating to this commission, but the armorials and *imprese* make it quite clear who the items were intended for.[43] They may have been commissioned when Isabella d'Este passed through Pesaro on her way to Rome in 1525, when she was lavishly entertained by her daughter Eleonora and son-in-law Francesco Maria. Many of the items in this set have subjects taken from Ovid's *Metamorphoses*, and the woodcuts in the Venice translation of 1497 often supply the basic composition, suggesting that Nicola owned a copy of this book. Other designs of his are based on drawings or engravings by contemporary artists, Marcantonio Raimondi, Giulio Romano and Raphael, among others.[44] Two of the surviving Este plates have biblical subjects, and the rest are classical. Many of these plates and bowls have a central area inhabited by Isabella's coat of arms and supporters, leaving the painter with the considerable technical problem of producing a legible image of complex activity in an annulus surrounding a completely different subject. For example, a plate with images taken from the *Metamorphoses* has, in the centre, the Gonzaga coat of arms impaling d'Este and surrounded with putti. All around this are stories relating to Apollo: he triumphs over the dead monster Python in the left-hand quadrant, while above him, Cupid prepares to instil love for Daphne in his heart. At the bottom of the plate is Daphne's father, the river god Peneus, and middle right, Apollo pursues Daphne, who is turning into a laurel.[45] Other plates handle the coat of arms differently. One features Isaac and Rebecca embracing, watched through a window by the Philistine king Abimelech. The Gonzaga/Este coat of arms is hanging on the wall. The entire scene, apart from the coat of arms, is based on a fresco by Raphael in the Vatican, or more probably on a preparatory drawing of Raphael's that Nicola had borrowed, or even bought.[46]

Another Urbinese majolica painter, Francesco Xanto Avelli, active 1520–42, was also working at the peak of this particular craft, and producing complex mythological scenes. Xanto's first unequivocally signed and dated work was made in Urbino in 1530–31, and he appears to have remained based in the city until at least 1542, the date of his last signed work. Like Nicola, he was unusually well read for an artisan, though only in Italian; he had read Virgil and Ovid in translation and was very familiar with Petrarch and Ariosto.[47] It is clear from the work of both men that they interacted with the contemporary art world, and that their products were among the most prestigious decorative items in sixteenth-century Italy.

14

The Later della Rovere Dukes

Guidobaldo II became duke in 1538. He followed family tradition by fighting for Venice, but he was less valued than his father. The early portrait by Bronzino, discussed in the last chapter, indicates his aspiration to military success, but in 1539 Guidobaldo's personal fee was 4,000 ducats with 100 men-at-arms and 100 lances in peacetime, with ten captains leading the infantry (at 15 ducats a month in peace and 25 in wartime), for a 19,000 ducat fee.[1] In 1532, his father had been able to negotiate a fee of 50,000 ducats.[2]

The pope, Paul III, having been baulked of marrying his illegitimate son Pier Luigi Farnese to Giulia Varano and putting him into Camerino as its count in 1534, returned to the attack at the end of 1538, after the death of Francesco Maria, and assembled an army to take Camerino by force. Venice and the emperor were both embroiled in a war against the Turks and offered no help, so Guidobaldo settled for selling the duchy of Camerino for 78,000 scudi, but with a full investiture of his own ducal status as a sweetener, and retreated to Pesaro.

The marriage with Giulia Varano, which Francesco Maria had considered such a coup, had only produced a daughter, Virginia.

A son was born but did not survive. Giulia's portrait by Titian (or his workshop), painted in 1545/7, shows a rather tentative-looking woman, portrayed seated, in three-quarters profile, which had become the standard format for representing aristocratic women.[3] She is wearing red, which seems to have been her favourite colour, since a letter survives, written in 1541, asking their factor in Venice to source cloth 'of the most bright and lively scarlet which can be found' for a new dress. The monogram 'G.G.' (Guidobaldo & Giulia) is embroidered on her sleeves, bodice and skirt.[4] She died in 1547, aged twenty-three.

Guidobaldo was thus free to look around for a second wife, and remarried the following year. He chose Vittoria, daughter of Pier Luigi Farnese, who by then was Duke of Parma, and thus granddaughter of Pope Paul III, a recognition that the Farnese star was still in the ascendant. The betrothal was a spur to a round of redecoration and refurbishment in the palace, including a new chapel by the *studiolo*, decorated by Federico Brandani.[5] Palace graffiti suggest how much this marriage meant both to Guidobaldo and to his household: he was standing looking down from the duke's loggia to see the arrival of his new wife and her entourage, and wrote on the wall '1548. 21 hours. The duke saw his wife. May her arrival be happy, and endure for always.' Meanwhile, somebody else recorded that she actually came through the door an hour later.[6] Her portraits suggest a woman who would on the whole rather have been a nun – she dresses in plain black, and wears a veil over her hair – but she gave him the needed son, Francesco Maria II, born in 1549, and two more daughters, Isabella and Lavinia. The couple were together for twenty-six years. Guidobaldo commissioned another portrait from Titian in the early 1550s, which echoes the father-and-son portrait of Federico da Montefeltro with the first Guidobaldo, since in it he is shown in civilian dress, but with his armour and helmet beside him, and little Francesco Maria II, aged about three or four, reaching up towards his father's hand.

25. The Villa Imperiale, a house for entertaining, commissioned by Eleonora Gonzaga as a gift to her husband, with gardens on two levels.

26. Agnolo Bronzino, portrait of Guidobaldo II della Rovere, aged eighteen; poised to defy his father.

27. Titian's portrait of Francesco Maria della Rovere, an experienced warrior in his prime, displaying a collection of commander's batons from his various commissions.

28. Detail of Titian's portrait of Eleonora Gonzaga (1536/7). Her seated, three-quarters pose had become standard for the portrayal of noble ladies.

29. Further della Rovere patronage of Titian: the famous *Venus of Urbino*, bought by Guidobaldo.

30. *opposite* Detail of Titian's portrait of Guidobaldo II as an adult, holding a commander's baton.

31. Majolica plate celebrating the transition of the dukedom from Montefeltro to della Rovere, before 1508.

FRĀCESCO MARIA
.II. DVCA· VI· DI·
VRBINO

FIDERICVS·VBALDVS· IOSEPH·PRINCEPS·VRB

LIVIA· DELLA· RO
VORE· DVCHESSA
D'VRBINO

32. A print of the ducal family, suggesting that the existence of an heir was widely advertised.

33. *overleaf* Vittoria della Rovere and her husband, Grand Duke Ferdinand II, in the 1630s, by Justus Sustermans, who was court painter to the grand dukes of Tuscany.

34. Federico's Duomo acquired a new façade in the eighteenth century, by Camillo Morigia.

35. One of the most distinguished modernist buildings in Urbino: Giancarlo de Carlo's Magistero. Its dramatic glass fan is invisible from the city.

In 1556, Guidobaldo completed one of his major projects, which he had been working on for ten years, overhauling the citadel and fortifications of the coastal town of Senigallia, which his father had got back from the Medici in 1524. It had originally been built for Giovanni della Rovere by Baccio Pontelli, but needed to be altered to answer the new challenges of artillery warfare. He also instituted a college of gunnery there. Otherwise, his main architectural project was improving the palace of Pesaro, with Girolamo Genga and his son as architects and decorators.[7] The white and gilt stucco ceilings are decorated with grotteschi, and all his *imprese*: Montefeltro eagles, ermines and grenades borrowed from Federico, della Rovere oaks, goalposts, and twin temples of honour and virtue.[8] In 1558, he took service with Philip II to safeguard the Spanish king's interests in Italy, and in the same year Charles V gave him the Order of the Golden Fleece.

The dukes of Urbino were no longer humanists, but they were not uncultivated. They were significant patrons of painting, the performing arts and music. Guidobaldo II also had a passion for horses.[9] His patronage of painters was extensive. Like his father, he was a great admirer of Titian, but he also supported a major painter born in Urbino itself, Federico Barocci (*c.* 1533–1610), who came from a family otherwise famous for making clocks and scientific instruments. According to his well-informed seventeenth-century biographer, Giovanni Pietro Bellori, the young Barocci keenly studied the Titians in the ducal collection[10] before developing a style of his own, marked by luminously brilliant colour and suave brushwork. Like many ambitious artists, he went to Rome, under the protection of Cardinal Giulio della Rovere, Guidobaldo's younger brother. Though he was very successful there, he developed a serious illness and returned to Urbino, where he recovered and built up his practice again, communicating with his patrons by letter. In at least two of his Crucifixions, he honours his birthplace by depicting the familiar outline of Federico's Ducal Palace in the landscape behind the sacred drama.[11]

Apart from his patronage of painters, Titian and Barocci in particular, Guidobaldo was also keenly interested in music, as were his children.[12] A major composer, Dominique Phinot, was associated with the court at Pesaro for a considerable part of his career.[13] In 1559, another composer, Costanzo Porta, dedicated a book of madrigals for five voices to Virginia, Guidobaldo's daughter by Giulia Varano, who was herself a singer.[14] Between 1542 and 1616, the della Roveres received dozens of dedications from a wide range of contemporary Italian musicians.[15] Virginia Vagnoli, a renowned Sienese soprano, spent several years at the della Rovere court in Pesaro, where she was the most prominent musician. The Pesaro poet Ludovico Agostini, who was in love with her, made her the chief character in the musical scenes of his most ambitious work, *Le giornate soriane*, an idealized description of a group of Guidobaldo's courtiers banqueting, hunting and singing madrigals in the hills around Pesaro, a sort of della Rovere *Book of the Courtier*, though, unlike Castiglione's famous work, it was not a success, and did not reach print until 2004.[16] Several other musicians served the court for many years, including Jachet Bontemps, an organist, Stefano de Ferrari, a celebrated lutenist, Paolo Animuccia, master of the chapel, and other singers and instrumentalists.

One notable literary recruit to the court was the poet Bernardo Tasso, who was joined there by his young son, the future major poet Torquato Tasso, in 1557. He was working on his enormous epic poem, *Amadigi*, but also made himself available as a humanist, discussing the merits of ancient and modern poets with the more scholarly members of the court. Torquato studied alongside the ducal heir, Francesco Maria II, and moved with the court between Urbino and Pesaro. A variety of literary figures frequented the court, and guided both Tasso's and Francesco Maria's early education in contemporary culture, such as the courtier-poet Girolamo Muzio, until the Tassos left for Venice in 1560 so that Bernardo could supervise the printing of *Amadigi*. Tasso's continued sense of indebtedness and connection with the della Roveres is witnessed by Urb. Lat. 413, a manuscript of the first draft of the first two cantos of *Gerusalemme Liberata*, written in 1575 in his own hand and dedicated to Guidobaldo II. Tasso's pastoral play *Aminta* was staged for the Carnival in Pesaro in 1574.

One area of della Rovere patronage that has left a substantial heritage is armour. Guidobaldo amassed a remarkable collection. In the sixteenth century, armour was increasingly used for the display of princely magnificence, and not simply as a protection in battle, where it was less and less useful as projectile weaponry improved. As Marina Belozerskaya observes, 'no other attire so cogently expressed strength and nobility, chivalry, and the revival of the valour of ancient heroes and statesmen'.[17] There was a new fashion for parade armour in the antique style, based on statues of emperors and other Roman art, together with surviving examples of Greek and Roman armour, fancifully reinterpreted. Guidobaldo II had a complete suit of 'Roman style' armour made for him in 1546 by Bartolomeo Campi of Pesaro, who proudly noted that he had achieved it in only two months.[18] Guidobaldo became governor of the Venetian armies that year, so it was perhaps made in a hurry for some parade or ceremonial.[19]

One of the first works to be signed by the most famous armourer of Milan, Filippo Negroli, is a burgonet, or visored helmet, made for Francesco Maria I in 1532, which was much admired because the armourer had contrived the appearance of curly hair.[20] Negroli also made an armour of mail and plate for Francesco Maria, which shows a mixture of 'all'antica' features with influence from a type of armour popular in the Islamic world. A portrait of Guidobaldo, which is now in Vienna, shows him in civilian dress, but with a suit of armour by Filippo Negroli arranged behind him, parts of which have survived.[21] The Metropolitan Museum of New York describes it as 'one of the finest made and most imaginatively designed Renaissance parade armors in the all'antica (antique) style'. It has a helmet made of a grotesque dragon head, and a cuirass decorated with two giant bat wings covered in eyes.[22]

Francesco Maria II is represented in armour shortly after he returned to Urbino having participated in the destruction of the Turkish fleet at the battle of Lepanto in October 1571, in a painting by Federico Barocci. The breastplate from this armour survives, and is also in the Metropolitan Museum; its considerable thickness suggests that it was armour for use, not parade armour, despite its fine chased decoration.

Francesco Maria was carefully educated: he was taken to Venice aged fifteen, where his taste for painting was noticed by Titian.[23] At sixteen, he asked his father if he could take service at the imperial court, but Guidobaldo preferred to send him to Spain, to his own employer, Philip II. He was welcomed at the Spanish court and felt at home there, and stayed for two and a half years. He fell in love with a Spanish girl, Magdalena de Girón, daughter of the Count of Osuna, and wrote to his father to say that he meant to marry her. He was sufficiently fixated on this woman to commission a portrait of her, which is still in Pesaro. Though Guidobaldo himself had similarly been in love with Clarice Orsini as a young man and forced to marry Giulia Varano, that did not make him any more sympathetic to his son's romance, and he demanded that Francesco Maria return to Italy.

Francesco Maria notes in his autobiography that when he came back to Pesaro in 1568, he studied mathematics with Federico Commandino.[24] This suggests that he was rather more intellectual than his father and grandfather, since Commandino, a native of Urbino, was an extremely learned mathematician and humanist. He was visited there in 1563 by one of the most noted English scientists of the day, John Dee, who was travelling in Italy.[25] Dee brought the Italian a manuscript of a mathematical treatise translated out of Arabic into Latin, which they both believed was based on a lost work by Euclid, translated out of Greek into Arabic (though it is now thought the author was a twelfth-century Muslim scientist from Baghdad).[26] They eventually co-published this work at Pesaro in 1570, in separate Latin and Italian editions.[27] It was most probably Francesco Maria who acquired one of the most important manuscripts in the library, the oldest and most inclusive version of Leonardo da Vinci's treatise on painting, probably put together by his student and heir Francesco Melzi, which has a lot to say about geometry, perspective and optics.[28]

Meanwhile, Guidobaldo organized a match for his son with Lucrezia d'Este, the sister of Alfonso II, Duke of Ferrara. She brought a hefty dowry of 150,000 scudi, which went some way towards solving a financial crisis in the duchy, and was probably why he insisted on the match.[29] The wedding was celebrated by proxy in Ferrara in January 1570 (Francesco Maria arrived only during Carnival) and was solemnized by Lucrezia's triumphal arrival in Pesaro in January 1571. This marriage crowned Guidobaldo's long-standing friendship with the Ferrarese court, which also had musical consequences, since the Este court was a great centre for musical innovations and particularly associated with the development of the madrigal.

Unfortunately, the relationship was doomed from the start. Lucrezia may have helped with the duke's financial worries, but she was fifteen years older than her bridegroom, thirty-six to his twenty-one. Nobody, of course, had asked Lucrezia what she thought about it; and when she married, she was in love with Count Ercole Contrari. She was a sophisticated, highly musical woman, and Francesco Maria was a rather odd young man. He had inherited his mother's religiosity, and was an obsessive list-maker, who compulsively recorded his own life in minute detail.

In 1571, the Venetian ambassador noted of Francesco Maria, 'his excellency plans to undertake the profession of arms himself'. He took a lot of exercise, and studied the technicalities of warfare, such as ballistics and fortification.[30] That year, the young prince participated in one of the most important naval battles of the sixteenth century, Lepanto, where the fleet of the Holy League, under the leadership of Don John of Austria (well known to him from his sojourn at the Spanish court), decisively defeated the Turks. This was the last major engagement fought by galleys. Francesco Maria fought under Don John in the admiral's frigate, and distinguished himself. When a reckoning was made, the Christian fleet had taken 117 galleys and 20 galliots, and sunk or destroyed about fifty other ships. Ten thousand Turks were taken prisoner, and many thousands of Christian slaves were rescued. About 7,500 Christians were killed, as against 30,000 Turks, and the battle effectively ended the Ottomans' incursions into Christian territory. But strangely, despite his extensive training and his family tradition, Francesco Maria never fought again. Though the Venetian signoria considered appointing him commander-in-chief in 1575, no agreement could be reached about terms.[31] He was not offered a condotta by any of the family's traditional employers until 1582, when he was hired by the Spanish king, though never, in the event, asked to take the field.

A year after Lepanto, in 1572, Lucrezia had a bad cold, and went back to Ferrara on the excuse of wanting a change of air. She never returned. She resumed her affair with Contrari, though when her brother Alfonso found out about it, he had the man strangled in his presence.[32] Lucrezia then began another affair, with Count Luigi Montecuccoli.[33] In 1578, the incompatible couple were granted a separation but not an annulment, which meant that since they were Catholics, neither of them could remarry. All Francesco Maria could do was wait, and pray for his wife to die. She saw no particular reason to oblige him, and lived on until 1598, by which time he was nearly fifty.

In 1574, Guidobaldo II died and Francesco Maria II succeeded to the dukedom. The della Roveres had finally produced a book-ish duke. Unfortunately, he had the same old problem as his predecessors: he had no son. Not counting children who died in infancy, the seven dukes of Urbino between them sired thirteen legitimate daughters and only five sons. Only Francesco Maria I was survived by more than one boy-child.

The new duke was cold, solitary and self-absorbed. He liked to make lists, whether of meals he had eaten, or animals he had killed (hunting was a favourite pastime), to observe facts. It was hunting that drew the duke to Castel Durante (now Urbania), where game was easily found. Federico da Montefeltro had built a deer park and lodge, the Barco, about a kilometre from the centre of Urbania, on the road leading to Sant'Angelo in Vado, for recreation, and Francesco Maria had it updated by Girolamo Genga for his own use. He also had Genga overhaul Francesco di Giorgio's ducal palace (which now houses a Museo Civico with a fine collection of paintings). He balanced the state budget by cutting back expenditure, and in 1579 sold the dukedom of Sora, the della Rovere patrimonial territories in the south of Italy, to Pope Gregory XIII for his son Giacomo Boncompagni, which brought him the hefty sum of 100,000 ducats.[34]

The celebrated biologist Ulisse Aldrovandi dedicated his enormous *De animalibus insectis* to Francesco Maria, witnessing to his interest in scientific observation. He was certainly a notable patron of scientists and technicians, and his other great interest was Aristotle.[35] His autobiography – the manuscript of which is in the Biblioteca Oliveriana in Pesaro – and his diary reveal his scientific temperament in that he observes natural phenomena of all kinds, but he never says how he feels about anything.[36]

Francesco Maria enjoyed theatricals, which, as in his father's time, were staged in the Great Hall at Pesaro, and he was a voracious reader. In 1585, he noted that he had finished reading the complete works of Aristotle, with the help of a local humanist, Cesare Benedetti, a task that had taken them fifteen years (Duke Federico had also read Aristotle with the assistance of a scholar).[37] He began to assemble a whole new library of printed texts; his librarian, Benedetto Benedetti, wrote repeatedly to Venice, Florence and Frankfurt (which was already issuing annual catalogues of available books in connection with the famous Frankfurt Book Fair), sending lists of what they were looking for.[38] He had a taste for architecture, and indulged his passion for solitude by designing a series of secluded retreats for himself.[39] He also laid out an extensive pleasure garden at Urbino, a formal garden that included choice fruit trees, a pergola, hedges and flower beds, and a *boschetto* on a hill planted with seventy elms, even though he seldom visited the city. In the eighteenth century, this became the garden of the Albani, who, since their ranks included a pope with an interest in restoring architecture, did much to preserve it. But it was destroyed in the 1930s when a school was built on the site.[40]

In 1581, there was a strange, rather sad moment. Ferdinand II of the Tyrol was amassing an Armoury of Heroes to add to the various collections at Schloss Ambras, near Innsbruck, the first systematic collection of armour ever made. Francesco Maria sent a helmet said to have belonged to Duke Federico (though it actually dated from the mid-sixteenth century), and armour belonging to Francesco Maria I, the 'curly-haired' helmet, and a cuirass.[41] Ferdinand was a little disappointed, but he was delighted also to receive six oil-on-copper miniatures, five of dukes of Urbino, and a sixth of a duchess (most probably Battista). Versions of Guidobaldo II and Oddantonio survive. The first duke's portrait was based on the blond barefoot youth in Piero della Francesca's *Flagellation*, and it would be a good guess that Federico and Battista's images were taken from the famous diptych. Francesco Maria also evidently commissioned a set of dukes for himself (together with duchesses), because they are listed in a Pesaro inventory made in 1623–4. It is strange to think of this childless man accumulating images of his forebears, but he clearly did, since there is another fancy portrait of Oddantonio in the Palazzo Ducale, Urbania, also from the late sixteenth century, which probably similarly formed part of a series.[42] Michel de Montaigne saw it when he visited Urbino in 1581, a visit that was not a success: he was not impressed by the palace, and nobody could find the key to the library.[43]

In 1597, Francesco Maria and the people of his duchy received a chilling reminder of the insecurity of their position. Alfonso d'Este II died, childless, having made determined efforts to secure the succession on his cousin Cesare, with the heartfelt assent of his people. The pope, then Clement VIII, was having none of it. He excommunicated Cesare, and sent an army of 30,000 to Ferrara. Cesare was forced to surrender, and the dukedom of Ferrara devolved to the Papal States. Francesco Maria was in exactly the same position. His father's younger brother, Cardinal Giulio Feltrio della Rovere, had had two illegitimate sons, later legitimized. One became an abbot, but the other, Ippolito della Rovere, was a layman, and married. He was about of an age with Francesco Maria, or perhaps some years younger. He had a son, Giulio, and several daughters. Ippolito's wife had died giving birth to Giulio, so the girls had been packed off to be brought up in the convent of Santa Caterina at Pesaro. Francesco Maria must have been forced to recognize that he would have no more chance of raising up Giulio as his heir than Alfonso had had of promoting Cesare.

Fortunately, at this anxious moment, Lucrezia died, in 1598. Francesco Maria's diary suggests a complete lack of feeling on his part, but since he doesn't seem to have set eyes on his wife since 1573, this is hardly surprising. Whenever he appeared in public after that, people shouted, 'Your Highness, get a wife!' ('Serenissimo, moglie!'). In 1599, the year after Lucrezia's death, Francesco Maria made an emergency marriage to the oldest of his girl cousins, Livia della Rovere, who was fourteen, thus thirty-six years his junior. The marriage was as disastrous as his first. The duke was old before his time, reserved and solitary, and Livia not unreasonably resented being made to marry an elderly man who had not the slightest interest in her. However, she seems to have done her best to adapt, since she is recorded as going deer-hunting with him, but there was no attraction between them. A double portrait by Federico Barocci sets out the story: the duke hangs over his young wife, pointing insistently to a sprig of oak, representing the della Rovere line.

She looks up from her book to stare at it: clearly, this marriage was all about the succession.[44]

Francesco Maria was far too self-absorbed to change his ways. He wanted a son; a wife was merely a means to an end. In 1601, there was a major crisis when he uncovered a plot, instigated by his bride's father, Ippolito della Rovere, to depose him on grounds of incompetence, which also involved his own chief engineer and architect, Muzio Oddi. Ippolito was forbidden the duchy, and Oddi was imprisoned in Pesaro, where he remained until 1609, after which he was exiled to Milan.[45] This incident further soured relations between Francesco Maria and his wife. Additionally, he had always been very close to his mother, Vittoria Farnese, who had acted as his duchess whenever he needed a woman to preside, and he did sometimes listen to her advice. The dowager did her best to protect and support her daughter-in-law, but when she died at the end of 1602, Livia was left friendless.

After six years of marriage, Livia's only child, Federico Ubaldo, was born on 16 May 1605. As on the previous occasion when the succession was hanging by a thread, there was a rash of commemorations of the precious son, as if some kind of sympathetic magic was being attempted. He was painted as a baby in gold-encrusted swaddling clothes by Federico Barocci, as a toddler by Claudio Ridolfi and Carlo Ceresa, and as a sickly-looking little boy by Claudio Ridolfi (twice). At least two churches in the vicinity of Pesaro acquired altarpieces showing the young Federico Ubaldo amid a protective cloud of saints.[46] There is also an anonymous engraving showing the parents, Francesco Maria, looking younger, thinner and healthier than his portraits, and Livia, with the precious son between them, aged about two, a hopeful, dynastic image. But the paintings do not suggest a robust, active, promising child.

The celebrations at Urbino following Federico Ubaldo's birth included a pageant celebrating the glories of Federico da Montefeltro, a baroque celebration of a Renaissance prince. It was devised by the Dominican Agostino Petretti, and clearly held the implication that those days would come again.[47] In the evening, the guests were summoned by a trumpet to crowd to the windows and balconies of the palace in order to witness a masque in the piazza. This had been decorated with woodland scenery, rising to a central mountain peak representing the Apennines. There was a cave near the top of it, containing elephants and classical trophies, with a broken bust of the Carthaginian general Hasdrubal, who had been defeated nearby at the Battle of the Metaurus in 207 BC. Two vast oak trees represented the della Roveres, with shepherds grouped picturesquely under their shade, playing musical instruments. A pageant passed slowly across the scene: first, the triumph of Fame. There was a black, crowned, Montefeltro eagle at the front, and behind it, figures of Fame, Time and Truth. The next car carried shields with the armorials of Duke Federico and the sovereigns associated with him, and representations of his honours, the golden rose, the Blessed Sword and commander's baton, the Garter, and so forth. The third was drawn by four horses, and ornamented with cornucopias and ducal *imprese*, surmounted by Justice, Bravery and Prudence. On foot came men carrying the banners and ensigns of the cities Federico had conquered, and lastly there was a car representing martial glory, carrying Pallas, and a pile of books with the motto, 'Minerva's liberal arts his victories did crown'.[48] This was followed by the return of all these allegorical entities to perform a ballet, and finally by fireworks. One of the reasons this has some importance is that because Francesco Maria proposed to fill the palace with guests, for perhaps the only time in his reign, he must have given the old building some attention before they arrived. Certainly, one of his odder initiatives was to have the fountain in the hanging garden turned into a highly ingenious refractive sundial, but there was probably some more practical refurbishment.[49]

Though Francesco Maria seems to have tried to take a more active part in the affairs of the dukedom after the birth of his son, he soon began to relapse into his old solitary ways. Clearly, he had not found begetting an heir particularly congenial, and the chance of any further children of the marriage with Livia was minimal. He lost interest in hunting, but took up horse-breeding, and spent more and more of his time in Castel Durante, where his stud was kept. He had his books brought there from Pesaro, and spent more and more of his time in seclusion, reading and discussing philosophical and theological topics with a select group of monks. He built himself a library there in 1607–9 to house his 13,000 printed books, in a park attached to the Palazzo Ducale, and dreamed of handing the dukedom over to his son. The child was only one when Francesco Maria created a council of state, selected from each of the cities in his dukedom, with the excuse that they could govern should a regency be necessary. He then withdrew completely from public life, so that, in effect, the regency began while he was still alive.

He seems to have had little faith in the capacities of Duchess Livia, perhaps because she had received a limited education in a convent, or because he disliked her, or because he distrusted her father. She was allowed to care for her son as a small child, but his education was entrusted to Countess Vittoria Tortora Ranuccio Santinelli, the wife of Francesco Maria's chief steward, and not to his mother. Federico Ubaldo was not overtaxed. His father left a memorandum of advice, which told him that since the Spanish kings were paying him a pension, he needed to learn Spanish, but otherwise, Italian would suffice. But the most important thing to remember was that he should marry the sister of the Grand Duke of Tuscany.[50] When he was ten, Federico Ubaldo was sent to Florence, to his Medici future in-laws, and Livia was left to lead a very lonely and isolated life at Castel Durante. She wrote her son a series of loving letters, suggesting that she would have been an affectionate mother to him if the duke had permitted it.[51]

Once again, an early marriage was an urgent necessity. Federico Ubaldo was betrothed to the Grand Duke's sister, Claudia de'

Medici, when they were both four. Unfortunately, he was not turning out well. Because he was a delicate child, he had been cosseted and indulged, and a cold, distant father plus an effectively absent mother must have been destabilizing. When he came of age and returned to Urbino, Francesco Maria realized with dismay that his son was weak, self-indulgent, and thoroughly spoilt. He was completely unable to cope with the boy, and Duchess Livia, living virtually under house arrest, was unable to help.

Federico Ubaldo and Claudia married in 1621, when he was sixteen, she seventeen. The lasting memorial of this wedding is the Porta Valbona, the principal entrance to the historic centre of Urbino, designed and built for the occasion by a local architect, Sigismondo Albani. Despite all he knew about his heir, Francesco Maria nonetheless abdicated in his favour in November 1621. This was perhaps a mixture of selfishness on the one hand, and on the other a vague hope that responsibility would sober his son up. The suite of pictures from the triumphal erection to welcome the new duchess in the principal square survive, and now hang in the Pasquino gallery of the Ducal Palace at Urbino. The painters, Claudio Ridolfi and Girolamo Cialdieri di Bartolomeo, offer the young Claudia de' Medici a series of vignettes of her predecessors, who are represented as stateswomen. Battista Sforza, wife of Federico da Montefeltro, is shown orating before Pius II. Elisabetta Gonzaga, wife of Guidobaldo da Montefeltro, is resisting all persuasions to a political divorce, and Caterina Cibo, mother of Guidobaldo II's first wife, is shown heroically defending her daughter, the heiress of Camerino. Thus the actual histories of previous Urbino brides tell a story of women educated to rule, which is specifically addressed in this series of tableaux, and perhaps suggests that whoever designed the *apparato* had hopes that Claudia would make up for her new husband's deficiencies.

Dukedom, unfortunately, went to the still-teenaged Federico Ubaldo's head. Like most of his family, he loved music, and he enjoyed the company of actors and, still more, actresses. He installed an actress called Argentina as his mistress and, in defiance of custom, took to acting himself.[52] However, he spent enough time with his wife to get her pregnant. A child was born in the second year of the marriage, though with the bad luck that seems to have attended the dukes in dynastic matters, she was a daughter, Vittoria della Rovere.

The year after that, 1623, Federico died, aged only eighteen. Autopsy revealed an infected lung, and water on the brain, and he seems to have had a stroke. He had made such a mess of things during his short reign that Francesco Maria had willy-nilly to emerge from his retirement and take over as duke, in the bitter knowledge that the dukedom would lapse on his death.

A few weeks after Federico's death, Vittoria and her mother moved to Florence, and on 19 April 1626, Claudia de' Medici married Leopold V, the Archduke of Austria, and moved to Innsbrück permanently, leaving her daughter to be raised by the Medici. When Leopold died in 1632, Claudia became regent in the name of her son Ferdinand Charles, and held the post until 1646. She died at Innsbrück in 1648, having clearly been another educated and effective woman, though, unfortunately, not at Urbino.

Vittoria was brought up in the Servite convent of La Crocetta, much patronized by the Medici ladies. Grand Duchess Maria Maddalena's youngest daughter, Anna de' Medici, joined her there. It was a most unusual convent, which the ladies used as a court, where they talked night and day, exchanged clothes, jewellery and secular books, enjoyed music and theatrical performances, and went in and out at will.[53] When she was seventeen months old, on 20 September 1623, she was engaged to her first cousin, the future Grand Duke of Tuscany, Ferdinando II de' Medici (1610–70), thirteen years her senior, ugly and homosexual. The magnificent frescoes of the Museo degli Argenti in the Pitti Palace were created in honour of the wedding, but the marriage was not a happy one. The bride was pretty, plump and deeply pious, whereas Ferdinando was interested in science and technology. In

1657, he and his younger brother Grand Prince Leopoldo founded the Accademia del Cimento in order to research new scientific methods and to attract scientists to Florence. Vittoria herself was not uneducated: she was taught Latin, Spanish and French, and when she was thirty-one, an ambassador to Florence noted that she was eloquent, and had 'a full understanding of contemporary historical events'.[54] She was also taught music, and as an adult was an informed and sophisticated patron. Contemporaries spoke of her with respect. The incompatible couple quarrelled over the upbringing of their son, Cosimo III de' Medici, a future Grand Duke of Tuscany: Ferdinando wanted a modern, science-based education for his son, while Vittoria was principally concerned to instil her own religious principles, in which she was successful. The last straw that ended the marriage was catching her husband in bed with a page.[55]

Back in Urbino, the aging Francesco Maria had taken up the title of duke again, but as there was no further hope for a male heir, he gave his duchy to Pope Urban VIII in 1625. The pope's nephew Taddeo Barberini then took control of the duchy, which was annexed to the Papal States after Francesco Maria's death at Urbania in 1631. Livia della Rovere was left a widow aged forty-six. She left Castel Durante and retired to her father's estate of Castelleone di Suasa, where she lived as a recluse until her death in 1641. She left all her property to her granddaughter, who thus inherited the vast ducal art collection, which she transferred to Florence.

Because she was estranged from her husband, Vittoria maintained a court of her own, chiefly at the Villa del Poggio Imperiale just to the south of Florence, which was notable for the patronage of women artists, musicians, poets and playwrights. She loved music, and was particularly concerned to support women musicians: in 1644, the Venetian composer Barbara Strozzi dedicated her first book of madrigals to the grand duchess.[56] A number of women writers also dedicated books to her, and she was first patroness of the first literary academy exclusively for women, the Assicurati of Siena, from 1654.[57] She was a significant patron and collector of art, which seems to have been the other consolation of her life besides religion. Though she valued her della Rovere heritage, and hung paintings by Raphael, Titian, Barocci and others at Poggio Imperiale, she made extensive collections of her own, frequently turning to the portraitist Justus Sustermans for pictures of herself and others. The exchange of portraits was an aspect of seventeenth-century diplomacy, and she had herself painted more than eighty times. She collected religious paintings, and was the most important patron of the Florentine artist Carlo Dolci.[58] She also liked still lifes. Vittoria accumulated a sizeable library, by no means all of it religious, and was particularly interested in writing about women rulers and in political memoirs.[59]

Though she has been portrayed as a gloomy bigot by a number of Medici historians, the last della Rovere was a sophisticated and highly cultivated woman, who was admired by contemporaries as an effective ruler.

15

The Eighteenth Century: Clement XI & The Stuarts

E ven before the last duke's death in 1631, Urbino was coasting into provincial decline, since Francesco Maria II seldom set foot there after 1605. After 1625, when he resigned his dukedom, the palace was in the charge of a papal legate, who divided his time between Urbino and Pesaro. Graffiti in the palace suggest that life there under the papal legates was stupefyingly dull. Someone, driven mad by 'Urbino's windy hill', scratched a heartfelt little poem into a wall:

> It is Cloud-Cuckoo-Land
> Every hour blown by wind
> No more can I withstand
> I will surely lose my mind
> Year of our Lord 1666, Aug. 18.[1]

Another graffiti from 1678 simply says, 'Ah, if I could go to Pesaro, what a pleasure it would be!'[2]

Meanwhile, outside the palace walls, life went on. Urbino was home to a series of important mathematicians from the days of Duke Federico onwards, and there was a good deal of technical and scientific activity in the town.[3] From the second half of the sixteenth century onwards, Urbino produced world-famous clocks and scientific instruments: Simone Barocci in particular was one of the few artisans capable of making experimental prototypes to a scholar's design, and Galileo was among his clients.[4] There was a scientific learned society in the town, the Accademia degli Strumenti. The most commercially successful new development was the manufacture of brass pins, made by a process invented in the eighteenth century by an Urbinate, Domenico Antonio, which became a sizeable industry. The town was also home to a literary society, the Assorditi.

Urbino's fortunes looked up again in 1700, when Gian Francesco Albani, from a local patrician family, became pope, taking the name of Clement XI. He viewed the Catholic Church as a spiritual and cultural entity rather than a political or military power, and while he certainly advanced the interests of his family, he was profoundly concerned for the dignity of the Church. His art patronage was less of grand new projects, in the mode of Sixtus IV, than of the restoration and refurbishment of Christian and classical monuments.[5] He was scholarly, a patron of the arts and sciences, and he took a great interest in the Vatican library and the archaeology of Rome. He was also patriotic towards the city of his birth, and lavishly endowed the family library, originally created by his grandfather. By 1800, it held about thirty thousand books, which meant there was still a great library in the town through the eighteenth century, made available to scholars.[6] About a third of the collection is now the Clementine Library of the Catholic University of America in Washington, having been sold up in the nineteenth century. In 1703, the pope sent Mgrs Origo and Lancisi to make a survey of Urbino, and on the basis of their work initiated a repair and rebuilding project.[7] The architect Carlo Fontana was sent from Rome to restore the cathedral and the Ducal Palace. As with his work on Roman monuments, Clement's restoration of the Urbino palace was tactful. His intention was always to restore with as little damage to the original fabric as possible. He put his mark, the Albani triple mountain and star, on small details (such as the pillars at the entrance and the top of the well in the courtyard), but refrained from large-scale interventions. He also had the church of San Bernardino, the bishop's palace and the Palazzo Communale overhauled.

One room on the piano nobile of the Urbino palace, richly decorated with the emblems of the Montefeltro and della Rovere families by the *stuccatore* Federico Brandani, is known as the Sala de Re. The plasterwork was commissioned by Guidobaldo II as part of a redecoration undertaken before his second marriage, to Vittoria Farnese, but it was subsequently renamed for a royal guest, James Francis Edward Stuart, the rightful king of England by descent. James's father, James II of England, had been ousted in 1688 in favour of his Protestant daughter Mary and her husband, William of Orange. After the disastrous Jacobite Rising of 1715, James was forced to leave France, which was allied with England and Holland, and found the pretender a diplomatic embarrassment. Clement XI offered him a refuge in Rome, but after a few months suggested that he might care to move his entourage to the palace at Urbino, which had recently been restored. The prince agreed, and the pope sent decorators off post-haste with quantities of furniture and a random collection of tapestries from the papal collection. Clement spent more than 2,200 scudi on the restoration, decoration and furnishing of the palace, probably the first major overhaul it had had since the birth of Federico Ubaldo nearly a hundred years previously.

When the palace was ready, the exiles set off in a procession of carriages, and arrived at Urbino in July 1717. This was by far the most exciting thing to happen in Urbino for quite some time, and he was met in the piazza by an assembly of local worthies. James occupied the entire suite of rooms overlooking the Cortile di Pasquino, which became his guard chamber, presence chamber, privy chamber and bedroom. The reason the Sala de Re has been particularly associated with James is that the décor includes unicorns, which, since unicorns support the arms of Scotland, made it appropriate for a Stuart. James used the room, which opened off his bedroom, as his private office, and wrote letters there.[8] The papal legate, Alamanno Salviati, who remained to keep an eye on the situation and act as liaison with Rome, lived in Duke Federico's apartments.[9] One of the Jacobites has left a description of how the palace struck him:

> The apartments are numerous and large. The stair straitly. You have his statue on the first turn. The chimneys, windows and doors are all of hewn stone curiously cutt in diverse shapes... there's a great sale [saloon] a hundred and twelve feet in length... in this sale there is a statue of the present pope sett up at the charge of this city.[10]

The first statue mentioned is of Federico in Roman armour carved by Girolamo Campagna, set in a niche at the top of the first flight, which was put there in 1604 by Francesco Maria II – his head is tilted so that his right profile is not visible. The second is a statue of Clement XI, who had abundantly earned the gratitude of the citizenry, which is by Bartolomeo Pincelotti: it is now outside, in the Largo Clemente XI.

At first, the exiled prince was enchanted by the size and grandeur of the palace, but the downsides began to multiply. Urbino was very remote, and perched on top of a steep hill, hopelessly inconvenient if one's idea of an excursion is driving in a carriage, which was axiomatic for an eighteenth-century nobleman. On feast days, James would drive to the Duomo in a coach and six, escorted by courtiers on horseback, and attended by liveried postillions. He could have walked from the palace to the cathedral in less than a minute.

On fine days, James went down to the Cappuccini monastery in the valley, and coursed hares with his 'two clever little Danish doggies'.[11] When it was wet, he played battledore and shuttlecock in the huge, under-furnished rooms. In the evenings, he might play cards with the ladies of Urbino. It was an empty, uneventful, acutely depressing life, where nobody had enough to do, and music was the principal form of entertainment: James was successfully converted to a love of Italian music from his previous French taste after the Duke of Mar arrived with quantities of new music from the latest operas.[12] Mar mused in a letter, 'I do not wonder the people of this country give themselves to music, architecture etc., since they are in a manner out of communication with the world, and must have things not depending on it to entertain themselves.' [13]

The approach of winter revealed another downside of the palace at Urbino: the large rooms are freezing cold, and there are very few fireplaces. Aristocratic life in the eighteenth century was conducted in warmer rooms, wearing thinner clothes, than it had been in the days of Federico. The following spring, James admitted defeat. Negotiations has been proceeding for his marriage, and so he left Urbino and went back to Rome with his new bride, Clementina Sobieska, where Clement put the Palazzo Muti at their disposal. He would live there for the next forty-seven years, till his death in 1766.

James was gloomy, dull and reserved, but Urbino society was doubtless sorry to see him go. However, the Albani remained faithful to their city of origin. Clement XI ensured the wealth of his family by assigning his brother a fiefdom (Soriano nel Cimino) and by appointing two of his nephews cardinals. Cardinal Annibale Albani, the elder of the two, held several important positions in the Curia before his death in 1751. In 1737 he decided to embellish Urbino by donating a statue of Pope Alexander VIII to the town, which was placed near the magnificent Albani family palace on what is now the Via Donato Bramante.

In 1668, Pietro da Cortona, one of the greatest painters of his time, had been commissioned to produce cartoons of the Apocalypse as models for the projected mosaic decoration of the first chapel on the right of St Peter's Basilica in Rome. The painter died in the following year and the work was completed by his pupil Ciro Ferri. The paintings themselves were abandoned and put into store. Annibale Albani heard about them, and ordered them to be taken to Urbino, where they were fitted into the domed roof of the chapel of Santa Chiara, where Duke Francesco Maria I della Rovere and his wife, Eleonora Gonzaga, were buried. Annibale's other gifts to the city include a small bronze statue of St Crescentinus, the patron saint of Urbino, found during the renovation of Santi Apostoli in Rome, also undertaken by the Albani.

Clement XI further adorned Urbino with an antiquarian status symbol, a red granite Egyptian obelisk, which was erected in front of the church of San Domenico. This was pieced together from five different fragments, two of which come from a pair of obelisks from Sais, a town in the Nile Delta, which were commissioned by Pharaoh Wahibre *c.* 580 BC. They were taken to Rome in the late first century, and used to decorate the Temple of Isis there. One of them toppled for some reason, and broke into three pieces, which were rediscovered on the site of the Iseum, near Piazza della Minerva, by Giovanni Pietro Bellori in 1676, and acquired by the other Albani cardinal, Alessandro, who is best remembered for the collection of ancient statues he gathered in his Roman villa. Another of the fragments that make up the obelisk as it is now is from an obelisk of Rameses II, most of which is in the Villa Celimontana in Rome.[14] When Clement became pope, he had the obelisk constructed from these bits and pieces, and decided it should go to Urbino. His nephew Cardinal Annibale organized the transport, and it arrived in Urbino in 1737.

Another eighteenth-century addition to the city was the renovation of Francesco di Giorgio's fifteenth-century Duomo. It was given a new west front, designed by Camillo Morigia, and completed in 1782. An earthquake in 1789 brought down the cupola, and necessitated major reconstruction, undertaken by Giuseppe Valadier, hence the overall neoclassical appearance of the building as it is today. Due principally to the Albani, the eighteenth century was kind to Urbino. It was a century of restoration and consolidation, which protected the town's Renaissance identity.

16

The Last Duke of Urbino

The palace at Urbino fell on hard times after the Albani interventions of the eighteenth century. When Napoleon reached Urbino in 1798, he transferred the city government to the palace. In the course of the nineteenth century, some of the building became a prison (and remained a prison at least until the 1880s), and other areas were requisitioned for the police and other functionaries, the vice-legate's apartments, barracks for Swiss guards, a theatre, a Monte di Pietà, archives, schoolrooms, stores, private flats, and the town academies.[1] However, there was one important new intervention in the town, which had nothing to do with the prefect in charge. Theatre and opera had become a principal form of entertainment in nineteenth-century Italy. Urbino was no exception, and the fine Teatro Raffaello Sanzio was built between 1845 and 1853, on top of Francesco di Giorgio's fifteenth-century ramp.

Though a variety of nineteenth-century English and American visitors to Italy made it as far as Urbino, they were on the whole unimpressed. An American artist makes it clear that a visit to Urbino in the 1880s was quite an adventure: 'we started and we wound and wound ever up to Gubbio, and down again across a valley, and then came a climb. Two oxen were added and we mostly walked, and up and up we went till at last the high pass opened, and away above was Urbino, beyond another vine-filled valley, the city stretching from mountain to mountain, built on mighty arches'.[2] When Edith Wharton visited thirteen years later, in 1896, she similarly found that 'for the last six miles or more of the drive our horses had to be reinforced by oxen'.[3] The roads were not significantly improved until the general improvement of the Italian highway network at the end of the 1960s.[4]

In an essay, *Euphorion*, the Italophile Englishwoman Vernon Lee, who visited Urbino in 1883, describes the town as 'small and lost among the Umbrian bandits'. She sets her ghost story, 'Amour Dure', in Urbino in winter (though she herself visited in spring).[5] Her hero is a romantic young Polish historian, who finds the town suffocatingly provincial, but also, in the most literal sense, haunted by the past. He is lodging with an antique dealer, so he finds himself surrounded by the rubble of the Renaissance: old carved chairs, *cassoni* and alleged Raphaels. The palace is 'a superb red brick structure, turreted and battlemented… from whose windows you look down upon a sea, a kind of whirlpool, of melancholy grey mountains. Then there are the people, dark, bushy-bearded men, riding about like brigands, wrapped in green-lined cloaks upon their shaggy pack-mules; or loitering about.' She writes of dark, narrow streets, shuttered windows. In her tale, the castle is haunted by the ghost of an invented, superlatively evil former duchess, Medea da Carpi, executed in 1582, who successfully seduces the young Pole and brings about his death.

Vernon Lee's contemporary, Joseph Henry Shorthouse, seems to have been even more spooked by Federico's palace than she had been. His historical novel *John Inglesant*, published in 1881, was much read in its day, and, like Lee, he seems to have found the palace a literally haunting place, seductive and vicious: 'It is impossible to dwell in or near this wonderful house without the life becoming affected, and even diverted from its previous course, by its imperious influence... together with this delight to eye and sense there is present to the mind a feeling, not altogether painless, of oppressive luxury, and of the mating of incongruous forms, arousing as it were an uneasy conscience, and affecting the soul somewhat as the overpowering perfume of tropical vegetation affects the senses... the indweller, whose intellect was mastered by the genius of the architecture, found his simplicity impaired, his taste becoming more sensuous and less severely chaste, and his senses lulled and charmed by the insidious and enervating spirit that pervaded the place.'6

John Addington Symonds, the Italophile poet and cultural historian, also visited Urbino in the 1880s, and found it more to his taste, but what he records is bleakness and emptiness, the shabby, run-down remains of former grandeur. 'Wandering now through these deserted halls, we seek in vain for furniture or tapestry or works of art... If frescoes adorned the corridors, they have been whitewashed; the ladies' chambers have been stripped of their rich arras. Only here and there we find a raftered ceiling, painted in fading colours, which, taken with the stonework of the chimney, and some fragments of inlaid panel-work on door or window, enables us to reconstruct the former richness of these princely rooms... The impression left upon the mind after traversing this palace in its length and breadth is one of weariness and disappointment.' He also records that part of the structure was still being used as a prison, and the hanging garden (which had been covered over with lead in the eighteenth century) as an exercise yard: 'paced in these bad days by convicts in grey canvas jackets'.7

Like Vernon Lee, Edward Hutton, writing in 1913, focused on the dismalness of the climate. 'Bleak and rain-sodden, battered by the wind, burnt by the sun, Urbino seems the last place in Italy to have nourished a court renowned for its grace and courtesy.'8 But for Hutton, as for Symonds, the palace is not sinister, merely sad. The miscellaneous offices of the Napoleonic era were still in evidence. 'In spite of all the patronage and splendour of the

Counts and Dukes of Urbino, there is little enough left to-day in their city to remind us of the hosts of artists they entertained at their court and employed in decorating the magnificent palace where they lived, and the churches they endowed or protected. The palace is, indeed, spoiled and changed... As you wander to-day through those corridors, out of which the beautiful rooms open, so bare now, or turned to the meaner uses of our time, through the doorways and past the mantelpiece with their friezes of dancing angels or vines carved by Domenico Rosselli, you come at last to the little study of Duke Federigo, where the walls, all of intarsia, once shut out for him the noisy world of battle and intrigue.'[9]

Urbino, then, was shabby and decayed before the First World War, a city and palace with a glorious past, but with no obvious future. The first major intervention that led to its renaissance was the decision to turn part of the palace into the National Gallery of the Marche, officially established by royal decree on 7 March 1912. The great ducal collections had been dispersed, mostly to Florence and Rome, in the seventeenth century, but at the unification of Italy in 1861, the evaporation of the Papal States had put the new Italian government in charge of a vast collection of art that needed to be catalogued, housed and, in many cases, restored.[10] The first pictures to come into the palace therefore were ones that belonged to ecclesiastical institutions in the Marche that had been suppressed in 1861, when an 'Istituto di Belle Arti' was created to house them in a disused church. In 1912, they were handed over to the new gallery. Among other items, the Uccello predella, the Ideal City panel, and two Titians, originally part of a processional standard belonging to the Confraternity of Corpus Domini, were brought to the palace, while two works by artists with strong associations with the dukes of Urbino were bought for the collection by the Ministry of Public Instruction, a *Madonna and Child* by Giovanni Santi and a *St Francis* by Federico Barocci. Luigi Serra, director of the gallery from 1915 to 1933, fought doggedly to increase the importance of the collection. He persuaded the Duomo to let the gallery have Piero della Francesca's *Flagellation* and Timoteo Viti's Arrivabene altarpiece, and in 1915 he acquired two fine paintings by Luca Signorelli, which had been made for the Confraternity of the Holy Spirit. Piero's *Madonna of Senigallia* came to the gallery in 1917. The tapestries after designs by Raphael, which are now in the Throne Room, arrived in 1923. They date from the seventeenth century, and three of them are English, while the other four were made in France.[11] Serra also put the whole collection on a more scholarly footing. In 1927, the state recognized the growing importance of the Gallery by sending Raphael's *La Muta* to join the collection. In 1934, under Serra's successor, the Barberini Gallery in Rome was persuaded to sell the double portrait of Federico and Guidobaldo and fourteen of the 'Illustrious Men' to the Italian state, and they were returned to Federico's *studiolo* (the rest, unfortunately, had been inherited by a different branch of the family, and sold to the Louvre in 1861, so they could not be recovered).[12]

The rediscovery of Urbino went hand in hand with the twentieth-century rediscovery of Piero della Francesca, since there was an obvious trail to the Galleria Nazionale in Urbino via Arezzo, Borgo Sansepolcro and Monterchi. By 1930, Baedeker, the classic traveller's guide of the early twentieth century, says, 'a visit to Urbino affords perhaps a more vivid idea of the Renaissance than many hours spent in Florence' (though the first edition of 1909 is much more lukewarm), and the more curious, and more aesthetically aware, had taken note. The first hotel to open in Urbino was the Albergo Italia, which for decades was the Mecca of all English visitors. Clive and Vanessa Bell went to Urbino in 1913, Adrian Stokes in 1925: he wrote to Ben Nicolson (responding to the latter's drawings of Urbino made in 1962), '[the palace] gave me the greatest architectural kick I have ever had'.[13] When the painter David Russell stayed at the Albergo in 1955, he leafed through the visitors' book and found it full of the names of people he knew.[14] My husband, visiting the art historian Hugh Honour in the 1970s, remembers his remarking that the problem with Urbino in the 1950s was that if you arrived and found someone already ensconced in the Albergo whom you particularly wished to avoid, there was no acceptable alternative.

The man, above all, who made Urbino what it is today was Carlo Bo. He was a professor of modern languages, an anti-fascist intellectual from Milan, who became rector of the Free University of Urbino in 1947. This institution had decayed along with the rest of the city. It had few resources when he took over, there were fewer than 140 students, and only one large building.[15] Bo was a visionary, however, with a dream of the transformation of his moribund 450-year-old university into one of the great institutions of Italy and the world.

In 1944, during the German occupation of Italy, Bo had found himself fighting alongside Giancarlo de Carlo, who was then the second most important figure in the Milan resistance movement. Once the war was over, de Carlo began practising as an architect, and in 1951 Bo called him to Urbino to restructure the university's crumbling headquarters. In 1958, de Carlo was asked to propose a structural plan for the renovation of Urbino, which took him six years to achieve. Since de Carlo called for a considerable degree of restriction on the private use of land, and the concentration of resources for the public good, his ideas were thought practically communist, and generated a great deal of public debate. However, there was no discord between town and gown. The mayor of Urbino, an ex-miner and pragmatic politician called Egidio Mascioli, understood what Bo was trying to achieve, and they worked together until the 1970s, by which time student numbers had jumped to 10,000. The enrolment is now 20,000 – an influx of talented young people, which has revitalized the city and given it purpose. It is for this reason that Bo has been referred to in print as 'the last Duke of Urbino', not entirely in jest: the money the students bring with them, just by living their lives, are the equivalent of Federico's *condotte*.[16]

The university impinges relatively little on the visitor's experience because the residential colleges are a complex of modern buildings by de Carlo on the Colle dei Cappuccini, ten minutes to the south-west of the city centre, and invisible from it. They are, in themselves, some of the most important and interesting post-war buildings in Italy: a university city, conceived as a parallel to the palace, and similarly organized as an ideal city.[17] Additionally, the university has restored many valuable buildings in the historic centre, saving them from abandonment and destruction, and preserving street façades while unobtrusively building in everything a modern university needs behind them. Creating a university in a small medieval town without destroying its integrity is a challenge many European cities have faced, few more successfully.[18] Three complex restructurings have been made within the old centre, all designed by de Carlo: the Law Faculty (completed in 1973), the Magistero (1976) and the Business School (opened in 2000–1). The Business School was created within the Palazzo Battiferri, the childhood home of one of the great woman poets of sixteenth-century Italy, Laura Battiferri Ammannati.[19] The most interesting is the Magistero (School of Education), which was built on the site of an eighteenth-century convent. Once within the high old walls, which have been preserved, it opens out into an extremely complex and subtle five-storey structure with a huge, amphitheatre-like semicircular fan of glass, which gives natural light from above to the big meeting rooms, and is visible only from outside the city. The Magistero takes advantage of the sloping site, so one enters at fourth floor level, with most of the building actually beneath one.

Much of de Carlo's efforts in the city centred on revitalizing the Mercatale, the threshold to the Renaissance city. He achieved the very considerable feat of reopening Francesco di Giorgio's magnificent spiral ramp up to the palace, while simultaneously conserving the splendid neoclassical theatre, Teatro Sanzio, which had been built on top of it, and he constructed underground parking and a coach station – the unglamorous practical underpinnings needed to accommodate visitors in the age of the car. The experience of arriving at Urbino today is the result of his work.

The palace also benefited from this atmosphere of renewal. In 1938, the city was designated as the headquarters for the new Soprintendenza alle Gallerie e alle Opere d'Arte delle Marche, with Pasquale Rotondi, who wrote the first major study of the architecture of the palace, as Soprintendente per i Beni Culturali. A Special Law for Urbino was enacted in 1968, when Federico's infill under the Ducal Palace area threatened to subside: this state subsidy paid for strengthening and consolidating the ground and financed basic repairs to the roofing and masonry.[20] A sum of 3.5 billion lire was made available, part to be spent on basic facilities such as sewers, part for the restoration of the Ducal Palace and other major buildings, and part to help private citizens restore houses in run-down areas of the city.[21] Extensive restorations were carried out by the Soprintendenza ai Monumenti after serious damage was caused to the fabric by earthquakes and earth tremors that shook the Marche from January to July 1972, and special grants were made to cope with the disastrous effects on the building's fabric. They financed basic repairs to the roofing and masonry of the Ducal Palace, and the complete renovation of the *studiolo*.[22] The results were presented to the public in a great exhibition in 1973, and tourism became more of a feature of the local economy as the city was renewed.

In 1970, Giancarlo de Carlo noted that Urbino was drawing in only about 30,000 visitors a year, and only 20 per cent of those were foreigners – thus, only about 6,000 travellers thought the journey worth their while.[23] But this was beginning to change, particularly for English speakers. The first chapter of Sacheverell Sitwell's *Great Houses of Europe*, published in 1961, was devoted to the Ducal Palace, and it featured extensively in Kenneth Clarke's *Civilisation*, filmed between 1966 and 1969.[24] In 1971, Michael Levey, then Keeper of the National Gallery, wrote a rapturous landmark article on Urbino in the *Sunday Times* – though it is clear from the photographs that accompany his words that the *torricini* and the loggias were still masked in scaffolding, and that much of the structure was still in need of consolidation and conservation.[25] The reopening of the palace after restoration, the renewal of the fabric of the city's buildings more generally, the revitalization of its identity, and an increasing number of hotels brought a welcome rise in visitor numbers, though it still remains a niche destination. Whereas Florence, Siena, Perugia and Assisi all cluster on the western side of the Apennines, with easy connections between them, Urbino lies east of the mountains. It remains a place of pilgrimage for people who are moved by the Italian Renaissance, and find there a sense of connection to the past that can hardly be equalled by any other city in Europe.

Bibliography
Picture Credits
Notes
Index

Bibliography

Agostini, Ludovico, *Le Giornate Soriane*, eds Laura Salvetti Firpo and Franco Barcia (Roma: Salerno, 2004).

Alberti, Leon Battista, *On Painting and On Sculpture*, ed. and trs. Cecil Grayson (London: Phaidon, 1972).

Albury, W.R., 'Castiglione's "Francescopaedia": Pope Julius II and Francesco Maria della Rovere in "The Book of the Courtier",' *The Sixteenth Century Journal*, 42.2 (2011), pp. 323–47.

Alexander-Skipnes, Ingrid, '"Bound with Wond'rous Beauty": Eastern Codices in the Library of Federico da Montefeltro', Mediterranean Studies 19 (2010), pp. 67–85.

Allegretti, Allegretto, 'Ephemerides Senenses', in Ludovico Antonio Muratori (ed.), *Rerum Italicarum Scriptores* 23 (Milano: Societas Palatinae, 1733), coll. 767–860.

Ames-Lewis, Francis, *The Library and Manuscripts of Piero di Cosimo de' Medici* (New York and London: Garland, 1984).

Ames-Lewis, Francis, 'Nicola da Urbino and Raphael', *The Burlington Magazine*, 130, no. 1026 (1988), pp. 690–92.

Arbizzoni, Guido, 'L'orazione di Martino Filetico in morte di Gentile Brancaleoni', *Res publica litterarum* 16 (1993), pp. 145–58.

Arbizzoni, Guido, et al., *Pesaro nell'età dei Della Rovere*, 2 vols (Venezia: Marsilio Editore, 2001).

Aristotle, *Nicomachean Ethics*, trs. H. Rackham (Cambridge, MA: Harvard University Press/ London: William Heinemann Ltd, 1934).

Baiardi Cerboni, Anna (ed.), *I Giardini del Duca* (Milano: Silvano Editore, 2018).

Baiardi Cerboni, Giorgio, Chittolini, Giorgio, and Floriani, Piero (eds), *Federico di Montefeltro: lo stato, le arti, la cultura*, 3 vols (Roma: Bulzoni, 1986).

Baldasso, Renzo, 'Portrait of Luca Pacioli and Disciple: A New, Mathematical Look', *The Art Bulletin*, 92.1/2 (2010), pp. 83–102.

Baldi, Bernardino, *Versi e prose, di monsignor Bernardino Baldi da Vrbino abbate di Guastalla* (Venezia: Francesco de' Franceschi, 1590).

———, *Della vita e de fatti di Giudobaldo da Montefeltro, Duca d'Urbino*, 2 vols (Milano, Giovanni Silvestri, 1821).

————, *Vita e Fatti di Federigo di Montefeltro Duca di Urbino*, 3 vols (Roma: Alessandra Ceracchi, 1824).

————, *Le vite de' matematici: Edizione annotata e commentata della parte medievale e rinascimentale*, ed. Elio Nenci (Milano: FrancoAngeli, 1998).

Baratin, Laura, Bertozzi, Sara and Moretti, Elvio 'The Geomorphological Transformations of the City of Urbino: The Design of the City Analysed with GIS tools', *Ricerca Scientifica e Tecnologie dell'Informazione*, 5.1 (2015), pp. 41–60, p. 49.

Battifferi, Laura, *Laura Battiferra and Her Literary Circle: An Anthology*, ed. and trs. Victoria Kirkham (Chicago: Chicago University Press, 2006).

Battisti, Eugenio, *Piero della Francesca*, 2 vols (Milano: Electa, 1992).

Baxandall, Michael, 'Bartholomaeus Facius on Painting: A Fifteenth-Century Manuscript of the *De Viris Illustribus*', *Journal of the Warburg and Courtauld Institutes*, 27 (1964), pp. 90–107.

Bayer, Andrea (ed.), *Art and Love in Renaissance Italy* (New Haven and London: Yale University Press, 2008).

Beecher, Donald, and Ciavolella, Massimo (trs.), Annibal Caro, *The Scruffy Scoundrels* (Waterloo: Wilfred Laurier University Press, 1981).

Bei, Leonello, and Cristini, Stefano, *La doppia anima: La vera storia di Ottaviano Ubaldini e Federico da Montefeltro* (Apecchio, Urbania: Associazione amici della storia di Apecchio, 2000).

Bei, Leonello, and Cristini, Stefano, *Vita e gesta del Magnifico Bernardino Ubaldini della Carda* (Apecchio, Urbania: Associazione amici della storia di Apecchio, 2015).

Bell, Susan Groag, *The Lost Tapestries of the City of Ladies* (Berkeley: University of California Press, 2004).

Belozerskaya, Marina, *Rethinking the Renaissance: Burgundian Arts Across Europe* (Cambridge and New York: Cambridge University Press, 2002).

Belozerskaya, Marina, *Luxury Arts of the Renaissance* (London: Thames & Hudson, 2005).

Bembo, Pietro, *I duchi di Urbino: De urbino ducibus liber*, ed. Valentina Marchesi (Bologna: I Libri di Emil, 2010).

Benelli, Francesco, 'Diversification of Knowledge: Military Architecture as a Political Tool in the Renaissance. The Case of Francesco di Giorgio Martini', *RES: Anthropology and Aesthetics*, 57/58 (2010), pp. 140–55.

Bennett, J. M. et al. (eds), Sisters and Workers in the Middle Ages (Chicago: University Press, 1994).

Benzi, Fabio, 'Baccio Pontelli, Francione e lo studiolo ligneo del Duco di Montefeltro a Urbino', *Storia dell'arte*, 102, n.s. 2 (2002), pp. 7–22.

Benzoni, Gino, 'Livia della Rovere, Duchessa di Urbino', *Dizionario Biografico degli Italiani*, 65 (2005, online).

Bertelli, Carlo, *Piero della Francesca*, trs. Edward Farrelly (London: BCA, 1992).

Bertozzi, Luigi (ed.), *Rime del conte Antonio di Montefeltro* (Rimini, Marsoner e Grandi, 1819).

Bianucci, R., A. Perciaccante, and O. Appenzeller, '"From father to son": Early Onset Gout in Guidobaldo I da Montefeltro, Duke of Urbino (1472–1508)', *European Journal of Internal Medicine*, 36 (December 2016), pp. 28–30.

Baiardi, Giorgio Cerboni, Chittolini, Giorgio and Floriani, Piero (eds.), *Federico di Montefeltro: lo stato, le arti, la cultura* (Rome: Bulzoni Editore, 1986), III, pp. 19–49.

Bober, Phyllis Pray, and Rubinstein, Ruth *Renaissance Artists & Antique Sculpture: A Handbook of Sources* (London: H. Miller, 1987).

Bonfatti, Luigi, *Memorie storiche di Ottaviano Nelli, pittore eugubino: illustrate con documenti* (Gubbio: Tipografia Magni, 1843).

Bonvini, Marinella Mazzanti, *Battista Sforza Montefeltro: una 'principessa' nel Rinascimento italiano* (Urbino: QuattroVenti, 1993).

Borchert, Till-Holger (ed.), *The Age of Van Eyck: The Mediterranean World and Early Netherlandish Painting* (Ghent and Amsterdam: Ludion, 2002).

Borgarino, Paola, 'Giancarlo de Carlo's University Colleges in Urbino. Studies and Analysis for the Conservation Plan', *Ge-conservación/Conservação*, 11 (2017), pp. 286–91.

Bornstein, Daniel, 'The Wedding Feast of Roberto Malatesta and Isabetta da Montefeltro: Ceremony and Power', *Renaissance and Reformation*, NS 12.2 (1988), pp. 101–17.

Bradford, Sarah, *Cesare Borgia* (London: Futura, 1981)

Brown, David Alan (ed.), *Virtue and Beauty: Leonardo's Ginevra de' Benci and Renaissance Portraits of Women* (Princeton: Princeton University Press, 2003).

Bullough, G., 'The Murder of Gonzago', *The Modern Language Review*, 30.4 (1935), pp. 433–44.

Burke, Peter, *The Fortunes of The Courtier: The European Reception of Castiglione's*

Cortegiano (University Park: Pennsylvania State University Press, 1996).

Bury, Michael, and Kemp, Martin 'An Urbino Provenance for the Toulouse "Boarhunt"', *The Burlington Magazine*, 133, no. 1060 (1991), p. 452.

Butler, Kim E., 'Giovanni Santi, Raphael, and Quattrocento Sculpture', *Artibus et Historiae*, 30, no. 59 (2009), pp. 15–39.

Caldari, Claudia, Mochi Onori, Lorenza and Peruzzi, Marcella (eds), *Ornatissimo codice: la biblioteca di Federico di Montefeltro* (Milan: Skira, 2008).

Caldelli, Elisabetta, 'Antiporte e clipei iscritti: suggestioni per una ricerca', in *La catalogazione dei manoscritti miniati come strumento di conoscenza. Esperienze, metodologia, prospettive*, ed. Silvia Maddalo and Michela Torquati (Roma: Istituto storico italiano per il Medio evo, 2010), pp. 217–28.

Callmann, Ellen, 'Lo Sport Aristocratico della Caccia: Una "spalliera" per Federico da Montefeltro', *Bollettino d'Arte*, Series 6.65 (1991), pp. 67–70.

Campani, I.A., *Opera Omnia* (Venezia: Bernardino Vercellensis, 1502).

Campbell, Caroline, *Love and Marriage in Renaissance Florence: The Courtauld Wedding Chests* (London: The Courtauld Gallery, 2007).

Campbell, Stephen J., '*Pictura* and *Scriptura*: Cosmè Tura and Style as Courtly Performance', *Art History*, 19.2 (1996) pp. 267–95.

Campbell, Stephen J. and Cole, Michael W., *A New History of Italian Renaissance Art* (London: Thames & Hudson, 2012).

Campbell, Thomas, *Tapestry in the Renaissance: Art and Magnificence* (New Haven and New York: Metropolitan Museum of Art and Yale University Press: 2002).

Campofregoso, Battista, *De Dictis Factis Memorabilibus Collectanea*, trs. Camillo Ghellini (Paris: Galliot du Pré, 1518).

Carlisle, Barbara, 'Pageants and Painting: The Theatrical Context of High Renaissance Painting', *The Centennial Review*, 24.4 (1990), pp. 459–74.

Carpinello, Mariella, *Lucrezia d'Este. Duchessa di Urbino* (Milano: Rusconi, 1988).

Castigione, Baldassare, *The Book of the Courtier*, trs. George Bull (London: Penguin Books, 1976).

Centanni, Monica, 'Elisabetta Gonzaga come Danaë nella medaglia di Adriano Fiorentino (1495)', *La rivista di engramma*, 106 (2013) pp. 107–25.

Chadwick, J. and Mann, W.N. (trs.), *Hippocratic Writings* (Harmondsworth: Penguin, 1978).

Chambers, David, and Martineau, Jane (eds), *Splendours of the Gonzaga* (London: Victoria & Albert Museum, 1981).

Chambers, D.S., *Patrons and Artists in the Italian Renaissance* (Basingstoke: Macmillan, 1970).

Chapman, Hugo, Henry, Tom and Plazzotta, Carol, *Raphael: From Urbino to Rome* (London: National Gallery, 2004).

Cheles, Luciano, *The Studiolo of Urbino: An Iconographic Investigation* (Wiesbaden: Reichert, 1986).

Chomentovskaja, O., 'Le comput digital: Histoire d'un geste dans l'art de la Renaissance italienne', *Gazette des Beaux-Arts*, 20 (1938), pp. 157–72.

Christiansen, Keith, *Piero della Francesca: Personal Encounters* (New York: Metropolitan Museum of Art, 2013).

Clark, Kenneth, *Piero della Francesca* (London: Phaidon, 1951).

Clarke, Georgia, *Roman House – Renaissance Palaces: Inventing Antiquity in Fifteenth-Century Italy* (Cambridge: Cambridge University Press, 2003).

Cleri, Bonita, and Eiche, Sabine (eds), *I della Rovere nell' Italia delle Corti*, 4 vols, II: *Luoghi e opere d'arte* (Urbino: QuattroVenti, 2002).

Clifford, Timothy, and Mallet, J.V.G., 'Battista Franco as a Designer for Maiolica', *The Burlington Magazine* 118, no. 879 (1976), pp. 387–410.

Clough, Cecil H., 'Sources for the History of the Court and City of Urbino in the Early Sixteenth Century', *Manuscripta*, 7 (1963), pp. 67–79.

——, 'Cardinal Bessarion at the Court of Urbino', *Manuscripta*, 8 (1964), pp. 160–71.

——, 'Sources for the Economic History of the Duchy of Urbino, 1474–1508', *Manuscripta*, 10 (1966), pp. 3–27.

——, 'The Albani Library and Pope Clement XI', *Librarium: Zeitschrift der Schweizerischen Bibliophilen*, 12.1 (1969), pp. 14–21.

——, 'Federigo da Montefeltro's Patronage of the Arts, 1468–1482', *Journal of the Warburg and Courtauld Institutes*, 36 (1973), pp. 129–44.

——, 'Federico da Montefeltro's Concept and Use of History', *Pariser Historische Studien*, 47 (1998), pp. 297–314.

Clough, Cecil H., (ed.), *Cultural Aspects of the Italian Renaissance* (Manchester: Manchester University Press, 1976).

——, *Duchy of Urbino in the Renaissance* (London: Variorum Reprints, 1981).

——, 'Federigo da Montefeltro: The Good Christian Prince', *Bulletin of the John Rylands University Library of Manchester* 67, no. 1 (1984): 293–340.

——, 'Federico da Montefeltro and the Kings of Naples: A Study in Fifteenth-Century Survival', *Renaissance Studies*, 6.2 (1992), pp. 113–72.

——, 'Art as Power in the Decoration of the Study of an Italian Renaissance Prince: The Case of Federico Da Montefeltro', *Artibus et Historiae*, 16, no. 31 (1995), pp. 19–50.

Cohen, Simona, 'Elisabetta Gonzaga and the Ambivalence of Scorpio in Medieval and Renaissance Art', *Magic, Ritual, and Witchcraft*, 13.3 (2018), pp. 408–46.

Colantuono, Anthony D., *Titian, Colonna and the Renaissance Science of Procreation: Equicola's Seasons of Desire* (Farnham: Ashgate Publishing Limited, 2010).

Corones, Anthony, Pont, Graham and Santich, Barbara (eds), *Food in Festivity* (Sydney: Symposium of Australian Gastronomy, 1990).

Corp, Edward T., *The Jacobites at Urbino: An Exiled Court in Transition* (Basingstoke: Palgrave Macmillan, 2009).

Cox, Virginia, 'Leonardo Bruni on Women and Rhetoric: *De studiis et litteris* Revisited', *Rhetorica*, 27, no. 1 (February 2009), pp. 47–75.

——, 'Gender and Eloquence in Ercole de' Roberti's Portia and Brutus', *Renaissance Quarterly*, 62.1 (2009), pp. 61–101.

——, 'Cicero at Court: Martino Filetico's *Iocundissimae disputationes*', in Gesine Manuwald (ed.), *The Afterlife of Cicero*, BICS Supplement (London: Institute of Classical Studies, 2016), pp. 46–66.

——, *A Short History of the Italian Renaissance* (London: I.B. Tauris, 2016).

Cusick, Suzanne, *Francesca Caccini at the Medici Court: Music and the Circulation of Power* (Chicago: University of Chicago Press, 2009).

da Bisticci, Vespasiano, *The Vespasiano Memoirs: Lives of Illustrious Men of the XVth Century*, trs. William George and Emily Waters (London: Routledge, 1926).

Dacos, Nicole, *La découverte de la 'Domus Aurea' et la formation des grotesques à la Renaissance* (London: Warburg Institute/ Leiden: Brill, 1969).

Damianaki, Chrysa, *The Female Portrait Busts of Francesco Laurana* (Rome: Vecchiarelli Editore, 2000).

D'Amico, Jack, 'Drama and the Court in "La Calandria"', *Theatre Journal*, 43.1 (1991), pp. 93–106.

da Montefeltro, Federico, *Lettere di Stato e d'Arte*, ed. Paolo Alatri (Roma: Storia e Letteratura, 1949).

d'Antoni, Anthony V., and Terzulli, Stephanie L., 'Federico di Montefeltro's Hyperkyphosis: a Visual-Historical Case Report', *Journal of Medical Case Reports*, 2:11 (2008).

da Vinci, Leonardo, *The Notebooks of Leonardo da Vinci* II, ed. Jean Paul Richter (New York: Dover, 1970).

de Beatis, Antonio, *The Travel Journal of Antonio de Beatis*, trs. J.R. Hale (London: Hakluyt Society, 1979).

de Carlo, Giancarlo, *Urbino: The History of a City and Plans for its Development*, trs. Loreta Schaeffer Guarda (Cambridge, MA: MIT Press, 1970).

de' Cavalieri, Pius Franchi (ed.), *Claudii Ptolemaei Geographiae: Codex Urbinas Graecus 82* (Leiden: Brill; Leipzig, Harrassowitz, 1932), 2 vols in 4.

Dee, John, *Libro del modo di diuidere le superficie attribuito à Machometo Bagdedino. Mandato in luce la prima volta da m. Giouanni Dee da Londra, e da m. Federico Commandino da Vrbino* (Pesaro: Girolamo Concordia, 1570).

Degli Arienti, Giovanni Sabadino, *Gynevera de le clare donne di Joanne Sabadino de li Arienti*, eds C. Ricci and R. Bacchi della Lega (Bologna: Romagnoli-Dall'Acqua, 1888).

D'Elia, Anthony F., *Pagan Virtue in a Christian World: Sigismondo Malatesta and the Italian Renaissance* (Cambridge: Harvard University Press, 2016).

della Chiesa, Francesco Agostino, *Theatro delle Donne Letterate con un breve discorso della preminenza e perfettione del sesso donnesco* (Mondovì: Giovanni Gislandi & Giovanni Tomaso Rossi, 1620).

della Rovere, Francesco Maria, *Discorsi militari dell'eccellentiss. sig. Francesco Maria 1. Dalla Rouere duca d'Vrbino. Ne i quali si discorrono molti auantaggi, & disuantaggi, della guerra, vtilissimi ad ogni soldato* (Ferrara: Dominico Mammarelli, 1583).

de' Medici, Lorenzo, 'Criteria for Paintings', from *Opera*, in Creighton E. Gilbert, *Italian Art 1400–1500, Sources and Documents* (Englewood Cliffs: Prentice-Hall, Inc., 1980).

Dennistoun, James, *Memoirs of the Duke of Urbino, Illustrating the Arms, Arts and Literature of Italy*, ed. Edward Hutton, 3 vols (London: Bodley Head, 1909).

De Pieri, Filippo, 'Visualizing the Historic City: Planners and the Representation of Italy's Built Heritage: Giovanni Astengo and Giancarlo De Carlo in Assisi and Urbino, 1950s–60s', in John Pendlebury, Erdem Erten, J. Peter Larkham (eds), *Alternative Visions of Post-War Reconstruction Creating the modern townscape* (Abingdon: Routledge, 2014), pp. 54–71.

de' Reguardati, F.M., *Benedetto De' Reguardati da Norcia* (Trieste: Lint, 1977).

Diller, Aubrey, 'The Greek Codices of Palla Strozzi and Guarino Veronese', *Journal of the Warburg and Courtauld Institutes*, 24.3/4 (1961), pp. 313–21.

Dionisotti, Carlo, '"Lavinia venit litora": polemica virgiliana di Martino Filetico', *Italia medioevale e umanistica*, 1 (1958), pp. 283–315.

Ebreo, Guglielmo, *De practica seu Arte Tripudii*, ed. Barbara Sparti (Oxford: Clarendon Press, 1993).

Edelheit, Amos, 'Human Will, Human Dignity, and Freedom: A Study of Giorgio Benigno Salviati's Early Discussion of the Will, Urbino 1474–1482', *Vivarium*, 46 (2008), pp. 82–114.

Eiche, Sabine, 'Francesco Maria II della Rovere as a Patron of Architecture and His Villa at MonteBerticchio', *Mitteilungen des Kunsthistorischen Institutes in Florenz*, 28.1 (1984), pp. 77–108.
———, 'Francesco Maria II della Rovere's Delizia in Urbino: The Giardino di S. Lucia', *The Journal of Garden History*, 5.2 (1985), pp. 154–83.
———, 'Girolamo Genga the Architect: An Inquiry into His Background', *Mitteilungen des Kunsthistorischen Institutes in Florenz*, 35.2/3 (1991), pp. 317–23.
———, (ed.) *Ordine et Officij de Casa de lo illustrissimo signor duca de Urbino* (Urbino: Accademia Raffaello, 1999).

Einstein, Alfred, *The Italian Madrigal*, 3 vols (Princeton: Princeton University Press, 1983).

Eisenbichler, Konrad, 'Bronzino's Portrait of Guidobaldo II della Rovere', *Renaissance and Reformation*, NS 12.1 (1988), pp. 21–33.

Ellis, Robinson, 'Vita Donati', *Appendix Virgiliana sive carmina minora Vergilio adtributa* (Oxford: Clarendon Press, 1963).

Ettlinger, Helen S., 'The Question of St. George's Garter', *The Burlington Magazine*, 125 (1983), pp. 25–9.
———, '*Visibilis et Invisibilis*: The Mistress in Italian Renaissance Court

Society', *Renaissance Quarterly*, 47.4 (1994), pp. 770–92.

Evans, Mark L., '"Uno maestro solenne": Joos van Wassenhove in Italy', *Nederlands Kunsthistorisch Jaarboek*, 44 (1993), pp. 75–110.

Falvo, Joseph D., 'Urbino and the Apotheosis of Power', *Modern Language Notes*, 101.1 (Jan. 1986), pp. 114–46.

Farago, Clare, *Leonardo da Vinci's "Paragone": A Critical Interpretation with a New Edition of the Text in the Codex Urbinas* (Leiden: Brill, 1992).

Feliciangeli, Bernardino, *Sulla monacazione di Sveva Montefeltro-Sforza, Signora di Pesaro* (Pistoia: Fiori, 1903).
———, 'Alcuni documenti relativi all'adolescenza di Battista e Costanzo Sforza', *Giornale Storico della Letteratura Italiana* 41 (1903), pp. 304–17.

Fildes, Valerie A., *Wet Nursing: A History from Antiquity to the Present* (Oxford: Basil Blackwell, 1988)

Filetico, Martino, *Iocundissimae disputationes*, ed. and trs. Guido Arbizzoni (Modena: Fondazione Scavolini, 1992).

Fiore, Francesco Paolo, and Tafuri, Manfredo (eds), *Francesco di Giorgio Architetto* (Milano: Electa, 1993).

Fiore, Francesco Paolo (ed.), *Francesco di Giorgio alla corte di Federico da Montefeltro. Atti del Convegno Internazionale di Studi (Urbino, 11–13 ottobre 2001)*, 2 vols (Firenze: Leo Olschki, 2004).

Folin, Marco (ed.), *Courts and Courtly Arts in Renaissance Italy* (Woodbridge: Antique Collectors Club, 2011).

Fornaciari, A., 'L'esplorazione della tomba di Federico II da Montefeltro: notizie preliminari', *Archeologia Postmedievale*, 4 (2000), pp. 211–18.

Fossier, François, 'Nouvelles recherches sur la bibliothèque du Pape Clément XI Albani', *Journal des savants* (1980), pp. 161–80.

Franceschini, Gino, 'La morte di Gentile Brancaleoni (1457) e di Buonconte de Montefeltro', *Archivio Storico Lombardo*, n.s. 2 (Jan 1, 1937), pp. 489–500.
———, 'Violante Montefeltro Malatesta. Signora di Cesena', *Studi Romagnoli*, 1 (1950), pp. 133–90.
———, 'Di Sveva Montefeltro Sforza, Signora di Pesaro', *Studia Picena*, 25 (1957), pp. 133–57.
———, *Figure del Rinascimento Urbinate* (Urbino: S.T.E.U, 1959).

Frank, Martin, 'Mathematics, Technics, and Courtly Life in Late Renaissance Urbino', *Archive for History of Exact Sciences*, 67.3 (2013), pp. 305–30.

Franklin, Carmela Vircillo, '"Pro communi doctorum virorum comodo": The Vatican Library and Its Service to Scholarship', *Proceedings of the American Philosophical Society*, 146.4 (2002), pp. 363–84.

Fraser Jenkins, A. D., 'Cosimo de' Medici's Patronage of Architecture and the Theory of Magnificence', *Journal of the Warburg and Courtauld Institutes*, 33 (1970), pp. 162–70.

Frick, Carol Collier, 'The Downcast Eyes of the Women of the Upper Class in Francesco Barbaro's *De Re Uxoria*', *UCLA Historical Journal*, 9 (1989), pp. 8–31.

Fried, Johannes, *Donation of Constantine and Constitutum Constantini* (Berlin and New York: Walter de Gruyter, 2007).

Fritelli, Ugo, *Giannantonio de' Pandoni detto "Il Porcellio"* (Firenze: Paravia, 1900).

Gaugelli, Gaugello, 'De vita et morte illustris D. Baptistae Sfortiae comitissae Urbini', *Canzone di Ser Gaugello de la Pergola*, ed. Adolfo Cinquini (Roma: Tip. S.C. de Prop. Fide, 1905).

————, *Il Pellegrino* (Napoli: Ed. Scientifiche Italiane, 1991).

Gaye, Johann Wilhelm, *Carteggio inedito d'artisti dei secoli XIV, XV, XVI: pubbl. ed ill. con documenti pure inediti*, 3 vols (Firenze: G. Molini, 1839–40).

Ginzburg, Carlo, *Indagini su Piero: il Battesimo, il ciclo di Arezzo, la Flagellazione di Urbino* (Torino: Einaudi, 2008).

Giovannini, Auretta, 'Una guida di Urbino di Papa Albani', in *Notizie da Palazzo Albani*, 1 (1973), pp. 49–53.

Girolamo Maria, Fra, 'Cronaca da Fra Girolamo Maria da Venezia', *Rerum Italicarum Scriptores*, 21.4, ed. Giuseppe Mazzatinti (Città di Castello: S. Lapi, 1902).

Goldthwaite, Richard, *The Building of Renaissance Florence: An Economic and Social History* (Baltimore and London: Johns Hopkins University Press, 1980).

Gombrich, E. H., 'Light, Form and Texture in Fifteenth-Century Painting', in his *The Heritage of Apelles* (Oxford: Phaidon, 1976), pp. 19–35.

Grendler, Paul F., *Schooling in Renaissance Italy* (Baltimore & London: Johns Hopkins University Press, 1989).

Gronau, Georg, *Documenti artistici Urbinati* (Firenze: G.C. Sansoni, 1936).

Grossi, Carlo, *Degli uomini illustri di Urbino comentario* (Urbino: V. Guerrini, 1819).

Guerriero de' Berni da Gubbio, Ser, *Cronaca di Ser Guerriero da Gubbio*, ed. Giuseppe Mazzatinti, *Raccolta degli Storic*, 21.4 (Citta di Castello: S. Lapi, 1902).

Guidi, José, 'Thyrsis ou la cour transfigurée', in A. Rochon and A. Fontes-Baratto (eds), *Ville et campagne dans la littérature italienne de la Renaissance*, 2 vols (Paris: Centre de Recherche sur la Renaissance Italienne, Université de la Sorbonne Nouvelle, 1977), II, pp. 141–86.

Hadeln, Detlev, 'Zum Datum der Bella Tizians', *Repertorium für Kunstwissenschaft*, 32 (1909), pp. 69–71.

Hale, J.R., *War and Society in Renaissance Europe* (London: Fontana, 1985).

Hara, Maria Yoko, 'Capturing Eyes and Moving Souls: Peruzzi's Perspective Set for *La Calandria* and the Performative Agency of Architectural Bodies', *Renaissance Studies*, 31.4 (2017), pp. 586–607.

Hay, Denys, 'The Manuscript of Polydore Vergil's "Anglica Historia"', *The English Historical Review*, 54, no. 214 (1939), pp. 240–51.

Hankins, James, 'Machiavelli, Civic Humanism, and the Humanist Politics of Virtue', *Italian Culture*, 32.2 (2014), pp. 98–109.

Helfenstein, Eva, 'Lorenzo de' Medici's Magnificent Cups: Precious Vessels as Status Symbols in Fifteenth-Century Europe', *I Tatti Studies in the Italian Renaissance*, 16.1/2 (2013), pp. 415–44.

Hendy, Philip, *Piero della Francesca and the Early Renaissance* (London: Weidenfeld and Nicolson, 1968).

Herrick, Marvin T., *Italian Comedy in the Renaissance* (Urbana: University of Illinois Press, 1966).

Hessler, Christiane J., 'Dead Men Talking: The Studiolo of Urbino. A Duke in Mourning and the Petrarchan Tradition', in Karl E. Enenkel, and Christine Göttler (eds), *Solitudo: Spaces, Places, and Times of Solitude in Late Medieval and Early Modern Cultures* (Leiden: Brill, 2018), pp. 365–404.

Hobbes, Thomas, *Leviathan* (London: Andrew Crooke, 1651).

Hofmann, Heinz, 'Literary Culture at the Court of Urbino During the Reign of Federico da Montefeltro', *Humanistica Lovaniensia*, 57 (2008) pp. 5–60.

Höfler, Janez, *Der Palazzo Ducale in Urbino unter den Montefeltro (1376–1508)* (Regensburg: Schnell & Steiner GmbH, 2004).

Hofmann, Heinz, 'Literary Culture at the Court of Urbino during the Reign of Federico da Montefeltro', *Humanistica Lovaniensia* 57 (2008), pp. 5–60.

Holcroft, Alison, 'Francesco Xanto Avelli and Petrarch', *Journal of the Warburg and Courtauld Institutes*, 51 (1988), pp. 225–34.

Hollingsworth, Mary, *Patronage in Renaissance Italy: From 1400 to the Early Sixteenth Century* (Baltimore: Johns Hopkins University Press, 1994).
———, *The Medici* (London: Head of Zeus, 2017).

Hub, Berthold, and Polalli, Angeliki (eds), *Reconstructing Francesco Di Giorgio Architect* (Frankfurt am Main: Peter Lang, 2011).

Hunt, Janin, and Carlson, Ursula, *Mercenaries in Medieval and Renaissance Europe* (Jefferson, N.C.: McFarland & Company, Inc., 2013).

Hutton, Edward, *Cities of Romagna and the Marches* (London: Methuen, 1913).

Jeffreys, Joyce, 'Ducal Palace, Urbino', in Sacheverell Sitwell (ed.), *Great Houses of Europe* (London: Weidenfeld and Nicolson, 1961), pp. 18–27.

Jerome, St, *Select Letters*, ed. and trs. F.A. Wright (London: William Heinemann, 1933).

Johns, Christopher M.S., 'Papal Patronage and Cultural Bureaucracy in Eighteenth-Century Rome: Clement XI and the Accademia di San Luca', *Eighteenth-Century Studies*, 22.1 (1988), pp. 1–23.

Johnson, Geraldine A., and Sara F. Matthews Grieco (eds), *Picturing Women in Renaissance and Baroque Italy* (Cambridge: Cambridge University Press, 1997).

Jones, P.J., *The Malatesta of Rimini and the Papal State: A Political History* (Cambridge: Cambridge University Press, 1974).

Jones, Roger, and Penny, Nicholas, *Raphael* (New Haven: Yale University Press, 1983).

Joost-Gaugier, Christiane L., 'Lorenzo the Magnificent and the Giraffe as a Symbol of Power', *Artibus et Historiae*, 8, no. 16 (1987), pp. 91–9.

Kallendorf, Craig W. (ed. and trs.), *Humanist Educational Treatises* (Cambridge: Harvard University Press, 2002).

Karamanou, Marianna, et al., 'Toxicology in the Borgias Period: The Mystery of Cantarella Poison', *Toxicology Research and Application*, 2 (2018), pp. 1–3.

Kent, F.W. and Elam, Caroline, 'Piero del Massaio, painter, mapmaker and military surveyor', *Mitteilungen des Kunsthistorischen Institutes in Florenz*, 57.1 (2015), pp. 64–89.

Kidwell, Carol, *Pietro Bembo: Lover, Linguist, Cardinal* (Montreal: McGill–Queen's University Press, 2004)

King, Catherine, 'Architecture, Gender and Politics: The Villa Imperiale at Pesaro', *Art History*, 29.5 (2006), pp. 796–828.

King, David A., 'The Star Names on Three 14th Century Astrolabes', in Menso Folkerts (ed.), *Sic itur ad astra: Studien zur Geschichte der Mathematik und Naturwissenschaften* (Wiesbaden: Harrasowitz, 2000), pp. 307–33.
———, 'The Astrolabe Depicted in the Intarsia of the Studiolo of Archduke Federico of Urbino', in Flavio Vetrano (ed.), *La Scienza del Ducato di Urbino* (Urbino: Accademia Raffaello, 2001), pp. 110–11.

King, Margaret L., and Rabil, Albert (eds), *Her Immaculate Hand: Selected Works By and About the Women Humanists of Quattrocento Italy* (Binghamton, N.Y: Center for Medieval & Early Renaissance Studies, 1983).

Kirkbride, Robert, *Architecture and Memory: The Renaissance Studioli of Federico da Montefeltro* (New York: Columbia University Press, 2008).

Kite, Stephen, *Adrian Stokes: An Architectonic Eye: Critical Writings on Art and Architecture* (London: Taylor and Francis, 2017).

La France, Robert G., 'Exorcising the Borgia from Urbino: Timoteo Viti's Arrivabene Chapel', *Renaissance Quarterly*, 68 (2015), pp. 1192–226.

Lanciarini, Vincenzo, *Il Tiferno Metaurense*, eds E. Catani and W. Monacchi, rev. edn, 2 vols (Sant'Angelo in Vado, comune, 1988).

Larner, John, *The Lords of Romagna: Romagnol Society and the Origins of the Signorie* (London: Macmillan, 1965).

Lavallaye, Jacques, *Les primitifs flamand: I, Corpus de la peinture des anciens Pays-Bas meridionaux au quinzieme siecle, VII: Le Palais Ducal d'Urbin* (Bruxelles: Centre national de recherches Primitifs flamands, 1964).

Lavin, Marilyn Aronberg, 'The Altar of Corpus Domini in Urbino: Paolo Uccello, Joos Van Ghent, Piero della Francesca', *The Art Bulletin*, 49.1 (1967), pp. 1–24.
———, 'Piero della Francesca's Flagellation: The Triumph of Christian Glory', *The Art Bulletin*, 50.4 (1968), pp. 321–42.
———, 'Piero della Francesca's Montefeltro Altarpiece: A Pledge of Fidelity', *The Art Bulletin*, 51.4 (1969), pp. 367–71.

Lee, Vernon, *Hauntings: Fantastic Stories* (London: W. Heinemann, 1890).

Lees-Milne, James, *The Last Stuarts* (New York: Charles Scribner's Sons, 1984).

Levey, Michael, 'Urbino', *The Sunday Times Magazine*, March 21, 1971, pp 12–25.

Lingo, Stuart, *Federico Barocci: Allure and Devotion in Late Renaissance Painting* (New Haven and London: Yale University Press, 2009).

Liotta, Michela, 'Il magnifico "errore" di Francesco di Giorgio Martini', *Atti del Convegno di studi storici, La rocca di Sassocorvaro. Ricerche su un enigma di architettura, 24 ottobre 1993* (http://www.tecnologos.it/Articoli/artocoli/numero_003/Francesco.asp).

Lombardi, Francesco Vittorio, *Le Torri del Montefeltro e della Massa Trabaria* (Rimini: Bruno Ghigi Editore, 1981).

Lorenzetti, Giulio, *Venezia e il suo estuario*, 3rd edn (Rome: Istituto Poligrafico dello Stato, 1963).

Luzio, Alessandro, and Renier, Rodolfo (eds), *Mantova e Urbino: Isabella d'Este ed Elisabetta Gonzaga nelle relazioni famigliari e nelle vicende politiche* (Mantua: L. Roux e c., 1893).

McClure, Ian, 'Titian's "Portrait of Guidobaldo II della Rovere"', *Yale University Art Gallery Bulletin* (2016), pp. 53–61.

Mack, Charles R., *Pienza: The Creation of a Renaissance City* (Ithaca: Cornell University Press, 1987).

McKean, John, 'Il Magistero: De Carlo's Dialogue with Historical Forms', *Places*, 16.1 (2004), pp. 54–63.

McKendrick, Scott, 'The "Great History of Troy": A Reassessment of the Development of a Secular Theme in Late Medieval Art', *Journal of the Warburg and Courtauld Institutes*, 54 (1991), pp. 43–82.

MacKinnon, Nick, 'The Portrait of Fra Luca Pacioli', *The Mathematical Gazette*, 77, no. 479 (1993), pp. 130–219.

McManamon, John M., S.J., *Funeral Oratory and the Cultural Ideals of Italian Humanism* (Chapel Hill and London: University of North Carolina Pres, 1989).

McRoberts, David, 'Dean Brown's Book of Hours', *Innes Review*, 19 (1968), pp. 144–67.

Majanlahti, Anthony, *The Families Who Made Rome: A History and a Guide* (London: Pimlico, 2006).

Mallett, Michael, *The Borgias: The Rise and Fall of a Renaissance Dynasty* (London: Bodley Head, 1969).
———, *Mercenaries and Their Masters: Warfare in Renaissance Italy* (London: Bodley Head, 1974).

Mallett, Michael, and Hale, J.R., *The Military Organisation of a Renaissance State: Venice c.1400 to 1617* (Cambridge: Cambridge University Press, 2009).

Mamini, Marcello, *"Udirai melodia del bel sonare". Federico di Montefeltro e la musica* (Urbino: QuattroVenti, 2007).

Manchisi, Michele, 'Angelo Galli e i codici delle sue rime', *Giornale storico e letterario della Liguria* 9 (1908), pp. 257–310.

Mann, J. G., 'The Sanctuary of the Madonna delle Grazie, with Notes on the Evolution of Italian Armour During the Fifteenth Century', *Archeologia*, 80 (1930), pp. 117–42, fig. 1.
———, 'A Further Account of the Armour Preserved in the Sanctuary of the Madonna delle Grazie near Mantua', *Archaeologia*, 87 (1938), pp. 311–51.

Martines, Lauro, *Power and Imagination: City-States in Renaissance Italy* (London: Peregrine Books, 1979).

Mazzini, Franco, *Urbino: I Mattoni e le pietre*, 2nd edn (Urbino: Argalia Editore, 2000).

Meihuizen, Nicholas, *Yeats and the Drama of Sacred Space* (Amsterdam: Rodopi, 1998).

Modesti, Adelina, *Women's Patronage and Gendered Cultural Networks in Early Modern Europe: Vittoria della Rovere* (New York and London: Routledge, 2020).

Monfasani, John, 'Alexius Celadenus and Ottaviano Ubaldini: An Epilogue to Bessarion's Relationship with the court of Urbino', *Bibliothèque d'Humanisme et Renaissance*, 46.1 (1984), pp. 95–110.

Monreal, Ruth, 'Una biografia in versi; gli epigrammi di Giovanni Battista Valentini, detto il Cantalicio, sulla vite e le gesti di Federico de Montefeltro', *Studi Umanistici Piceni* 22 (2002), pp. 129–57.

Montaigne, Michel de, *The Works of Montaigne*, trs. William Hazlitt (London: John Templeman, 1832).

Montano, Marco, *Herode Insano*, ed. Alberto Gregorini (Rocca S. Casciano: Capelli, 1898).

Montoli, Cecilia, 'The Production of Illuminated Manuscripts in Florence and Urbino', in Marcello Simonetta, *Federico da Montefeltro and his Library* (Milano: Y Press SRL, 2007), pp. 41–9.

Moranti, Luigi, *La Confraternita del Corpus Domini di Urbino* (Bologna: Il Lavoro, 1990).

Mortimer, Ian, *The Fears of Henry IV: The Life of England's Self-made King* (London: Jonathan Cape, 2007).

Motta, Uberto, *Castiglione e il mito di Urbino: Studi sulla elaborazione del "Cortegiano"* (Milano: Vita e pensiero, 2003).

Mozzarelli, Cesare (ed.), *'Familia' del principe e famiglia aristocratica*, 2 vols (Roma: Bulzoni, 1988).

Mulazzani, Germano, 'Observations on the Sforza Triptych in the Brussels Museum', *The Burlington Magazine*, 113, no. 818 (1971), pp. 252–3.

Müntz, E., 'L'atelier de tapisseries d'Urbin', in *Les archives des arts: Recueil des documents inédits ou peu connus*, 1 (1890), pp. 42–4.

Muzio, Girolamo, *Historia di fatti di Federico da Montefeltro duca d'Urbino* (Venice: Gio. Battista Ciotti, 1605).

Nardini, Luigi, *Le imprese o figure simboliche dei Montefeltro e dei della Rovere* (Urbino: Soc. tip. ed. urbinate, 1931).

Nenci, Elio (ed.), *Bernardino Baldi (1553–1617) studioso rinascimentale* (Milano: FrancoAngeli, 2005).

Norris, Christopher, 'Titian: Notes on the Venice Exhibition', *The Burlington Magazine for Connoisseurs*, 67, no. 390 (1935), pp. 127–31.

Norton, Paul F., 'The Lost Sleeping Cupid of Michelangelo', *The Art Bulletin*, 39.4 (1957), pp. 251–7.

Oakeshott, Ewart, *European Weapons and Armour: From the Renaissance to the Industrial Revolution* (Guildford: Lutterworth Press, 2008).

Ombrosi, Luca, *Vita dei Medici sodomiti* (Roma: Canesi, 1965).

O'Neill, John P. (ed.), *From Filippo Lippi to Piero della Francesca: Fra Carnevale and the Making of a Renaissance Master* (New Haven and London: Yale University Press, 2005).

Paltroni, Pierantonio, *Commentari della vita e gesta dell'Ill.mo. Federico Duca d'Urbino*, ed. Walter Tommasoli (Urbino: Argalia, 1966).

Panizza, Letizia (ed.), *Women in Italian Renaissance Culture and Society* (Oxford: Legenda, 2000).

Panicali, Roberto, *Orologi e orologiai del Rinascimento italiano. La scuola urbinate* (Urbino: QuattroVenti 1988).

Panzini, Franco (ed.), *Giardini delle Marche* (Jesi: Banca delle Marche, 1998).

Paolini, Devid, 'Madonna Gentile Feltria de Campofregoso, Alphonso Hordognez y la traducción italiana de *La Celestina*', *eHumanista*, 19 (2011), pp. 260–95.

Papini, Roberto, *Francesco di Giorgio Architetto*, 3 vols (Florence, Electa Editrice, 1946).

Parker, Holt, 'Costanza Varano (1426–1447): Latin as an instrument of state', in Laurie Churchill *et al.* (eds), *Women Writing Latin*, 3 vols (London: Routledge, 2002), III, pp. 31–53.

Parroni, Piergiorgio, 'Maestri di grammatica a Pesaro nel Quattrocento', *Res Publica Litterarum*, 5 (1982), pp. 205–19.

Pearson, S.C., 'The Convent of Santa Chiara in Urbino: A New Chronology of its Construction and Patronage', *Architectural Histories*, 3.1 (2015), pp. 1–5.

Pellecchia, Linda, 'Architects Read Vitruvius: Renaissance Interpretations of the Atrium of the Ancient House', *Journal of the Society of Architectural Historians*, 51.4 (1992), pp. 377–416.

Pempi, Marcella, 'The library of glorious memory', in Marcello Simonetta, Federico da Montefeltro and his Library (Milano: Y Press SRL, 2007), pp. 29–39.

Pennell, Joseph, *The Adventures of an Illustrator, Mostly in Following his Authors in America & Europe* (Boston: Little, Brown & Co., 1925).

Perini, Erica, *La signoria dei Brancaleoni di Casteldurante* (Firenze: Firenze Atheneum, 2008).

Pernis, Maria Grazia, 'Ficino's Platonism and the Court of Urbino: The History of Ideas and the History of Art', Columbia University PhD, 1990.

Pernis, Maria Grazia, and Adams, Laurie Schneider, *Federico da Montefeltro and Sigismondo Malatesta: The Eagle and the Elephant* (New York: Peter Lang, 1996).

Peruzzi, Marcella, *Cultura, potere, immagine. La Biblioteca di Federico di Montefeltro* (Urbino: Accademia Raffaelo, 2004).

Petretti, Agostino, *Serenissimae quercus noui germinis in honorem triplicis quercus noua descriptio a f. Augustino Petreto Regiensi, Sacri Ordinis Praedicat. ... In solemnitate baptismi serenissimi principis disputationi tradita. Serenissimo d.d. Francisco Mariae sexto Vrbinati duci dicata* (Urbino: Bartolomeo and Simon Ragusi, 1605).

Piazzoni, Ambrogio M. (ed), *La Bibbia Di Federico Da Montefeltro - Commentario al Codice* (Modena: Franco Cosimo Panini, 2005).

Piccolomini, Aeneas Sylvius, *Commentarii* (Frankfurt: Aubri, 1614).
———, *The Commentaries of Pius II*, trs. Florence Alden Gragg, 5 vols (Northampton: Smith College, 1937–1940).

Pieraccini, Gaetano, *La stirpe de' Medici di Cafaggiolo*, 3 vols (Florence: Nardini, 1986).

Pinetti, Angelo, 'L'Umanista Ludovico Odasio alla Corte dei Duchi d'Urbino', *Archivio Storico Lombardo*, ser. 3, 5 (1896), pp. 355–80.

Pinti, Paolo, *Lo stocco pontificio: immagini e storia di un'arma* (2001, online).

Piperno, Franco, *L'immagine del duca: musica e spettacolo alla corte di Guidubaldo II duca d'Urbino* (Firenze: Leo S. Olschki Editore, 2001).

Pope-Hennessy, John, 'Whose Flagellation?', *Apollo*, 124 (1986), pp. 162–5.

Porta, Costanzo, *Di Constantio Porta da Cremona il primo libro di madrigali a cinque voci novamente da lui composti et per Antonio Gardano stampati et dati in luce* (Venezia: Antonio Gardano, 1559).

Prendilacqua, Francesco, *Intorno alla Vita di Vittorino da Feltre* (Como: Carlo Franchi, 1871).

Pyhrr, Stuart W., Godoy, José-A. and Leydi, Silvio, *Heroic Armor of the Italian Renaissance: Filippo Negroli and His Contemporaries* (New York: The Metropolitan Museum of Art, 1998).

Raggio, Olga, and Wilmering, Antoine M., *The Gubbio Studiolo and its Conservation* (New York: Metropolitan Museum of Art, 2000).

Ratti, Nicola, *Della famiglia Sforza*, 2 vols (Rome: Presso Il Salomoni, 1794–1795). *Restauri nelle Marche: testimonianze acquisti e recuperi* (Urbino: Arti Grafiche Editoriali, 1973).

Reti, Ladislao, 'Leonardo da Vinci and Cesare Borgia', *Viator* 4.4 (1973), pp. 333–68.

Reynolds, L. D. (ed), *Texts and Transmission* (Oxford: Oxford University Press. 1983).

Richardson, Carol M. (ed.), *Locating Renaissance Art* (New Haven and London: Yale University Press, 2007).

Roberts, Sean, 'Poet and "World Painter": Francesco Berlinghieri's Geographia (1482)', *Imago Mundi* 62.2 (2010), pp. 145–60.

Rodocanachi, Emmanuel, *Rome au temps de Jules II et de Leon X* (Paris: Hachette, 1912).

Roeck, Bernd, *Piero della Francesca e l'assassino* (Torino: Bollati Boringhieri, 2007).

———, 'Die Kosten der Kunst: Ein bisher unbekanntes Inventar der Besitztümer Federico da Montefeltros und Ottaviano Ubaldinis della Carda', *Zeitschrift für Kunstgeschichte*, 73.2 (2010), pp. 169–86.

Roman, Nathalie, 'Collaborations artistiques et leadership: le cas du Breviaire du Blanche de France (Rome, Biblioteca Apostolica Vaticana, ms Urb. Lat. 603)', *Convivium*, 4.2 (2017), pp.132–55.

Rose, Paul Lawrence, 'Commandino, John Dee, and the *De superficierum Divisionibus* of Machometus Bagdedinus', *Isis*, 63.1 (1972), pp. 88–93.

Rosenberg, Charles M. (ed.), *The Court Cities of Northern Italy: Milan, Parma, Piacenza, Mantua, Ferrara, Bologna, Urbino, Pesaro and Rimini* (Cambridge: Cambridge University Press, 2010).

Rotondi, Pasquale, *The Ducal Palace at Urbino* (New York: Transatlantic Arts, 1969).

Roullet, Anne, *The Egyptian and Egyptianizing Monuments of Imperial Rome* (Leiden: Brill, 1972).

Rubin, Patricia, *Giorgio Vasari: Art and History* (New Haven: Yale University Press, 1995).

Ruda, Jeffrey, 'Flemish Painting and the Early Renaissance in Florence: Questions of Influence', *Zeitschrift für Kunstgeschichte*, 47.2 (1984), pp. 210–36.

Russell, David, *Self-Portrait of the Painter* (lulu.com, 2009).

Ryder, Alan, *The Kingdom of Naples under Alfonso the Magnanimous* (Oxford: Clarendon Press, 1976).

———, *Alfonso the Magnanimous: King of Aragon, Naples, and Sicily 1396–1458* (Oxford: Oxford University Press, 1990).

Sabadino degli Arienti, Giovanni, *Gynevera de le clare donne di Joanne Sabadino de li Arienti*, eds C. Ricci. and R. Bacchi della Lega (Bologna: Romagnoli-Dall'Acqua, 1888).

Sabbattini, Nicola, *Pratica di fabricar scene, e macchine ne' teatri* (Pesaro: Flaminio Concordia, 1637).

Salmi, M., 'Gli affreschi del Palazzo Trinci a Foligno', *Bollettino d'Arte*, 13 (1919), pp. 153–9.

———, *Piero della Francesca e il Palazzo Ducale di Urbino* (Firenze: Le Monnier, 1945).

Sangiorgi, Fert (ed.), *Documenti Urbinati: Inventari del Palazzo Ducale (1582–1631)* (Urbino: Accademia Raffaello, 1976).

Santi, Giovanni, *Federico di Montefeltro, Duca di Urbino: Cronaca*, ed. Heinrich Holzinger (Stuttgart: W. Kohnhammer, 1893).

Santoni-Rugiu, Paolo, and Massei, Alessandro, 'The Legend and the Truth About the Nose of Federico, Duke of Urbino', *British Journal of Plastic Surgery*, 35 (1982), pp. 251–7.

Santucci, Giovanni, 'Federico Brandani's Paper Model for the Chapel of the Dukes of Urbino at Loreto', *The Burlington Magazine* 156, no. 1330 (2014), pp. 4–11.

Sarti, Raffaella, 'Renaissance Graffiti: The Case of the Ducal Palace of Urbino', in Sandra Cavallo and Silvia Evangelisti (eds), *Domestic Institutional Interiors in Early Modern Europe* (London: Routledge, 2016), pp. 51–82.

———, 'Felice dolc aventuroso loco': Courtly Life, the Courtier's Model and the Myth of Urbino in the Graffiti of the Palazzo Ducale', *Journal of Early Modern Studies*, 9 (2020), pp. 163–92.

Savelli, Renzo, 'Notizie Storiche', in D. Giuseppe Ceccarelli, Giancarlo Gori, and Simona Salvatori (eds), *Fossombrone nel Ducato di Federico: Segni di un'epoca e di una cultura* (Fossombrone: Comune, 1982).

Saviotti, Alfredo, *Una rappresentazione allegorica in Urbino nel 1474* (Arezzo: Accademia Petrarca di lettere, arti e scienze, 1920).

Scaglioso, Carolina, 'Le Assicurate di Siena (1654–1704?): un'Accademia al femminile tra identità e appartenenza', *Educazione Permanente Numero monografico* (1997), pp. 1–183.

Scarpacci, Silvia, 'La conservazione delle opere d'arte ad Urbino, dall'Unità d'Italia alla nascita della Galleria Nazionale delle Marche', *Il capitale culturale*, 4 (2012), pp. 197–216.

Scatena, Giovanni, *Oddantonio da Montefeltro, 1° duca di Urbino* (Roma: E. Paleani, 1989).

Schabacker, Peter, and Jones, Elizabeth, 'Jan van Eyck's "Woman at Her Toilet"; Proposals Concerning Its Subject and Context', *Annual Report, Fogg Art Museum* (1974–1976), pp. 56–78.

Schäpers, Maria, *Lothar I. (795–855) und das Frankenreich* (Wien: Böhlau Verlag, 2018).

Schmarsow, August, *Melozzo da Forlì: Ein Beitrag zur Kunst und Kulturgeschichte* (Berlin: Spemann, 1886).

Schrader, Laurentius, *Monumentorum Italiae quae hoc nostro saeculo et a christianis posita sunt, libri quatuor* (Helmstedt: Jakob Lucius, 1592).

Schrenck van Notzing, Jakob, *Die Heldenrüstkammer (Armamentarium heroicum) Erzherzog Ferdinands II. auf Schloss Ambras bei Innsbruck*, ed. Bruno Thomas (Osnabruck: Biblia Verlag, 1981).

Sforza, Alessandro, *Il Canzoniere*, ed. Luciana Cocito (Milan: Marzorati editore, 1973).

Sforza, Giovanni, *La patria, la famiglia e la giovinezza di papa Niccoló Quinto* (Lucca: Giusti, 1884).

Shaw, Christine, and Mallett, Michael, *The Italian Wars, 1494–1559* (London and New York: Routledge, 2017).

Shearman, John, 'The Logic and Realism of Piero della Francesca', in Antje Kosegarten and Peter Tigler (eds), *Festschrift Ulrich Middeldorf* (Berlin: W. de Gruyter, 1968), pp. 180–6.
——, 'Raphael at the Court of Urbino', *The Burlington Magazine*, 112, no. 803 (1970), pp. 72–8.

Sherrill, Tawny, 'Fleas, Furs, and Fashions: Zibellini as Luxury Accessories of the Renaissance', *Medieval Clothing and Textiles*, 2 (2019), pp. 121–50.

Shorthouse, Joseph Henry, *John Inglesant*, 2 vols (London: Macmillan, 1881).

Siebenhüner, Herbert, 'Die Bedeutung des Rimini-Freskos und der Geisselung Christ des Piero della Francesca', *Kunstchronik*, 8 (1954), pp. 124–6.

Sikorsky, Darius, 'Il palazzo ducale di Urbino sotto Guidobaldo II (1538–74): Bartolomeo Genga, Filippo Terzi e Federico Brandani', in Maria Luisa Polichetti (ed.), *Il palazzo di Federico da Montefeltro: Restauri e ricerche* (Urbino, QuattroVenti 1985), pp. 67–90.

Simonetta, Marcello, *Federico da Montefeltro and his Library* (New York: Y Press, 2007).
——, *The Montefeltro Conspiracy: A Renaissance Mystery Decoded* (New York: Doubleday, 2008).

Soil, Eugène, *Les Tapisseries de Tournai, les Tapissiers et les Hautelissiers de cette Ville: Recherches et Documents sur l'histoire, la Fabrication et les Produits des Ateliers de Tournai* (Tournai: Vasseur-Delmée, 1892).

Stein, Arnold, 'Yeats: A Study in Recklessness', *The Sewanee Review*, 57.4 (1949), pp. 603–26.

Stornajolo, Cosimus, *Codices Urbinates Graeci* (Rome: Typis Vaticanis, 1895).
———, *Codices Urbinates Latini* 3 vols. (Rome: Typis Vaticanis, 1902–1921).

Stourton, James, *Kenneth Clark: Life, Art and Civilisation* (London: William Collins, 2016).

Stras, Laurie, *Women and Music in Sixteenth-Century Ferrara* (Cambridge: Cambridge University Press, 2018).

Streeton, Noëlle L.W., 'Jan van Eyck's Dresden Triptych: New Evidence for the Giustiniani of Genoa in the Borromei Ledger for Bruges, 1438', *Journal of the Historians of Netherlandish Art*, 3.1 (2011), pp. 1–16.

Swain, Melissa, 'Spousal Sovereignty: The Ruling Couple and Its Representations in Quattrocento Italy, with Special Reference to Federico da Montefeltro (1422–1482) and Battista Sforza (c. 1446–1472)', New York University PhD, 2016.

Symonds, John Addington, 'The Palace at Urbino', in *Italian Byways* (London: Smith, Elder & Co, 1883), pp. 129–53.

Syson, Luke, and Thornton, Dora, *Objects of Virtue: Art in Renaissance Italy* (London: British Museum Press, 2001).

Tasso, Bernardo, *L'Amadigi* (Venezia: Gabriele Giolito, 1560).

Teague, Walter Dorwin, 'Enrico Bernardi, Master Intarsiatore', *Craft Horizons*, 11.2 (1951), pp. 8–12.

Tenzer, Virginia Grace, 'The Iconography of the Studiolo of Federico da Montefeltro in Urbino', Brown University PhD, 1985.

Thomas, William, *The historie of Italie: a boke excedyng profitable to be redde: because it intreateth of the astate of many and diuers common weales, how thei haue ben, [and] now be gouerned* (London: Thomas Berthelet, 1549).

Thornton, Dora, *The Scholar in his Study* (New Haven: Yale University Press).

Tick Bowers, Jane, and Judith Tick Bowers (eds), *Women Making Music: The Western Art Tradition, 1150–1950* (Chicago: University of Illinois Press, 1986).

Tocci, Luigi Michelini, 'I due manoscritti urbinati dei privilegi dei Montefeltro con una Appendice Lauranesca', *La Bibliofilia*, 60 (1958), pp. 206–57.
———, 'Agapito bibliotecario docto: biblioteca urbinate alle fine del Quattrocento', in *Collectanea Vaticana in honorem Anselmi M. Card. Albareda a Bibliotheca Apostolica edita*, (Città del Vaticano: Biblioteca Apostolica Vaticana, 1962).
———, 'Ottaviano Ubaldini della Carda e una inedita testimonianza sulla battaglia di Varna (1444)', *Studi e testi*, 277 (1964), pp 97–130.
———, *Il Dante Urbinate della Biblioteca Vaticana-codice Urbinate Latino 365* (Città cel Vaticano: Biblioteca Apostolica, 1965).

Tommasoli, Walter, *La Vita di Federico da Montefeltro, 1422–1482* (Urbino: Argalia Editore, 1878).

Tonelli, Luigi, *Tasso* (Torino: Paravia, 1935)

Torres Santo Domingo, Nuria, '500 años del primer libro impreso en caracteres móviles árabes. 500 Years of the First Arabic Printed Book by Movable Type', *Pecia Complutense*, 11(21) (2014), pp. 1–20.

Touring Club Italiano, *Marche* (Milano: Editore Cernusco, 1979).

Valazzi, Maria Rosaria, *Itinerari Rovereschi nel Ducato di Urbino* (Urbino: QuattroVenti, 1981).

Vasari, Giorgio, *Le vite de' più eccellenti pittori, scultori ed architettori*, ed. Gaetano Milanesi, 9 vols (Firenze: G.C. Sansoni, 1878–1906).
———, *On Technique*, trs. Louisa S. Maclehose (London: J.M. Dent, 1907).

Vasić Vatovec, Corinna, *Luca Fancelli, architetto. Epistolario Gonzaghesco* (Firenze: Uniedit, 1979).

———, 'La villa di Rusciano', in *Filippo Brunelleschi, la sua opera e il suo tempo* (Firenze: Centro Di, 1980), pp. 663–77.

Vernarecci, Augusto, 'Della colpa e prigionia di Muzio Oddi', *Nuova rivista misena*, 2 (1889), pp. 103–8.

Verstegen, Ian, 'Guidobaldo II della Rovere in European Perspective', *Yale University Art Gallery Bulletin, European Art* (2016), pp. 42–52.

Vertova, Luisa, 'Restorations in the Marches', *The Burlington Magazine*, 116, no. 853 (1974), pp. 229–33.

Vitali, Carlo, 'Musica e musicisti alla corte di Federico III da Montefeltro', *Il Flauto dolce*, 9 (1983), pp. 3–6.

Warnke, Martin, 'Individuality as Argument: Piero della Francesca's Portrait of the Duke and Duchess of Urbino', in Nico Mann and Luke Syson (eds), *The Image of the Individual: Portraits in the Renaissance* (London: British Museum Press, 1998), pp. 81–90.

Webb, Jennifer D., 'The Making of the Montefeltro: Patronage of the Arts and Architecture during the Reign of Federico Da Montefeltro and Battista Sforza', Bryn Mawr PhD, 2006.

———, 'All Is Not Fun and Games: Conversation, Play, and Surveillance at the Montefeltro Court in Urbino', *Renaissance Studies*, 26.3 (2011), pp. 417–40.

Weidhaas, Peter, *A History of the Frankfurt Book Fair* (Toronto: Dumdum Press, 2007).

Welch, Evelyn, 'The Art of Expenditure: The Court of Paola Malatesta Gonzaga in Fifteenth-Century Mantua', *Renaissance Studies*, 16.3 (2001), pp. 306–17.

Westfall, Carroll William, *In this Most Perfect Paradise: Alberti, Nicholas V, and the Invention of Conscious Urban Planning in Rome, 1447–1455* (University Park, PA and London: The Pennsylvania State University Press, 1974).

Wharton, Edith, *My Dear Governess: The Letters of Edith Wharton to Anna Bahlmann*, ed. Irene Goldman-Price (New Haven and London: Yale University Press, 2012).

Wilson, Timothy, *Ceramic Art of the Italian Renaissance* (London: British Museum Publications, 1987)

Wood, Jeryldene M. (ed.), *The Cambridge Companion to Piero della Francesca* (Cambridge: Cambridge University Press, 2002).

Woods-Marsden, Joanna, '"Ritratto al Naturale": Questions of Realism and Idealism in Early Renaissance Portraits', *Art Journal*, 46.3 (1987), pp. 209–16.

Woodward, William Harrison, *Vittorino da Feltre and Other Humanist Educators* (Cambridge: Cambridge University Press, 1905).

Yeats, William Butler, *A Vision: The Revised 1937 Edition*, eds Margaret Harper and Catherine Hall (New York: Scribner, 2015).

Zampetti, Pietro, *Gli affreschi di Lorenzo e Jacopo Salimbeni nell'oratorio di San Giovanni di Urbino* (Urbino: Ist. statale d'arte, 1956).

Zippel, Giuseppe, 'Artisti alla corte Estense nel '400, *L'Arte*, 5 (1905), pp. 405–7.

Picture credits

1 dvoevnore/Shutterstock

2 Bridgeman Images

3 Raffaello Bencini/Bridgeman Images

4 Bridgeman Images

5 Carlo Grifone/Wikimedia

6 DeAgostini/Getty Images

7 SuperStock/Alamy

8 Chris Hellier/Alamy

9 RMN-Grand Palais/Dist. Photo SCALA, Florence

10 akg-images/MPortfolio/Electa; akg-images/DeAgostini Picture Lib/M. Carrieri

11 Alamy/Wikimedia

12 Metropolitan Museum of Art/Wikimedia

13 Bridgeman Images

14 Sailko/Wikimedia

15 DeAgostini/Getty

16 Bridgeman Images

17 DeAgostini/Getty

18 Galleria Nazionale delle Marche

19 Bridgeman Images

20 Sepia Times/Universal Images Group/ Getty

21 The Picture Art Collection/Alamy

22 Salting Bequest/V&A

23 Uffizi/Wikimedia

24 Google Art Project

25 Wikimedia

26 Bridgeman Images

27 Bridgeman Images

28 Bridgeman Images

29 Bridgeman Images

30 Yale University Art Gallery/Gift of Mrs Catherine B. Hickox

31 Soulages Collection/V&A

32 Colnaghi/British Museum

33 The National Gallery, London/akg

34 Veniamin Kraskov/Shutterstock

35 Archivio Università degli studi di Urbino Carlo Bo

Notes

Preface

1 The only exception seems to be a three-quarter representation in a manuscript miniature in Città del Vaticano Urb. Lat. 93, f. 7v (see https://spotlight.vatlib.it/humanist-library/feature/federico-s-portrait).

2 Stourton, p.334.

3 Fornaciari, pp.211–18.

The Origins of the City of Urbino

1 Mazzini, p.51.

2 There are arguments for both, since the deal was of obvious benefit to both sides. See Fried.

3 Hobbes, p.286.

4 *De falso credita et ementita Constantini Donatione declamatio*, written 1440.

5 Fabrizio Fenucci, 'Notes on Federico da Montefeltro's Emblems', in Simonetta 2007, pp.81–2.

6 *Inferno* 79, 74–5: 'l'opere mie / non furon leonine, ma di volpe'.

7 Teodolinda Barolini, '*Inferno* 27: Disconversion', *Commento Baroliniano*, Digital Dante, https://digitaldante.columbia.edu/dante/divine-comedy/inferno/inferno-27/

8 Larner, pp.44, 89.

9 The earliest Dante is Vatican, Biblioteca Apostolica Urb. Lat. 366; the others, from the end of the fourteenth century, are Urb. Lat. 367 and 378. The two Petrarch volumes are now bound together as Urb. Lat. 1171.

10 Dennistoun II, pp.110–11.

11 Oxford, Bodleian Library Canoniciani Italiani 50.c, f. 167v, Bertozzi.

12 Giorgio Nonni, 'Le rime di Angelo Galli et il Codice Piancastelli 267 (Forlì V 87)', in G. Baiardi Cerboni, II, pp.327–46.

13 *Tractatus de re bellica spirituali per comparationem temporalis.* Manuscripts are Urb. Lat. 880 and Paris, Bibliothèque Nationale Lat. 16436.

1   **Gubbio, Urbino & Mercatello**
    1422–1431

1   Luigi Michelini Tocci, in Baiardi Cerboni I, p.304.

2   Giacomo Bandino Zenobi, 'Tra famiglia e "familia": i bastardi delle case signorili di area marchigiana', in Mozzarelli II, pp.415–35.

3   Franceschini 1959, p.10.

4   Paltroni, p.42. Bei and Cristini (2000) argue that Bernardino was Federico's true father.

5   Paltroni, pp.67–8, n.2.

6   Clough 1984, p.325, Piccolomini 1937–40, IV, 302.

7   Thomas, p.204.

8   Luzio and Renier, p.77, n.1.

9   Bei and Cristini, 2015 and 2000.

10 Dennistoun, I, p.45.

11 Arbizzoni 1993, p.145.

12 Clough 1984, pp.293–340.

13 Leonardo Bruni's text and translation is in Kallendorf, pp.92–125, p.125.

14 'Ioanna Aledusia Bartholomeo Brancaleoni fidissimo coniugi et sibi huius oppidi principi monumentum pietatis vivens fecit'. Inscription reproduced in Perini, p.72.

15 Baldi 1824, I, p.11.

16 Franceschini 1959, pp.12–13.

17 Paltroni, p.44; 'singulare et virtuosa madonna de grande intellecto et non de minore animo, la quale lo vece educare tanto virtuosamente quanto fusse pusibile a dire'.

18 Swain, p.47, n.52.

2   **Growing Up:**
    Venice & Mantua
    1432–1437

1   Clough 1998, p.300.

2   Guerriero, pp.49–50.

3   Raggio and Wilmering, p.114.

4   Baldi 1826, I, p.12.

5   Della Chiesa, p.269, Molly Bourne, 'The Art of Diplomacy: Mantua and the Gonzaga, 1328–1630', in Rosenberg, p.149.

6   Bourne, pp.148, 153.

7   Woodward, pp.31–3.

8   Woodward, p.33, n.1.

9   D'Elia, pp.89–90.

10 Grendler, p.334.

11 D'Elia, p.31.

12 Prendilaqua, p.49.

13 Baldi 1824, I, p.14, 'Nell' armeggiari, negli esercizi cavallereschi, à quale già per l'età cominciava ad addattarsi, ebbe per maestro supremo Gianfrancesco medesimo, e dopo lui que' Cavaliari, che in quello fioritissima Conte, è dedita agli esercizi dell'arme, come in una onoratissima Scuola a gran numero si trattenevano'.

14 Da Bisticci, p.99.

3   **Dutiful Son**
    1437–1444

1   Paltroni, p.47.

2   Mallett and Hale, p.69.

3   Hale, p.55.

4   Pyhrr, pp.28, 29.

5   Mann 1930, fig. 1, and 1938, pl. cII [after cleaning].

6   Compare Mann 1938, figs. 3–9, 67–71, esp. fig. 69.

7   Hale, p.54.

8   Tommasoli, p.42.

9   'Oratio magnifice ac illustrissime domine Baptiste sororis comitis Urbini ad imperatorem quando fuit in Urbino' is in Bologna, biblioteca universitaria 170, f. 70v. Trs King and Rabil, pp.35–8.

10   Bonfatti, pp.23–4.

11   Tommasoli, p.42.

12   Ratti, II, p.106. Parker, pp.39, 47–8.

13   Dati mentions his hair colour: Lavin 1968, p.332, n.55.

14   D'Antoni and Terzulli, Lavin 1969, p.367: 'In every sense it can be said that Piero painted two portraits, one of Federico and one of his armor. The suit, in fact, was probably set up in the artist's studio where he could inspect it at his leisure.'

15   Zampetti.

16   Raggio and Wilmering, p.21, Paltroni, pp.53–4.

17   Giorgio Nonni, 'Le rime di Angelo Galli et il Codice Piancastelli 267 (Forlì V 87)', in G. Baiardi Cerboni II, pp.327–46, contains many of his poems, mostly love poems. Urb. Lat. 699 is the principal manuscript.

18   Manchisi, pp.257–8. Contrary to what is generally thought about Italian honour-culture, it was perfectly possible for an ex-ducal mistress to make a good marriage. Ettlinger 1994, p.771.

19   Tommasoli, p.19.

20   Franceschini 1959, p.22.

21   Ryder 1976, pp.27, 77.

22   Clough 1992, pp.113–72.

23   Dennistoun I, p.52.

24   Tommasoli, p.41.

25   'ob violatum pudicitiam feminarum': Ser Guerriero, p.982.

26   Franceschini 1950, p.137.

27   Dennistoun I, p.53, Campofregoso, p.282v.

28   Jones, p.191. Franceschini 1959, pp.35–8, prints Federico's long letter, a masterpiece of libellous eloquence, accusing Sigismondo of a revolting array of crimes.

29   Assembled in Scatena, pp.89–103, esp. 100. See also Roeck 2007, pp.33–6.

30   Pernis and Adams, p.14.

31   Paltroni, p.68.

32   Hankins, pp.98–109.

33   Cox, 2016, p.60.

34   Paltroni, p.68.

35   Tommasoli, p.66.

36   Franceschini 1950, p.176: 'contra voluntatem Sanctissimi D.N. tyramnice teneat et occupet dictus Federicus… cum nullam concessionem aut titulum'.

4   Taking Control
1444–1450

1   Dennistoun I, p.213.

2   Clough 1966, pp.14–15.

3   Angelo Turchini, 'Sigismondo e Federico', in Fiore I, pp.27–48.

4 Mallett 1974, pp.70, 82, 102.

5 Mallett 1974, p.104.

6 'my deeds were not those of the lion but those of the fox' (*Inferno* 27, 74–5).

7 Baldi 1824, p.63. Franceschini 1957, p.136.

8 Tommasoli, p.68.

9 Franceschini 1950, p.141.

10 Clough 1992, p.158.

11 Tommasoli, p.52.

12 Agnesina was betrothed by 1446, probably in 1442, when her father sought the marriage of his son Oddantonio to Cecilia Gonzaga, for which see Scatena pp.52–62.

13 Franceschini 1959, pp.34–5, Pernis and Adams, p.28.

14 Clough 1992, p.113.

15 Franceschini 1950, pp.141–2.

16 Franceschini 1950, pp.144, 175–9.

17 Franceschini 1950, pp.143–4.

18 Welch, p.308.

19 Jones, p.197, Franceschini 1950, pp.144, 163.

20 Tocci 1958, p.253.

21 Luigi Michelini Tocci, 'Federico da Montefeltro e Ottaviano Ubaldini della Carda', in G. Baiardi Cerboni, I, pp.297–344.

22 Pernis and Adams, p.23.

23 As translated by Dennistoun I, p.50.

24 Hofmann, p.26: 'sic bene partita est regni communis utrique'.

25 Concetta Bianca, 'La presenza degli umanisti ad Urbino nella seconda metà del Quattrocento', in Fiore I, pp.129–45.

26 Hofmann, p.31: 'sic puer his, quoniam pacis tutabitur ortum / interitum exosus, donando vincet honestis / quamlibet ingeniis studiorum cultor eorum / quae quondam Augustus mira est virtute sequutus'.

27 Jones, pp.216–17, and more fully Franceschini 1957, pp.143–54.

28 Feliciangeli 1903a, and for Violante's letter to Francesco Sforza, Franceschini 1957, pp.182–3.

29 Dennistoun I, p.98.

30 Pernis and Adams, p.22.

31 Webb 2006, pp.45–6.

32 For Gentile's active role in governing, see Perini, pp.72–4.

33 Belozerskaya 2002, pp.207–8.

34 Paltroni, p.54.

35 Papini II.2, p.28.

36 Muzio, p.364.

37 Mortimer, pp.302–3.

38 Mallett, 1974, p.213.

39 Santoni-Rugiu and Massei, pp.251–7.

5   Consolidation
1451–1460

1 Westfall.

2 'Donna d'animo fecondo, ma Corpo per la soverclia grassezza sterile' (Baldi 1824, II, p.36).

3 Simonetta 2007, p.20.

4 Hollingsworth 1994, p.4.

5 Jones, pp.198–200.

6   Ryder 1990.

7   Da Vinci II, pp.22–3.

8   Matteo Ceriana, 'Fra Carnevale and the Practice of Architecture', in O'Neill, p.103.

9   Hale, p.157.

10 Hale, p.49, Mallett 1972, p.165.

11 Hunt and Carlson, pp.143–4.

12 *Spingardi* were a new weapon invented by the condottiere Bartolomeo Colleoni in the mid-1460s: they were mounted on gun carriages and discharged a ball about the size of a plum; a foreshadowing of the future development of light artillery (Dennistoun I, p.189).

13 Clough 1998, p.307; Dennistoun I, p.249.

14 The one on the title page of Urb. Lat. 151 is brownish, represented as clearly metallic, perhaps meant for bronze. Others, in Urb. Lat. 52 and 185, are lead-grey, and another in 328 is white.

15 Aristotle, *Politics*, VII, 14.

16 Nardini, p.12.

17 Cheles, pp.74, 78.

18 Arbizzoni 1993, L'orazione di Martino Filetico in morte di Gentile Brancaleoni: 'et suis propemodum vos oculis cariores habebat' (he is addressing Buonconte), p.148.

19 'Che non altramente che ingenerato me avesse teneramene me amava', Franceschini 1937, p.490.

20 Franceschini 1937, pp.492–3.

21 Mazzanti, p.31.

22 Cox 2016, pp.46–66.

23 Baldi 1824, II, p.48, Clough 1992, pp.122–3.

24 'Io conosco che per li peccati miei nostro Signore Dio me ha tolto un occhio et questo figliolo che era la vita mia et el contentamento mio et de i sudditi miei, che io non seppi mai volere cosa de lui chel non fessa segondo el mio desiderio.' Franceschini 1937, p.499.

25 Tocci in G. Baiardi Cerboni, I, p.308.

26 '… e morte di grazessa come lu doctore diche che era facta tanto grassa et grossa che era una cosa mostruosa a vedere.' Quoted in Franceschini 1937 p.489.

27 Padua, Biblioteca del Seminario, MS 84, ff. 1–4v.

28 'Temperata, prudente, humile e sagia… benigna, honesta, alma gentile' (lines 53, 78). Sforza, pp.226–30.

29 Arbizzoni 1993, p.146: 'uxor erat Domino Gentilis nomine patri / tu Gentilis eris filia cara patri'.

6   **Battista: 1460–1472**

1   Degli Arienti, p.292.

2   Bornstein, p.103.

3   See King and Rabil, pp.36–7; Cox 2009a, pp.47–75.

4   Dennistoun I, pp.429–31 prints two of her sonnets to Malatesta, and a Latin letter to Pope Martin V.

5   Parroni, p.206.

6   Cox 2009b, p.46. See also Parker, in Churchill.

7   Mazzanti, pp.40–1. See Feliciangeli, 1903b, pp.311–12.

8   Archivio di Stato di Milano, Potenze
    Sovrano. No. 1475. Other authors
    (Battista Contessa di Montefeltro).
    One such letter, signed by Battista,
    was written to Bianca Maria Sforza
    and dated December 9th, 1458.

9   Feliciangeli 1903b, p.315.

10 De'Reguardati, pp.366–8, documents
    128, 129.

11 Mulazzani, pp.252–3.

12 Mauro Lucco, 'Burgundian Art for
    Italian Courts: Milan, Ferrara,
    Urbino', in Borchert, pp.108–17,
    p.113.

13 Joanna Woods-Marsden, 'Portrait of
    the Lady, 1430–1520', in Brown (ed.),
    p.67, observes that blonde hair was *de
    rigueur* in Italian portraits of young
    women until around 1490.

14 Degli Arienti, p.290: 'Fu de mediocre
    statura, biancha de carne et fresca
    come viva rosa; hebbe belli et
    modestissimi occhii, quali raro
    dimostravano non cognoscere bene
    che fusse al suo pudico conspecto.
    Havea bella mano et candidi denti.
    Fu de natura et complexione più
    presto sanguinea, che altro; presto
    alcuna volta, per qualche offensione,
    se adirava, ma presto la ira se partiva.'

15 See also Frick.

16 Quoted in Adrian Randolph,
    'Regarding Women in Sacred Space',
    in Johnson and Grieco, p.35.

17 Guerriero, p.69.

18 Ebreo, pp.248–9.

19 Cox 2016, p.151.

20 'Temperat atque pedes Tersicore ipse
    tuos', Mazzanti, p.49.

21 Graham Pont, 'In Search of the
    Opera Gastronomica', in Corones I,
    pp.114–24, p.118.

22 Baldi 1824 II, p.51, records the
    acquisition of the small outpost. It
    was little more than a hamlet: in 1371,
    twenty families lived there. By 1439
    and again in 1458, it was occupied by
    Malatesta forces. Lombardi, p.38.

23 Several examples of these letters may
    be found in Archivio di Stato di
    Milano, Potenze Estense. Marca.
    No.143 (1450–1458), which contains
    fragments of three letters sent to
    Francesco Sforza explaining the
    threat posed by Sigismondo
    Malatesta and dated May 5th, 1460,
    June 25th, 1460, and July 6th, 1460.

24 Degli Arienti, pp.296 and 294: 'Molte
    volte, quando per varie expeditione el
    duca suo marito existendo in campo,
    essa seco dimorava cum virile animo,
    senza alcuno timore, de la qual cosa
    forsi qualche inprudente la
    imputava… troppo proveduta et
    saghace, che bastarebbe havesse
    gubernato el regno di Franza.'

25 Tommasoli, p.128.

26 Tommasoli, p.119.

27 Pernis and Adams, p.9.

28 Ceriana in O'Neill, p.111.

29 Guerriero, p.72.

30 Feliciangeli 1903b, p.315, Mazzanti,
    pp.36–7.

31 Dennistoun I, pp.126–7. Mallett,
    1972, p.199, comments that slipped
    discs and joint trouble were common
    results of riding, and sometimes
    falling, in heavy armour.

32 *Divae Baptistae cohortatio quod Romae
    Federicum imperatorem et coniugem
    non invenerit*, Urb. Lat. 373,

Biblioteca Apostolica Vaticana, ff. 115v–117r. See Mazzanti, pp.96–7 and Fritelli.

33 Quoted in Ratti, II, pp.128–9.

34 See Mazzanti, pp.95–101. See also Ratti, who goes to great lengths to track down documentation of Battista's activities in Rome esp. II, p.135, n.14.

35 Pearson, p.2.

36 Da Bisticci, p.106.

37 Mack.

38 Mazzanti, pp.100–1.

39 Arbizzoni, 1992, 'Introduzione', pp.26–7.

40 Mazzanti, p.127.

41 Dionisotti reconstructs the two opposing lobbies of humanists, for and against instruction in Greek, esp. p.312.

42 'Gratias ago quom id intelligo quod nesciebam. Sed, si placet, hodiernae disputationi finem imponamus. Sum enim regis legatos auditura, quos heri multo vesperi ad nos ventasse non ignoratis.' See Arbizzoni 2003, pp.171, 229.

43 Arbizzoni 2003, p.172.

44 Gaugelli 1905, III:19–27, p.19.

45 Arbizzoni 2003, p.107.

46 *La prima, che Demostene e Platone*
Par ch'abbia avanti e legga anche
Plotino
D'eloquenza e savere al paragone
Ben potrà star con l'Orator d'Arpino
Moglie fia d'un invitto altro campione
Fedrigo Duca dell'antica
Urbino (*Tasso*, canto 44, stanza 57, p.270).

47 Marcella Peruzzi, 'The Library of Glorious Memory: History of the Montefeltro Collection', in Simonetta 2007, pp.29–35, p.29.

48 Simonetta 2007, pp.146–9.

49 Martin Davies, 'Non re n'è ignuno a stampa: The Printed Books of Federico da Montefeltro, in Simonetta 2007, pp.63–79, p.64.

50 Degli Arienti, *Gynevera*, p.296.

51 Fildes, p.49.

52 Degli Arienti 301, writes, 'her daughters were adorned with different clothes, beautiful garments, and gems, in which she took great pleasure'.

53 Pernis and Adams, p.51.

54 For Lilio Tifernate see Lanciarini I, p.399 n.3. Paolini presents evidence for Gentile's humanist studies.

55 Pernis and Adams, p.52.

56 'Nihil fuit familiarius neque amantius amicitia qua Batista et ego eramus conjuncti', da Montefeltro, p.162.

57 See Urb. Lat. 373.

58 Degli Arienti, p.297.

59 Monfasani, pp.95–110.

60 Fabrizio Fenucci, 'Notes on Federico da Montefeltro's Emblems', in Simonetta 2007, pp.81–7, p.83. See also Santi, XII.56, p.115.

61 Mallett 1972, p.195.

62 Dennistoun I, p.212. Santi, XII.57, p.117; 'sol ne porrtava a casa lalta gloria / che piu che altro tesoro ha el nome bello'.

63 Grossi, p.28.

64 Delio Proverbio, 'The Diaspora of the Hebrew Manuscripts: from Volterra

to Urbino', in Simonetta 2007, pp.51–61.

65   Touring Club Italiano, p.242.

66   Hollingsworth 2017, pp.163–4.

67   Pernis 1990, p.30, Vasić Vatovec, pp.663–77.

68   For a more extensive discussion see Mazzanti, pp.162–75.

69   Gaugelli, VI.

70   Dennistoun I, p.214.

71   Da Montefeltro, p.6.

72   Illustrated Wood, p.102.

73   Chadwick and Mann, pp.170–1.

74   McManamon, p.113.

75   Motta, pp.89–90.

76   Ellis, pp.9–21.

77   Redacted by Baldi in the sixteenth century, in Baldi 1821, I, p.5. The story is told at length by Bembo, p.139.

78   *Del modo di regere e di regnare.* The presentation manuscript is New York, Pierpont Morgan Library, M. 731, and it was later published, in 1517.

79   Diego Zancani, 'Writing for Women Rulers in Quattrocento Italy: Antonio Cornazzano', in Panizza, pp.57–74.

7   Magnificence
1472–1482

1   *Feltria*, Vat. Urb. Lat. 710:
Ipse domum rediens primum vacua atria lustrat,
Mox semota petens, clausis de more fenestris,
In luctu et lacrymis, nigra in veste sedebat.
Pullati incedunt comites, famulique minores,
Ac nigra sunt mensi mantilia, nigra supellex
Et thalamum infaustum velamina nigra tegebant.

2   'non potui non vehementer angi'. Hessler, p.386.

3   Clough 1966, p.14.

4   Tommasoli, p.129.

5   Clough 1973, p.131.

6   Edelheit, pp.82–114.

7   Urb. Lat. 227.

8   Saviotti.

9   Einstein I, p.35.

10   Tommasoli, p.251.

11   Baldi 1824, III, p.241: 'Usuncassano potentissimo Re di Persia nel mandar, che fece Ambasciatori a'Potentati Cristiani, ordinò loro particolarmente che da sua parte lo visitassero, e gli presentassero ricchissimi doni: il che fecero essi diligentemente'.

12   Joost-Gaugier, p.94.

13   Rotondi, pp.86–90.

14   Eiche 1999, p.25; Pernis and Adams, pp.17–18.

15   Vitali, pp.3–6.

16   'Bella gerit, musasque colit', Franco Piperno, 'Italian Courts and Music', in Folin, pp.78–89; p.85. See also Mamini.

17   Urb. Lat. 1411, ff. 7r–9v.

18   Tommasoli, p.275. Santi, XVIII:71, p.139.

19   Simonetta 2008, p.56.

20   Mallett 1972, p.100, Simonetta 2008, p.35.

21   Simonetta 2008, pp.69–71.

22   Simonetta 2008, p.126.

23   Simonetta 2008, p.139.

24   Allegretti, coll. 783, 796.

25   Dennistoun I, p.249.

26   Mallett 1972, p.197.

27   Pinti.

28   Simonetta 2008, p.170.

29   Simonetta 2008, p.204.

30   Simonetta 2008, p.180.

31   Simonetta 2007, p.22.

32   Dennistoun I, p.259.

33   Franceschini 1950 p.140.

34   Franceschini 1950, p.188.

35   Clough 1984, p.296.

36   Bornstein, p.106.

37   Jones, p.295 n.5; and see p.251 for his mistress and children, and n.3 for Elisabetta's daughter, Battista.

38   Franceschini 1950, 140.

39   Pearson, pp.4–5.

40   Clough 1984, p.348, from MS Urb. Lat. 490.

41   'Questo fu uomo virtuosissimo, litterato, honesto amatore della religione e di tutti li buoni costumi, havendo tutte le buone parte che deva havere un vero duca', Girolamo Maria, Fra, p.102.

8   The Palace at Urbino

1   *Nicomachean Ethics*, IV.2.v–xvi [1122]. The word translated 'magnificence' is 'megaloprepeia'.

2   Fraser Jenkins, p.162. For additional information about the classical origins for magnificence, see Clarke, pp.54–65.

3   Piccolomini 1614, p.49.

4   Goldthwaite, p.83.

5   Martines, p.310.

6   Clough 1992, pp.144–9.

7   Christoph Luitpold Frommel, 'Il Palazzo Ducale di Urbino e la nascita della redisenza principesca del Rinascimento', in Fiore I, pp.167–96; p.167.

8   Maria Giannatiempo López, 'Antefatti al palazzo di Federico: ritrovamenti, ipotesi', in Fiore I, pp.147–66; p.150.

9   Höfler, p.287 (document of 3 June, 1443).

10   López, in Fiore I, pp.157–64.

11   Pernis and Adams, p.25.

12   Santi XIV.56, pp.22–30. 'La donde, el Conte, de infinite amore/ ardendo, a aedificar prima in Urbino / Incomicio vi cum supremo core,/ non aedifitio humano anzi divino,/ un gran palazzo, el qual a simil terra/si como lui e stato un chiar distino,/ pero che quanto el cierchio della terra/ gira, secondo che ognun parla e dice,/ piu bella cosa a se dentro non serra.'

13   Höfler, p.98.

14   Rotondi, pp.23–4.

15   Gronau, p.vii.

16   Da Bisticci, p.100.

17   'Aulam regionum omnium pulcherrimam edificiorum arte tota designaret, atque ibi edificandae praefuisset.' The inscription is given by Gaye, I, p.276.

18 Roberta Martufi, 'Il giardino pensile del palazzo ducale di Urbino', in A. Cerboni Baiardi, pp.89–100.

19 Philip Jacks, 'The Renaissance Prospettiva', in Wood, pp.115–33; p.122.

20 Baratin, p.49.

21 Sarah Edwards, 'La Scala Elicoidale: The Spiral Ramps of Francesco di Giorgio. An Architectural Re-Invention', in Hub and Polalli, pp.107–26.

22 Goldthwaite, p.83.

23 Tenzer, pp.334–5, 409.

24 Simonetta 2008, p.56.

25 This is suggested by Pernis and Adams, p.17.

26 Folin, p.26.

27 Pernis 1990, pp.5–9, 84–7.

28 Thornton, p.1.

29 Marcello Toffanello, 'Ferrara: the Este Family', in Folin, pp.181–202; p.186.

30 Vasari 1907, p.305.

31 Benzi, pp.7–22.

32 D. King 2001, pp.110–11.

33 D. King 2000, p.323.

34 Baldi 1590, p.536.

35 Kirkbride.

36 Schrader, pp.283–4, Lavallaye, pp. 102–4.

37 Hessler, pp.365–404.

38 Vasari 1907, p.263.

39 Teague, p.11; *Restauri*, pp.603–4.

40 Vasić Vatovec, pp.238–40, Caroline Elam, 'Mantegna at Mantua', in Chambers and Martineau, pp.15–25, p.21.

41 Dacos, pp.58–9; Lorenzetti, p.332.

42 Castiglione, p.41.

43 de' Medici, p.129.

44 Hendy, p.25.

45 Da Bisticci, p.100.

46 Raggio and Wilmering, p.123.

47 Jacks, 'The Renaissance Prospettiva', in Wood, pp.115–33, p.118.

48 Sangiorgi, pp.43, 63.

49 Jacks, 'The Renaissance Prospettiva', in Wood, p.237, n.10.

50 Tenzer, pp.157–9.

51 Christiansen, p.19.

9 Gubbio and Beyond: Other Architectural Projects

1 Raggio and Wilmering, pp.52–5.

2 Giangiacomo Martines, 'La Costruzione del Palazzo Ducale di Gubbio: Invenzione e Preesistenze', in G. Cerboni Baiardi II, pp.171–86, p.171; Francesco Paolo Fiore, 'Francesco di Giorgio a Gubbio', in *idem*, II, pp.151–70, p.161.

3 Raggio and Wilmering, p.72.

4 Luzio and Renier, p.74.

5 Dennistoun I, pp.172–3.

6 Benelli, pp.140–55.

7 Nicholas Adams, 'La Rocca Ubaldesca di Sassocorvaro: ?Anni settanta-ottanto del XV secolo e sgg.', in Fiore and Tafuri, pp.211–17.

8 Edwards, in Hub and Polalli, pp.107–26.

9 Liotta.

10 Savelli; Anna Cerboni Baiardi, 'Dal giardino sognato al giardino da sogno', in A. Cerboni Baiardi, pp.11–40, p.18.

11 Nicholas Adams, 'La rocca di San Leo', in Fiore and Tafuri, pp.218–23.

12 Roberta Martinis, 'Un Architettura con un cielo in mezzo: Francesco di Giorgio nel Palazzo Milanese di Federico da Montefeltro', in Hub and Polalli, pp.133–62; pp.140–2.

13 Pellecchia, p.379.

14 Santucci, pp.4–11.

15 C. King, pp.815–18.

16 Panzini, pp.148–57.

17 Paolo dal Poggetto, 'La diffusione del verbo raffaelesco: la Villa Imperiale; l'attività di Raffaellino del Colle', in Arbizzoni 2001, II, pp.203–46.

18 Panzini, pp.158–62.

10 Federico as Patron of the Arts

1 S. Campbell, p.269. For the Latin text, see Zippel, pp.405–7.

2 Tim Benton, 'Bramante and the Sources of the Roman High Renaissance', in Richardson, pp.251–90; pp.257–9.

3 Chapman, pp.15–33.

4 Butler, p.18.

5 Chapman, p.16.

6 Matteo Ceriana, 'Fra Carnevale and the Practice of Architecture', in O'Neill, pp.97–136, p.98.

7 Ceriana, in O'Neill, p.103.

8 Maria Giannatiempo López, 'Antefatti al palazzo di Federico: ritrovamenti, ipotesi', in Fiore, pp.147–66.

9 Salmi, pp.153–9.

10 Rotondi, pp.21–2.

11 C. Campbell, pp.30–47.

12 Illustrated in Mazzanti, p.80. When he married Gentile his famous nose was intact, so the *cassone* cannot be hers. The second is in the Victoria and Albert Museum.

13 Deborah L. Krohn, 'Rites of Passage: Art Objects to Celebrate Betrothal, Marriage and the Family', in Bayer, pp.60–7; p.64.

14 Now in Musée des Augustins de Toulouse.

15 Bury and Kemp, p.452; Sangiorgi, p.272, no. 944.

16 Sangiorgi, p.64; Callman, pp.67–70.

17 Vasari, 1878–1906, II, pp.147–8.

18 Angelo Galli wrote two poems to accompany it, in Urb. Lat. 699, f. 18, printed by Dennistoun I, pp.436–7.

19 There is an example in the Archaeological Museum of Bologna, inventory no. MCA-NUM-22732.

20 Clark, Siebenhüner, pp.124–6, Battisti.

21 'Nella sagristia… la Flagellazione di N.o Sig.re alla colonna, con disparte li nostri ser.mi duchi Oddo Antonio, Federico e Guid'Ubaldo di Pietro Dall' Borgo.' Quoted by Ginzberg, p.50, n.97.

22 Bertelli, pp.124–5.

23 Lavin 1968, p.332.

24   St Jerome, *Letters*, no. 22, § 30
     (Wright pp.52–159).

25   Pope-Hennesey, pp.162–5.

26   Jane Bridgeman, 'Troppo belli e
     troppo eccellenti', in Wood,
     pp.76–90; p.81.

27   Chambers and Martineau, pp.9–10.

28   Lavin 1969, p.369, Philip Jack 'The
     Renaissance Prospettiva', in Wood,
     pp.115–33; p.119.

29   Clough 1984, p.317; Shearman 1968,
     p.185.

30   Clough 1984, p.313.

31   Simonetta 2008, p.186.

32   Clough 1984, pp.314, 317.

33   Bertelli, p.136.

34   Joanna Woods-Marsden, 'Piero della
     Francesca's Ruler Portraits', in Wood,
     pp.91–114; p.94.

35   On the Senigallia Madonna, see
     Hendy, pp.117–18.

36   Vat. Urb. Lat. 193 f. 114 r–v,
     Stornajolo 1902–21, III, p.199.

37   'Ast Petrus nervos mihi dat cum
     carnibus ossa, / Das animam,
     Princeps, tu deitate tua; / Vivo igitur,
     loquor et scio per me posse moviri
     [sic]; / Gloria sic Regis praestat et
     artifi'. Woods-Marsden, p.211.

38   *Epigrams*, X.32 '…Ars utinam mores
     animumque effingere posset!/
     pulchrior in terris nulla tabella foret.'

39   Simonetta 2008, pp.13, 119.

40   J.M. Fletcher, 'Isabella d'Este, Patron
     and Collector', in Chambers and
     Martineau, pp.51–63; pp.56–7.

41   Lucco, 'Burgundian Art for Italian
     Courts: Milan, Ferrara, Urbino', in
     Borchert, pp.109–17, p.110.

42   Raggio and Wilmering, p.19.

43   Woods-Marsden, p.211.

44   Charles Rosenberg, 'The Double
     Portrait of Federico and Guidobaldo
     da Montefeltro: Power, Wisdom and
     Dynasty', in G. Baiardi Cerboni, II,
     pp.213–22.

45   Rotondi, figs 167, 168.

46   Alberti, p.60.

47   Damianaki.

48   Brown, p.14.

49   Now in Niedersächsisches
     Landesmuseum, Hamburg.

50   Woods-Marsden, 'Portrait of the
     Lady, 1430–1520' in Brown,
     pp.64–87; p.64.

51   de Carlo, p.17.

52   Rotondi, p.52, and fig. 116.

53   Woods-Marsden, in Wood,
     pp.91–114; pp.108–9.

54   Woods-Marsden, in Wood, p.121.

55   Now 87 in the Galleria Nazionale
     delle Marche.

56   Ruda, pp.210–36.

57   Streeton, pp.1–16.

58   Belozerskaya 2002, p.11.

59   Rubin, p.4.

60   Santi, XXII:92, pp.120–1.

61   Baxandall, p.102.

62   Clough 1992, pp.113–72.

63   Now in the Kunsthalle, Bremen.

64   Schabacker, pp.56–78.

65   Vasari, 1878–1906, I, p.184.

66   Elena Parma, 'Genoa: Gateway to the
     South', in Borchert, pp.94–107; p.95.

67 Belozerskaya 2002, p.78.

68 Roeck 2010, p.186.

69 Helfenstein, p.431.

70 Da Bisticci, p.101.

71 Margaret L. Koster, 'Italy and the North: A Florentine Perspective', in Borchert, pp.78–90; p.90. Gombrich, p.20.

72 Lavallaye, pp.45, 46, 50, 90–2.

73 McRoberts, p.166.

74 Evans, p.82.

75 Lavin 1967, p.2.

76 Lavin 1967, p.9.

77 Lavin 1967, p.10: 'sua fatigha per depignare la tavola de la fraternita'.

78 See the Confraternity of Corpus Domini records, Libro B, carta 75r: 'Eadem 7 de marzo 1474 florini quindece doro contanti da nostro Illustre Signore [Federico da Montefeltro] a Guido de Menghaccio per detta fraternita per aiutorio de la spesa de la tavola…'; quoted in Moranti, p.217.

79 Lavin 1967, p.22.

80 Chomentovskaja, p.172. Joos van Ghent also used the finger-counting gesture in his portrayals of Saint Thomas Aquinas, Boethius, and Duns Scotus in Federico's *studiolo*.

81 Evans, pp.87–8. Other arrangements have been suggested.

82 Fletcher, in Chambers and Martineau, p.52.

83 Ames-Lewis 1984, p.14.

84 Evans, p.92.

85 Evans, p.97. Conversely, Clough has argued that Pedro Berruguete was never in Urbino at all: 1981, no X, pp.1–10.

86 Webb 2011, pp.422–3.

87 Baldi 1590, p.537: 'Questo [studio] oltra gli scorniciamenti di legno dorati, tarsia, & altri ornamenti, e diviso in alcuni spatii, ne'; quali per mano di Timoteo Viti, famoso pittore di quei tempi, sono dipinti una Pallade con l'egida, un' Apollo con la lire, a le nove Muse ciascuna col suo proprio instrumento.'

88 Gaugelli 1991, p.34.

89 Luzio and Renier, pp.75–6.

90 McKendrick, p.773.

91 Clough 1992, p.128.

92 T. Campbell, p.55.

93 Belozerskaya 2005, pp.110–11.

94 Ceriana, in O'Neill, p.115.

95 Baldi, 1590, p.553.

96 … hic aditus sunt mille atque ostia mille,
Quae ducunt, Cretae tanquam labyrintus, ad amplae
Interiora domus; miro caelata labore
Marmore de pario postes et limina cernes;
Stant aulae innumerae fulgentes marmore et auro.Schmarsow, pp.75–6.

97 'rutilo fulgentia in auro'. Campani VII, p.23.

98 Belozerskaya 2002, p.105.

99 T. Campbell, p.199. De Beatis, p.95.

100 Belozerskaya 2002, p.115.

101 'Spesso in la sala vedi adornamento / De panni razi, che mai fuor più belli'.

102 'opera bellissima e vaga'. Clough 1973, p.139.

103 'mal condizionato e straciato'. Sangiorgi, p.217.

104 Da Bisticci, p.101. Müntz, pp.42–4.

105 Dennistoun I, p.150.

106 Sangiorgi, pp.216–17.

107 Castiglione, p.41.

108 Fletcher, in Chambers and Martineau, pp.53–4.

109 Clough 1998, p.311, Schmarsow, p.75.

110 Clifford Brown, 'Lo insaciabile desiderio nostro de cose antique: New Documents on Isabella d'Este's Collection of Antiquities', in Clough 1976, pp. 324–53; pp.333, 338–9, 350.

111 Da Bisticci, p.101.

112 Bober and Rubinstein, pp.82–3, Syson and Thornton, pp.97–8.

11 Urbino: The Ducal Library

1 Peruzzi, *Cultura*.

2 Da Bisticci, pp.102–5.

3 Franklin, p.368.

4 Reynolds, pp.13–14.

5 It is one of three gospel books known to have been made for him. Schäpers, p.585.

6 Cecilia Montoli, p.41; Caldelli, pp.217–28.

7 Pempi, 'The library of glorious memory', in Simonetta, 2007, p.36.

8 The 'bibliographic canon' Parentucelli drew up for Cosimo is published in Giovanni Sforza, 1884, pp.359–81. Da Bisticci notes that this 'canon' also served to guide the libraries of the duke of Urbino and the Sforzas (pp.102–3, 114).

9 Peruzzi, *Cultura*, pp.35–8.

10 Urb. Lat. 732, 'Carmen de laudibus Divi Principis Federici', lines 10–14. For his presence at Urbino, see Tocci, 'Ottaviano Ubaldini della Carda', p.102.

11 'Federico da Montefeltro: Portrait of a Renaissance Man', Simonetta, 2007, p.22.

12 Hofmann, pp.5–60.

13 Monreal, pp. 129–57.

14 Davies, pp.63–79.

15 Bell, 'Medieval Women Book Owners', in Bennett et al., p.144.

16 Roberts, pp.145–60. The Urbino copy is Urb. Lat. 273. A special prologue by Berlinghieri, 'Juno's Apology to Jove for the Death of Duke Federico' tells us that it missed its mark.

17 Kent and Elam, pp.64–89.

18 Campbell and Cole, p.211.

19 Duke Federico, for example, commissioned a set of eleven pieces representing the Trojan War from Jean Grenier of Tournai in 1476, which were admired by both Isabella d'Este and Vespasiano da Bisticci (Campbell and Cole, p.234; see also Soil). Bell, pp.44–5, gives evidence for moving tapestries from residence to residence.

20 Piazzoni.

21 Montoli, in Simonetta, p.42.

22 Tocci, 1965.

23 Simonetta 2008, p.140.

24 Roman, pp.132–55. For Federico's relations with Naples, see Clough 1992, pp.113–72.

25 Clough, 'Federico da Montefeltro', p.120.

26 Roman, in *Convivium*, 4.2 (2017), p. 135.

27 Pempi, p.30. The text of the letters is in Peruzzi, *Cultura, Potere*, pp.127–8.

28 Diller, pp.313–21.

29 De' Cavalieri.

30 Clough 1964, pp.160–71; Monfasani, pp.95–110.

31 Alexander-Skipnes, pp.67–85.

32 Peruzzi, *Cultura*, discusses the library's organization, placement within the palace, and the role of the librarian in selecting and displaying works for visitors.

33 Pempi, p.32. See Eiche 1999, pp.131–2.

34 Stornajolo 1895, p.xiii.

35 See now Maria Moranti, 'Organizzazione della Biblioteca di Federico da Montefeltro', in Baiardi, et al., pp.19–49.

36 Tocci 1962, p.261 n.l.

37 Webb 2006, p.75.

38 A book-shaped case used for storing manuscripts, documents and old or precious books; named after the Swedish naturalist Daniel Solander (1733–82), who catalogued the natural history collections of the British Museum.

39 Pempi, p.32.

40 Tocci 1962, pp.245–89.

41 Martelli, in Simonetta, pp.41–50, discusses the history of the scriptorium and who worked there, and highlights the political contexts that informed Federico's choice of illuminators and scribes.

42 Peruzzi, *Cultura*, p.65 n.19.

43 Caldari et al., p.39 n.39. He used Urb. Lat. 342 to recover the word 'cucita' in Juvenal, *Saturae* V.17: 'in a very ancient text of Juvenal which the very learned Guidobaldo, prince or duke of Urbino, brought out of his splendid collection of books' (Juvenalis codice pervetere quem doctissimus princeps aut dux Urbinatium Guido de pulcherrima sua librorum supellectile prompserit).

44 Where it is MS. Vit. 22/1.

45 Reti, p.342.

46 Hay, p.243.

47 Farago.

48 Pempi, p.36.

49 *Pratica di fabricar scene, e macchine ne' teatri* (Pesaro: Flaminio Concordia, 1637).

50 Davies, 'Non re n'è ignuno a stampa: the printed books of Federico da Montefeltro', in Marcello Simonetta, *Federico da Montefeltro and his Library* (Milano: Y Press SRL, 2007), pp.63–79, p.64.

12 Guidobaldo

1 Pinetti, p.355–80.

2 Dennistoun, I, pp.297–8.

3 Eiche, 1999, p.87. See Dennistoun, *Memoirs* I, p.310.

4 Carlisle, pp.326–8.

5 Luzio and Renier, pp.8, 12, 293–5.

6 Bembo, p.192.

7 Colantuono, p.190.

8 Luzio and Renier, p.88.

9 Bianucci, pp.28–30.

10 Clough 1966, p.8.

11 Mallett, 1969, p.11.

12 'hoc fugienti fortunae dicatis'.

13 Centanni, p.123.

14 Bembo, p.200.

15 There is a copy in the great library, transcribed from a later printed edition of 1509, so made after Guidobaldo's death (Urb. Lat. 257).

16 Mackinnon, p.140. Baldasso, pp.83–102, argues that this is in fact Guidobaldo, but without reference to any other images of the duke.

17 Mackinnon, p.139.

18 Baldi, 1998, pp.330–45, at p.344.

19 Hay, pp.240–51.

20 Dennistoun I, p.361.

21 Dennistoun I, p.377.

22 Norton, p.251.

23 Mallett 1969, p.174.

24 'El pontefice se contenta dispensar el matrimonio del Duca per essere impotente, e far lui Cardinale; la moglie si dara' ad un baron in Franza.' Luzio and Renier, p.141.

25 Bembo, pp.194–6.

26 Mallett, 1969, p.183, Bradford, p.207.

27 Norton, p.252. The letter is in Gaye, II, p.54. See Brown, in Clough 1976, pp.333, 338–9, 350.

28 La France, p.1207.

29 Dennistoun II, p.33, from the diary of Marino Sanudo.

30 Ettlinger 1983, pp.25–9.

31 Clough 1963, p.77.

32 La France, p.1212.

33 Dennistoun II, p.31.

34 Rodocanachi, pp.82, 398.

35 Torres Santo Domingo, pp.1–20.

36 Jones and Penny, p.5.

37 Cohen, p.417.

38 Shearman 1970, p.75.

39 La France, p.1219.

40 Falvo, pp.133–40, Guidi, pp.141–86.

41 Castiglione, p.13.

42 Castiglione, p.32.

43 Luzio and Renier, p.172.

44 Kidwell, p.122.

45 Albury, p.325.

46 Castiglione, p.44.

47 Castiglione, pp.40, 41.

48 Clough 1966, pp.18, 8.

49 Burke, pp.158–62.

50 Castiglione, pp.344–5.

51 Stein, p.603.

52 Meihuizen, pp.108–9. Yeats, p.82.

53 Albury, pp.326–7.

13 Francesco Maria della Rovere

1 Dennistoun II, p.314.

2 Dennistoun II, p.429.

3 Bradford, p.249.

4 Dennistoun II, p.315.

5 Shearman 1970, pp.77–9.

6 Dennistoun II, pp.317–18.

7 Vasari, 1878–1906, VI, p.317.

8 Majanlahti, p.84.

9 Dennistoun II, p.324.

10 Dennistoun II, p.339.

11 It was probably Niccolò Grasso's *Eutychia*, since the principal characters in this play are natives of Urbino. Herrick, pp.75–6.

12 D'Amico, pp.93–106.

13 Hara, pp.586–607.

14 T. Campbell, p.201.

15 Chambers and Martineau, pp.xxi and 102.

16 Luzio and Renier, pp.230–4.

17 C. King, p.798.

18 Paolo dal Poggetto, 'La diffusione del verbo raffaelesco: la Villa Imperiale; l'attività di Raffaellino del Colle', in Arbizzoni 2001, II, pp.203–46.

19 Thomas, p.214.

20 Thomas, pp.213–14.

21 Urb. Lat. 372; printed ed. Montano. Other plays in the library include Urb. Lat. 759, 760, 761, 764, which is the unique manuscript of Annibal Caro's popular comedy *Gli Straccioni*, made for Vittoria Farnese della Rovere (Beecher and Ciavoletta, p.viii), 765, 766, 775.

22 Dennistoun III, p.163, Eiche 1984, p.81, notes that this was still the case in the time of Francesco Maria II.

23 Simonetta 2008, p.121.

24 Mallett and Hale, p.290.

25 Shaw and Mallett, pp.152–3.

26 Shaw and Mallett, pp.182–3.

27 Dennistoun III, p 22.

28 T. Campbell, p.4.

29 Mallet and Hale, p.292.

30 Della Rovere.

31 Vasari, 1878–1906, VI, p.276.

32 Eisenbichler, p.28.

33 Pyhrr, p.123.

34 Sherrill, pp.121–50.

35 Panicali, pp.101–9, studies clocks depicted in Titian portraits.

36 Hadeln, pp.69–71, and McClure, p.56.

37 Bullough, pp.435–6.

38 Karamanou, pp.1–3.

39 Wilson, pp.148–50.

40 Syson and Thornton, p.216.

41 Vasari, 1878–1906, VI, p.581, and Clifford and Mallet, pp.387–410.

42 Wilson, p.44.

43 J.V.G. Mallet, 'The Gonzaga and Ceramics', in Chambers and Martineau, pp.39–53.

44 Ames-Lewis 1988, pp.690–2.

45 Chambers and Martineau, pp.175–6.

46 Chambers and Martineau, p.178.

47 Holcroft, pp.225–34.

14 The Later della Rovere Dukes

1 Mallett and Hale, p.300; Dennistoun III, p.88.

2 Mallett and Hale, p.297.

3 Norris, p.128.

4 Dennistoun III, p.100.

5 Sikorski, pp.67–90. Rotondi, p.99.

6 Sarti 2020, p.183.

7 Eiche 1991, pp.317–23.

8 Marcello Luchetti, 'Le imprese dei della Rovere: immagini simboliche tra politica e vincente familiari', in Arbizzoni 2001, I, pp.57–93.

9 Dennistoun III, p.88.

10 Lingo, pp.19, 177.

11 Lingo, p.104 (in Genoa Cathedral) and Luciano Archangeli, 'La pittura di Barocci e dei barocceschi a Pesaro', in Arbizzoni 2001, II, pp.181–201, p.186 (in the Prado, Madrid).

12 Piperno.

13 Roger Jacob, 'Dominique Phinot, a Franco-Netherlandish Composer of the Mid-Sixteenth Century', in Clough 1976, pp. 423–39; pp.426–7. He was executed for homosexual activities c. 1558.

14 Porta.

15 Franco Piperno, 'Musiche e Musicisti attorno ai Della Rovere', in Arbizzoni 2001, II, pp.375–402, 399–402.

16 Agostini.

17 Belozerskaya 2005, p.138.

18 Oakeshott, p.201. Now in the Royal Armouries, Madrid.

19 Pyhrr, pp.281–3.

20 Pyhrr, p.41.

21 Pyhrr, p.147.

22 Pyhrr, pp.123, 136.

23 Dennistoun III, pp.130–1.

24 Dennistoun III, pp.134–5.

25 Rose, pp.88–93.

26 Abu-Bekr Muhammed ben Abdelbaqi el-Bagdadi (d. 1141). The translator was Gerald of Cremona (d. 1187), and Dee had found a fourteenth-century manuscript of the

work, which he had transcribed (Rose, p.90).

27 Dee.

28 Farago, based on Urb. Lat. 1270.

29 Santucci, p.7.

30 Frank, pp.309–10.

31 Mallett and Hale, p.307.

32 Stras, pp.182–3, 295.

33 Tonelli, p.72. See also Carpinello.

34 Santucci, p.7.

35 Frank, p.306.

36 Pesaro, Biblioteca Oliveriana MS 384, ff. 219–29. The diary is Firenze, Biblioteca Magliabechiana 25, no. 76.

37 Frank, p.312.

38 It was founded by 1462, and in the sixteenth century was the most important book fair in Europe. See Weidhaas.

39 Eiche 1984, pp.77–108.

40 Eiche 1985, pp.154–83.

41 Belozerskaya 2005, pp 135–9, and Schrenck van Notzing, no. 23.

42 Clough 1995, p.38.

43 Montaigne, p.592.

44 Illustrated in dal Poggetto, p.37.

45 Vernarecci: 'Della colpa e prigionia di Muzio Oddi', pp.103–8, 122–6.

46 One is by Gian Giacomo Pandolfi, in the Chiesa san Filippo at Sant'Angelo in Vado, another by Alessandro Vitali at the parish church of Montebello-Orciano. See Benedetta Montevecchi, 'Immagini di un piccolo duca : Federico Ubaldo Della Rovere nella pittura del primo ventennio del Seicento', in Cleri and Eiche II, pp.223–44.

47   Petretti.

48   Dennistoun III, pp.178–9.

49   Panicali, pp.120–9.

50   Dennistoun III, pp.192–3.

51   Benzoni.

52   Dennistoun III, p.205.

53   Cusick, p.264.

54   Pieraccini II, p.507.

55   Ombrosi, p.33.

56   Ellen Rosand, 'The Voice of Barbara Strozzi', in Tick and Bowers, p.174.

57   Scaglioso, p.9.

58   Modesti, p.133.

59   Modesti, pp.8–10.

15   **The Eighteenth Century: Clement XI & the Stuarts**

1   'È un paese da cùcù / ove il vento ogn'hora stà / sopportar nol posso più / perderei la sanità / anno Dni 1666 die 18 Aug.' Sarti 2020, p.182.

2   Sarti 2020, p.185.

3   Enrico Gamba, 'Bernardino Baldi e l'ambiente tecnico-scientifico del Ducato di Urbino', in Nenci, pp.339–51, and Vetrano.

4   Panicali, p.55.

5   Johns, p.1.

6   Clough 1969; Fossier, pp.161–80.

7   Giovannini, pp.49–53.

8   Corp, p.38.

9   Corp, p.39.

10   Corp, p.41.

11   Lees-Milne, p.29.

12   Corp, pp.76–85.

13   Mar to Innes, 24 Dec. 1717. Corp, p.32.

14   Roullet, p.76.

16   **The Last Duke of Urbino**

1   Sarti 2009, pp.51–82.

2   Pennell, p.129.

3   Wharton, letter 1 May, 1896.

4   de Carlo, pp.113–15.

5   First published in 1890 in Lee, pp.3–58, p.6.

6   Shorthouse II, pp. 109–10.

7   Symonds, pp.149–50, 153.

8   Hutton, p.276.

9   Hutton, p.287.

10   Scarpacci, pp.197–216.

11   T. Campbell, p.202.

12   Lavallaye, pp.84, 119.

13   Kite, p.64.

14   Russell, p.65.

15   McKean, p.60.

16   McKean, p.61.

17   Borgarino, pp.286–91.

18   De Pieri, pp.54–71.

19   Battiferri.

20   Vertova, pp.229–33.

21   de Carlo, p.113.

22   Documented in *Restauri*.

23   de Carlo, p.22.

24   Jeffreys, pp.18–27.

25   Levey, pp. 12–25.

Acknowledgements

My primary debt is to my college, Campion Hall, Oxford, for many serendipitous conversations, and much specific help. I also need to thank the staff of the Bodleian and Sackler Libraries, who have done wonders with providing books and scans in what has been a very difficult year. A host of kind individuals have answered questions, notably Fausto Calderai, Edward Coulson, Peter Davidson, Matthew Dunch SJ, Anthony d'Elia, Mark Edwards, Alastair and Cecilia Hamilton, Adam Hanna, Alexandra Harris, Daniel Höhr, John McKean, Melanie Marshall, Tessa Murdoch, Loredana Polezzi, Alan Powers, Louisa Riley-Smith, James Stourton, Laura Tosi, Dora Thornton, and Jeremy Warren. I am very grateful to them all.

My dedication reflects an older debt, to Professor Sir Duncan Rice, former Principal of the University of Aberdeen.

Index

(*Federico da Montefeltro, Duke of Urbino, is referred to in the index as Federico*. Page numbers in *italic* refer to illustrations.)

A

abbess of Santa Chiara. see Varano, Elisabetta (Malatesta)

Albani, Gian Francesco. see Clement XI, Pope

Alberti, Leon Battista, 151, 162, 192, 204
  On the Art of Building, 144, 152, 160, 219

Aldobrandini, Ippolito. see Clement VIII, Pope

Alexander VI, Pope (Rodrigo Borgia), 119, 172, 241, 246, 247–252, 284

Alexander VII, Pope (Fabio Chigi), 231

Alexander VIII, Pope (Pietro Vito Ottoboni), 309

Alfonso V, King of Aragon, King of Naples, 49, 56, 72, 84, 147, 156, 183, 197, 199, 215, 222

Alidosi, Francesco, Cardinal of Pavia, 265

armour, 41–44, 291–292, 296

artillery. see guns and gunnery

astrolabe, 157

astrology, and Ptolemy's theory of human body, 254

Avelli, Francesco Xanto, 286

B

Baedeker Guide entries on Urbino, 315

Baldi, Bernardino, biography of Federico, 35, 38, 59, 71, 78, 121, 148, 149, 154, 158, 163, 188, 206, 208, 245

Barbari, Jacopo de,' portrait of Fra Luca Pacioli, 244

Barberini, Maffeo. see Urban VIII, Pope

Barocci, Ambrogio, 153, 212

Bell, Clive, 315

Bell, Vanessa, 315

Bembo, Bonifacio, portraits of Francesco and Bianca Maria Sforza, 58, 194

Bible, Federico's copy, 221

Bisticci, Vespasiano da (Federico's book-purveyor), 39, 100, 122, 125, 128, 147, 152, 163, 201, 203, 205, 210, 215, 217, 221, 227

Bo, Carlo, 316

Boniface VIII, Pope (Benedetto Caetani), 19

book collections. see also libraries (rooms and buildings)
  Federico, 99–101, 106, 215

Francesco Maria II, 216, 231, 293, 295, 300
Guidobaldo I, 229
kinds of libraries, 216
physical beauty of books, 220
Book of the Courtier. see Castiglione, Baldassare
Borgia, Alfonso de. see Callixtus III, Pope
Borgia, Cesare
  audience with Julius II and Guidobaldo I (1503), 210, 251
  commissions plan of Urbino city walls from Leonardo da Vinci (1502), 150
  death (1507), 250
  ejected from Urbino by Guidobaldo I, 257
  gifts Michelangelo's 'Sleeping Cupid' to Guidobaldo I, 247
  murders Venanzio Varano (1507), 264
  occupies Urbino (1502-3), 248–250, 254, 262
  ransacks Gubbio ducal palace (1502), 167
  ransacks Urbino (1502), 210, 229, 254, 256
  Romagna campaign (1500), 248
Borgia, Lucrezia, 247
Borgia, Rodrigo. see Alexander VI, Pope
Bracciolini, Poggio, 204, 216
  Florentine History, 100, 218
Brancaleoni, Gentile. see Montefeltro, Gentile da (Brancaleoni), Duchess of Urbino
Braschi, Giovanni. see Pius VI, Pope
Brera Madonna. see Francesca, Piero della
breviary, Federico's, 222
Bronzino, Agnolo, 174
  portrait of Guidobaldo II, 278, 287

C

Caetani, Benedetto. see Boniface VIII, Pope
Callixtus III, Pope (Alfonso de Borgia), 241

Campagna, Girolamo, 308
Fra Carnevale. see Corradini, Bartolomeo di Giovanni
Carpaccio, Vittore, Young Knight in a Landscape, 259, 260
cassoni (large storage chests), 180–181
Castel Durante
  Brancaleoni rule, 27, 168
  deer park, 239, 295
  Ducal Palace, 168, 230
  Federico Count of, 156
  Federico's architectural projects, 165, 168–169
  Federico's hunting lodge, 182
  Francesco Maria II's preference for, 230, 300
  Guelph/Ghibelline conflict (1277), 168–169
  Guidantonio da Montefeltro captures (1424), 28
  Guidobaldo Is triumphal pageant (1483), 238
  library, 231
  majolica production, 283
  previous name (Castel delle Ripe), 168
  rebuilding and renaming (1284), 168
Castiglione, Baldassare, 9, 161, 211, 251, 252, 268
  Book of the Courtier, 72, 255–258, 260, 268, 290
ceramics. see majolica
Charles I, King of England, 251
Charles V, Holy Roman Emperor, 274, 279, 284, 287, 289
Charles VII, King of France, 242
chests (cassoni), 180–181
Chigi, Fabio. see Alexander VII, Pope
Christian humanism, 154
Cibo, Giovanni Battista. see Innocent VIII, Pope
Cicero, Marcus Tullius, 53, 116
Clarke, Kenneth, 318
Clement VII, Pope (Giulio de' Medici), 274, 277–278

Clement VIII, Pope (Ippolito
    Aldobrandini), 297
Clement XI, Pope (Gian Francesco
    Albani), 160, 174, 306–307, 309, 310
Cognac, League of. see League of Cognac,
    War of
Colonna, Oddone. see Martin V, Pope
condotta commissions and contracts
    ('condotte')
    Antonio da Montefeltro, 127, 240
    Federico, 14, 57–58, 72–73, 90, 113, 115,
        117, 119–120, 126, 133, 134, 135, 145,
        183, 187, 223, 236
    Francesco Maria I, 294
    Guidobaldo I, 229, 236–237, 240,
        246–247
    length of term, 57
    Sigismondo Malatesta, 65–66, 72
    Roberto Malatesta, 135
    profitability of, 56, 89, 115, 120, 145,
        187, 217, 229, 236, 246
    system of, 56–57
condottieri (mercenary captains). see also
    mercenaries
    artillery usage, 74–75
    captains and princes, 25, 33, 38, 42,
        49, 57, 63, 65, 124, 134, 144, 187,
        188, 194, 197, 268
    cautious approach to waging war,
        58
    chivalry, 67
    Federico's career as condottiere, 14,
        42, 49, 52, 58, 65–66, 72–75, 90,
        115, 116, 151, 217, 222
    Guidobaldo I's career as, 236, 245–
        247, 260
    handguns usage, 75–76
    Montefeltri family tradition, 22
    physical courage, 14
    rights and responsibilities, 56–57
    wives of, 29, 82, 91–92, 95, 237
Corradini, Bartolomeo di Giovanni (Fra
    Carnevale), 164, 178–179, 182
Cosmography. see Ptolemy
Cox, Virginia, 53

D

da Vinci, Leonardo, 73, 150, 229, 230,
    244, 293
Dante
    Antonio da Montefeltro's copies of
        Divine Comedy, 21
    'Famous Men' series, 204
    in Federico's book collection, 99, 221
    and Guelph/Ghibelline conflict, 19
    Montefeltro family references in
        Divine Comedy, 19, 59
De Carlo, Giancarlo, 316–318
Dee, John, 292
della Carda, Ottaviano Ubaldini
    (Federico's possible brother), 26, 30,
    31, 41, 63, 65, 66, 71, 78, 89, 91, 94, 96,
    99, 100, 101, 102, 104, 108, 110, 113, 115,
    116–117, 119, 121, 136, 138, 139, 154, 157,
    165, 169, 181, 183, 187, 190, 192, 197,
    200, 203, 206, 223, 229, 236, 239, 240,
    241, 246
della Gatta, Bartolomeo, 229
    portrait of Guidobaldo I, aged six,
        192, 236
della Rovere, Claudia (Medici), Duchess
    of Urbino, 300–301
della Rovere, Eleonora da (Gonzaga),
    Duchess of Urbino, 174, 263, 265, 271,
    272, 273, 277, 279, 281, 285, 310
della Rovere, Federico (son of Francesco
    Maria I), 267
della Rovere, Federico Ubaldo, Duke of
    Urbino
    betrothed to Claudia de' Medici
        (1609), 300–301
    birth (1605), 160, 298, 307
    birth celebrations (1605), 298–299
    death (1623), 302
    Duke of Urbino (1621-3), 301
    lives in Florence (1615-21), 300
    marries Claudia de' Medici (1621), 301
    portraits, 298
    upbringing (1605-21), 300–301
della Rovere, Francesco. see Sixtus IV,
    Pope

della Rovere, Francesco Maria I, Duke of
      Urbino
   armour, 291–292, 296
   and battle of Pavia (1525), 273–274
   birth (1490), 239
   Cardinal Alidosi murder, trial and
      acquittal (1511), 265–267
   Carpaccio's *Young Knight in a
      Landscape* portrait (1510), 259
   Castiglione's *Book of the Courtier*,
      255, 258
   character, 261–262
   children, 267, 272
   commands Holy League forces against
      Turks (1538), 281
   condotto fee, 287
   death (1538), 281–282
   Duke of Urbino (1508), 167, 260, 261
   dukedom lost (1516), 270
   dukedom regained (1521), 272
   education, 261
   excommunication (1516), 270
   excommunication lifted (1521), 272
   Federico's coffin opened (1512), 138,
      187
   Filippo Negroli armour (1532),
      291–292
   first army command (1506), 259
   in France (1502-4), 262–263
   Giovanni Andrea murder (1507),
      263–264
   Guidobaldo I's heir, 247, 252, 259, 263
   Italian War of 1521-26 (Four Years'
      War), 273–274
   Julius II and, 252
   Knight of the Garter (1509), 265
   League of Cognac, War of (1526-30),
      274–277
   Leo X and (1515-21), 269–272
   marries Eleonora Gonzaga (1508),
      263, 264
   Ottaviano Petrucci and, 253
   Pesaro granted (1512), 173, 230, 268
   Pesaro Villa Imperiale residence,
      272–273
   Prefect of Rome (1501), 247
   Raphael's *Young Man with and Apple*
      portrait (1505-6), 254
   Romagna campaign (1509), 264–265
   Titian paintings collection, 279–280
   Titian portrait (1536), 279–280
   Urbino escape (1512), 230, 248, 262
   victories over France and Holy Roman
      Empire (1512), 268
della Rovere, Francesco Maria II, Duke
      of Urbino
   autobiography, 292, 295
   battle of Lepanto (1571), 292, 293–294
   becomes Duke (1574), 294
   birth (1549), 288
   book collection, 216, 230, 293, 295
   burial place, 169
   Castel Durante library, 231
   character, 295
   collects paintings of ancestors, 296
   commissions portrait of Duke
      Oddantonio (1581), 184
   courts Magdalena de Girón (1565-8),
      292
   death (1631), 169, 210, 230, 231, 305
   death of Lucrezia (1598), 297
   decline of Urbino, 305
   education, 290, 292
   hunting, 295
   installs statue of Federico (1604), 308
   interests, 295–296
   John Dee visits (1563), 292
   lack of heir, 294
   last Duke of Urbino, 231, 305
   lives in Spain (1565-8), 292
   majolica plate celebrating wedding to
      Livia (1599), 284
   Marco Montano's *Herode insano*
      performed for, 273
   marries Livia della Rovere (1599),
      284, 297
   marries Lucrezia d'Este (1570), 293
   orders portrait of Federico (1581), 184
   Polydore Vergil's English history
      acquired (1613), 245

portraits, 288, 292, 297, 298

reclusiveness, 169, 299–300

resigns duchy to Urban VIII (1625), 303, 305

resumes dukedom after death of son (1623), 302, 303

scholarship, 230

sells Sora dukedom to Gregory XIII (1579), 295

son. see della Rovere, Federico Ubaldo

threat from Clement VIII (1597), 297

thwarts coup plot (1601), 298

withdraws from public life (1606), 299–300

della Rovere, Giovanna (da Montefeltro) (Federico's daughter), 97, 102, 118, 188, 239, 252, 253

della Rovere, Giovanni (Federico's son-in-law), 117, 118, 188, 239, 247

della Rovere, Giuliano. see Julius II, Pope

della Rovere, Giulio Feltrio, Cardinal (son of Francesco Maria I), 279, 289, 297

della Rovere, Guidobaldo II, Duke of Urbino

acquires Villa Miralfiore palace, Pesaro (1559), 174

Agnolo Bronzino portrait, 278, 281, 287

armour collection, 291–292

becomes Duke (1538), 287

children, 287

commissions Battista Franco's Trojan War drawings (1545), 284

commissions Sala de Re plasterwork (1548), 307

condotto fee, 287

contrasts his virility with impotent Guidobaldo I, 278–279, 281

courts Clarice Orsini (1532), 279, 292

death (1574), 294

death of Giulia (1547), 287

father threatens to disinherit (1532), 279

hostage in Venice (1527), 277

love of horses, 289

marries Giulia Varano (1534), 279, 281, 287

marries Vittoria Farnese (1548), 160, 288, 307

Order of the Golden Fleece given by Charles V, 289

patron of arts and music, 289

portraits, 291, 296

refortifies Senigallia (1556), 289

sells Camerino duchy to Paul III (1538), 287

service with Phillip II (1558), 289

Tasso's *Gerusalemme Liberata* draft gifted to, 219, 290–291

della Rovere, Guilia (Varano), Duchess of Urbino, 278, 281, 288, 292

della Rovere, Livia, Duchess of Urbino, 284, 297, 298, 303

della Rovere, Lucrezia (d'Este), Duchess of Urbino, 293, 294, 297

della Rovere, Vittoria (Farnese), Duchess of Urbino, 99, 160, 174, 284, 288, 298, 307

d'Este, Lucrezia. see della Rovere, Lucrezia (d'Este), Duchess of Urbino

di Bartolomeo, Maso, 74, 179

di Francesco, Giovanni, 181, 182

di Giorgio Martini, Francesco, 30, 137, 138, 150, 153, 155, 156, 160, 164, 166, 169–171, 173, 178, 190, 192, 193, 197, 213, 219, 228, 295, 310, 311, 317

Divine Comedy. see Dante

E

Edward IV, King of England, 12, 118–119, 131, 190, 251

Elisabetta, abbess of Santa Chiara. see Varano, Elisabetta (Malatesta)

Eugenius IV, Pope (Gabriele Condulmer), 33, 39, 49, 54, 60–62, 89

F

'Famous Men' series. see Wassenhove, Joos van

Farnese, Alessandro. see Paul III, Pope

Farnese, Vittoria. see della Rovere, Vittoria (Farnese), Duchess of Urbino

Feltre, Vittorino da, 31, 36, 36–39, 46, 53, 64, 158, 205, 224

Ferdinand Charles, Archduke of Austria, 302

Ferdinand I (Ferrante), King of Naples, Duke of Calabria, 73, 78, 117, 119, 126, 128, 130, 132, 193, 206, 215, 236, 242

Ferdinand II, Archduke of Austria, Imperial count of Tyrol, 296

Ferdinand II, King of Aragon, 190, 256

Ferrante, Duke of Calabria. see Ferdinand I (Ferrante), King of Naples, Duke of Calabria

Filetico, Martino, 77, 79, 83, 87, 91, 92, 93, 94, 95, 97, 98, 99, 102

Five Regular Solids. see Francesca, Piero della

Flagellation of Christ. see Francesca, Piero della

Florentine History. see Bracciolini, Poggio

Fossombrone, Federico's architectural projects, 170–171

Four Years' War. see Italian War of 1521-26

Francesca, Piero della
    Brera Madonna, 42, 186, 200
    double portrait (diptych) of Battista and Federico da Montefeltro, 9, 58, 63, 93, 160, 193, 197
    Federico's patronage, 177, 180, 197, 213
    On the Five Regular Solids, 244
    Flagellation of Christ, 161, 184, 188, 296, 315
    hand as space-defining motif, 205
    Madonna of Senigallia, 188, 315
    portrait of Battista da Montefeltro, 85, 190, 195
    portrait of Federico, 46, 190, 192, 194
    skill in rendering perspective, 164, 179
    slow worker, 202
        treatise on perspective, 163, 218–219
        twentieth century rediscovery, 315

François I, King of France, 271, 273

Frederick I Barbarossa, Holy Roman Emperor, 18

Frederick III, Holy Roman Emperor, 173

G

Gabrieli, Giovanni, 53

Garter, Order of, 12, 118–119, 265

Geography. see Ptolemy

Ghibellines. see Guelph/Ghibelline conflict

giraffes as status symbols, 120–121

Girón, Magdalena de, 292

Gonzaga, Elisabetta. see Montefeltro, Elisabetta (Gonzaga), Duchess of Urbino

Gregory I (the Great), Pope, 219

Gubbio
    Antonio da Montefeltro dies in (1500), 240
    cathedral, 103
    Cesare Borgia's occupation, 167
    Ducal Palace, 101, 103, 110, 149–150, 165–167
    Ducal Palace garden, 149
    Ducal Palace intarsia panels, 42, 124, 164, 168
    Ducal Palace *studiolo*, 139, 159, 161, 167, 205, 206
    Federico born in (1422), 20
    Federico receives vicariate of (1447), 62
    Federico's architectural projects, 165–167
    Guidobaldo I's tour of (1482), 236
    majolica production, 283
    Montefeltro rule begins (1387), 21
    patron saint (Bishop Ubaldo), 103

Guelph/Ghibelline conflict, 19, 27, 28, 56, 168–169

guns and gunnery, 73–77, 96, 129

H

Hawkwood, Sir John, 187
Henri II, King of France, 69
Henry II, King of England, 255
Henry IV, King of England, 68
Henry VII, King of England, 207, 245, 251
Henry VIII, King of England, 265, 274
Historie of Italie. see Thomas, William
Hoby, Sir Thomas, 257
Honour, Hugh, 315–316
humanism
    Christian, 154
    Federico and, 39, 52, 106, 173
    princely patronage, 73, 261, 289
    women humanists, 84, 240
humanist education, 37–38, 45, 64, 78, 83,
    88, 102, 110, 144, 215, 217, 226, 229,
    235, 237
humanist politics, 52–53
humanist rivalries, 94–95, 96
humanist scholars, 17, 22, 36, 62, 63, 92,
    95, 102, 103, 104, 107, 109, 113, 120,
    121, 156, 158, 177, 188, 197, 199, 204,
    216, 218, 223, 228–229, 241, 245, 290,
    292, 295
Hutton, Edward, 313

I

ideal city, concept of, 93, 157, 161–164,
    257–258, 315, 317
Innocent VIII, Pope (Giovanni Battista
    Cibo), 237, 241
Institution of the Eucharist. see
    Wassenhove, Joos van
Italian War of 1521-26 (Four Years' War),
    273–274

J

James II, King of England, 307
James II, King of Scotland, 74

jousting, 68
Julius II, Pope (Giuliano della Rovere),
    119, 172, 211, 250–252, 255, 256, 258,
    259, 261, 263, 264, 266, 268, 269

L

La Muta. see Raphael
Landino, Cristoforo, 102
Laurana, Luciano, 147, 148, 150, 151, 156,
    163, 167, 190, 193
League of Cognac, War of (1526-30),
    274–277
Lee, Vernon, 312
Leo X, Pope (Giovanni de' Medici), 172,
    209, 269, 272, 278
Leopold V, Archduke of Austria, 302
Lepanto, battle of (1571), 292, 293–294
Levey, Michael, 318
libraries (rooms and buildings). see also
    book collections
    Castel Durante, 231
    Palazzo Ducale, 215–231
Life of Pontormo. see Vasari, Georgio
Lives of the Painters. see Vasari, Georgio
Lodi, Peace of (1454), 77
Lothar, Holy Roman Emperor, 216, 222
Louis X, King of France, 108
Louis XII, King of France, 262

M

Madonna of Senigallia. see Francesca,
    Piero della
Madonna with Chancellor Rolin. see van
    Eyck, Jan
majolica, 282–286
Malatesta, Battista (da Montefeltro)
    (Federico's aunt), 29, 36, 45, 81, 82, 98
Malatesta, Elisabetta (da Montefeltro)
    (Federico's daughter), 93, 102, 135, 137,
    184, 249

Malatesta, Sigismondo, 13, 34, 38, 48, 50, 51, 53, 55, 56, 59, 60, 61, 65, 72, 81, 87, 88, 89, 94, 98, 100, 102, 125, 130, 135, 153, 170

Martin V, Pope (Oddone Colonna), 21, 27, 28, 29, 33, 48, 49, 117

Mary II, Queen of England, 307

Mascioli, Egidio, 316

Matthias Corvinus, King of Hungary, 75

Maximilian I, Holy Roman Emperor, 256, 268

Medici, Cosimo I de,' Duke of Florence, 60, 86, 143, 144, 179, 198, 218

Medici, Giovanni de.' see Leo X, Pope

Medici, Guiliano de.' see Clement VII, Pope

Medici, Lorenzo I de, Lord of Florence, 14, 73, 104–105, 107, 121, 126–128, 130, 134, 160, 162, 163, 189, 201, 221, 236, 270, 274

Medici, Lorenzo II de,' Lord of Florence, Duke of Urbino, 277
  captain-general of the Church (1516), 270
  captures Urbino (1516), 270–271
  death (1519), 271
  Duke of Urbino (1516), 270
  Prefect of Rome (1516), 270
  wounded during conflict with Francesco Maria I (1516), 271

Medici, Vittoria de,' Duchess of Tuscany (daughter of Federico Ubaldo), 302–304

Mercatello, 27, 30, 45, 48, 165, 169, 181, 186, 188, 197

mercenaries. see also condottieri (mercenary captains)
  armour, 41–44
  armoured mercenary's retinue, 41
  Christian piety, 93
  employment, 21, 105, 271
  German landsknechts, 274, 276
  looting, 105–106
  Swiss, 276
  units ('lances'), 41

Metamorphoses. see Ovid

Milan, Palazzo Salvatico, 173

Montefeltro, Agnesina da (Federico's daughter), 102

Montefeltro, Agnesina da (Federico's half-sister), 29, 59, 60, 102

Montefeltro, Antonio da (Federico's illegitimate son), 68, 72, 77, 89, 94, 95, 102, 108, 118, 127, 134, 136, 190, 224, 238, 244

Montefeltro, Antonio II da, Count of Urbino, 20, 21, 27, 33

Montefeltro, Antonio II da, Count of Urbino (Federico's grandfather), 35, 145

Montefeltro, Battista da. see Malatesta, Battista

Montefeltro, Battista da (Sforza), Duchess of Urbino (Federico's second wife)
  appearance, 85
  betrothed to Federico (1457), 81
  biography, 85
  birth (1446), 72, 90
  books and reading, 100–101, 115
  brother. see Sforza, Costanzo
  character and attributes, 81
  children, 12, 90, 102, 103
  dancing prowess, 87
  death (1472), 108, 113, 156, 166
  death mask, 109
  and della Francesca's Brera Madonna, 186
  distinguished female lineage, 82–84
  double portrait with Federico (della Francesco), 9, 58, 63, 193–198, 280
  duchess's suite in Palazzo Ducale, 147, 256
  education, 78, 95, 102
  effects of pregnancies on health, 90
  father. see Sforza, Alessandro
  and Filetico's Iocundissimae disputationes (1462-3), 94–99, 102
  fondness for Gubbio, 166
  founds Urbino Monte di Pietà (1468), 103

funeral (1472), 109–110
funeral oration (Giannantonio
    Campano), 92, 109–110, 121, 209
granddaughter. see Colonna, Vittoria
jewellry, 200
leadership qualities, 88, 102
marries Federico (1460), 11, 81, 86–87,
    100, 145, 166, 173
meets Buonconte da Montefeltro
    (Federico's son) (1456), 78
meets Pius II (1461), 91–93
name saint, 187
objects associated with, 181, 183
piety, 93
portrait bust, 193
portraits, 85, 190, 192–197, 296, 301
posthumous narratives, 110
posthumous role model for women,
    111–112
public speaking, 33
ruling partnership with Federico,
    97, 197
successful marriage with Federico, 82
and Tasso's *Amadigi* (1559-62), 99
Montefeltro, Caterina da (Federico's
    stepmother), 28, 29, 44, 45
Montefeltro, Costanza da (Federico's
    daughter), 72
Montefeltro, Elisabetta da (Gonzaga),
    Duchess of Urbino (wife of
    Guidobaldo I), 167, 171, 181, 238, 242,
    248–252, 254, 256, 260, 263, 264,
    270, 301
Montefeltro, Federico da, Duke of
    Urbino, activities
book collecting, 99–101, 106
education, 31, 36–40
founds Urbino Poor Clares convent
    (1445), 92
jousting, 68
military career. see military career,
    campaigns and battles *below*
ruling partnership with Battista, 97, 102
travel, 66
writing, 13

Montefeltro, Federico da, Duke of
    Urbino, architectural projects
Battista's suite at Palazzo Ducale,
    89–90
Castel Durante, 168–169
deer park and lodge, 295
financing of, 65
Fossombrone, 170–171
Gubbio, 165–168
library, 22
Mercatello, 170
Milan, Palazzo Salvatico, 173
Palazzo Ducale, first phase, 145–147
Palazzo Ducale, second phase,
    147–148
Palazzo Ducale, third phase,
    148–151
post-1474 projects, 115
Sala delle Veglie, 256
San Leo, 171–173
Sassocorvaro, 169–170
studiolo, 156–160
Montefeltro, Federico da, Duke of
    Urbino, biography and literary
    references
Angelo Galli's poetry, 47
Bernardino Baldi's biography (c 1600),
    38
Cronache Malatestiane, 26
Giovanni Santi's chronicle, 63
Pierantonio Paltroni's biography,
    26, 47
Porcellio Pandoni's epic poem (*Feltria*)
    (1461-75), 91
Walter Tommasoli's biography, 50
Montefeltro, Federico da, Duke of
    Urbino, family
brother (possible). see della Carda,
    Ottaviano Ubaldini
cousin. see Varano, Elisabetta
    (Malatesta)
daughters (illegitimate). see
    Montefeltro, Gentile da (1448-
    1529); Montefeltro, Gentile da
    (b 1457-60?)

daughters (legitimate). see
   della Rovere, Giovanna (da
   Montefeltro); Montefeltro,
   Agnesina da; Montefeltro,
   Costanza da (1460-1)
father. see Montefeltro, Guidantonio
   da
father (rumoured). see della Carda,
   Bernardino
foster mother. see Brancaleoni,
   Giovanna (degli Alidosi)
Ghibelline allegiance, 56
granddaughter. see Colonna, Vittoria
grandmother. see Montefeltro,
   Giovanna da (Gonzaga)
half-brother. see Montefeltro,
   Oddantonio da
need for legitimate heir, 12, 71, 89
son (legitimate). see Montefeltro,
   Guidobaldo I da
sons (illegitimate). see Montefeltro,
   Antonio da; Montefeltro,
   Buonconte da
wives. see Montefeltro, Battista da
   (Sforza); Montefeltro, Gentile da
   (Brancaleoni)
Montefeltro, Federico da, Duke of
   Urbino, health
   ankle fracture after falling through
      upper floor (1477), 125
   gout, 88
   jaw infection (1433), 9, 30
   loss of right eye (1450), 69
   physical injuries, 14
   slipped disc (1460), 91
   spinal disfigurement, 46
Montefeltro, Federico da, Duke of
   Urbino, life events (chronological
   order)
   born (1422), 26
   rumours about his parentage (1422-),
      26
   legitimized (1424), 28-29
   lives with Brancaleoni relatives in
      Mercatello (1427-33), 29-31

betrothed to Gentile Brancaleoni
   (1430), 28
hostage in Rimini (1432), 34
hostage in Venice (1433-4), 31, 34, 46
lives in Mantua (1434-7), 36
marries Gentile Brancaleoni (1437),
   45, 47
birth of Buonconte (1442), 48
and Oddantonio's assassination
   (1444), 50-51
ruler of Urbino (1444), 51-53
banishes half-sisters (1446), 59
excommunicated by Eugenius IV
   (1446), 61
thwarts assassination plot (1446), 59
birth of Guidobaldo I (1472), 103
excommunication lifted by Nicholas
   V (1447), 62
friendship with Ottaviano della Carda
   (1447-), 62-63
loses right eye during joust (1450),
   69
consolidates power (1451-60), 71-79
death of Buonconte (son) (1458), 78
death of Gentile (1458), 79
marries Battista Sforza (1460), 11, 81,
   82, 86-87, 100, 145, 166, 173
birth of Giovanna (1464), 97
siege of Volterra (1472), 108-113
invested as Duke of Urbino (1474),
   118
death and funeral (1482), 135-139
Montefeltro, Federico da Duke of
   Urbino, military career, campaigns
   and battles (chronological order).
   see also condotta commissions and
   contracts ('condotte'); condottieri
   (mercenary captains)
   first army (1437), 41
   first suit of armour (1437), 42-44
   assumes father's military
      responsibilities (1438), 44
   defends Urbino (1438-42), 48
   captures San Leo fortress (1441),
      48

serves under Francesco Sforza (1443), 49

career as condottiero (1444-), 57–59

feud with Sigismondo Malatesta (1444-63), 56, 65, 88, 96, 98

first independent condotta (1444), 57

Gabrieli revolt suppressed (1444), 53

guns and gunnery (1449-), 73–77, 96, 129

allies with Alfonso V, King of Naples (1451), 72

siege of Volterra (1472). see Volterra, siege of (1472)

campaign against Florence (1478-79), 128–131

Montefeltro, Federico da, Duke of Urbino, personal attributes and image
appearance, 46–47
cleanliness, 44
commemorative pageant (1605), 299
comparison with Cicero, 53, 95
crafting of image, 31, 52
eye for the ladies, 67–70
fastidiousness, 44
foremost condottiero, 52
good Christian prince, 13, 52
Greek language prowess, 94
handwriting, 39
hidden side, 14
honesty, 58
humanist associations, 223
humanist prince, 39, 52, 106
humanist taste, 173
humanist warrior, 11
ideal virtuous ruler, 13, 52–53
legitimization of rule, 52–53
magnificence, 113–139
Oddantonio contrasted with, 13
posthumous reputation, 14
Renaissance prince, 13, 299
respect for accomplished women, 31
ruthlessness, 14
scientific approach to warfare, 59
self-made man, 35

studiolo as expression of character and self-image, 158
trustworthiness, 58
weakness for women, 67–70
youthful appearance, 46–47
Montefeltro, Federico da, Duke of Urbino, personal possessions and associated objects
armour, 41–44
astrolabe, 157
bath-house, 44
Bible, 221
Blessed Sword and Hat from Pope Sixtus IV, 131
book collection, 99–101, 106, 215–231
breviary, 222
copy of works of Virgil, 100
emblems (imprese), 11, 22, 35
giraffe, 120–121
helmet, 296
special saddle with leg support, 128
Montefeltro, Federico da, Duke of Urbino, persons associated with
Baccio Pontelli (architect), 148–149
Francesco di Giorgio Martini (architect). see di Giorgio Martini, Francesco
Piero della Francesca. see Francesca, Piero della
Angelo Galli (secretary), 22
Luciano Laurana (architect). see Laurana, Luciano
Vespasiano da Bisticci (book-purveyor). see Bisticci, Vespiano da
Montefeltro, Federico da, Duke of Urbino, portraits and statues
Brera Madonna (della Francesca), 42
double portrait with Battista (della Francesca), 9, 58, 63, 193–198, 280
reading, with Guidobaldo I (van Wassenhove), 11–12, 191, 219, 315
statue in Roman armour (Girolamo Campagna), 308
as young man (Salimbeni brothers) (1416), 47

Montefeltro, Federico da, Duke
of Urbino, titles and awards
(chronological order)
Compagnia della Calza (1433), 35
fiefdom of Mercatello (1437), 45
lord of Urbino (1444), 12
vicariates of Urbino, Gubbio and
Cagli (1447), 62
duke of Urbino (1474), 12
Order of the Ermine (1474, 12
Order of the Garter (1474), 12, 118–119
styles and titles inscription (1476),
155–156
Montefeltro, Gentile da (Brancaleoni),
Duchess of Urbino (Federico's first
wife), 12, 28, 31, 45, 47, 48, 55, 56, 66,
71, 77, 79, 81, 89, 114, 146, 181, 190
Montefeltro, Gentile da (Federico's
illegitimate daughter), 102
Montefeltro, Giovanna da (Federico's
daughter). see della Rovere, Giovanna
(da Montefeltro)
Montefeltro, Giovanna da (Gonzaga),
Countess of Urbino (Federico's
grandmother), 102
Montefeltro, Guidantonio da, Count of
Urbino (Federico's father), 13, 21, 25,
27, 28, 29, 30, 33, 35, 44, 47, 48, 49,
52, 81, 82, 103, 136, 138, 145, 166
Montefeltro, Guidobaldo I da, Duke of
Urbino (Federico's son), 235–237,
260
adopts Francesco Maria I della
Rovere as heir, 239, 246
artists associated with, 178
baptism (1472), 103
besieged in Bibbiena (1498), 246
betrothed to Elisabetta Gonzaga, 237
betrothed to Lucrezia of Aragon
(1474), 237
birth (1472), 110, 138
Bologna campaign (1506), 258–259
burial place, 138
captured and ransomed during Orsini
campaign (1497), 246

Cardinal Bessarion's *Fridericus*
dedication, 116
and Castiglione's *Book of the Courtier*,
255–258
childhood, 235
confirmed as Federico's heir (1482),
136
confirms Francesco Maria I della
Rovere as heir, 263
Corte Alta as favoured residence, 171
death (1508), 110, 240, 259–260, 283
description, 235, 236
early years of reign, 237
education, 102, 229
entertains Lucrezia Borgia (1501), 247
Federico safeguards his succession,
115
and Federico's loss of right eye, 68
first army command (1488), 237
founds University of Urbino (1507),
259
funeral (1508), 260
funeral oration, 110
gift of gold chain from Sixtus IV
(1477), 127
gout, 240
Gubbio's decline, 167
impotence, 239, 279, 281
informed of Federico's death (1482),
136
invested as Duke (1482), 236
jewellry, 201
Julius II visits (1506), 256
leadership qualities, 247
library, 229
marries Elisabetta Gonzaga (1488),
181, 238
mathematics prowess, 163
Michelangelo's 'Sleeping Cupid'
gifted by Cesare Borgia (1502),
247
Officina degli strumenti scientifici
(Office of Scientific, 259
ousted by Cesare Borgia (1502), 167,
248, 254, 261

portraits, 11–12, 127, 191, 203, 206, 219, 240, 244, 254, 315

Prefect of Rome, 247

Raphael portrait (1506), 240, 254

restored as Duke (1503), 210, 229, 250–252

sexual probity, 241

succession worries, 247

Montefeltro, Oddantonio da, Count and Duke of Urbino (Federico's half-brother)

Angelo Galli secretary to, 22

assassinated (1444), 12, 50–51, 136, 145, 184

as blond youth in della Francesca's *Flagellation of Christ*, 184

born (1428), 13

burial place, 52

character blackened, 50–51

Count of Urbino (1443), 49

Duke of Urbino (1443), 49–50, 144

education, 45

and Eugenius IV, 60

Federico paints him as bad ruler, 13, 52–53

Federico's possible complicity in assassination, 52

financial laxity, 55

Francesco Maria II commissions portrait (1581), 184

heir to dukedom, 44

only son of Guidantonio, 29

persons associated with, 59

portraits, 296

shortcomings as ruler, 237

Montefeltro, Ringarda da (Malatesta), Countess of Urbino (Guidantonio's first wife), 13

Montefeltro, Sveva da. see Sforza, Sveva

Montefeltro, Violante da, abbess of Corpus Domini, Ferrara (Federico's half sister), 29, 59, 61, 89, 136

Montefeltro da, Buonconte (Federico's illegitimate son), 48, 72, 73, 77, 81, 84, 89, 115, 190, 224

N

Napoleon (Bonaparte), 311

Negroli, Filippo, 291

Nicholas III, Pope (Giovanni Orsini), 276

Nicholas V, Pope (Tommaso Parentucelli), 62, 65, 71, 73, 163, 170, 179, 204, 216, 218

'Nicola da Urbino,' 284–285

Nicolson, Ben, 315

O

On the Art of Building. see Alberti, Leon Battista

Orsini, Clarice, 279, 292

Orsini, Giovanni. see Nicholas III, Pope

Ottoboni, Pietro. see Alexander VIII, Pope

Ovid, 286

Metamorphoses, 285

P

Pacioli, Fra Luca

and Piero della Francesca, 244

Summa de Arithmetica, 163, 244

Summary of arithmetic, geometry, proportions and proportionality, 244

Pacioli, Fra Luca, Jacopo de Barbari's portrait of, 244

Palazzo Ducale (Urbino), 168, 173

Alberti's description (1469), 151

armamentum, 157

armariolum, 157

bench, 153

caldarium, 155

cassoni, 181

cassoni (large storage chests), 180–181

Clarke's *Civilisation*, 318

context for building of, 143–145

Cortile d'Onore, 154

courtyard, 152
daily life, 122–124
decline and renewal (1800-present),
    311–319
decoration, 147
facciata ad ali, 153
Federico's initials, 148
Federico's rebuilding, 144–152
frigidarium,, 155
garden, 149
grenade motifs, 77
guardaroba, 152, 155, 158, 164, 228
hygiene, 123
and James Francis Edward Stuart (The
    Old Pretender), 307–309
library, 215–231
National Gallery of the Marche (1912),
    314–315
neviera, 155
'ostrich room,' 145
Palazzetto della Iole, 101, 146, 147,
    180, 212
private and public areas, 151–154
restorations in 1960s and 70s, 318–319
Risciolo, 150, 151
sala, 152
Sala degli Affreschi, 146, 180, 182
Sala degli Angeli, 148, 152, 164
Sala dell' Alcova, 77, 146
Sala della Iole, 146
Sala della Udienza, 155
Sala delle Veglie, 256
salotto, 152
Sitwell's *Great Houses of Europe*, 318
spalliera, 181
stables (Data), 150
studiolo, 154
studiolo. see *studiolo*
tempietti, 154
Throne Room, 148, 154, 192
Throne Room History of Troy
    tapestries, 207–210
torricini, 149, 151, 154
torricino, 155
upper loggia, 197

Palazzo Salvatico (Milan), 173
Parentucelli, Tommaso. see Nicholas V,
    Pope
Paul II, Pope (Pietro Barbo), 103, 130
Paul III, Pope (Alessandro Farnese), 279,
    287, 288
Pavia, battle of (1525), 273–274
Pembroke, Philip Herbert, 4th Earl of, 251
Pembroke, William Herbert, 3rd Earl
    of, 251
Pepin III (the Short), King of the Franks,
    16, 18
Pesaro
    Alessandro Sforza lord of, 60, 62, 72,
        81, 89, 173
    Battista in, 83–84, 94, 181
    Battista's rule, 29
    Camilla Sforza's rule, 112
    Cesare Borgia captures, 248
    della Rovere ducal court moved to,
        160, 168, 174
    Federico in, 51
    Francesco Maria I dies in (1538),
        281–282
    Francesco Maria I lord of, 230, 268,
        270
    Francesco Maria II in, 292–293,
        295–300
    Giovanni Sforza lord of, 238
    Great Hall, 295
    Guidobaldo II in, 287, 289–290
    location, 173, 273
    Lucrezia d'Este's entry (1571), 293
    Malatesti alienated from, 83
    Malatesti family alienated from, 60
    preferred to Urbino, 305
    printing, 253
    Santa Caterina convent, 297
    siege of (1516), 270
    Sigismondo Malatesta attempts to
        recover (1448), 65–66, 72
    Tasso in, 290–291
    Villa Imperiale, 173, 272–273
    Villa Miralfiore, 174–175
Philip II, King of Spain, 289, 294

Piccolomini, Enea. see Pius II, Pope

Pisanello (Antonio di Puccio Pisano), 183, 185, 193, 194, 199

Pius II, Pope (Enea Piccolomini), 14, 26, 50, 62, 92, 109, 144, 153, 154, 204, 250, 301

Pius VI, Pope (Giovanni Braschi), 174

Pontelli, Baccio, 148–149

popes, rise to political primacy in Western Europe, 15–21

pottery. see majolica

printing, establishment of, 121–122

Ptolemy
astrological associations with human body, 254
Cosmography, 223
Geography, 228
in *Studiolo*, 157, 204, 228

R

Raphael
father of (Giovanni Santi), 63, 178, 238, 253
first documented work (1501), 253
first painting to reach England (*St George and the Dragon*), 251
La Muta, 315
life and career, 253
and 'Nicola da Urbino,' 284, 285
payment for cartoons for Acts of the Apostles tapestries, 209
portrait of Guidobaldo I, 240
portraits of Guidobaldo and Elisabetta da Montefeltro, 254
possible portrait of Eleonora Gonzaga, 263
silver basins designed by, 271
St George and the Dragon, 251
takes over father's workshop (1500), 178
tapestry designs, 315
training in Urbino, 177–178
in Vittoria della Rovere's collection, 303
Young Man with an Apple, 254, 259

Robert I, King of Naples, 180

Roselli, Domenico, 193, 197, 212

Russell, David, 315

S

Sackville, Thomas, 257

San Leo, 172–173

San Leo, Federico's architectural projects, 171–173

Santi, Giovanni. see also Raphael, 63, 116, 118, 124, 146, 178, 188, 206, 238, 250, 253

Sassocorvaro, Federico's architectural projects, 169–170

sculpture, 179, 188, 208, 212, 230

Serra, Luigi, 314–315

Sforza, Alessandro, Lord of Pesaro (Battista's father), 60, 62, 65, 72, 78, 79, 81, 83, 85, 87, 89, 173

Sforza, Battista. see Montefeltro, Battista da (Sforza), Duchess of Urbino

Sforza, Bianca Maria (Visconti), Duchess of Milan, 57, 77, 83, 94, 111, 189, 194, 195

Sforza, Costanza (Varano), Duchess of Milan (Battista's mother), 46, 60, 62, 65, 78, 83, 84, 85, 87, 89, 90

Sforza, Costanzo, Lord of Pesaro and Gradara, 90, 94, 95, 98, 108, 195, 238

Sforza, Francesco, Duke of Milan, 49, 57, 66–67, 72, 78, 83, 84, 88, 111, 119, 125, 189, 194, 196, 198, 274

Sforza, Ludovico ('il Moro'), Duke of Milan, 74, 126, 130, 134, 207, 242, 268

Sforza, Sveva (Federico's half-sister), 29, 59, 61, 65

Shorthouse, Joseph Henry, 312

Sigismund, Holy Roman Emperor, 38, 83

Sitwell, Sacheverell, 318

Sixtus IV, Pope (Francesco della Rovere), 14, 108, 109, 112, 117, 118, 126–128, 130–133, 149, 154, 166, 191, 202, 204, 205, 211, 236, 242, 269, 306 *spalliere* (decorative wall-mounted panels), 181

St George and the Dragon. see Raphael

St Mark the Evangelist. see Wassenhove, Joos van

Stephen II, Pope (Orsini), 17

Stokes, Adrian, 315

storage chests (*cassoni*), 180–181

Strozzi, Barbara, 303

Stuart, James Francis Edward (The Old Pretender), 307–309

studiolo (Palazzo Ducale)
    assassination of Oddantonio da Montefeltro, 145
    decoration, 145
    description, 155–156
    doors, 152
    expression of Federico's character, 158
    furniture, 157–159
    intarsia panels, 11, 42
    masculine space, 158
    observatory, 124
    panelling, 164
    pictures in, 190
    portraits, 11, 31, 37, 315
    restorations in 1960s and 70s, 318
    Temple of the Muses (*Tempietto*), 206

Summa de Arithmetica. see Pacioli, Fra Luca

Sustermans, Justus, portraits of Vittoria della Rovere and husband Grand Duke Ferdinand II of Tuscany, 304

Sylvester I, Pope, 17

Symonds, John Addington, 313

Syrlin, Jörg, 204

T

Talbot, Mary, 251

Talbot, Sir Gilbert, 251

tapestries, 207–210

Thomas, William, 257
    Historie of Italie, 26

Titian
    della Roveres' liking of, 280–281, 289, 292, 303
    in National Gallery of the Marche, 314
    portrait of Charles V, 279
    portrait of Eleonora Gonzaga, 279, 281
    portrait of Francesco Maria I, 279–280
    portrait of Giulia Varano, 287
    portrait of Guidobaldo II, 281
    portrait of Guidobaldo II and Francesco Maria II, 288
    portraits of beautiful ladies, 279–280
    Venus of Urbino, 181

U

Ubaldo, Saint, patron of Gubbio, 103

Urban VIII, Pope (Maffeo Barberini), 159, 303

Urbino
    Baedeker Guide entries, 315
    decline and renewal (1800-present), 311–319
    early history to Renaissance, 15–22
    hotels, 315
    as ideal city, 161–164, 257–258
    location, 319
    marketplace (Mercatale), 150, 152, 317
    modern growth of tourism, 318–319
    Montefeltro rule begins (1378), 20
    printing, establishment of, 122
    quintessential Renaissance city, 319
    restoration during eighteenth century, 310
    restorations in 1960s and 70s, 317–319
    and W. B. Yeats's 'The People,' 258
    writings by nineteenth-century English and American visitors, 311–314

Urbino, buildings
    Albergo Italia, 315
    Palazzo Battiferri, 317
    Teatro Raffaello Sanzio, 311

Teatro Sanzio, 317

Urbino, churches and religious
  establishments
  Cathedral (Duomo), 106, 116, 122,
    127, 138, 184, 308, 310, 315
  Duomo, 154
  San Bernardino, 138
  San Domenico, 149
  Santa Chiara, 79, 109, 124, 137, 149,
    184, 196, 225, 230, 249, 310

Urbino, Counts of (dates of birth,
  succession, death)
  Antonio II da Montefeltro (b 1348,
    s 1363, d 1404). see Montefeltro,
    Antonio II da, Count of Urbino
  Guidantonio da Montefeltro (b 1377
    s 1403 d 1443). see Montefeltro,
    Guidantonio da, Count of Urbino
  Oddantonio da Montefeltro (b 1428
    s 1443 d 1444. see Montefeltro,
    Oddantonio da, Count and Duke
    of Urbino

Urbino, Dukes of (dates of birth,
  succession, death)
  Oddantonio da Montefeltro (b 1428
    s 1443 d 1444. see Montefeltro,
    Oddantonio da, Count and Duke
    of Urbino
  Federico III da Montefeltro (b 1442
    s 1444 d 1482). see Montefeltro,
    Federico da, Duke of Urbino
  Guidobaldo I da Montefeltro (b 1472
    s 1502 (deposed and restored
    1502) d 1508). see Montefeltro,
    Guidobaldo I da, Duke of Urbino
  Cesare Borgia (b 1475 s 1502 deposed
    1538). see Borgia, Cesare
  Francesco Maria I della Rovere (b 1490
    s 1508 (deposed 1516-19) d 1538).
    see della Rovere, Francesco Maria
    I, Duke of Urbino
  Lorenzo II de' Medici (b 1492 s 1516
    d 1519). see Medici, Lorenzo II de,'
    Duke of Florence and of Urbino
  Guidobaldo II della Rovere (b 1515

  s 1638 d 1574. see della Rovere,
    Guidobaldo II, Duke of Urbino
  Francesco Maria II della Rovere
    (b 1549 s 1508 (abdicated 1621-3)
    d 1631). see della Rovere, Francesco
    Maria II, Duke of Urbino
  Federico Ubaldo della Rovere (b 1605
    s 1621 d 1623). see della Rovere,
    Federico Ubaldo, Duke of Urbino

Urbino, Palace. see Palazzo Ducale
  (Urbino)

Urbino, University of
  foundation, 259
  as ideal city, 317
  modern building, 11, 316–318
  Palazzo Bonaventura, 145

V

van der Weyden, Rogier, 198
  Sforza Triptych, 85
van Eyck, Jan, 195, 197–200
  Madonna with Chancellor Rolin, 199
Varano, Elisabetta (Malatesta), abbess of
  Santa Chiara (Federico's cousin), 60,
  92, 109, 124
Vasari, Georgio, 156, 159, 162, 173, 178,
  182, 200, 264, 280, 284
  Life of Pontormo, 278
  Lives of the Painters, 198
Venice
  Ca' d'Oro, 35
  Federico in (1443-4), 31, 34, 46
  Francesco Maria I fights for, 273–277
  Francesco Maria I in (1538), 281
  Francesco Maria II in (1564), 292
  Guidobaldo I fights for, 246
  Guidobaldo I in (1502), 249
  Guidobaldo II fights for, 278, 287
Venus of Urbino. see Titian
Virgil, 38, 64, 158, 205, 227, 286
  Aeneid, 46, 112, 183
  Donatus's life of, 110
  Federico's copy of works of, 100

quotations from, 38
Visconti, Bianca Maria. see Sforza, Bianca Maria, Duchess of Milan
Visconti, Filippo Maria, Duke of Milan, 33, 42, 57, 63, 67, 100
Viti, Timoteo, 178, 206, 250, 254, 264, 315
Vitigis, Ostrogothic king, 16
Volterra, siege of (1472), 14, 104–107, 109, 120, 126, 148, 225

young Guidobaldo, 11, 46, 157, 191
portrait of Guidobaldo I, 235
portrait of Virgil, 204–206
St Mark the Evangelist, 202
Wharton, Edith, 312
William III, King of England, 307
wives of condottieri, 29, 82, 91–92, 95, 237
women artists, writers and musicians, 303–304
women humanists, 84, 240

W

warfare. see armour; guns and gunnery; mercenaries
Wassenhove, Joos van, 11, 178, 192, 198–205, 213
'Famous Men' series, 189, 203–205
Institution of the Eucharist, 191, 203
portrait of Federico reading, with

Y

Yeats, W. B., 'The People,' 258
Young Knight in a Landscape. see Carpaccio, Vittore
Young Man with an Apple. see Raphael